MEMOIRS

OF

JAMES BEGG, D.D.

JAMES BEGG, D.D.

MEMOIRS

OF

JAMES BEGG, D.D.

*MINISTER OF NEWINGTON FREE CHURCH,
EDINBURGH.*

BY

THOMAS SMITH, D.D.
PROFESSOR OF EVANGELISTIC THEOLOGY, NEW COLLEGE,
EDINBURGH.

Including Autobiographical Chapters by Dr. Begg.

IN TWO VOLUMES.

VOL. I.

EDINBURGH:
JAMES GEMMELL, GEORGE IV. BRIDGE.
1885.

Ballantyne Press
BALLANTYNE, HANSON AND CO.
EDINBURGH AND LONDON

PREFACE TO VOL. I.

NOTWITHSTANDING a very general opinion that it is undesirable to add unduly to the number of published biographical books, there was a universal feeling, not only among the personal friends of Dr. Begg, but among a large portion of the general community of our country, that a "Life" of him should be written. Application was made to me to undertake the work. With a sincere desire to aid thus in perpetuating the memory of my friend, yet with much reluctance, arising from an appreciation of the difficulties of the task, I assented to the proposal, and now I am very glad that "half of my heavy task is done."

I have not had any aid from journal or diary, and very little from correspondence, to "make Dr. Begg his own biographer." So far as I know, Dr. Begg never kept any journal, and although he wrote innumerable *notes* in reply to innumerable inquiries, he wrote very few *letters*; nor did he preserve the notes or letters which he received. I do not know that the paucity of material of this kind is very much to be regretted, as it is a very imperfect idea that can be formed of a man's actual life from his own daily retrospect recorded during the last quarter of an hour in each day.

The first four chapters of this volume consist of an autobiographical fragment. The reader will see that it is very diffuse, and that its author designed his Memoirs to be on a large scale—to be, in fact, a "History of His Life and Times." The chapters immediately following (V.-XI.) are a sort of running comment upon these, and it will probably be considered that they also are chargeable with undue diffuseness. My only apology is that I thought it right to accommodate my part of the work to the portion executed by my friend, and of which mine was designed to be a continuation.

In addition to the chapters which Dr. Begg had prepared for the press, he had had copied a considerable number of papers designed to be incorporated with his autobiography. These I have inserted at their proper places.

I have now to make a few additions and corrections:—

1. In connection with the monument of Dr. and Mrs. Begg of New Monkland (p. 43), I have had forwarded to me two letters from a bank agent at Airdrie, from which it appears that one of Dr. Begg's sons, Mr. William Begg, deposited with him a sum of money to provide for the maintenance in perpetuity of his grandparents' monument.

2. I have through inadvertence spoken of the Dean of Faculty, who had so much to do with the Auchterarder and other cases, as Mr. Charles Hope. It should have been Mr. John Hope.

3. I have with some difficulty procured a copy of the "Anti-Patronage Library," spoken of in page 403. I find that it was not published until 1842. The letter on that page is therefore misplaced. The "Library" contains an abridgment of Dr. Begg's pamphlet on patronage, published in 1839.

4. To avoid periphrasis, I have spoken throughout of the subject of the memoir as Dr. Begg. This was occasionally somewhat awkward. But I thought it, upon the whole, better to designate him by the title by which he was so generally known. In point of fact, he did not acquire that title till a time subsequent to that to which the present volume relates.

I have only further to express my best thanks to many friends who have rendered me valuable aid, and in particular to several gentlemen to whom I took the liberty of making application without having any proper right, on the ground of friendship, to make it. In every case such applications have been kindly and favourably responded to.

And now I present the first instalment of my work to the public, with the promise that, if God spare me in life and health, the second portion of it shall follow without very long delay.

I have no right to deprecate criticism, as my task was voluntarily undertaken; and I am painfully conscious of many defects and imperfections in my execution of it.

T. S.

CONTENTS.

CHAP.		PAGE
I.	BIRTH AND EARLY DAYS	1
II.	COLLEGE LIFE IN GLASGOW AND EDINBURGH	44
III.	MY LICENSE, ORDINATION, AND EXPERIENCE AS AN ASSISTANT AT NORTH LEITH, AND A MINISTER OF CHAPELS AT DUMFRIES AND EDINBURGH	81
IV.	TRANSLATION TO PAISLEY — MINISTER OF A CITY CHARGE	107
V.	DR. BEGG'S FAMILY—HIS CONNECTION WITH GREENOCK	114
VI.	SCOTTISH PAROCHIAL SCHOOLS	126
VII.	GLASGOW UNIVERSITY	134
VIII.	GLASGOW DIVINITY HALLS	140
IX.	LICENSE AS A PREACHER—ASSISTANT AT NORTH LEITH—CHARACTER OF HIS PREACHING	157
X.	CHAPELS OF EASE—CALL TO MAXWELLTOWN—MINISTRY THERE	166
XI.	LADY GLENORCHY'S CHAPEL, EDINBURGH	180
XII.	TRANSLATION TO PAISLEY AND MINISTRY THERE	202
XIII.	PAISLEY MINISTRY CONTINUED—CHURCH EXTENSION	212
XIV.	FIRST SPEECH IN THE GENERAL ASSEMBLY	228

CHAP.		PAGE
XV.	THE YEAR 1833	250
XVI.	THE YEAR 1834	265
XVII.	PRESENTATION TO THE PARISH OF LIBERTON	291
XVIII.	MINISTRY AT LIBERTON	307
XIX.	CHURCH CONTROVERSIES	316
XX.	CHURCH EXTENSION MOVEMENT	332
XXI.	NON-INTRUSION CONTROVERSY	351
XXII.	THE BEGINNING OF THE END	405

DR. BEGG'S BIRTHPLACE.

MEMOIRS OF JAMES BEGG, D.D.

Autobiographical.

CHAPTER I.

BIRTH AND EARLY DAYS.

I WAS born in the manse at New Monkland on the 31st October 1808. There are two parishes of the name of Monkland, distinguished as New and Old. They are situated in the north-eastern district of Lanarkshire, extending from the Clyde eastward to the boundary of the county. They originally formed only one extensive parish, but were divided into two parishes called New and Old Monkland, in 1640. The whole district was called Monkland, because it was once the property of the monks of Newbattle Abbey in Midlothian. New Monkland, in which I was born, is about ten miles in length and seven in breadth, being bounded by Old Monkland and Cadder on the west, by Shotts on the south, Slamannan on the east, and Cumbernauld and Kilsyth, in the county of Dumbarton, on the north. Airdrie, now a very thriving town, is in the parish, and the old great middle turnpike road from Glasgow to Edinburgh passes through Airdrie, the distance from Edinburgh being thirty-two miles, and that from Glasgow nearly eleven. The district is high and somewhat bleak, but tolerably well cultivated and wooded, and very healthy and bracing. Although there is no hill or mountain in the parish, the church and manse occupy an elevated position, and from the church-gate the distant chimneys and smoke of Glasgow are clearly seen; whilst, on the other hand, in passing along the Edinburgh and Glasgow Railway near Croy, or the Caledonian Railway near Coatbridge, the old parish church of New Monkland, a plain but commodious structure with a stunted spire, is visible on the rising ground. The manse is at a little distance towards the east, the parish school-house and teacher's house standing between. The manse was enlarged during my father's incumbency, and the glebe extended to eleven acres.

The parish was somewhat famous, and suffered severely, during the Covenanting period. The people of New Monkland sent a detachment of men to the battle of Bothwell Bridge, John Main, elder, Ballochnie, being the standard-bearer. He carried a handsome yellow silk banner emblazoned with inscriptions and emblems in gold, which is still preserved by his descendants, and which I have often seen—indeed, which I got some time ago repaired. The principal motto on the flag is, "EAST MONKLAND FOR CHURCH AND STATE, ACCORDING TO THE WORD OF GOD AND THE COVENANT," and there is the representation of a Bible, a crown and thistle, with the motto, *Nemo me impune lacessit*, and under it a hand grasping a drawn dagger. Eleven men from New Monkland were killed at Bothwell Bridge, including Andrew Yuill, the gardener of Rochsoles, which is close to my father's manse, and others with names and from places still equally well known in the parish. Eight were made prisoners, and nineteen were fined in considerable sums. Dreadful hardships were endured in New Monkland during the Covenanting period. An old writer says:—

"For the space of ten years, the parish, with little exception, was at the mercy of the military, who wantonly wasted and plundered, and took a pride in their cruelties. . . . Troops of dragoons frequently came to the parish, under pretence sometimes of seeking arms, and sometimes to hinder conventicles; but their chief end was plunder, which, when they collected, they would have compelled the people to furnish horses to convey to head-quarters at Hamilton. The cruelties they exercised during such marauding are indescribable. When those whom they designed to seize upon had made their escape, they seized their cattle. When not hunted after by the military, they were frequently, upon reports and information, called before the Sheriff and other courts, where they were fined and forced to come under bonds and engagements contrary to their consciences, and which to many of them were more grievous than all the losses they had sustained. Few parishes were more harassed, for when the military were in the neighbourhood they seldom failed to pay East Monkland a visit either going or returning. On one occasion the curate at Cumbernauld brought two hundred dragoons to search for men in the woods, and when they found none they quartered themselves upon the inhabitants, and consumed everything at their pleasure. The laird of Monkland was subjected to forfeiture, and that most unjustly. . . . His son was obliged to sell the half of his estate after the Revolution."

These facts may account for the strong Presbyterianism of the district, for the welcome with which the Revolution was greeted, and for the circumstance that in both of the Monklands the 600 merks were paid to the patrons under the Act 1690, so that Queen Anne's Act restoring patronage did not take effect in them. In both of these parishes the heritors and elders still[1] "propose" the minister for the acceptance of the congregation, and to this probably may be traced the fact that my father was ever a parish minister there.

At the time when I was born the district was tranquil and comparatively thinly peopled—there was little stir or enterprise; but the discovery of coal and iron has since added enormously to the surrounding wealth and population. The southern district especially is now densely peopled. My

[1] This was of course written before the Patronage Abolition Act of 1874.—T. S.

father was minister of the New Monkland for upwards of forty years, having been previously for a short time assistant at St. Ninians, and afterwards for seven years, with much acceptance, minister of the Calton Chapel, Glasgow. He was born at Douglas in the upper ward of Lanarkshire, and both his father and mother were stern Reformed Presbyterians. There are still favourable recollections of the family in that district. My grandfather is said to have been a man of much excellence; and Dr. Symington of Paisley told me that my grandmother was distinguished for her knowledge of the Bible above almost all the women he ever knew. She was so determined a Reformed Presbyterian, however, that she would never go to hear her son preach, he having at an early period joined the Established Church. All my relatives by that side were nearly equally determined Covenanters. Although they came to live in the manse occasionally, and although everything was pleasant as amongst friends, they would never enter the parish church, but doggedly walked two miles to the Reformed Presbyterian chapel at Airdrie. These are amongst my earliest recollections; and although, as a little boy, I did not understand these controversies, I remember holding these friends in decided veneration. Their conduct and determination gave me even then a strong impression of the importance of fixed principles. It is one of my oldest recollections that I asked one of my uncles, who was a Reformed Presbyterian elder, why he did not go to the parish church; when I received in the most solemn manner the following answer, "Thou shalt not hear the instruction which causeth to err from the words of truth." How astonished these people would have been, had they been now alive, at some very different characters who affect at present to be the standard-bearers of Reformed Presbyterian orthodoxy! The older "Cameronians," as they were called at that time, were a noble race, and the very stringency with which they adhered to what they regarded as fixed principles, avoiding, like Davie Deans, "right-hand extremes and left-hand defections," was very remarkable, and a peculiar glory in the race of Scotchmen. I have always felt it to be an honour to have some of this blood running in my veins.

My mother's name was Mary Mathie. She was daughter of a merchant in Greenock, and was born in Manse Lane in 1777. She was a woman of great amiability and considerable humour, a person of excellent sense and devoted Christian principle, an excellent manager of domestic affairs, but very quiet and retiring. She was in some respects a considerable contrast to my father. This often happens, and with great advantage. My father was a man of a strong and determined nature, although also kind and considerate, and possessed of very noble qualities. He possessed great natural talent and sagacity, high Christian principle, and was one of the most popular preachers in the West of Scotland in his day. He retained his popularity to the last. His church, which contained upwards of 1000 people, was filled every Sabbath, and many people regularly came great distances, some of them seven and eight miles, to attend public worship. The recollection of his ministry is still strong in the district, and no doubt will be heard of in eternity. He was one of the best specimens of the old parish minister, and had vast local influence for good. The church bells were rung thrice every Sabbath by a curious but excellent old character called William Brownlee, a worthy sample of the old Scotch beadle, who took as deep an interest in everything parochial, as if he had been the minister himself. Before the third bell began, the people were seen flocking in their Sabbath dresses with the utmost gravity from all quarters to the church. When William Brownlee, with his picturesque broad blue bonnet, came round for the Bible, before beginning to ring the bell for the third time, my father was in the habit of asking him what o'clock it was; and I have heard him answer, with the greatest solemnity, "It's jist seven minutes and three quarters frae the oor, if I'm no mista'en, for I wouldna like to tell a lee." These peaceful and striking Sabbaths never can be forgotten. They are the glory of Scotland; and it is impossible to deny that if the system of parochial subdivision and thorough Scriptural instruction had only received justice and kept pace with the population, we should have had, by the blessing of God, a model country in a far higher degree than statesmen have ever imagined. To have powerful Christian men acting in manageable districts everywhere, backed by public authority, surrounded by a loving and devoted people, preaching the doctrines of the Gospel with all earnestness from Sabbath to Sabbath and from house to house, was a blessing of inestimable value, and a marked contrast to much that we see at present under pretence of "progress." My father was a thoroughly devoted evangelical minister, and his time was entirely engrossed with preaching, visiting, catechising, managing the poor, attending Presbyteries, assisting at communions, and generally promoting the temporal and spiritual interests of all around. There are some features of his private character, moreover, that are specially worthy of notice, for his religion was not of the shallow and inconsistent type so often met with at present. He had the greatest abhorrence of debt, and when, after his death, we advertised for his creditors, there was found to be nothing due but the bill of the doctor who attended him on his death-bed. My subsequent experience in life has proved that this is by no means a common thing, although there is no clearer precept in Scripture than "Owe no man anything." Very few seem to square their expenditure rigidly by their income, "paying as they possess," as the Scotch people say; although there is no other way of being thoroughly honest. A universal system of ready-money payment in all domestic transactions would remove one of the greatest evils and sources of discomfort, although some people seem to take their debts very coolly. We have heard of a Scotch woman, to whom a neighbour said, "Ephie, I wonder hoo ye can sleep wi' sae muckle debt on your head;" to which Ephie quietly answered, "I can sleep fu' weel, but I wunner *they* can sleep that trust me!" My father was most particular in making statements as to matters of fact, and if we made an assertion in an apparently careless or exaggerated way, he instantly cross-questioned us, to see that we had sufficient ground for what we said, and that it was neither untrue nor exaggerated. He was very bold, and would say nothing behind a man's back which he was not prepared to say to his face. At the time of what were called the Radicals, when I was very young, my father, although always an advocate for reasonable reform, yet because some of them maintained theories of spoliation to be promoted by force and civil war, and were supplying themselves with pikes and other instruments, denounced them from the pulpit, and declared that it was an attempt on the part of "the scum of the earth" (this was said with great emphasis, and I yet remember it distinctly) to become rulers of the nation. It was alleged at that time that some of the leaders of the Revolutionists in Airdrie were proposing to divide the different estates. Each was making his selection of a considerable property in the neighbourhood —some were for Airdrie House, others for Cavinhill, others for Rochsoles. One of them said, "John, I think I would just be contented wi' your house and garden." "*My* house!" exclaimed John, with the utmost astonishment and indignation. "Are you going to become a public robber?" "The case being altered, that alters the case." They were very violent, and threatened to shoot all who should oppose them, and my father among the rest. He adopted his measures at once, sent away his family, but set the enemy at defiance himself. I remember well being sent as a child, in a cart covered with blankets, with all the rest of the family, to the neighbouring manse of Slamannan, ten miles distant, and inland, far from the scene of strife. The minister, Mr.

Robertson, was a quiet and comfortable bachelor, and received us with great hospitality. But my father himself would not move, lived in the manse, continued to denounce what he regarded as unsound views from his pulpit, and walked the streets of Airdrie as if nothing were happening. After a time the storm blew over, and we returned in safety and comfort to our old residence, whilst the ordinary routine of parish action proceeded as before. A thoroughly evangelical preacher, my father entered more fully than many do at present into all the details of duty and sin, "breaking sanctification small," as Dr. Chalmers was in the habit of phrasing it. Airdrie was chiefly at that time a place of weavers, and some of them had stolen the yarn of the Glasgow manufacturers. I have the most vivid recollection of my father preaching on this with great earnestness and emphasis in a sermon from the text, "Let him that stole steal no more." The general population was, in ordinary times, very quiet and orderly; and family worship, or, as it was called, "taking the books," was almost universally observed. But there were a few noted and less satisfactory characters in the parish, and amongst the rest a well-known drunkard called Willie Paul, who was the terror of the children as he reeled home at night. At length the news was spread through the parish that Willie, in one of his drunken fits, had fallen into an empty coal-pit and was drowned. This produced a deep sensation, and the following Sabbath I remember most vividly my father's sermon on the text, "At the last it biteth like a serpent, and stingeth like an adder." As a decided Presbyterian, he stoutly maintained his own opinion. He hated all mere partisanship in Church Courts, and never allowed himself to become a mere follower of men. But yet, at the same time, he never carried public discussions into private life; and I have heard him say that, if he was brought into collision with any of the brethren in public debate in the Presbytery or Synod, he not only endeavoured to avoid mere personality, but he contrived as soon as possible to see them, so as to remove any feeling of asperity, and to have friendly conversation on other subjects. His rule was, moreover, never to desert a friend in difficulty, or to admit any one in whom he had confidence to be wrong until he was proved to be so. A remarkable case of this kind occurred, which I have often heard him mention. The celebrated Dr. Mackinlay of Kilmarnock did what is generally held to be a very imprudent thing, namely, married his own servant. There were circumstances connected with the marriage which gave rise to remark; as, for example, that on his marriage jaunt he was alleged to have worn a coat with metal buttons, and some other similar circumstances of which a handle might be made. But my father, who had investigated the whole matter, was convinced that there was nothing in it but a proceeding of doubtful prudence and taste, and especially that there was nothing morally wrong. He therefore stood bravely by the doctor, as did all his own numerous congregation at Kilmarnock. He went as usual to assist him at his communion, when others refused, till the cloud had passed away, which it did afterwards most thoroughly. "A friend in need is a friend indeed." On the arrival of my father at Kilmarnock, he announced to Dr. Mackinlay that he would do the whole usual work of his assistants single-handed. And I often heard him mention that, accordingly, he preached twice on the Thursday, twice on the Saturday, exhorted ten tables, and preached in the evening on Sabbath, and wound up all by preaching twice on the Monday. Some one who was present at the ten tables declared, that the longer he spoke, he spoke the better. On one occasion a warm admirer of his said that he had "a Bothwell Brig face;" and he was just the man to carry out his resolution in such circumstances with heroic determination. He was a great advocate for punctuality in keeping appointments, and reckoned the waste of other people's time, by keeping them waiting, little better than a breach of the eighth commandment. Whilst abundantly frank and outspoken in proper circumstances, no one referred more frequently to, or understood better the propriety of, the proverb—"A fool uttereth all his mind, but a wise man keepeth it in till afterwards." He had a stern dislike of all meretricious modes of courting popularity, of all innovations in worship. Hence his successful struggle in favour of the old form of the communion table, in opposition to the administration of the sacrament in pews, as a violation of the original institution of the Lord's Supper, and inconsistent with the very appearance of a feast or sacrament of communion. Hence his struggle, along with others, which was also crowned with success, against the organ in St. Andrew's Church, Glasgow, as inconsistent with Presbyterian principle, as a restoration of part of the Temple service, as opposed to the simplicity and spirituality of New Testament worship, and fitted seriously to divide the Church. Hence his contention against the painted window representing Christ blessing children in St. Enoch's Church, Glasgow. Hence his dislike to the whole modern system of certificates carried about by preachers, as if they were a kind of servants in quest of situations, as derogatory to the license which they have received after thorough study and examination, from a Presbytery, and as no real proof of their qualifications. I remember a preacher who had been in the parish for some time on one occasion applying for a certificate, expecting, no doubt, a towering enumeration of all his qualities. My father simply wrote, "I certify that —— is a member of this congregation, and that he is free from scandal or any ground of Church censure, so far as I know." I do not know whether he used the certificate or not. Probably he did not. But this system of carrying about a sheaf of certificates, which was then only beginning, has now grown into a gigantic abuse. The people and preachers are equally to blame for this. It is said that a Scotch client on one occasion, hearing his case defended by an eloquent lawyer, exclaimed, "I aye kent that I was ill-used, but I never kent *how* ill-used I was until I heard yon man speak." So, many of our preachers may well say, "We always knew, or at least hoped, that we were very clever fellows; but we did not know, and people will never suspect, how clever we are, except by our certificates."

My father said that in his younger days he was rather delicate. His constitution, however, must always have been good; his voice was singularly clear and powerful, and by his plain and wholesome diet and quiet life in the country he became, by the blessing of God, strong and robust. Indeed, he was a strong man till very advanced in years, and died at his post with unclouded intellect, and scarcely diminished strength, at eighty-three. He had an amazing knowledge of the Scriptures. Not only could he quote them easily and accurately, but his knowledge of them was most minute. For example, in quoting from the book of Job, he could tell whether it was Job himself, Bildad the Shuhite, Zophar the Naamathite, Eliphaz the Temanite, or Elihu, the son of Barachel the Buzite, that spoke; although at the same time he had a great contempt for all knowledge of the Scriptures which had not a special reference to matters vital and of eternal interest. He was a great walker, not keeping a horse. I have repeatedly walked with him to Shotts, Slamannan, and Hamilton, distances varying from eight to ten miles. His chief business at Hamilton was to attend the Presbytery, although on one occasion I went with him there to be introduced to the then Duke of Hamilton, who examined me in Horace, and gave me a bursary in Glasgow College. I remember still the fear and trembling with which I was ushered through several apartments in the Palace of Hamilton into the presence of the great man, who rather plumed himself upon his scholarship, and the delight with which I heard the expression of his Grace's satisfaction.

To Shotts and Slamannan my father went to preach on the days of the communion, and I sometimes went with him. But in every case we walked home again after the work of the day was over, the distance altogether being from sixteen to twenty miles. His preaching on these occasions was very powerful. Although I knew some of the sermons beforehand, having heard them before, I always listened to them with fresh interest, and the more pathetic or alarming passages always came with fresh power. He preached without a note before him, but not without thorough preparation. He was a great advocate for this mode of preaching, and an admirable model of it. He deeply regretted the gradual prevalence of a different method, as fitted to weaken the power of the pulpit. It may suit men of genius, but in the case of ordinary men and ordinary people it is much less effective for good. Some one asked him on one occasion whether there was any good reason for the change in the case of common preachers, when he answered with his usual decision and in strong Doric, "The reason is doon-richt laziness."

In my young days the mass of the people of that district, with the exception of those resident in Airdrie, which was then only a small village, belonged to the rural population. There were a number of small proprietors scattered through the parish, commonly called in Scotland "bonnet lairds." Most of them were very respectable people, although their means were at that time very limited. The discovery of iron, which has since brought such a vast population to the district, has since enriched many of them. Coals were then abundant, and the indication that iron existed under the surface was even then evident in some places by the red colour of the water, although the matter excited little attention. In particular, there was a well in the parish strongly impregnated with sulphur and iron, called the "Virtue Well," to which the people resorted, with little idea of the immense wealth that was stored up beneath the surface. Coatbridge at that time had only a few houses. Amongst the first persons to make the discovery that iron existed, and might be of great value, were the family of the Bairds, whose remarkable rise from high respectability in common life into prodigious fortunes I remember. The result has been almost incredible in certain instances. For example, it is said that one piece of moss land was bought at that time for £300, and that out of it £100,000 worth of iron has since been taken. In my early days, however, nothing of all this great wealth existed. But although not very rich, some of the small lairds were remarkably litigious. Although my father was the sort of local judge and general arbiter, yet one or two of them ruined themselves by prolonged cases in the civil courts. My father remonstrated strongly with them. The matters in debate were often very trifling, as a gravestone in the churchyard, or a seat in the church, or a precise boundary. One of them, in answer to these remonstrances, said with great emphasis, "I really dinna ken ony greater pleasure on earth than a weel-gawin'[1] law-plea." That same man ruined himself by this insane love of litigation. He was forced to part with a very comfortable property, and left his family in penury.

These were the exceptions, however; the mass of the people being very respectable and well behaved. I believe many of them were true Christians. They were most regular attenders on public worship. The intelligence exhibited at the public examinations held by my father in the different districts, their love of Divine ordinances, the heartiness of their singing the praises of God, in which they were led by a most exemplary and intelligent precentor, called Ebenezer Patterson, a thorough and enthusiastic musician, were all extremely refreshing and symptomatic of good. Large gatherings of people assembled at the communion seasons, a peculiarity which still exists in the north of Scotland. Be-

[1] That is, "well-going."—T. S.

sides much week-day preaching by able ministers on such occasions, the church was crowded on the Sabbath during the long but deeply interesting service, whilst five or six sermons were at the same time preached to an immense congregation at "the tent." The effect of all this I believe to have been on the whole very beneficial, notwithstanding the ridicule of Burns, and the comparative coldness of later times. All my own earliest and most solemn impressions of Divine things were connected with these memorable scenes, although they were much deepened and confirmed afterwards by the early death of one of my sisters, and by other circumstances.

Apart from other considerations, these great and memorable seasons of communion were of much value, by breaking in upon the routine of the ordinary Sabbaths, confirming at the mouths of many witnesses the great truths of the Gospel, giving the people of the whole district an opportunity of hearing the most powerful preaching, and refreshing and stimulating the ministers themselves by pleasant and edifying intercourse with each other. The alleged drawbacks to the system were as nothing in comparison with these great and manifest advantages.

Some of the able men who assisted my father from year to year at the communion were very remarkable. Dr. Scott of Greenock interchanged services regularly with my father. He was a grave and able man, and had collected a large and deeply attached congregation in the Middle Church of Greenock, in the ministry of which Dr. Cunningham afterwards acted as his colleague. I have still a vivid recollection of a sermon he preached on one of these occasions on the text—"How shall we escape if we neglect so great salvation?" He dwelt with peculiar power and emphasis on the word "neglect," showing that men required simply to do nothing, only to let the matter alone, to secure their final destruction. Being condemned already, they had merely to allow the day of grace to pass away unimproved, and their ruin was certain. Simple as the truths are, they came with peculiar force from the lips of Dr. Scott. The following passage in regard to him is from the pen of Dr. Cunningham:—

"Dr. Scott was possessed in an eminent degree of almost all those qualifications which render a minister of the Gospel a workman that needeth not to be ashamed,—excellent talents, extensive information, very high attainments in personal holiness, a thorough knowledge of the Word of God, sound and comprehensive views of Christian doctrine, great practical acquaintance with the effects of the truth on the minds of men of different characters and in different circumstances, and much Christian wisdom in rightly dividing the Word of Truth, so as to make it bear most directly and successfully upon the minds of those whom he addressed.

"I had not the happiness of knowing him until after he had been laid aside from the discharge of public duty, but it was my privilege for several years to act as his assistant, and to minister among his flock; and I can truly say of him, as Burnet did of Leighton, that 'I have the greatest veneration for his memory, and that I reckon my knowledge of him among the greatest blessings of my life, and for which I know I must give an account to God in the great day.' I had an opportunity of witnessing, and I think it proper to bear testimony to, his singular freedom from those feelings which, even among good men, sometimes disturb the cordial and affectionate harmony that ought to subsist between an aged pastor and his assistant and successor, his profound and lively interest in the spiritual welfare of his flock, manifested in every way that was practicable, and especially in habitual prayer that the blessing of God might rest upon them, and his holy and magnanimous disregard of everything but what might tend most to promote the glory of God in the salvation of their souls. From peculiar circumstances, he was placed in a situation in which he was called upon, after he had been laid aside from public duty, to choose between securing what he reckoned a pure dispensation of Christian truth to his flock, and the accomplishment of an object which must have been dear to his strongest natural affections, and he never hesitated which side to choose. He continued, while he lived, to act firmly and conscientiously, under the conviction that he was bound to have for his first object the spiritual welfare of the flock over which the Holy Ghost had made him overseer, whatever sacrifices this might require at his hand."[1]

In the life of one of his most excellent hearers, to whom his ministry was much blessed, we find the following:—

"Mrs. Johnstone always enumerated among her most precious means of spiritual instruction, the ministry of her beloved pastor, the late Rev. Dr. Scott, which she long enjoyed and highly prized, particularly the discourses he preached for many years every alternate Wednesday forenoon. She would say, 'He frequently seemed to be allowed to catch a glimpse, as it were, within the veil, as the spirit of grace and supplication was largely poured out upon him when he brought us to the mercy-seat where grace reigns, and with a fluency and copiousness of expression peculiarly his own, made our requests known unto God, carrying us, through our Advocate with the Father and glorious High Priest, into the holiest of all, that we might receive those gracious communications which would prepare us for entering His glorious presence in Heaven. Then he exhibited in a manner peculiarly convincing and attractive the doctrines of the Cross, unfolding to the eye of faith the dignity and glory of the person of Christ, the nature and perfections of God, as seen in Him in whom the fulness of the Godhead dwells, setting forth what debtors we are to sovereign kindness, and proving from the Word of Truth the suitableness to our utter helplessness and spiritual destitution of all the offices which Christ sustains, as well as of all the relations in which He is revealed.'

"She often spoke of the remarkable blessing which flows from sanctified affliction, as eminently qualifying her pastor to direct and comfort many in their day of distress, by pointing them to the fountain of consolation from which he had been enabled to draw all his support, under manifold, continued, and complicated trials. She would say, 'Dear Dr. Scott has been called to drink largely of the cup of affliction,

[1] Preface by Dr. Cunningham to a volume of sermons of Rev. Dr. John Scott, Greenock, pp. 4, 5. Edinburgh: Oliver & Boyd, 1839.

but in the school of experience and of Christ "he has learned in whatsoever state he is therewith to be content;" like his blessed Master, "learning obedience by the things he has suffered;"' and would go on to observe, 'Ministers who are faithful need not escape trial and suffering, for the Scripture has it, "And whether we be afflicted, it is for your consolation and salvation, which is effectual in the enduring of the same sufferings which we also suffer; or whether we be comforted, it is for your consolation and salvation."'"[1]

Yet, like most of the other excellent men of this stamp that I have met with, Dr. Scott had a great deal of innocent humour, and told a story with much zest. I remember his telling one of a sailor who came to be married, and when asked if he would take the woman to be his lawful and married wife, he hesitated, looked blank, and said, "I would like to know first what you are going to say to *she*." On another occasion when the woman was asked if she would obey, and did not at once answer, the sailor exclaimed, "Leave that to me, sir."

Dr. Love of Anderston also was a regular assistant. He is well known to have been a man of high spirituality and great mental power. He was an early secretary of the London Missionary Society. He was a slow and solemn but very impressive preacher. Some one has said that his sermons consisted of a strong view of the attributes, with "a use" of terror. His sermon on the Revolution, on the text, "He is terrible to the kings of the earth," is very powerful.

In the Appendix to Dr. Scott's life it is said :—

"Those who knew Dr. Love in the pulpit only could not conceive of him as he appeared in the social circle, modestly conspicuous for Christian cheerfulness and Christian courteousness; and, when he chose, contributing in a singularly engaging manner to rational and profitable enjoyment. Much as his society was sought by eminent ministers and Christians

---

[1] Memoir of the late Mrs. Ann Johnstone, Willow Park, Greenock, pp. 35-37. Second edition. Edinburgh: Oliphant & Sons, 1846.

of almost every denomination, and much as his ministerial labours were increased with his advancing years, he continued to secure leisure to cultivate the favourite classical studies of his youth, and also to read with delight some of the most celebrated works of the Greek Fathers; and though about the same time he was not chosen to fill the theological chair of a northern university when he submitted to a comparative trial, the electors declared him to be 'worthy of the highest literary honours,' and a sister university, not long after, conferred on him the highest degree in divinity.

"Thus distinguished for talents and literary acquirements in ministerial duties and in social life, Dr. Love was still more distinguished, in secret and in private, as a man who lived to God, and 'walked with God.' Frequently as he worshipped the Supreme Being, he habitually guarded against 'drawing nigh to Him with his mouth, and honouring Him with his lips, while his heart was far from Him.' He anxiously sought a sense of the Divine presence in his devotions, how short soever, and diligently watched for the tokens of it. He gratefully acknowledged them when perceived, and the least diminution of them he as tenderly lamented; nor, for near thirty years, was he either frequently or long deprived of this his richest enjoyment, even amid sharp trials and depressing infirmities." [1]

Such was another of the men by whom the large congregations at New Monkland were roused and led during the seasons of communion. I remember well that grave and sweet old face relaxing into the utmost tenderness, and the quiet and genial humour with which this Elijah-like man told pleasant, interesting, and profitable stories, and enjoyed a hearty laugh.

Mr. Bower of Old Monkland was an extremely popular minister, and a great preacher in the tent. He carried on long dialogues in his sermons, which were extremely fascinating to the people. William Anderson was the village innkeeper, and he, on his own behalf, was anxious, as the afternoon wore on, that some one should preach in the tent who

---

[1] Appendix to volume of sermons by Dr. John Scott: Memoir of Dr. John Love, p. 488.

was less popular, that the people might adjourn for their simple refreshment in his hostelry. It is said that on one occasion he was looking out of his door, with blank and unavailing anxiety, and seeing one stray man approaching from the preaching ground, he eagerly asked, "Are they no moving yet?" To which the reply was, "Mr. Bower has ta'en the tent, and they'll no be moving for an hour yet." It is a pity that samples of that old and effective kind of preaching have not been preserved. I only remember the introduction of one of Mr. Bower's sermons. The text was, "Blessed are the dead that die in the Lord," and Mr. Bower proceeded to say, "When a man dies people say to one another, 'When did he die? What did he die of? Was he long ill? What family has he left? Has he left any money? Who has he left it to?' But, alas! alas! how few ask the question, 'Did he die in the Lord?'" He also was a considerable humourist. Indeed, it may be almost taken as an axiom, that there can be no thoroughly great man without some sense of the ludicrous, for everything has a ludicrous side, and a man cannot see all the sides of any truth, unless he sees this amongst the rest. Like the ministers of those days, Mr. Bower was a man of great influence at Old Monkland, and exercised a general superintendence of all things in his parish. Curious cases were sometimes brought before him. I remember his telling of one woman who came to complain that her husband did not give her enough to eat, and in proof of this she brought the actual porridge that was to serve for her breakfast, and did this more than once. Whereupon Mr. Bower at length exclaimed, "If ye bring them any more I'll sup them." He at the same time thought that she ought to manifest more respect to her husband, and reminded her of Sarah, who "honoured her husband, calling him lord," upon which the woman exclaimed, with the utmost scorn and disdain, "John Tamson my lord, bonny my lord!" Mr. Bower disliked very much new and ranting tunes, and preaching on one occasion in a church where the precentor was alleged to be fond of novelties, he leant over the pulpit after giving out the psalm, and giving him a smart tap with the psalm-book on the head, said, "Now come, gie us nane o' your lilts." It was a practice in those days for some of the people to stand up during the sermon to shake off a tendency to drowsiness, but with poor human nature this was sometimes made a means of indulging vanity and a spirit of display. On one occasion a man who had got a very smart and rather gaudy vest stood up more than once, and threw back his coat apparently to let the vest be seen. Mr. Bower said at length, "Noo, John, ye had better sit doon; we have a' seen your braw waistcoat." The system of public rebuke in the church still continued, and on one occasion, calling up for some offence a woman named Janet Greenhorn, he began by saying "Janet Greenhorn," and with emphasis began, "Nae Greenhorn in sin." Preaching, it is said, at one time, of Peter weeping, he said, "Now observe this was not a woman, for everybody kens that there's sometimes little between their greeting and their laughing." These were the eccentricities, however, of a truly able and very popular man. My father heard him preach his first sermon, from the text, "Thou shalt remember all the way which the Lord thy God led thee these forty years in the wilderness, to humble thee and to prove thee, to know what was in thine heart, whether thou wouldest keep His commandments, or no" (Deut. viii. 2). The first words of his first public prayer were, "Lord, we pray for all men, from Pharaoh riding in his gilded chariot to the maid that is behind the mill."

Mr. Bower had a beadle who was a considerable character, as many of the old beadles were. On one occasion he said to the minister, in reference to the grave-digging, which was also part of his function, "Trade's very dull the noo; I hae na buried a leevin cratur for three weeks." It reminds us of the language of the poet—

> "See yonder maker of the dead man's bed,
> The sexton, hoary-headed chronicler,
> Of hard unmeaning face, down which ne'er stole
> A gentle tear."

This same beadle, who was very much an eye-servant, was appointed to watch the gooseberries during the days of the communion, when, amongst a multitude of worthy people, some doubtful characters came about. On one occasion, when the beadle saw some one coming out of the manse, and therefore likely to observe and report, he exclaimed, with the greatest apparent zeal, to strangers going near the garden, "How daur ye touch the minister's grosets?" but as soon as the manse people had again vanished out of sight, he proceeded to add, in an undertone, "Tak a pickle for a' that." Mr. Bower had no children of his own; but a young relative of the name of James (or, as he was more generally called, Jamie) Hamilton stayed with him. The minister was very indulgent. Jamie was a great pickle, and gave poor Mr. Bower a great deal of trouble. He gave himself out as a kind of doctor, and, out of pure mischief, made absurd prescriptions, which sometimes had only the effect of making bad worse. Occasionally he took fits of running away, and Mr. Bower had much trouble in hunting him out and bringing him back. On one occasion, it is said, he went to Edinburgh, took up his quarters in a hotel, calling himself Captain Hamilton. After much trouble Mr. Bower found where he was, arrived at the hotel, and demanded whether a Mr. Hamilton was there. The waiter said, "There's a Captain Hamilton here." Mr. Bower, entering into the humour of the joke, immediately said, with great briskness, "Will you be good enough to tell him that Major Bower has come?"

Dr. Mackinlay of Kilmarnock was one of the leading assistants both at Old and New Monkland on those sacramental occasions. He was certainly a most powerful preacher, and I have the most vivid recollection still of the sermons that I heard him preach to large crowds in the open air. One was upon the text "Prepare to meet thy God, O Israel" (Amos iv. 12), and the other on "Awake, thou that sleepest, and arise from the dead, and Christ shall give thee light" (Eph. v. 14). There was something singularly imposing in Dr. Mackinlay's appearance. He was a born orator. His manner, voice, and matter, all conspired to produce a great effect. From the time of his entering the tent or pulpit, you were struck with him as no ordinary man; and his various, solemn, perfectly self-possessed, and lively manner sustained the attention throughout. It might be said of him, in the words of Milton in regard to one of his heroes—

"All gave attention mute, and he began."

The caricatures of him given by Burns, who had evidently heard him, and deals with him as a man of great power and celebrity, convey a tolerably good impression of the general effect of his preaching. The following statement is founded in truth, although, of course, it is distorted and exaggerated:—

"Hear how he clears the points of faith
  Wi' rattlin' and wi' thumpin'!
Now meekly calm, now wild in wrath,
  He's stampin' and he's jumpin'!"

There was a considerable art in effective tent-preaching, with which, however, except in the North of Scotland, very few of our Scotch ministers are now familiar. The great secret was to keep well within the tent, and to use it as a speaking-trumpet. In this way a man with a clear voice could speak to a great multitude. It was not a tent such as the military use, for covering both the people and minister, but simply an upright enclosed pulpit with a book-board and small canopy, and it was upon the whole admirably adapted for the purpose in view. Skilfully employed by a man accustomed to it, thousands could be addressed with the greatest ease, whilst the exercise of the lungs in the open air is much less exhausting than in a crowded meeting within doors. I have heard my father's voice distinctly nearly half a mile away on a still Sabbath. The exercise, however, had its difficulties. When the day was stormy, the ordeal was sometimes trying even for the experienced. The rule of the tent was that a minister continued till the next arrived. It is said that on one occasion, when the wind was blowing hard in the mouth of the tent, a worthy minister began to hesitate about going up the steps to continue the exercise, whereupon one of the worthy old women who generally clustered round, and were notable at all tent-preachings, said, "Gang up, man, gang up; is it no said that ye should spend and be spent?" To which he quietly remarked, "It's quite true, my good woman, but no a' in ae day." It was in connection with this form of preaching that the dislike of the common people to reading sermons came out into greatest prominence. The well-known story of the man who had a portion of his sermon blown away out of the tent, and to whom one of the hearers on handing it back said, "There's your fourthly," is an illustration of this. This feeling prevailed in the strongest form in the district about which I am writing, and at the time to which my narrative relates, I remember well the pungent remarks of the people on the subject: "Hoo can we mind the minister's sermon, if he canna mind it himsel'?" was the constant theory. It was regarded as a kind of imbecility not to be able to speak "without the paper." It was supposed to prove that colleges were after all of no value. The idea was that a "college-bred man" should be able to speak as often and as long as was necessary. This was the great purpose of college training. On one occasion when my father was from home, which was very seldom, he sent a youthful substitute, who turned out to be very conceited, and a slavish reader. A poem was sent to my father on his return home. I wish I could give the whole of it, but after a high eulogium on my father's preaching ability, and the effect of this both in promoting spiritual good, and in producing a reaction against weaker men, the anonymous author went on to say:—

> "The ither Sabbath I did mark,
>   The conduct o' yon braw young spark;
> He slipped the Bible in the dark,
>   Thought nane would see.
> Awa wi' siccan smuggled wark,
>   It's no for me.
> An' thinkin' he wad no be seen,
> Did something in the Bible preen;[1]
> But, ah! there were ower mony een
>   On him that glanced,
> And ca'd it weak and unco mean,
>   What he advanced.
> I never likit sermon readin',
> It's but a dry and sapless feedin',
> Sae tell yon chiel for to be heedin'
>   If he comes back;
> His sermons dress in ither cleadin'
>   Than white and black."

Dr. Mackinlay was an admirable sample of the method of preaching without reading, and Dr. Chalmers an equally remarkable illustration of the opposite method. Dr. Chalmers, however, was an exception to all rules, and it is simply absurd on the part of men of little talent and dull mediocrity to say, "We will read our sermons, because Dr. Chalmers did so." A sermon to be read with effect should be most powerful, "every sentence the weight of a talent." If it were possible to have an average of men of the power and eloquence of Dr. Chalmers, they might adopt any course they pleased. But as the whole experience of the world in past ages, and the experience of all other kinds of oratory at present prove, a man as a general rule loses immense advantage by reading sermons, provided always he will take sufficient previous pains in the way of preparation. This must be assumed on both sides. It is not to be forgotten that there is such a thing as extemporaneous writing, as well as extemporaneous

---

[1] *I.e.*, "pin."

speaking, and one is, to say the least of it, quite as dull and intolerable as the other.

Turning to the ministers of that period at New Monkland, Dr. Gardiner of Bothwell was a regular assistant at the communion. Many of my readers know that he afterwards made a great figure in what was called the " Moderatorship Controversy," and that he is only lately deceased. He was a man of strong constitution, of good sense and sound doctrine, but not a remarkably popular preacher. In seconding the motion for his appointment as Moderator in 1837, my father said:—

"That gentleman is well qualified to occupy the Moderator's chair, and if he is called to it, I feel assured that he will discharge his duties with ability and dignity. I have had every opportunity of being acquainted with Dr. Gardiner, and know him to be a man most distinguished for his character, talents, and acquirements. During more than twenty-five years he has been a member of the Presbytery of Hamilton, and he at all times has attended most regularly and most minutely to the business of that court. I know his steady and unwavering zeal in behalf of the best interests of the Church of Scotland, and especially of that noble and patriotic scheme of Church Extension in which we are so happily engaged," &c.

A very different man in some respects, although less publicly known, was Dr. Hodgson of Blantyre—a great ally of my father's in the Presbytery of Hamilton and other Church Courts, although he did not often preach at New Monkland. He was a great scholar and an eloquent preacher—a devoted minister—and at the same time a man of much wit and vigour of mind. In the debate in the General Assembly on the communion table, some one had said that it was a small matter. Dr. Hodgson exclaimed, "Principles are never small, although deviations from them often seem of little importance. There is a river which at its source a child may step across, but on its vast expanse, when it approaches towards the sea, all the navies of the world may ride." He only published one sermon, so far as I know, a sermon preached at the opening of the Synod of Glasgow and Ayr, on the text, "They stoned Stephen, calling upon God and saying, Lord Jesus, receive my spirit." But this sermon contains many fine passages, and amongst the rest the following in regard to Scotland:—"There is a land of small extent, whose shores have been pronounced inhospitable, whose sky has been described as ever foul with clouds, and whose surface is drenched by frequent rains. And yet to this country the eyes of Europe have been directed, assembled senates have made choice of it when in a high debate they considered the advantages of knowledge, and orators have delighted to expatiate upon it as the land of educated men." Dr. Hodgson was famous at repartee. He was once travelling on the outside of a coach, when a man began to speak disparagingly of John Knox. Dr. Hodgson suddenly turned round, and said, with the greatest gravity, "Sir, we have no men now-a-days like John Knox; he never opened his mouth but he blew down a cathedral!" He was a great friend of the late Dr. Clason, whom he familiarly called "Peter." On one occasion when Dr. Hodgson was telling a story, Dr. Clason said, "I think I have heard you tell that story before, Doctor." The Doctor promptly replied, with that strong and rich burr for which he was distinguished, "Very likely, Peter, every man has a limited number, you know. You have two, Dr. Russell (of Dalserf, a noted man also at that time) has five, and I have twenty-six." Some one hinted that they had heard him preach the same sermon before, when he quickly retorted, "Yes, and by the blessing of God, I hope you may live to hear it again." Some one heard Dr. Hodgson preaching on a Sacrament Sabbath evening, when a heavy-footed ploughman in the gallery left his seat about the middle of the sermon, and with heavy tramps made his way towards the door, disturbing the Doctor and the whole congregation. Dr. Hodgson immediately exclaimed, "Where did you learn that, sir? Did you learn it in your Catechism, or did your mother teach you it?" and he added, with great emphasis, "SIT DOWN, SIR." The man, entirely taken by surprise, instantly resumed his seat, and the congregation was no further disturbed. Dr. Hodgson's wife was rather a character, and often tried to measure swords with him in the way of wit, but, although a clever woman, seldom with much success. A preacher who told us the story once officiated at Blantyre. After the sermon, and on his return to the manse, Mrs. Hodgson ventured upon a few words in the way of commendation, whereupon the Doctor exclaimed, "Ann, that won't do; you couldn't judge of that sermon; you slept." Poor Ann was obliged to acknowledge that she had been overcome with sleep during part of the discourse, but she attempted to turn off the criticism, and stumbled out, "The spirit was willing." "Ah, but," said the Doctor, as quick as lightning, intercepting her quotation, "you are going to pervert that text, my dear; the inference is Watch therefore; you would make it Sleep therefore."

Dr. Macgillivray of Aberdeen was tutor at Craighead, above Bothwell Bridge, and attended for a little Dr. Hodgson's ministry during his latter days. On one occasion he called at the manse, and the Doctor being poorly, Mrs. Hodgson brought a dose of medicine, which the doctor had strictly ordered, but which Dr. Hodgson was most reluctant to take. Dr. Macgillivray says that "turning towards her with a queer twinkle in his large gloomy eyes, he said, 'Well, my dear, they say that man and wife are one; take you the medicine for me, and if it does you any good, I shall get the full benefit of it.'" Dr. Macgillivray speaks of his "humorous anecdotes and witty remarks," and adds:—

"His style of preaching was strictly expository, comparing Scripture with Scripture; turning up all the parallel passages, and commenting upon them as he went along. These comments were generally very striking, and applied sometimes with sudden and most telling force. During a great part of the time that I was in the way of attending his church, he went over the 50th Psalm in this way, confining himself to a couple of verses at a time. He drew the substance of his lecture out of the marginal references before him in the pulpit Bible. Although it is upwards of thirty years since I used to hear him, I remember well his magnificent descriptions of the Judgment Day, and his dramatic representations of the words and actions of the Judge, as, calling 'to the heavens from above and to the earth below,' He summoned His people to gather about Him, and to witness His judicial proceedings.

"But his prayers were to me more remarkable than his preaching. They were generally marked by a tone of sadness that was deeply impressive, and sometimes almost swelling out into a wail of despair. He seemed as if stretching up his hands to God out of a deep pit, from which there was scarcely any hope of escaping. It was touching and solemnising, but it was exceedingly depressing to hear him at times."

There were other men of less note who came to assist my father occasionally—such as Mr. Robertson of Slamannan, whose guests we youngsters were during the Radical outbreak—a good man, but stern; Mr. Watson of Cumbernauld; Mr. Proudfoot of Strathaven; Mr. Young of Chryston Chapel, who was poorly paid, and who, when asked if he intended to marry, said, "My horse won't carry double." They were worthy and excellent men in their own way, but not very popular. Some of the plain people said "they had nae affluence." The rest, although some of them are now nearly forgotten, were men of great eminence. They stood head and shoulders above the mass of the people and of ordinary ministers. They were men of great individuality and much vigour and influence, totally unlike the dull level of mediocrity to which our present system, or our more degenerate age, seems to be fast shaping down, in so far as the mass of our ministers are concerned.

To some this may seem the mere dream of childhood, but after a large experience of human life I am convinced that it is a sober reality, and that many of the ministers of the present day of considerable pretensions are not to be named beside their more powerful predecessors, whilst the rank and file of our present ministers are immensely inferior. These men besides were all great Church reformers, and had their wise schemes of Church reform and extension been adopted, most of our present evils would have been averted. But after all that has taken place, it is a problem of the greatest importance, Why has the relative position of the mass of the ministers of Scotland degenerated of late? We apprehend that two causes at least have had something to do with it. The talent of the country is drained by India and the Colonies, and by means of the Snell bursaries at Glasgow College; and the remuneration of ministers has in no respect kept pace with the progress of society. The result, however, if allowed to continue, will prove disastrous. It is a great calamity to a country when its ministers are men of little power and influence, when its priests are, as in ancient times, made of "the lowest of the people," and this evil seems now increasing in Scotland. Weak and unworkable theories are put forth, but in the meantime the old parochial system, which of old accomplished so much, was never extended to keep pace with the population, and now, amidst increasing heathenism and degeneracy, men of high talent and Christian power are failing.

In addition to the powerful ministers with whom I was thus brought into contact when a boy, I heard much from the conversation of these men of earnest and stalwart ecclesiastics in other districts, who are also now vanishing into the obscurity of the past. It is chiefly, I fear, their vigorous eccentricities that have caught hold of my memory.

There was Mr. Risk, of Dalserf, who when a lady of his congregation sent him a polite message that "he should clean his teeth," returned it by a suggestion that "she should scrape her tongue." When the people sent a deputation to ask him to be more evangelical in his preaching, he exclaimed, "What do you mean?" They said, "We mean you should tell us more about renouncing our own righteousness." Whereupon the minister tartly replied, "It is the first time I have heard that you had any righteousness to renounce."

Mr. Brisbane, of Dunlop, was a remarkable character, of whom we heard much, although his parish was at some distance. Many stories are told of his peculiarities. The late Mr. Brown, of Roslin, who was his assistant in his young days, wrote to me that he was a devoted minister, thoroughly evangelical, sound in the faith, an excellent classic scholar. He added, "I lived in the manse with him rather more than two years, and I look back on that part of my life as about the happiest I have spent. I had the entire charge of the parish, in so far as a probationer could take it. The population amounted to 1020. There were only two Dissenters in it, and these were Mr. Brisbane's two servants —an old confidential servant and her niece—but they both regularly attended the parish church." Mr. Brisbane was a strong adherent of the Evangelical party in the Church. Mr. Brown told me that he used to say of the sermons of some of the more extreme Moderates that "if they had not read them no person could have supposed that they had written them. They consisted chiefly or wholly of a dry morality which many of them did not understand or attempt to practise. In their harangues on morality they were guided more by the speculations of the infidel philosophers than by the announcements of the Word of God."

To illustrate this, one of the more extreme Moderates preached on a Fast Day for Dr. Clason, and an old man said to him, "Ye manna get yon man to preach ony mair." The Doctor asked for what reason; and the old man immediately replied, "He's far back, very far back in his information, yon man; he doesna ken that Adam's fallen yet." It must have been with some of this sort that Mr. Brisbane was surrounded. Some of them, it is said, were extremely anxious to get to the General Assembly every year by the resignations of their brethren, especially their Evangelical brethren, whose turn it was to go. One of them, by way of taking time by the forelock, came to Mr. Brisbane a good while before the election of members took place, and said, "Mr. Brisbane, it is your turn to go to the Assembly, and as you are getting up in years perhaps you don't care to go. It would be a great favour were you to resign and suggest that I should go in your place." Mr. Brisbane understood the matter thoroughly, and only quietly said, "I gut nae fish till I get them." The Moderate now waited until the election was over, and thinking that all was secure, now went over again to the manse of Dunlop, and announced to Mr. Brisbane that he had been elected, and there was now no difficulty in the way of the arrangement formerly proposed; whereupon Mr. Brisbane as coolly as ever remarked, "I keep my ain fish-guts to my ain sea-maws," and bowed him out of the room. One of his parishioners, who was not very steady, was constantly in the way of seeking to make reparation by asking a certificate in his fits of repentance, upon pretence that he was about to leave the parish and give no more annoyance. Mr. Brisbane at length handed him the following document:—

"I certify that the bearer (naming him) has too little grace to be good, and too little sense to be desperately wicked.
"THOMAS BRISBANE, Minister."

When the parishioner read the certificate, Mr. Brown says he instantly handed it back to Mr. Brisbane, and never returned for another. All who knew the man, and who heard of the certificate, admitted that the description was perfect. Mr. Brisbane sometimes amused himself by writing epitaphs for his friends. A preacher who was reputed to be very soft-hearted, and to make large use of Ralph Erskine's sermons in his preaching, came under the lash of Mr. Brisbane, who made in regard to him the following epitaph:—

> "Here lies interred
> A man of feeling,
> Who lived on love,
> And preached by stealing."

The late Mr. Fleming of Neilston long carried on a contest with his heritors about church accommodation. This was his great theme for years. One day when Mr. Brisbane was at Neilston, Mr. Fleming took him to the churchyard to show him what church accommodation he still required the heritors to furnish. Having done this he said to Mr. Brisbane, "I hear you have been making epitaphs for some of your friends, and I wish you would make one for me." Mr. Fleming's name was Alexander, and Mr. Brisbane was in the habit of familiarly calling him "Sanders." He immediately said, "We cannot make epitaphs for everybody, but how would this do for you?

> 'Welcome, Sanders, to your station;
> *Here* ye'll find accommodation.'"

Mr. Brisbane had a great dislike of all preaching that was not textual. On one occasion, after hearing a weak sermon from a young preacher, and being asked how he liked it, he exclaimed with great tartness, "The man might have said to the text at the beginning what he said to the folk at the end, 'We'll may-be meet again and may-be no.'" On another occasion he heard a sermon by a young minister on the text, "The angel did wondrously, and Manoah and his wife looked on." Some one said, "What did ye think of the sermon?" Mr. Brisbane said, "The sermon was not unlike the text; the lad did wondrously, and the text lookit on."

In this enumeration of remarkable ministers of this and the preceding period, I must not omit one of the most distinguished, namely, the Rev. Dr. Balfour of Glasgow. He was by much the most popular minister in Glasgow previous to the translation of Dr. Chalmers from Kilmany. By all accounts, and I heard of him from many quarters, he was a most eloquent preacher and an admirable man. He was my father's minister whilst he was a student, and he introduced him to his first charge as assistant at St. Ninian's by preaching an eloquent sermon on the text, "We have not followed cunningly devised fables." Dr. Love and he were extremely intimate; and in preaching a funeral sermon on the occasion of his death, Dr. Love wound up by saying that when he reached heaven he would not be long in looking round to welcome the triumphant embrace of Dr. Balfour.

In my father's house I heard a good deal of a previous generation of ministers, as well as of those then prominent in the West of Scotland. The most remarkable, probably, of these was Mr. Thom of Govan; more distinguished, however, by talent than by grace. It is said that on one occasion he was taking part in the ordination of a minister of whose ability he had not a very high opinion. The Presbytery being large, and it being difficult for all the ministers to reach the head of the one about to be ordained, so as to lay their hands upon it, Mr. Thom thrust out his stick and laid it on his head. When some of the ministers remonstrated with him for this extraordinary procedure he said, "It'll do weel eneuch; timmer to timmer." Mr. Thom was always at feud with the authorities of the College at Glasgow, and a volume of his works has been published containing some very pungent satires upon the professors. It contains also a specimen of his sermons, which are very peculiar. In the satires he criticises with great severity an address presented by the College to the Crown, and affects to have discovered, by its want of sense, grammar, and logic, that it must have been a forgery. There is also a letter bearing to be from one of the professors to a friend in the country, giving reasons why they had left the Blackfriars Church and set up a chapel for themselves within the walls of the College. The Professor tells his friend in confidence that they were shocked at the preaching in the Blackfriars Church, which spoke so plainly of sin and duty, and especially because when the minister spoke of drunkenness, Sabbath-breaking, and other vices, all the people turned and stared at the professors' gallery, as if they were the persons chiefly at fault. They resolved, therefore, to have a chapel where these things should not be spoken of, but where they should have treatises on the beauty of virtue, on virtue being its own reward, and other kindred philosophical subjects. Tradition reports that he maintained a similar warfare against the Glasgow magistrates. Standing on the street, it is said, one day with the Provost, who had risen from nothing, a little urchin came up begging, and being refused and driven away sternly by the Provost, Mr. Thom interposed and said, "Hey, laddie, there's a penny; ye'll maybe be Provost of Glasgow yoursel' yet."

Mr. Thom was fond of riding a good horse, and it is alleged that one of the magistrates said, "You're greater, Mr. Thom, than your Master, for He rode on an ass." Mr. Thom immediately retorted, "We would be willing enough to ride on asses too, but they're no to be got noo-a-days; they've made them all magistrates." Preaching before the magistrates on one occasion, it is said that he took for his subject the Ethiopian eunuch, and said amongst other things, "Suppose you saw one of our public authorities riding in his chariot, certainly not a very unlikely thing. But suppose you saw him reading the prophet Esaias, a highly improbable thing. But suppose, further, you were to say to him, 'Understandest thou what thou readest?' a highly necessary question in such circumstances. Do you suppose he would say, 'How can I except some man *guide* me?' This is the very last thing that would enter a modern magistrate's head. He would say, 'What right have you to ask? Go about your business.'" Preaching on another occasion before the magistrates, it is reported that he suddenly halted and said, "Dinna snore sae loud, Bailie Brown; ye'll wauken the Provost." And on another occasion still, it is said he called a dead halt, took out his snuff-box, tapped it on the lid, and took a pinch of snuff with the greatest deliberation. By this time the whole audience was agog with eager curiosity to know what was wrong. Mr. Thom, after a little, gravely proceeded to say, "My friends, I've had a snuff, and the Provost has had a sleep, and if ye like we'll just begin again." He was a great enemy to the American War, and crowds of people flocked from Glasgow to hear his sermons preached on the days of humiliation appointed by the Government in connection with successive defeats sustained by our troops in that struggle. He exercised a good deal of ingenuity in announcing these days of humiliation so as to retain his principles and yet obey the Government. On one occasion he said, "My people, ye're muckle thocht o'. The folk in London have committed a great sin, and they have sent me a letter asking me to call you together to pray for them." On another occasion he said, "I've been aye telling ye that ye are very wicked people, but I have a very serious thing to tell ye to-day. The news of your wickedness has reached as far as London, and I have a letter appointing ye to meet together for prayer and repentance." One of the neighbouring ministers of a small borough had fallen out with the magistrates, the ground of offence being that he did not pray for them in suitable terms. Mr. Thom was asked to preach on one occasion instead of him, and in his prayer he used the following expressions: "Pity the magistrates of this place; pity those that sit in council with them; have compassion on the people under their care."

The Rev. John Campbell of Renfrew was a man also

famous in his day, and we used to hear of him from some of the visitors at the Manse. Only two of his sayings I remember. In the General Assembly a very young elder, an advocate, had made a speech breathing anything but an evangelical flavour. Mr. Campbell rose and tersely said, "In the speech, Moderator, to which we have just listened, there was a good deal of the young man, not a little of the old man, very little of the new man." On another occasion a young aristocratic champion had been defending the law of patronage, and amongst other things had said that he gave thanks to God every day for the existence of such an excellent arrangement. Mr. Campbell in reply quietly said, "Moderator, there is some hope surely for the Church now. We are getting very devout and pious young men amongst us. Here's one, for example, that's thankful for very sma' mercies."

Of Mr. Oliphant of Dumbarton, also, whose fame is very widespread, we heard a good deal. He was a man of great excellence, but at the same time of considerable eccentricity. His Catechism on the Lord's Supper is very good indeed. My father used to tell that when any one said to him, "Such a man is a very fine man," he would say, "Is he very fine? What proof have ye of that? Had ye ever ony money transactions wi' him?" Many stories have been told of him; but the following, which we heard at that time, seem characteristic. He is said on one occasion to have borrowed half-a-crown from one of the elders before he entered the pulpit, and returned it immediately after the service was over. The elder expressed astonishment at the transaction, and asked what it meant. Mr. Oliphant said confidentially, "I think a man aye speaks baulder when he has siller in his pooch." My father once saw him go into the pulpit and discover that he had forgotten his spectacles. There were a number of elders round the pulpit, venerable men, each of them having on his nose what were formerly called "specs." Mr. Oliphant deliberately bent over and took the specs off the nose of one of these ancients, who looked up with great astonishment at what had taken place. But the minister without one word of explanation placed them on his own nose and gravely proceeded with the service. On another occasion, he happened to quote the passage in reference to the hairs of our head being numbered, and looking round at the circle of wigged elders, he added with emphasis, "Ay, and even of your wigs." Old Mr. Carrick, the banker, of Glasgow, in his own department seems to have been a somewhat similar character. He bought a great deal of land in New Monkland parish during the earlier days of my father's ministry. He came out in a postchaise, which met him at the outskirts of the town, that people might not suspect where he was going, and he brought his dinner with him in the form of hard-boiled eggs and bread. He was a man of much shrewdness, thoroughly honest, and a keen scrutiniser of bills, as well as of the solvency of those who subscribed them. He was in the habit of saying, when he was not prepared to honour a bill, simply, "It's no convenient," which must have come upon many hard-pressed merchants like the sound of doom. When asking about the pecuniary capabilities of people, if any one said, "He's a very rich man," Mr. Carrick would eagerly retort, "Hoo do ye judge that?" And if the answer was, "He keeps his carriage," the old man would quietly say, "That's nae sign ava'; the mair a man spends the less he has." On one occasion, when the same carriage argument was used to him, he impatiently exclaimed, "I dinna want to ken if he keeps his carriage; I want to ken if he can keep his feet."

But enough of such characters and of old reminiscences, although these quaint old figures often rise up still before me like a vision in the distance, and give a vivid idea of a power and energy that are gone. These are chiefly eccentricities, which one most easily remembers, but they were to a large extent, in most of these men, accompanied with thorough independence, real worth, and Christian excellence.

The union of church and school was another admirable feature of the parochial system. The teacher dealt with the young and the minister with the old, and under a harmonious agreement they worked to each other's hands for the purpose of bringing the whole population under enlightened Christian influence. Men speak of compulsory education, and most assuredly children should not be suffered to grow up in ignorance; but it is still better if no compulsion is required; and all my early recollections are connected with a state of things in which it would have been thought disgraceful for any child to be allowed to grow up in ignorance, and where ministers and teachers were most cordial fellow-workers in promoting the universal Christian instruction of the people.

Our parish teacher and my own instructor, the Rev. Hugh Watt, was a preacher of the Gospel. He discharged his various duties in the parish with great assiduity and faithfulness, and died only recently, at a very old age. He taught remarkably well, not only the elementary branches, but Latin and Greek, preparing young men for the college. He turned out a number of preachers. The late Dr. Black of the Barony, the present Rev. David Black, Tillicoultry, and many more, were amongst his pupils. We all held him in high esteem and veneration, although on proper occasions he did not spare the rod. The sentimental views of more recent times had then no existence. I look back with the utmost respect even to that venerable instrument "the tawse," and I am certain that society would be saved a good deal of trouble and much expense, not to speak of the many advantages to the people themselves, were the maxims of Solomon more literally observed, "He that spareth the rod hateth the child;" "Foolishness is bound up in the heart of a child, but the rod of correction will drive it away." How professedly Christian people can say they regulate their whole opinions and conduct by the Bible, and yet disregard one of its plainest precepts in regard to their children, we have never been able to understand. Very few prizes were given. So far as I remember, there was only one, viz., a prize to the scholar who could repeat the 119th Psalm without omission or alteration, and this prize I was happy enough to secure. It bore the following motto:—"To Mr. James Begg, for general eminence in repeating psalms." Mr. Watt was an inveterate smoker, and must have puffed away an immense quantity of money in the course of such a long incumbency. He and the Rev. Mr. Lawrie of Airdrie, and the Rev. Mr. Gibb of Holytown, who were all teachers in the neighbourhood, being all at the same time preachers of the Gospel, all of them occasionally officiated for my father during his rare absences from his own pulpit. They were all excellent and accomplished men, but none of them were remarkably popular as preachers; and indeed my father's people were very difficult to please. Mr. Gibb was a strong, raw-boned man, a sort of Dominie Sampson in appearance, but a great Hebrew scholar, and at the same time a man of much simplicity of character. He was always aiming unsuccessfully at being married, although with very limited means, and some people were alleged occasionally rather to practise upon his simplicity. "What letter was that you wrote recently?" said some one to Mr. Gibb. The simple man proceeded to tell the name of the young lady who was favoured with his correspondence. "Was there not a curious piece in the middle of it?" said the interrogator. Whereupon Mr. Gibb, to vindicate himself, and having a capital memory, proceeded to repeat the whole epistle, the contents of which were soon spread through the village. And yet, with all his simplicity, he was a man of great learning and mental force. I remember still a sermon of his on faith, although I must have been very young at the time, which gave me a clearer and more discriminating idea upon that subject than I previously possessed. Our worthy teacher, Mr. Watt, paid the greatest attention to Scriptural instruction and to our knowledge of the Catechism, as did also my father on the Sabbath evenings. We were then made to write down whatever we remembered of the sermon, and to repeat large portions of Scripture and of the Catechisms, together with the whole Book of Psalms. I derived more advantage from this than from any subsequent process of training, and I am certain that wherever these Sabbath-evening exercises are neglected or superseded by evening worship, the children suffer an unspeakable loss.

There were four chapels in the parish in addition to the parish church. All of them were in Airdrie. One of them was a chapel-of-ease, of which the Rev. Joseph Finlayson was minister, a man of some pretensions to literature, but by no means a successful minister. He must have been very ill-paid, and was understood to live chiefly on his own private resources. The Rev. Mr. Mushet of Shettlestone is alleged to have said that "naebody preached the Gospel so cheap as he did, except perhaps that ill-paid minister, Mr. Finlayson of Airdrie." The other chapels belonged to the New and Old Light Seceders and Reformed Presbyterians respectively. Mr. Duncanson, the New Light Seceder, was an accomplished man, and a diligent and respectable minister. Mr. Torrance, the Old Light minister, was also a very excellent and diligent minister, although more eccentric. Many stories were told of him, and no doubt some of them were exaggerated. He spoke with great familiarity and simplicity, both in preaching and prayer. Some one told me that they heard him in prayer most earnestly beg for favourable weather for maturing and gathering in the harvest, and he added with the greatest gravity, "For I was at the Shotts a few days ago, and the corn was as green as leeks."

He was alleged to have said that marriage was "like twa fir deals glued thegither, and whiles grooved." All the ministers lived in good neighbourhood, and many of the controversies which have since sprung up were then wholly unknown. The abolition of patronage and a system of parochial subdivision, both of which my father strongly advocated, would have probably united them all except the Reformed Presbyterians.

My father having a good manse and glebe, had no trouble in regard to his stipend, which was paid in slump by the College of Glasgow, who received all the surplus teinds. We always kept two or three cows and a quantity of poultry, over all of which my mother presided with much assiduity and skill. In those days to be an eminent housekeeper was reckoned a high and necessary qualification for any woman, but especially for the wife of a minister. More modern theories had not appeared; and Solomon's picture of a virtuous woman, who "openeth her mouth with wisdom, the law of kindness being under her tongue," and who is "not afraid of the snow for her household, for all her household are clothed in scarlet," was universally admired. My mother told us that, in connection with the boarding-school which she attended, she was trained in a knowledge of cookery, housekeeping, mending clothes, and, in a word, everything that is necessary to make domestic management successful. Under her kind and affectionate treatment we were brought up with great comfort, although in the plainest style. We had abundance of good porridge and milk for breakfast—a dish in which I have delighted ever since, and which I believe has done more to give bone and sinew to the Scotch people, and to make them the men they are, than all other material causes put together. Being somewhat distant from market, and sometimes entirely snowed up in winter, my father laid in large barrels of oatmeal. At the beginning of every winter, moreover, he killed, salted, and stored in barrels what was called a "mart," in other words, a fat bullock, and sometimes a couple of pigs, and these being scientifically dealt with by my mother's domestic wisdom, gave us, with the produce of the garden, abundant materials for warding off starvation during the whole winter. As boys, we not only took an interest in the cows and poultry, but were allowed to enjoy ourselves by keeping rabbits and pigeons, the latter being trained to great familiarity, so that they would alight on our hands. In this respect, it is of importance to indulge the innocent tastes of children; and I remember carrying these tastes to Glasgow, and gratifying them by cultivating acquaintance at the windows of our lodgings with the dingy pigeons of that great city. Our parish doctor was Dr. Tennant, a highly intelligent man and a skilful physician. Fortunately for himself, he had a small private property of considerable value in the parish, for the district was generally so healthy that I am afraid he never earned very much by professional remuneration.

The time was now approaching for my going to college, which I did at an early age. Although for seven years more I still came and went to New Monkland during the intervals of the sessions of college, my permanent connection with the place now began to be broken. We were then a large family of seven children, besides my father, mother, and two servants. Although I found Glasgow unhealthy, I continued to gather health anew, and, I trust, to make some intellectual and spiritual progress, during these pleasant summer vacations. These early scenes can never be forgotten. The farmers around—a most worthy class of people—were all glad to see the minister's children, and to give them of their good things. I, on the other hand, mixed freely with them, studying farming in so far as it was then practised, and trying my hand at all their occupations. I became pretty expert at all kinds of country labour, and I have never since lost a taste for country life, although I have had few opportunities of indulging it. I close this chapter with the following inscription over the grave of my excellent father and mother in New Monkland churchyard:—

"Here lie the Remains of

THE REV. DR. BEGG,

Late Minister of this Parish,

Who died on the 11th June 1845, in the 83d year of his age, and 52d of his ministry.

'An eloquent man, and mighty in the Scriptures.'

Also of M. MATTHIE, his Wife, who died in Aug. 1831, aged 54 years."

CHAPTER II.

COLLEGE LIFE IN GLASGOW AND EDINBURGH.

GLASGOW being within ten miles of my father's manse, I was taken there to attend college when only about twelve years of age. The date of my enrolment as a student at Glasgow is 1820. This is one of the defects of our Scotch system, for as the curriculum of study for a minister embraces eight years, there is a strong temptation to send boys to college before they can possibly have been grounded in elementary education, so as to secure their being licensed at anything like an early period of life. Much good might result from the establishment of a high class of intermediate schools in all small towns, such as the far-seeing John Knox projected three centuries ago, at which boys might attend for a couple of years between their leaving the parish schools and going to the universities. Besides, the present course of university education might be improved; and if, instead of only a winter session and a long summer vacation, there were two sessions of four months each, with six weeks or two months of interval between each, the professors would have no harder work than other men, whilst the studies of the young men might both be expedited, and in every way conducted with much greater advantage. By some such means the tedious eight years might be condensed into four, or, at all events, into six, with a number of manifest advantages to all parties. At present, unless a young man commence his public studies at twelve or thirteen, he has no great encouragement to begin them at all, and has strong inducements to look to some other profession. But what can a young man, or rather boy, know of his own mind at twelve or thirteen? And if he begins to think seriously of becoming a minister at a later period of life, when he can really say that he has formed a deliberate judgment, a large portion of the best part of his life must necessarily be over before he can enter into a pulpit. These matters very urgently demand consideration. We do not see why the Christian ministry should be subjected to such obvious disadvantages, without strong and determined efforts to secure reform on the part of those who have the means of redressing the evil.

All this becomes more striking when the utter neglect with which students are treated during their curriculum is taken into consideration. As a general rule, none of the public authorities ever ask theological students what their motives are for proposing to enter so sacred a calling as that of the holy ministry. No such questions are ever mooted until they are in the very act of being licensed or ordained. No one takes the least charge of their manners or morals whilst they attend at a Scottish university, facetiously called an " Alma Mater." They are allowed, in so far as the college authorities are concerned, to reside where they please, and to act in the intervals of the class as they please, without any one inquiring after them; and we have no doubt that the result in many cases is most prejudicial.

In regard to the college life of Edward Irving and his brother, Mrs. Oliphant, speaking of this very feature, justly says—

"The two lads were deposited in a lofty chamber in the Old Town near the College, to pursue their studies with such diligence as was in them. Even to such youthful sons, the Edinburgh University has no personal shelter to offer; then as now, the Alma Mater was a mere abstract mass of class-rooms, museums, and libraries, and the youths or boys who sought instruction there were left in absolute freedom to their own devices. Perhaps the youths thus launched upon the world were too young to take much harm; or perhaps the early necessity for self-regulation, imposed under different and harder circumstances than those which have brought the English public schools into such fresh repute and popularity, bore all the fruit which it is now hoped and believed to produce. But whatever be the virtues of self-government, it is impossible to contemplate without a singular interest and amaze the spectacle of those two boys, one thirteen, the other probably about fifteen, placed alone in their little lodging in the picturesque but noisy old town of Edinburgh, for six long months at a stretch, to manage themselves and their education, without tutors, without home care, without any stimulus but that to be received in the emulation of the class-room, or from their books and their own ambition."

My elder brother had gone to college the year before I went. We lived together consecutively in two different lodgings in the High Street—sad and dingy-looking places they now seem to me on inspecting them at this distance of time. But in the one case, the lodging was much better than the landlady, who took bouts of tippling, and sometimes served up our porridge almost in the form of raw meal and water, which the Scotch call "drammoch," whilst she occasionally equally miscooked our other food. We had not many companions, and at that time the system of smoking, which has become such a plague amongst our modern students, was all but unknown. Still, if something like the English system of "residence" is not to be adopted, all my recollections make me strongly in favour of a kind and vigilant superintendence of students, by persons properly authorised and qualified, in their lodgings as well as in their classes. A students' dining-hall has been proposed and partly secured. But what is wanted is properly arranged lodging or boarding houses for students, duly arranged and licensed by the College authorities. We do not see why retired ministers or Christian men should not preside over such establishments, as a great opportunity of usefulness.

Large houses could easily be fitted up for the purpose, and the affair managed both with economy and profit. Each student might have a separate bedroom, but all might have family worship and their meals together. Now that few of our students, moreover, act as tutors in families, by means of which their manners were brushed up and polished, this might also be a means of training them both in Christian principles and in the habits of civilised life. It would also afford ministers an opportunity of visiting the students pleasantly and seeing them together. One of the greatest practical mistakes the Free Church made was in rejecting the offer of £3000 by Lady Effingham to form the foundation of a fund for a students' pastor. In the Presbyterian Church of Ireland, connected with the Belfast College, they have, I think, a man called the "Dean of Residences," who gives an annual report in regard to the students' lodgings. This we hold to be a matter of the first importance. In other respects the Scotch system which then prevailed, and which we presume prevails still, had considerable advantages, especially to men of limited incomes. Our lodgings were very economical as to price, and we lived chiefly upon provisions imported from the manse. We got in from the country boxes of good things, including oatmeal, cheese, bacon, butter, eggs, and other provisions. We also had our clothes washed in the country, the Airdrie carrier taking them out and bringing them in from time to time. We got very little pocket-money, and we kept a regular account of how we spent all we got, to be exhibited to my father when he came to town, on our return home, or when we were in want of any more. We became rather adepts at housekeeping, purchasing with care and circumspection our own tea and sugar, &c. In connection with all this the plan of suppressing the old College of Glasgow at present, in order to make way for the new, has always seemed to me very doubtful policy. By all means let the grand new institution at the west end of Glasgow be erected, but why not continue the venerable old College also, and have thus two colleges and one university? Two are more needed now than one was when the present buildings were erected. The grounds might have been sold to the railway authorities, and still the class-rooms and a certain area preserved. This would not only have led to a wholesome competition between the Old and New Colleges, but the poorer class of students might still have found more economical lodgings in the neighbourhood of the old buildings. If talent is not hereditary or confined to any one rank, it is important to glean ardent students and able men from all classes of the community.

The chief way of travelling in those days from New Monkland to Glasgow was either by walking, by the Airdrie coach, or by the canal-boat from Airdrie to Glasgow, which was amazingly slow, but upon the whole not uncomfortable. We boys, however, in our periodical visits to New Monkland, generally walked, and although the distance was considerable, we thought nothing of it, started as gaily as larks, and were charmed to escape from the smoke and dust of Glasgow to the freshness of the country. Confinement, to which we were not accustomed, not to speak of our exercises, was not very conducive to health during the winter months, although I always recruited again at my father's house during the intervals, and went back in vigorous health after each summer's vacation. When we went first to Glasgow, we were introduced to a few friends whom my father and mother had previously known, and with whom we occasionally spent an evening, and especially the Saturday evenings, after we had finished our studies for the week. One of these was Mr. Reid, then editor of the *Glasgow Courier*, who was very kind and condescending to me, although such a mere boy. We were told that he had afterwards reported to my father that I was "a nice gash laddie." Other friends, of the name of Parker and Cuthbertson, were equally kind and attentive, and partly removed our feeling of loneliness as strangers in a strange town.

Speaking of editors, the great editor of Glasgow at that time and for years after, was Mr. Samuel Hunter, a portly and noticeable man, who established the *Glasgow Herald*. He was a minister's son, and a man of great sagacity. I have often heard of his mode of composing his articles, which really was a very suitable one. He spent the forenoon of every day in the Exchange, walking deliberately with his hands behind his back. He laid himself alongside of all the men who had the greatest reputation for sagacity, and after comparing notes with them, he digested the result into short pithy articles, in which the men of greatest authority saw and admired the reflection of their own wisdom. This, of course, required mental power and social position; but, constituted as human nature is, it was not only an easy, but a most successful way of accomplishing the result. Mr. Hunter was a bachelor and lived with his sister. He was in the habit of telling a story of what happened to him with one of the students. It seems to have been an object in those days to introduce students to editors, and one had been introduced to Mr. Hunter. Afterwards one of his relatives said to the great editor, "You were'na very attentive to yon student, although we gave him a letter of introduction to ye." "Yon student," retorted Mr. Hunter, "doesna need muckle attention; he'll tak' good care o' himself. When he cam' first, I asked him to his breakfast, and my sister had, amongst other things, a platefu' of eggs. The young man slippit roun' his hand, and took the biggest egg in the plate. Thinks I to mysel', My lad, ye'll dae. Ye're quite fit already to gang oot into the world." Mr. Hunter sat in St. Andrew's Church, under the ministry of Dr. Gibb. The church in Mr. Hunter's time and afterwards was very thinly attended, and when he was asked why he sat there, he said, "Oh, it's a fine kirk in the summer-time." He was a great conservative of the old school, but very fond of going to Moffat. He sometimes remained there inconveniently long, and the difficulty was to get him to see the necessity of coming back. It is alleged that on one occasion the following plan was adopted with success. A most violently radical article was written and inserted in only one copy of the paper, which copy was immediately despatched to Moffat. Mr. Hunter was thrown into a paroxysm of alarm, proceeded straightway to Glasgow and to the *Herald Office*, and was relieved to discover the actual state of the matter.

There were other notable public characters at that time in Glasgow, and they naturally attracted the notice of a lad from the country, quite as much as the classes at the College. Dr. Chalmers was then in the very zenith of his popularity. It was extremely difficult to get into his church. I remember worming my way through the dense crowd that besieged the building, getting up the gallery stair, and, as a little boy, clambering over the back part of the gallery, I saw and heard Dr. Chalmers for the first time. He is still vividly before my mind, breaking out into paroxysms of impassioned oratory, and actually foaming at the mouth. It was a scene never to be forgotten; although, at that time, I very little comprehended its true meaning. The style of preaching was very different from that to which I had been accustomed. The reading was close and fervent; it was "fell reading," as the old woman said; but I could make very little of it at that time, beyond seeing the general and evidently powerful impression made on the densely crowded congregation. This certainly was very remarkable. I had a full opportunity of knowing the great, amiable, and eloquent Doctor in subsequent years, and I cannot doubt that we have seen no man, "take him for all in all," like him in our day. There was then, however, a kind of human idolatry called forth by his amazing popularity in Glasgow, which was on one or two occasions most justly and effectually rebuked. It is said that Dr. Love went to preach for him on one occasion. The moment the venerable man was seen in the pulpit, a number of the people began quickly to retire, whereupon the Doctor exclaimed, in his grand and majestic voice, and with an air of authority which all who ever heard him must be able to imagine, "Brethren, we will not begin the public worship of God until the chaff blows off." On another occasion a bustling stranger came to the church, and said to a grave old member of the congregation whom he met, "Is Dr. Chalmers to preach?" to which the grave old man replied firmly but quietly, "No, the bit idol's no at hame the day." The blow told with effect. Edward Irving was at this time the assistant of Dr. Chalmers, and although he was eclipsed by the great luminary, his great talents were appreciated, whilst his remarkable appearance excited general notice. When he left Glasgow for London he preached on the text, "Finally, brethren, farewell." He said, amongst other things, with much modesty, "I don't say you have liked me, but I thank you that in the circumstances you have at least borne with me." We shall meet this great man again in other circumstances.

When I went first to the College, I attended chiefly on Sabbath the College chapel, the first establishment of which had been ridiculed by Mr. Thom of Govan. I found his theory pretty fully realised. He says in his caustic style:—

"We have, whatever may be said of us, a real though a general and philosophical religion; and had we a chapel where such of us as have been clergymen are to preach by turns, we will have discourses upon the dignity of human nature, upon disinterested benevolence, upon sympathy and propriety, upon living according to nature, and upon virtue's being a sufficient reward to itself. . . . It is a fixed maxim among us that 'that is always the best religion which takes the slightest hold on the heart, and the slighter the better.'

And though, with respect to the intention of the speaker, it is a very different religion which we have been hearing, we have, however, had the firmness to remain hitherto untouched and uncorrupted by it; and, though I say it, it is a great truth and no vain boast, that it will be difficult to find as many wise and good men in so narrow a place upon whom the vulgar and superstitious religion of the country hath taken so little hold."—*Thom's Works*, pp. 237-238.

The chief preachers in the College chapel were two, both of them very dry. One of them was afterwards suspected of being an Arian, and the other was a very uninteresting preacher. I had never before heard the same style of preaching. Such texts as the following were chosen, and indicate the general strain of the discourses, "A man that hath friends must show himself friendly." Of course we do not mean to say that an admirable and evangelical sermon may not be preached from any text in the Bible, and we are far from sympathising with the worthy old woman who, on hearing a minister give out as his text, "Work out your own salvation with fear and trembling," bitterly said, "I kent if there was an ill text in the Bible, he would be at it," although we understand her meaning. There is an extreme in the use of texts as well as of everything else, and "all Scripture is profitable." But the sermons in the College chapel at that time were dry and profitless—anything but evangelical. I therefore for a time went to various churches where the preaching was more in accordance with what I had previously heard. Dr. Anderson of the Relief Church in John Street, who still holds his place, was then a very popular preacher. Dr. Heugh of the Secession preached also with great clearness, and in a lively, interesting style, and had a large congregation. Dr. Muir and Dr. Wardlaw were both very acceptable. The man under whom I sat most during the latter part of my studies at Glasgow College was Dr. Brown of St. John's, who had been translated from

Tongland in Galloway to be successor to Dr. Chalmers. He was a truly excellent man, with a pleasant countenance and somewhat husky voice, but preached in the most earnest and impressive style. I vividly remember some of his sermons to the present hour.

Amongst other Glasgow characters at that time, of a very different stamp, was a street musician called "Blind Alick," a man who afforded great amusement to the students and other young people. He played with little skill on a fiddle, and sang his own songs, which were sufficiently curious. His practice was to prolong the fiddling in every case as long as each line lasted. Many of his lines were Alexandrine; but still he continued, whether tune or rhyme were in accordance with any rule of music or metre or the reverse. He always began by saying in a pompous style, "I am the author of all that I sing and say." I remember a portion of one of his songs:—

> "Come, all ye boys of Brittany,
>   A story I've got to tell,
>   Of the wars of Spain and Germany,
>   And how the town of Badajos fell.
>   There was the famous Alick Pattison,
>   A hero of renown,
>   Who was the first that did mount the walls of Badajos,
>   And the first that did tumble down.
>   I've travelled the whole world over,
>   And many a place beside,
>   But a more beautifuller city than Glasgow
>   I never saw, situated on the banks of that navigable river the Clyde."

Our professors for the first year were Mr. Josiah Walker for Latin, and Sir Daniel K. Sandford for Greek. It was said that Mr. Walker had been an exciseman, and he certainly wrote a good deal about Burns, who was probably the most remarkable member of the fraternity that ever existed in Scotland. Mr., afterward Sir Daniel, Sandford, was appointed in room of Mr. Young, an enthusiastic teacher of Greek, who died at that very time. Sir Daniel, who was also an able Greek scholar and a man of much general talent, did a good deal to promote the study of that noble language at Glasgow. In subsequent years Mr. Jardine was our Professor of Logic, a gruff plain man, but still very kindly to the young men, an admirable teacher, and a thoroughly evangelical elder of the Church. Mr. Milne taught us Moral Philosophy in a somewhat heathenish style, making man pass through all stages from savage to civilised, insisting on the progress of human nature, even in its primitive state, from worse to better, instead of from better to worse. In short, it was very much philosophy without the fall of man and apart from the Bible. Mr. Miller, who was a good deal of a character, taught Mathematics; and Mr. Meiklam, a man of fair ability, taught Natural Philosophy. At the end of my undergraduate course I took a degree in Arts, having passed what was called the Black Stone examination. This degree is dated the 9th of April 1824, I being at that time under sixteen years of age. Our teachers in Theology were Dr. Stevenson MacGill, Professor M'Turk in Church History, and Dr. Gibb in Hebrew. The two latter were very ordinary men, although kind and attentive to the students; but the former, although not possessed of the great talents of some men, was yet an able man, of much zeal and unction, most earnest for our progress and spiritual improvement. He certainly produced a very powerful effect, by the Divine blessing, upon the students, and had a great influence in afterwards improving the Church. He was a very spare man in appearance, and he used to give us kind advice on all subjects, including diet, recommending the students, amongst other things, to eat pease-brose, in imitation of his own example. It was thought to be a case like that of the celebrated Hugo Arnot of Edinburgh, also very thin, and who was found one day eating speldings, whereupon a wit remarked that "he was very like his meat." Dr. MacGill was an admirable critic of sermons, a very important department of professorial work. He insisted that the whole class should be present to hear his criticisms, and it was a most profitable exercise. I have seen him sit to hear four or five sermons in succession without taking a note, and then criticise the whole in detail with the most admirable discrimination and judgment. He was strong for short introductions, clear divisions, precise statements of doctrine, and accurate quotations of Scripture. He had the greatest abhorrence of high-flown language, and of some words that the students were fond of using; as, for example, Deity, and other words of heathen origin, which were then currently used by Moderate ministers. He was a man of great general philanthropy, took the deepest interest in social questions, and was the originator of the monument to Knox which stands in the Glasgow Necropolis. He was a copious writer on a variety of matters of general philanthropy. Perhaps no man did more in his day to turn the tide in Scotland in favour of Evangelism than Dr. MacGill. He was foremost in arguing against pluralities and other abuses in the Church, and I had great pleasure in having him to assist me afterwards in Paisley during the early period of my ministry.

A writer in an Irish theological journal gives the following interesting particulars in regard to Dr. MacGill, who was the theological instructor of Dr. James Buchanan, Dr. Candlish, and of many more who afterwards became useful, some of them distinguished, ministers of the Church of Scotland or in other bodies; for at that time some students of other bodies attended the Hall with us:—

"This eminent and godly professor exercised an influence so marked over the minds of our Irish Presbyterian students, from the time of his appointment in 1814 to the Divinity chair, that we have been at the pains to gather a few particulars concerning his history. He was the son of an extensive shipbuilder at Port Glasgow, where he was born on 19th January 1765. His mother was Frances Welsh, and derived her descent from John Welsh of Ayr, the son-in-law of John Knox. They were pious people, and were at great pains in directing the education of their son, particularly in Scriptural knowledge, though, as he himself records, he was settled in the ministry before he felt the power of religion in his soul. He was a most distinguished student, gaining prizes in all his classes, and resided as tutor in the family of the Hon. Henry Erskine, whose son, the late Earl of Buchan, was his pupil. It was while he was a student of theology that he made his first essay in authorship, publishing 'The Student's Dream'—an allegorical anticipation of the duties of a Christian minister—which was so highly popular that it was admitted into 'Macnab's Collection,' a well-known school-book at that time. He was licensed to preach in 1790, and was immediately offered the Chair of Civil History in St. Andrews, through the influence of the Hon. H. Erskine; but his love of the ministry led him to decline the tempting proposal. In 1791 he was settled in Eastwood, with the unanimous concurrence of the patron, Sir John Maxwell of Pollock, and the heritors, elders, and people. He became a popular minister, thoroughly evangelical, and specially interested in the religous welfare of the young. At the end of six years he became minister of the Tron Church, Glasgow, and on the death of Dr. Findlay—so well known by his able answer to Voltaire on the inspiration of the Scriptures—he succeeded, in 1814, to the Chair of Systematic Theology. He introduced a new era in the study of Divinity in the Scottish Colleges, and proposed methods for the regular superintendence of the students in religious knowledge, as well as in classical literature and philosophy. He exercised a very happy influence over their minds by his kindly intercourse with them in private. He published several able works, took a distinguished part in maintaining the charitable institutions of Glasgow, and was elected in 1828 to the Moderator's chair in the General Assembly. He died on 18th August 1840, in the seventy-sixth year of his age."

Whilst the retrospect of my studies under Dr. MacGill is

very pleasant, I cannot say, however, that the problem of theological training has yet been solved; and mainly for this reason, that the ultimate object of training men for the ministry is too much thrown into the background. To make learned and accomplished students is of great importance. To see that they are men of God, and thoroughly in earnest in regard to the great work of their future lives, is still more important. But the art of preaching has been very little made a matter of special study in connection with our theological training. It is not so in other departments, and it was not so, for example, by Mr. Cornelius Winter in the case of the students under his care, as described by Mr. Jay of Bath. In connection with theological lectures, however valuable, there is little training in the English Bible, in committing it to memory so as to quote it easily and accurately, or in the actual practice of public speaking, although this is to be the main business of our lives. In my day, as a voluntary exercise, we attended classes of elocution. But had I not received a thorough drilling in Bible knowledge at my father's house, I should have found myself very deficient in after-life. On the other hand, the early specimens of preaching which I heard from Dr. Scott, Dr. Love, Dr. Mackinlay, and my father made the deepest impression, and were probably best adapted for the ordinary purposes of proclaiming and expounding the Gospel with effect to all classes of the people. Such geniuses as Dr. Chalmers, however admirable, are no models for ordinary men.

During the intervals of the College sessions I did something in the way of teaching, which I found of advantage. We never understand a matter thoroughly until we try to communicate it to others. Moreover, during our sessions at the Hall we had two very instructive societies—the one a debating society, held in Campbell Street, and the other a preaching society, which met in Albion Street Chapel. In both societies we had some men who are still alive. Our debates, I think, were generally conducted in such a way as to strike the proper medium between not discussing questions thoroughly, and making ourselves partisans against our own convictions for the sake of victory. We discussed in the course of the winter a great many theological subjects with much profit. But I am convinced that, as a general rule, all such debates on the part of mere students should be conducted under the presidency of a minister or professor of experience, so that the question might be summed up with thorough knowledge and impartiality, and its true merits exhibited previously to the close of the debate. If such societies were managed in this way, we could imagine nothing more profitable, both in the way of arousing and informing the minds of young men. Our debating society met on a week-night evening, and every week during the session. The preaching society always met on a Saturday forenoon. After earnest prayer we preached sermons alternately, and then candidly, but often unsparingly, criticised one another's discourses. At these societies, Dr. Munro, late of Manchester, and others since known and useful, were distinguished. At the close of our session we sometimes had a frugal dinner-party, which to us was an occasion of great importance. Dr. Munro was a considerable poet, and on one of these occasions he wrote an invitation to Mr. Fairley, now of Mauchline, almost as quickly as I can speak it, as follows:—

> "My dear Mr. Fairley,
>   Thus briefly and barely
> I beg leave to say,
>   That to-morrow's the day
> When our preaching society,
>   Having had a satiety
> Of sermons this season,
>   Resolve, and with reason,
> To dine all together,
>   Come fair or foul weather ;
> And as you've had a share
>   Of our glory and care,

> Our sapient debating,
>   Our ranting and rating,
> Come share, to be brief,
>   Our turbot and beef.
> Believe me, and go,
>   Yours, ALEX. MUNRO."

As I had now nearly completed my studies at Glasgow, and was looking forward to getting, in a year or so, license from the Hamilton Presbytery, I thought it better to go to Edinburgh for a winter and study under Dr. Chalmers. By the kindness of the late Dr. Black of the Barony, I received the appointment of tutor in the family of the late excellent Mrs. Neilson, then of Millbank, Canaan. This sweet place, of considerable extent, afterwards became the property of Professor Syme. It was a delightful residence, with great privacy and an excellent library, and as the family, of truly Christian people, sat in Dr. Andrew Thomson's church, I had the privilege of hearing and knowing that truly great man, as well as Dr. Chalmers. He was an admirable every-day preacher and most faithful minister. It is sometimes amusing to hear the incredulity with which men who measure others by themselves listen to the statement that a man can at once do several things well. Dr. Andrew Thomson was a many-sided man, of great capacity, enthusiasm, and energy. It is marvellous that no life of him has ever been published, whilst innumerable lives of men not to be mentioned in the same twelvemonth with him have appeared. He had a rare combination of gifts, and was a man of great versatility and public spirit, a most powerful reasoner, a bold denouncer of sin, an inimitable story-teller, and a master of satire and ridicule. He was, besides, a great educationist and musician.

There are a few of Dr. Thomson's speeches recorded, but they give little idea of the power of the living man, whose appearance, voice, and manner all added greatly to the effect.

He made an admirable speech against pluralities, wherein he tells one or two good stories. At one part of the speech he says—

"When that amiable man, Dr. Walker, was presented to the church and parish of Colinton, he was violently opposed by the people. They did not think that he would be an edifying or useful minister to them, and therefore they resisted his settlement. The late Dr. M'Knight was anxious to conciliate them, and to render Dr. Walker's induction as smooth and pleasant as possible. And accordingly he went out on a Sabbath (that perhaps being his day for supplying the vacancy), and seeing in the churchyard a venerable, intelligent-looking man, whom he thought he might address as a leading person in the parish, he began to converse with him on the subject. He found all his arguments, however, quite fruitless. At last he told the man, as one of the most powerful recommendations of Dr. Walker as a learned and able man that could be given, that since he had been presented to the parish of Colinton the King had also given him a professorship in the University of Edinburgh. 'Has he, sir?' said the old man hastily but firmly, and looking on him with a keen and penetrating eye. 'That mak's the thing far waur. I see how it's to be now. He will just make a bye-job of our souls.'"

Again, speaking of the University of St. Andrews, he said—

"When an eminent literary character from England was paying a visit to that university, the Senatus, with their well-known hospitality, gave him an entertainment. After dinner this very appropriate toast was announced by the Principal, 'The Arts and Sciences;' on which Professor Brown, who was unfortunately rather deaf, rose and audibly repeated the toast in the altered phrase, 'Our Absent Friends.' (Peals of laughter.) Sir, one of the great objects we are aiming at in our motion is simply this, that the arts and sciences may not become absent friends in all our universities."

In the case of Little Dunkeld, where an attempt was made

to thrust in a Mr. Nelson, who could not speak a word of Gaelic, Dr. Thomson made a noble speech. He said—

"Why, sir, it is called the mouth of the Highlands, and surely it may be presumed that the mouth of the Highlands must have a Gaelic tongue in it." (A laugh.) He continued, "With respect to the presentee himself, I sympathise with him on the disappointment he must feel; but I will not allow my sympathies to get the better of my sense of duty to the Church and to the people. . . . He may be as great as his namesake, Lord Nelson (a laugh), the thunder of whose achievements roared from the Baltic to the Nile, whose fame circumnavigated the globe, and whose memory will be cherished as long as that country exists which he defended and adorned, and as long as there is a wave to dash upon its shores (hear, hear), but still he has no more Gaelic than his Lordship had, and therefore is as unfit to be minister of Little Dunkeld as would have been the Admiral. (A laugh.) He may be wiser than his teachers and than the ancients, but then he has no Gaelic. He may have more Greek and Latin than the professors under whom he studied these learned languages, but still he is ignorant of Gaelic. He may be a profounder theologian than was John Calvin himself, but the loss is he is void of Gaelic. His eloquence may be more splendid and overwhelming than that of my reverend friend Dr. Chalmers, but with all this he knows not a word of Gaelic (laughter), and that is sufficient to determine us against finding him a qualified presentee." Again, "I beg pardon of my Highland brethren around me for taking the liberty to say in their presence that I am not much in love with some peculiarities of the Highlanders. I hate the bag-pipe (loud laughter); I hate it mortally. The kilt I have always looked upon as a very cold, and not altogether a decent vestment (much laughter); and I must say that the Gaelic language, which has been so plentifully praised to-day, sounds—I suppose owing to my ignorance—very harsh in my ear, and really gives me pain. (Hear, hear.) But, sir, though I am not partial to these characteristics of the Highlanders, they have other properties, I confess, that attract me and secure my regard. As an admirer of nature, I delight in their mountains and glens, their streams and their lakes.

As a social being, my heart warms at the recollection of their generous hospitality. As a patriot, I admire the unconquerable valour they have ever shown in defence of their country. As a Christian, I love their immortal souls; and as a Christian minister, I feel myself bound and constrained to protect them, so far as I can, from all attempts to encroach upon their spiritual privileges and to impair their spiritual well-being. (Hear, hear.) And on this account it is that I stand up in the General Assembly this evening to oppose the measure contemplated by the complaining party at your bar and by their supporters in this house. Sir, I forbid the banns between Mr. Nelson, the presentee, and the parish of Little Dunkeld."

His speeches against slavery constituted the turning-point in the whole struggle. Dr. Chalmers and he made an admirable and almost irresistible combination, Dr. Chalmers beginning the debate in a powerful prepared speech, and Dr. Thomson concluding with a withering combination of argument, remonstrance, satire, and invective.

Dr. Thomson and Dr. Chalmers were the main agents, under the Divine blessing, of turning the tide in Scotland in favour of evangelical religion. When I went to Edinburgh, Dr. Thomson was in the very heat of the Apocryphal controversy, and his "Christian Instructor," in which he dealt out monthly chastisement to a crowd of culprits, was much admired by many, whilst by others it was keenly assailed with abuse. He was the open enemy of all corruptions in Church and State—a powerful and faithful preacher—an earnest promoter of education, and the fearless champion of all that was true, honest, lovely, and of good report. When he died, Dr. Chalmers exclaimed in preaching his funeral sermon, "If our next war is to be a war of principles, then before the battle has commenced our noblest champion has fallen." Both of these men had the true Presbyterian spirit, and they manifested an utter scorn for time-serving and vacillation. They had only one duty to discharge in regard to truth, namely, to defend it at all hazards, and one would as soon have expected to see Arthur Seat inverted as to find these men denying the principles of their whole lives to secure any object whatever. I had much pleasure in the society of both. I preached about a year after my arrival in Edinburgh, and on being licensed my first sermon was for Dr. Andrew Thomson on a week-day in the Old Church. For a long time I kept the note inviting me to do so. I shall always cherish the highest veneration for his memory.

There was a whole galaxy of great men at that time in all departments in Edinburgh. In addition to the eminent ministers I have mentioned, Dr. M'Crie was in his strength, and the students often went to hear him. I have still a vivid recollection of several of his sermons, and of the dignified manner and kindling eye with which he delivered them. I remember part of a description of drunkenness, even when not carried to excess. "The glory of man is reason, and whatsoever tends to dim the lustre of that crown is criminal. Next to reason the glory of man is the tongue, and whatsoever tends to make that tongue to falter is criminal. Whatsoever maketh a man slow to hear, swift to speak, swift to wrath, is criminal and savours of excess." At an after period I saw a good deal of the Doctor, and admired him very much. I am confident that he has been much misrepresented of late.

The Parliament House had many eminent men at this period. The students followed Cranstoun, Jeffrey, Moncrieff, and Cockburn, to hear them speak. The speaking of Jeffrey was almost matchless for fluency, coupled at the same time with elegance. From the rapid transitions which I have heard him make from subject to subject in taking up successive cases, he must have had an amazing memory. I never heard any one manage parenthesis better. I have heard him introduce a parenthesis—indeed he did it often—and have watched to hear if he would catch up the thread with accuracy; and he generally, if not always, succeeded with admirable adroitness. His speaking, although wonderful, was too minute for the House of Commons; and yet, even there he said some memorable things; as when he compared the Reform Bill, which included only the upper stratum of society, to the firmament spoken of in Scripture, which divided " the waters from the waters,"—the waters of a wholesome state of society from the underlying waters of revolution. He afterwards, in speaking on the Auchterarder case, dealt in his peculiar philosophical way with the precise degree of attraction and repulsion about certain men, although the true cause might not be fully ascertained or ascertainable. Cockburn was a different man, but also a very easy, eloquent, and imposing speaker. A story is told to illustrate the difference between the two. Jeffrey was examining a country witness in a case of alleged lunacy, and he asked in regard to the man in question, " Did you think him a man of sound intelligence ? was he *compos mentes*, &c. ?" All that he could get out of the witness was, " What's your wull, sir ?" Cockburn said, " Let me try him "—" Did ye ken this man ?"—" Ou aye," said the witness; " I kent him brawly."—" Did you think there was ony thing intil 'im ?" —" 'Deed no very muckle ; very little mair than the spoon put intil 'im."—" Would ye hae trusted 'im to sell a coo ?" —" 'Deed no ; ony butcher's laddie wud a' cheated 'im."— " That will do," said Cockburn. Cranstoun and Moncreiff were also well worth hearing ; although, as a general rule, they were not such favourites with the students. But there was one man that all were anxious to see, viz., Sir Walter Scott. He sat within the railings as one of the clerks of the Court of Session, with his dreamy eye and conical head, and we all looked in upon him from time to time with mysterious curiosity, the great secret, although guessed at, not having been avowed.

The University also had some striking men besides Dr. Chalmers, probably the chief of them being John Wilson, the editor of "Blackwood," and the author of the then famous "Noctes Ambrosianæ." His stalwart figure was well known on the streets of Edinburgh, and his lectures were very eloquent. His students were very fond of him, and he was very popular, upon the whole, over Scotland. Like Sir Walter Scott, he understood the peculiarities of Scotch feeling, even although he did not always sympathise with them. His impressive scene of the old Scotchman giving out the psalm is very characteristic:—

> " Within Thy tabernacle, Lord,
>   Who shall abide with Thee?
> And in Thy high and holy hill
>   Who shall a dweller be?"

It is said that one of the old-clothes-men that hang about the College said to him on one occasion (some say it was Cockburn), in a loud whisper, "Any old clothes?" to which he answered in an equal whisper, "No; have you?" It is alleged that some one else answered the same question on another occasion by saying, "I have nothing else."

The Presbytery of Edinburgh was a great place of resort by the students of theology. It was reckoned in those days an important part of our training to study the proceedings of church courts, and attending the Presbytery was regarded as one of the best methods of obtaining the necessary information. The Presbytery of Edinburgh met at that time in a small, obscure, but rather dignified hall, situated amongst the crowd of buildings recently swept away in front of the Industrial Museum. The leading men, besides Dr. Chalmers, were Dr. Inglis and Dr. Thomson, the respective leaders of the opposite parties. Dr. Inglis was a tall and dignified-looking man, but a man of great talent and weight. He was father to the present Lord Justice-General. He had a peculiar voice; indeed, as Lockhart in his "Peter's Letters" justly says, he had two voices—one a kind of squeak or high treble, the other a sort of low and solemn grunt. Nevertheless it was impossible to hear him speak without being impressed with a sense of his high talent, and that in the department of law he might have risen to high rank. He was greatly superior in principle to many in his own party. It is said that being once at a country sacrament, and hearing some doctrine of which he did not approve from one of the assistants, he deliberately took up his hat and walked off to the manse. When the service was over and the minister came in, he said, "Doctor, were you ill?" "No," said Dr. Inglis sternly, "I was not ill, but I was ill-pleased; and I wish you to understand that if the same doctrine is to be preached here again, I shall never come back." I heard him preach a very excellent sermon in his own church—the Old Greyfriars—on the text, "Work out your own salvation with fear and trembling, for it is God that worketh in you both to will and to do," &c. The church at that time was very thin, and it was alleged that a standing debate existed on this subject. The colleague of Dr. Inglis was Dr. Anderson, whom also I heard preach, a totally different kind of man—a man of considerable elocution and rhetoric, but of little solid talent. The debate was as to the cause of the poorly filled church. Some said the church was thin because of Dr. Inglis's want of *manner*, and some said it was because of Dr. Anderson's want of *matter*. It was like the case of "Jack Sprat, who could eat no fat, and whose wife could eat no lean;" and, at all events, the result was similar—"the platter was nearly clean." Dr. Inglis was the principal founder of our India Missions, and although a good deal of debate has arisen in regard to the theory upon which these missions are founded, viz., a system of education as contrasted with mere public preaching of the Gospel, this proved his missionary zeal, and the actual result has—without settling this precise question at issue—reflected permanent credit, under God, both upon the head and heart of Dr. Inglis.

The first day I entered the Presbytery of Edinburgh rather a scene occurred. It was during the heat of the Apocrypha controversy, in which Dr. Thomson took so prominent and effective a part. It so happened that the proof-sheets of one of the most sharp and pungent pamphlets on the other side were brought by mistake to the house of Dr. Thomson, instead of to that of the Rev. Henry Grey. The pamphlet in question was anonymous, but in this way, although of course he did not touch the proofs, he unexpectedly was forced to know that the true author was either the Rev. Henry Grey, or, as was more generally supposed at that time, one very nearly related to him. This led to very much keenness and strong feeling. Dr. Thomson defended his own position in the "Christian Instructor," coupled with an unsparing criticism of "Anglicanus," for this was the name assumed by the anonymous writer. He even dealt pretty plainly with "Anglicana," and one other still, supposed to be in the background, and whom Dr. Thomson styled "Anglicanum." The town was convulsed. It was the subject of universal conversation, and some of the windows were filled with caricatures representing the principal characters. The matter ultimately reached the Presbytery. It was referred to incidentally on the day when I first entered it. Mr. Marshall—who had just come from Glasgow to be minister of the Tolbooth Church, and who afterwards joined the Church of England, became a very High Churchman, and was buried, it was said, in his surplice—rose in a very solemn way to deplore the state of things which had thus arisen, and to beg Dr. Thomson to give up so painful a struggle altogether. Mr. Marshall at the same time added, that he tendered this advice entirely on general grounds, and admitted that he was quite ignorant of the true merits of the controversy. Dr. Thomson, who had been sitting all this time like a chained eagle, immediately rose with the greatest quickness and said, "Moderator, here is a curious thing. A new member comes into our Presbytery. He admits that he is utterly ignorant of the subject about which he presumes to speak, and yet he knows enough to give me an advice, and a very foolish one. Let me recommend him to obtain some knowledge of the question before he speaks on the subject again. He will then discover that he has made a complete mistake, and tendered his advice entirely to the wrong person." Poor Mr. Marshall looked very crestfallen, and no more was said. There were a number of subordinate men in the Presbytery, but of some mark; as, for example, Dr. M'Knight, son of the commentator, a man of considerable talent and wit. Dr. David Dickson of St. Cuthbert's, a man of great benevolence and excellence of character, and a most active parish minister, once came into the Presbytery rather in a hurry and sat down beside him; whereupon Dr. M'Knight jokingly said, in reference to an illustration of nouns in our Latin grammar, "*David*, a man's name; *animal*, a living creature." In the General Assembly, on one occasion, it was proposed to appoint a Psalmody committee. Dr. M'Knight quietly proposed that the following should be amongst the names on the committee: "Dr. Singer and Dr. Sangster, Mr. Piper of Fa-la (Falla), and Dr. Low Rhymer of Hand-in-tune" (Dr. Lorimer of Haddington). He was the true author of a joke that has often been published. When his colleague came in very wet on one occasion, he said, "Go into the pulpit and you'll be dry enough." Mr. Somerville of Currie, whom Dr. Thomson on one occasion termed "a gentle lamb from the sheep-walks of Currie," was a man of some note. He spoke with very considerable fluency, and was rather a noted character in the general community. He preached a public sermon in connection with the effort to finish the National Monument on the Calton Hill. His idea at that time was that the monument should be finished, although it has since been discovered that it makes Edinburgh more like Athens to allow it to continue as it is. Dr. Somerville chose for his text on that occasion, "What mean ye by these stones?" Dr. Gilchrist, the Presbytery clerk, formerly of Greenock, then of the Canongate, was an able man and a good deal of a character. I knew him well afterwards, and he was a most worthy, straightforward, kindly man, but peculiar. He published a volume of sermons which had little sale. Some one spoke to him on the subject of his volume. He said, "Oh, ye see, it was just to undeceive the family. They thocht" (he sometimes spoke in broad Scotch) "that there was a perfect fortune locked up in my manuscripts, and I just published a volume to convince them that they needna be looking for siller to that quarter." He once said to me, speaking of one of his co-presbyters, afterwards rather famous, "The Apostle speaks of itching ears, but there's another itch—the itch o' popularity. Our freen" (naming the minister) "has got it, and it's faur waur than the common itch. You can cure the common itch wi' butter and brimstone, but nae remedy has yet been discovered for the itch o' popularity."

During the same period I had an opportunity of hearing in all his glory the late Edward Irving. I had heard of him at a previous period, in the days of his comparative obscurity, when he was assistant to Dr. Chalmers in Glasgow; but now all the world had heard of his immense popularity in London. That popularity had been rather increased than otherwise by certain novelties of doctrine and practice which he was alleged to have introduced into his congregation. He had come down to attend the General Assembly, and as he was a man of immense physical power and extraordinary zeal and energy, he had resolved to preach every morning at six o'clock. These sermons began in St. Andrew's Church, but as it was completely mobbed, they were transferred to the West Kirk, which contains about three thousand people. Being anxious to hear this celebrated man, I was up every morning with the lark, and walked from Millbank, Canaan, into Edinburgh in time to secure admission to the church with the first of the crowd. Every corner of the immense building was crammed long before the commencement of worship. As soon as the hour struck, an unusually tall figure was seen emerging from the vestry, and making his way through the crowded aisles, towering above the people head and shoulders, like Saul. His hair was parted in front, and his beautifully chiselled face was somewhat marred by a remarkable squint in one of his dark expressive eyes. But otherwise he was very fine-looking. When he reached the pulpit, he solemnly opened the psalm-book, bent back its boards, turned up his cuffs and wristbands, and proceeded to read the psalm with a powerful and sonorous, but thoroughly modulated voice, which rivalled the deep bass of the finest organ. I often thought it was worth my whole journey to town, even at that early hour, to hear the way in which he rolled out the 45th Psalm, apparently one of his greatest favourites—

"O Thou that art the Mighty One,
Thy sword gird on Thy thigh."

I remember once, in the course of his sermon, his not only saying, but repeating, as if he relished its sweet rhythm, with marvellous intonation, "Her Nazarites were purer than snow; they were whiter than milk. They were more ruddy in body than rubies; their polishing was of sapphire." Although there was not much in the discourse that one could take away, yet it was admirably delivered, and excited an immense interest. Although it was not unusual to have it prolonged for nearly two hours, yet this was done without any of the people indicating a disposition to move.

In connection with this visit, Mr. Irving exhorted a table at St. George's, at which I was present, and this exercise was equally peculiar. It was a grand spiritual soliloquy, lasting for nearly an hour. It was said at that time by good authority that in private intercourse affectionate attempts were sometimes made by the older and more experienced ministers to wean him from his peculiarities. It was all in vain. A friend told me that he was present at a private party where Mr. Irving was stalking through the room and soliloquising in his usual marvellous way. Dr. Gordon, with his solemn manner and keen logic, endeavoured to arrest the progress of his discourse, and to bring him to the point. Mr. Irving suddenly turned round, stretched out his brawny arms, and exclaimed, "Gordon, you can argue, but you're but a child at discourse." Irving I believe was a truly good man, although in some respects sadly mistaken. No one can read his diary, as given by Mrs. Oliphant, without being persuaded of this, and also of his great kindness of heart. No one can read his sermons and works without seeing that he was a man of the most elevated spirit, and that few Scotchmen have ever existed who had so high and exalted a conception of all that is greatest and most glorious in our native land. How he would have scorned the idea of accommodating truth to circumstances, and with what indignant reproof did he denounce the idea that there could be any true education which was not saturated and pervaded by the truths of religion. No man ever wrote more nobly of the Book of Psalms, and I know from the testimony of Dr. Black of the Barony, who attended him on his death-bed, that he died a humble, self-renouncing, and hopeful Christian.

The theological course of Dr. Chalmers was extremely well worth attending, not only for the eloquence and power with which he expounded theological truth, and the deep interest which he took in all his students, but for the immense impulse which he gave to all who were capable of receiving it. The enthusiastic and unflagging action of the mind of Dr. Chalmers was something marvellous, and it was a most wholesome action to which to subject the minds of students. Immense good resulted from his class.

As I had been a member of a debating society in Glasgow,

I was anxious to see how such matters were conducted in Edinburgh. I therefore joined the Theological Debating Society connected with the University. I walked in and out from Millbank to attend its meetings, returning on many a dark night—on some nights so dark that I had to feel for the wall coming along by Bruntsfield Links. At this time there were very few lamps or buildings in that direction. This society met in one of the lower rooms of the University, and when I joined it, it was attended by some remarkable men who afterwards became famous, including the late Mr. Patrick (afterwards Professor) Macdougall, the late Rev. J. B. Patterson of Falkirk, and above all Mr. William (afterwards Dr.) Cunningham. The debates were conducted with remarkable ability. A list of the members of this association has recently been published, and I find that the date of my entry is November 21, 1828. The society was first instituted on the 23d November 1776, when Mr. John Gibson, its first secretary, delivered a discourse from 1 Cor. xiv. 12, "Seek that ye may excel, to the edifying of the Church." In its earlier days it was both a preaching and a debating society, and such men as Dr. Inglis, Dr. Chalmers, Dr. Welsh, and many more were afterwards members of it. It was broken up amidst the wreck of the Disruption, but has recently been revived. The first night I was present there was a discussion on what constituted one of the salient points of what was then designated the "Row heresy," namely, whether or not assurance was of the essence of saving faith. The debate was opened with very considerable talent in the affirmative by Mr. William Tait, son of the Rev. Mr. Tait of the College Church, an excellent man, but who had joined the Rowites, and was afterwards excluded from the Established Church of Scotland. As soon as Mr. Tait's speech was finished, up rose a tall young man with a frizzled head, and proceeded amidst deep attention to take his argument to pieces with great clearness, cogency, and power. This was

Dr. Cunningham, and it was the first time I had ever seen him. Although very young, his speaking had all the characteristics of his more advanced days. I have still a recollection of part of his argument. Said he—

"If a man makes the assertion, 'I shall dwell in the house of the Lord for ever,' that is an assertion which requires proof. Men may deceive themselves, and if it is not true of all men that they shall dwell in the house of the Lord for ever, this man must produce clear evidence that it is true of *him*. If the message of the Gospel were so framed as to specify the names of individuals, and to require all such simply to believe a fact in regard to themselves, that fact being clearly asserted in the Word of God, then undoubtedly assurance and faith would be the same thing—in other words, assurance would be of the essence of faith. But this is not the form in which the Gospel message comes to us. All are invited to receive and rest upon Christ, but no man is named, and no statement is made in regard to any individual apart from Christ, which he is called to credit simply as a fact. The Gospel call is that we should believe on the Lord Jesus Christ, receive and rest upon Him alone for salvation; and the Scripture proves that whilst this may be accompanied by immediate assurance, it may be done also in such a way as to secure salvation, whilst the blessed and full assurance of our personal interest in Christ does not exist, or may have existed and been withdrawn. The duty of seeking assurance, and not resting satisfied until it is obtained, is admitted, and ought to be earnestly preached; but it is not admitted, and it is only a confusion of ideas to say, that assurance and faith are the same thing."

I was extremely struck with this speech. It was delivered as easily, coolly, and powerfully as any speech I ever heard Dr. Cunningham deliver. That copious vocabulary of his, without any attempt at figure, anecdote, or illustration, was as remarkable at that time as afterwards, as well as his crushing logic. Some one has compared him to a "snow-plough," which powerfully removes obstructions and clears the way for itself and for others; and one has likened his style of speaking to the action of a "bone-mill," crushing down all intellectual obstacles with irresistible force. But perhaps the most interesting thing about him was the early maturity of his powers. He was an untiring reader of books, and had a memory of the most tenacious kind, the double effect of which was that everything was arranged and tabulated in his mind in the most perfect order, and he seldom changed his opinions. I saw much of him in afterlife. He was a man of decided Christian principle, amiability, and integrity, but in that first debate I had a very striking illustration of his ability and power of argument. The question was afterwards during the evening discussed with much earnestness and talent, and although appearing for the first time, I ventured to offer a few remarks on the subject, which were well received. The matter in debate was by no means new to me, in connection with the stirring discussions on the same subject in the West of Scotland. I had afterwards the honour to be one of the presidents of this Theological Debating Society.

Mr. Bullock, afterwards of Tulliallan, was a member of the society, and a man of great vigour and edge of mind. He said to me, "The great things to be studied in public speaking are plainness and pith." Some one asked him why he did not join the Moderate party in the Church; to which he quietly replied, "I have always had a belief in a future state." Some one was telling him of an adventure, as an illustration of his own talent. He had been on horseback, and night coming on unexpectedly, he lost his road, and did not know what to do. But it occurred to him just to throw the reins on the horse's neck and let him take his own course, and it so happened that he brought him safely home. "Now," said he to Mr. Bullock, "was not that a clever plan?" "Yes," said Mr. Bullock, "it was very clever on the part of the horse." A Leith merchant failed in business and then turned minister. Mr. Bullock quietly remarked, "It is said of Matthew the publican that he left all and followed Christ; but this is a case of an entirely opposite description. All has left this man before he has begun to follow."

During my residence at this time in Edinburgh, the subject of Roman Catholic Emancipation was keenly discussed, and immediately afterwards settled, as it now appears, to the permanent injury of the kingdom. Very great diversity of opinion then existed on the subject. Dr. M'Crie, Dr. Jones, Dr. Gordon, my father, and many others, were strongly opposed to the measure, and predicted the very results which have since occurred. On the other hand, Dr. Chalmers, Dr. Thomson, and the Whigs of the Parliament House were as strongly in its favour; and after Sir Robert Peel and the Duke of Wellington declared themselves prepared to admit Romanists into power, many of their party also changed along with them. I was present at the great meeting held in Edinburgh in favour of the Emancipation measure. Jeffrey spoke with his usual fluency and felicity of language. But the great speech of the meeting was that of Dr. Chalmers. The enthusiasm was immense, as he ran over a stream of concessions that he, in his simplicity, was willing to make. Let them get into Parliament—let them get to the very ear of the monarch, and so forth; but give them the Bible, and with that single instrument he would overthrow all the influence and policy of Rome! Looking back over the past, one cannot help wondering at the amiable credulity which dictated such a speech, in opposition to the essential principles of the Revolution Settlement, and at the shallow view which such a powerful man took of past history and experience, and of the craft and resources of the mystic Babylon. Her first cry is always equality, but she is only satisfied with absolute supremacy. At that time one asked Dr. Chalmers how it happened that the mass of the good people of Scotland were opposed to his views? He said, "They are not chemists. They cannot analyse the question. They can only smell it, and they smell Popery in it." As the "Times," however, was afterwards forced to admit that " the bigots were right," so the " smell " of the Scotch Covenanters, the result of dire experience, was more reliable than the philosophy of worthy Dr. Chalmers.

No doubt if the Church had been faithful the result might have been otherwise; but the Church has ever since been sinking into deeper apathy on the subject of Romanism, and now a disastrous crisis seems near. This very apathy has in no small measure been owing to the elaborate efforts made at the time to which I refer to persuade the people of the United Kingdom that Popery had essentially changed, and that the safeguards and other efforts in defence of Protestant truth and liberty found necessary in the days of our ancestors might now be dispensed with. Previous to that period the people of Scotland regarded Popery with singular horror and aversion, as a system subversive of Divine truth and human liberty—a bloody and intolerant superstition—the system described in the Revelation as "drunk with the blood of saints and of the martyrs of Jesus." They justly regarded it also as an impious superstition, not destined to be reformed but destroyed. They believed from Scripture, as experience has since proved, that it would become worse and worse. This was the unanimous impression of the older ministers, and of all the best of the people since I remember, and there cannot be a doubt that the discussions at the period to which I am referring, and the ground taken by such eminent men as Dr. Thomson and Dr. Chalmers at that period in regard to Popery, have since had a most disastrous effect in Scotland and in the United Kingdom.

Two very remarkable men visited Edinburgh at this time in connection with the Popish question, viz., Captain Gordon, afterwards M.P. for Dundalk, and the Rev. Nicholas Armstrong. They addressed several large public meetings and excited much interest. Captain Gordon was a robust, energetic-looking man, and spoke very well and fluently, dwelling chiefly on the Bible as the only rule of faith, and exposing the perversions of the Romish system. Mr. Armstrong was a tall, dark Irishman, and spoke with remarkable vehemence and energy. They both clearly indicated at that early period the course upon which the country had embarked, and the results which are now taking place around us, although multitudes regarded them as raising an entirely false alarm.

During my student life I acquired two lessons of considerable importance. The first is, that, as a general rule, it is a most unsatisfactory and unprofitable thing to go from church to church in quest of edification. Not only is your own mind apt to be unsettled by the constant variety, but even inferior sermons coming from a man to whose manner you are accustomed are often more instructive and satisfactory. No doubt students are prone to roam about amongst the churches. It is right that they should hear remarkable men, and to some extent they may undoubtedly derive advantage from this. But, as a general rule for all classes, and not least for students, "a rolling stone gathers no moss," and it is better to select a profitable ministry and adhere to it. Any advantage from variety, except in the cases referred to of peculiarly eminent men, is supplied at the communion seasons as they periodically return, when these are conducted according to the ancient practice of Scotland. This is a lesson, however, which one sometimes learns only by experience. I was brought to a determination to adhere to my own church, which, after I left the College chapel in Glasgow, was that of the excellent Dr. Brown of St. John's, by a peculiar incident. One day the Doctor was absent, and there came in his place a preacher whose discourse was extremely poor and unsatisfactory, and who uttered in a hard and most stentorian voice things which he expected to be pathetic. He reminded me forcibly of a story which I had heard of a man who was at a public catechising, when he was asked "Who was Pontius Pilate?" Being unable to answer, and at the same time rather dull of hearing, his next neighbour whispered to him "He was a Roman governor," upon which the man shouted out, to the great astonishment both of the minister and the congregation, "He was a roaring gommeral, sir!"

A story was told of Dr. Andrew Thomson. A preacher whom I knew, and who was not unlike the one I am now describing, was once preaching before Dr. Thomson, and was extremely anxious to know what the Doctor thought of his preaching. The Doctor at first evaded his hints, but when he found this would not do, he said, in his usual quick way, "Well, Mr. So-and-so, I think I can pay you the same compliment that was once paid to myself." "What was that?" eagerly inquired Boanerges. Dr. Thomson said, "I was once preaching on a fast-day at Kirkcaldy in the afternoon, Dr. Gordon having preached in the forenoon. Two men were going home from the church, and they began to talk to each other about the sermons. 'What thocht ye o' yon man in the forenoon?' said the one man to the other. 'Oh, he was a fine sensible man, a gran' preacher.' 'And what thocht ye o' that man in the afternoon?' said he. 'Aweel, I maun admit,' said the other, 'that yon man roared weel.'" So did the preacher, to whom I listened with inexpressible pain; and as Dr. Brown was not to be at home in the afternoon, I determined to improve the day by hearing some one better. What was my horror, when I went to another church, to see the same man go into the pulpit and repeat the same hideous performance, word for word, and roar for roar. I knew that this, at least, could not have occurred if I had adhered to my own church, and I determined to be very cautious in wandering for the future.

The second lesson was the importance of not studying during all hours of the night, but going early to bed and rising early. This, and living on porridge and other plain food, avoiding all tobacco and other narcotics or stimulants, have been the great lessons of my physical life. There is an immense temptation presented to students to work through all hours of the night, as it is more easy to keep their fires in at night than to get them lighted in the morning. Of course they cannot burn the candle at both ends, and therefore they must either sit up late or rise early. But the worst of it is not the late hours in themselves. If you study late at night and with any energy, you become feverish; and even when you get to bed, you toss about and are unable to sleep. Now without a reasonable measure of sound sleep robust health is impossible. On the other hand, if you work in the morning, you work with the full renovated vigour which a sound sleep has been the means, by the blessing of God, of imparting. I have no doubt also that you will be less disposed to indulge in cobweb subtleties and the production of German mist; whilst even if you become excited or feverish in consequence of earnest work, the exercise of the day will entirely restore the tone of the system, and enable you to sleep with all the placidity of a child. This, besides, is a matter of far greater importance than many suppose. A sound body is a great auxiliary to a sound mind, just as a great memory, although some undervalue it, is an immense auxiliary to a sound judgment. Some of the most powerful men of our day, Dr. Chalmers, Dr. Thomson, John Wilson, Dr. Cunningham, and others, have had a remarkably developed physical framework. Solomon says, "A cheerful heart doeth good like a medicine;" and I have no doubt that irritable nerves and an imperfect digestion on the part of Christian ministers are more frequent causes of personal discomfort and incapacity for work, nay, even of chronic mischiefs in congregations, than many suppose. No doubt the first matter of concern ought to be the state of the soul, a heart right in the sight of God, reconciliation with God, and a spirit of entire devotion to our Master's service. But these things being secured, we should seek to be enabled to serve God in every way with the very best of all things, including the best of health. Even Paul exhorted Timothy to use the necessary means to get rid of his feeble health and often infirmities.

CHAPTER III.

MY LICENSE; ORDINATION, AND EXPERIENCE AS AN ASSISTANT AT NORTH LEITH, AND A MINISTER OF CHAPELS AT DUMFRIES AND EDINBURGH.

THE date of my license by the Presbytery of Hamilton is June 10th, 1829. An excellent practice prevailed in those days, and I presume had been handed down from early date, of requiring all those who were about to be licensed, not only to pass through the ordinary examinations in the Presbytery, but to call on all the ministers separately at their own manses. The object of this was, that the ministers might have an opportunity of satisfying themselves, by personal examination, in regard to the spirit and attainments of those who were about to become licentiates of the Church. Like many of the other excellent rules of Presbyterianism, it implied that presbyteries should have only a limited number of members, and that the districts should be limited in extent. Whilst for the purpose of concentrating influence and producing popular effect, the larger presbyteries of the present day may be defended, it is certain that, for all the practical purposes of thorough oversight and mutual conference, the smaller presbyteries were much more efficient. Indeed, the true theory of Presbyterian oversight has been to a large extent forgotten in recent times, and the practical business of presbyteries either neglected, or conducted by means of boards and other exotic arrangements imported into the Presbyterian system, but which have marred its beauty and diminished its efficiency. Nothing could have been better than the now almost obsolete arrangement to which I have referred, by which the gifts and motives of aspirants to the ministry were submitted to the quiet scrutiny of such a variety of minds as were found in an average presbytery. This also gave the young men the great advantage of the paternal counsel and prayers of many ministers of Christ, before starting in public life. A friend of mine, of decided eminence, tells me that some of the best advice he ever received in life, was during the round of calls which he thus made. Being the son of one of the ministers, and knowing most of the members of Presbytery intimately, as well as residing for the time at a considerable distance, I fear I did not get the full advantage of this private ordeal; although I was subjected in public to a kind and painstaking scrutiny, through some parts of which, in the hands of such men as Dr. Russel and Dr. Hodgson, I passed with some little trepidation.

There was another laudable practice which prevailed in the Presbytery of Hamilton at that time, and which, for anything I know, was once common in Scotland generally By the ordinary method a preacher never faces anything like a living congregation until he is actually licensed. Unlike young doctors or lawyers, or any other professional men, he is at once launched from a mere round of studies into the actual business of his life-work, without guide or counsellor. In theory this is manifestly unsound, and I have no doubt it works most mischievously in practice. A system of clinical studies, actual preaching in public under a good preacher and successful minister, would be very beneficial. It would not only be sound in theory, but a totally different thing from the loose talking sometimes at present practised by students at mission stations without the slightest supervision or advice, and which only teaches young men the dangerous secret of keeping their mouths open without saying anything worthy of being listened to. This I regard as one of the most dangerous ordeals to which a young man intending to be a minister can be subjected. Out of it, it is scarcely possible for a young man to rise to the higher altitude of a good speaker or a vigorous preacher. The system to which I refer at Hamilton did not come up to the full requirements of the case. But it was an approximation to it. It seemed to acknowledge the principle for which I contend, and it was better than nothing. Perhaps it might be a relic of more sensible times. After a young man had preached all his other discourses before the Presbytery, and was about to give his "popular sermon" just previous to license, the bell of the church was rung to assemble the congregation. A number of worthy people seemed to be in the habit of coming together on such occasions to get the first hearing of the forthcoming preacher. The young man was required to go to the pulpit, and in the presence of a congregation, as well as of the Presbytery, to give a final proof of his gifts and aptitude to teach. I have the most vivid recollection of passing through this ordeal. The faces of the worthy old people who had come together to hear are still vividly before me. My "popular sermon" was on the text, "Wherefore, seeing we also are compassed about with so great a cloud of witnesses, let us lay aside every weight, and the sin that doth so easily beset us, and let us run with patience the race set before us," and I felt that it had a solemnising as well as stimulating effect to be brought thus face to face with an actual living congregation.

Previous to this I had only made one address to anything like a congregation—the general idea at that time being that a man should not preach till he was licensed, although I had acted as family chaplain, and in several other ways spoken in public. This address was made at a mission station in the Canongate. But now being licensed, I began my work at once; and it so happened that I was now carried away permanently from my native district, from the Presbytery of Hamilton and its associations, although my father's people, at a subsequent period, were anxious that I should become his assistant and successor. On a day of the same week in which I was licensed, I preached what was properly my first sermon in public, to a small audience in what was called the Old Church, Edinburgh, as a very unworthy substitute for Dr. Andrew Thomson. On the following Sabbath, instead of Mr. Bruce Cunningham, now of Prestonpans, I preached twice for Mr. Thomson in the parish church of Duddingston. Mr. Thomson is better known as having been an eminent painter than as a minister. His parish was small at that time, there being a chapel of ease in Portobello, where the mass of the population of the parish existed. I never heard Mr. Thomson himself preach, and I suspect that preaching was not his forte, but he was a singularly shrewd, genial, and accomplished man. He had such a remarkable genius for painting, that it is said, that from the snuffing of a candle applied by his thumb, he could make a tolerably good picture. Some of his landscapes are certainly very marvellous productions. He was not at home on the day that I preached, but at his own request I afterwards visited him at his manse. Mrs. Thomson conducted the psalmody on the day of my preaching, and being an excellent musician, and having trained a number to sing with her, the result was very pleasing and successful.

I determined from the first not to read my sermons. I knew, however, from what I had seen amongst the older ministers, and especially from what I had heard from my father, that to succeed in this a good deal of labour must be incurred. He was in the habit of saying, that he took ten days to commit his first sermon to memory, although his memory was certainly one of the best that I have ever heard of. This labour, however, I had reason to believe, would be well repaid in the long run, and I was determined, if spared, to face it. The truth is, one great mistake which many young men make, is in confounding wire-drawn talk with effective speaking, and in supposing that a sermon is committed to memory when they can only grope their way through it with much hesitation and difficulty, the eye being continually introverted on the MS. To commit a sermon properly to memory, a man should be so thoroughly master of it, as to speak it with the most perfect ease. The old preachers were in the habit of saying, that a preacher should be able to begin at any part of his sermon at a moment's notice, though wakened for the purpose out of his sleep. Some may call this mechanical and slavish, but it is the only way to success. It was only thus that Demosthenes, Cicero, and the great orators of old, succeeded; and it is thus, as a general rule, that great speakers in all departments succeed still. It is only when such a thorough mastery is obtained, that the preacher can be easy and natural, and that there can be real and effective speaking. By and by, of course, this can be done with much less elaborate preparation. A copious vocabulary is mastered, perfect self-possession is gained, and the art of speaking, in those endowed with proper gifts, comes to be as natural as the art of walking. But, in both cases, if we would ever succeed, we must "creep before we walk." We must never forget that God, both in nature and grace, works by means. Unless a man is willing to submit to great drudgery, both to secure present qualifications and for an ulterior end of the highest importance, he will never, as a general rule, be an effective preacher or speaker. Of course, after all, the most necessary thing is, to be entirely absorbed in our great work as ambassadors for Christ, to have always something of importance to say, and an earnest desire to say it with effect, for the glory of God and the good of souls. I succeeded tolerably well in my first two sermons at Duddingston, although my impressions of the great difficulty and importance of the work which I had taken in hand, and of my own unworthiness to perform it, were greatly deepened.

I preached again in the evening in the Canongate Chapel.

The commencement of a preacher's life is generally a matter of special interest to his immediate friends and companions, and some of mine were present at the evening worship. It so happened that the people of North Leith were anxious to obtain an assistant to their able and eloquent minister, Mr. (afterwards Dr.) James Buchanan. Somehow or other, they got word of this new preacher, and I had an application next morning to take the place. No man could be more comfortable than I was in Mrs. Neilson's family at Millbank. In a pecuniary point of view, I was asked to make a sacrifice, and I was under a strong temptation to continue in my quiet retreat, as we had an excellent theological library, and as I really had few sermons prepared except those that I had prepared for the Hall and the Presbytery. To take a few months of leisure and quiet study, before passing into actual work, seemed therefore very desirable, especially as I was very young. The offer, on the other hand, had some very favourable aspects. To obey what appeared to be a Providential call; to be associated with an eminent minister in the great work of the gospel; to have only partial duty, so as to have some reasonable time for preparation at first, were considerations with me of no small importance. I had always been taught to follow the leadings of Providence. Matthew Henry in his Exposition of the Shorter Catechism says, "Is man his own maker? No. Is he then his own master? No. Should he be his own carver? No." This must ever be regarded as of vital importance. The paramount consideration with me was, that as the Christian ministry was to be the object and work of my life, the sooner I threw myself into it the better, although I felt that it must be done with deep humility and earnest prayer. I therefore agreed to undertake the proposed duty, on the condition that the people were satisfied after hearing me preach in the afternoon of the following Sabbath. The new ordeal of preaching in such circumstances to such a vast congregation, consisting of nearly two thousand people, and a people accustomed to hear so eloquent a preacher as Dr. Buchanan, was a very trying one. It was very different from preaching in the little school-house in the Canongate, the little church of Duddingston, or even in the considerably larger Canongate Chapel. I remember well the full gaze of the vast congregation, as the new stranger mounted the pulpit stair and began the service; but I was graciously carried through with some measure of success. It was intimated to me that the arrangement was concluded, and an old elder gave me a few private words of special encouragement. I immediately left my kind friends and removed to a lodging on the road from Bonnington to Newhaven, at which I still look up in passing with special interest. Many an earnest day of study and prayer in that humble lodging! My duty was to preach every Sabbath afternoon. Besides this, I conducted a class of young people, which turned out very successful, and I visited and held meetings at Newhaven on the one hand, where, at that time, there was no place of worship; and on the other, at a place in Leith called the Peat Neuk, which had a very unsavoury reputation, and which gave me a tolerable insight, almost for the first time, into what have since been called the "lapsed masses" of our towns. Many of the houses which I visited there were very degraded, and some of the people, who even attended my meetings with tolerable regularity, were strange samples of the race. The work upon the whole was not encouraging, but I did not shrink from it. One extraordinary character, I remember, who lived by begging, had a great black patch over one of his eyes, as if he had lost the use of it. It never occurred to me that this could be a device to create sympathy and extort coppers. But some one gave me the hint that thus the case actually stood, and one night after the service I went quietly up to the man, and lifting the patch I saw his eye shining below as clear as a diamond. Of course, I admonished him in as kind and faithful a way as I could to adopt a more upright course for the future; but I was certainly a good deal taken aback by finding that I had such characters amongst my hearers. The Newhaven portion of my charge consisted of very different elements. It was altogether pleasant to work amongst the people there. There are no more respectable people in their own rank of life than the Newhaven fishermen, their wives and families. They are admirable attenders on public worship; they listened most earnestly, sang with great beauty and fervour, and their moral position stood exceptionally high. I found them extremely friendly, and I remember well an innocent but kind woman, when I was called away to Dumfries, earnestly asking how far away Dumfries was, and whether it was possible for her still to attend in the new congregation.

I was only about six months at North Leith, and the Session were good enough to give me a beautiful quarto pulpit Bible when I left, with the following inscription:—

"North Leith Session House,
29th April 1830.

"Sederunt—The Rev. James Buchanan, Moderator, &c., &c.
"*Inter alia,*—
"The Kirk-session, considering that the Rev. James Begg is about to leave the parish of North Leith with the view of being settled in Troqueer Chapel,—Resolved to return him their best thanks for his acceptable and useful labours as assistant to the Rev. Mr. Buchanan, and requested the Moderator to present Mr. Begg with a Bible, as a small token of their esteem for his character, and of their interest in his usefulness and prosperity as a Minister of Christ.
"Extracted from the Minutes of the Kirk-session.
"James Buchanan, *Moderator.*"

My transference to Troqueer or Maxwelltown, in the suburbs of Dumfries, was accompanied with some rather singular features. The first time that I entered the General Assembly as an auditor, that venerable Court met in a very small and confined place in St. Giles's, where there was scarcely any room for the general public. I forced my way, however, as a student, up into the little gallery available for strangers, and looking over to the area below, I saw the massive form of Dr. Chalmers, and the figures of many with whom I was afterwards brought into closer contact. This was the Assembly 1828. My old Professor, Dr. Stevenson Macgill, occupied the Moderator's chair. Dr. Chalmers sat as elder for the burgh of Anstruther Easter, and his influence, as well as that of the worthy Moderator, had evidently begun to be felt, for the subject of Church Extension was brought before this Assembly, and a committee was appointed, "to take such measures as to them may seem best calculated, by bringing the subject under the notice of the Government or otherwise, to procure ultimately a remedy for so alarming an evil." Still too much of the old spirit remained even in this Assembly. The subject being discussed was the propriety of erecting a chapel of ease in Maxwelltown, an important suburb of Dumfries, separated from that town only by the river Nith, there a considerable and important stream. The discussion about whether this chapel at Maxwelltown was to be sanctioned or not was long and keen, and from the papers of the Assembly for that year the merits of the debate come clearly out. All must now look back with astonishment at the violent resistance offered to this effort to extend the Established Church by the freewill offerings of the people.

From the statements made in the Assembly, it appears that the population of the district was 4301; the parish church contained 704 persons, and was somewhat distant from Maxwelltown. The people had raised £1250 to erect a chapel, but the Presbytery, by a majority, evaded their application, by declaring that a new parish church should be built to hold 1500 people. This, of course, would not have met the case, and besides it was stoutly opposed by some of the heritors. The matter in this form came before the Assembly, and a committee, of which Dr. Chalmers was a member, was appointed to consider it.

There was considerable difference of opinion in the committee, but by a majority they found that the Presbytery "ought not to have delayed in this case, and remit to them to proceed in terms of the Acts of Assembly," &c. The record of the Assembly bears that "after long reasoning," the reasoning to which I had listened, a motion to the same effect was adopted. The chapel was accordingly erected, and it was of this chapel that I was afterwards the first minister. The coincidence was curious.

As this brought me into the very heart of one of the great centres and strongholds of what was called the "Moderate" system of Church government in Scotland, initiated by Principal Robertson, and beginning to give way before the rising power of Dr. Chalmers, it may be of importance to enter into some detail regarding it. This system has been fruitful of sad results, which the country is only beginning now to discover, and in the south of Scotland it was at that time in almost unbroken strength.

(Take in sketch of Moderatism.)[1]

Such is an outline of the history. For a long time what was called the Moderate party had offered the most extraordinary and violent opposition to the erection of chapels of ease. They did not seem to have the slightest idea that, by first driving the people out of the Church by the forced settlements, and then keeping them out by refusing to sanction chapels, they were necessarily weakening their own position; they were, in fact, pursuing the very policy of the man in Hogarth, who was unconsciously sawing through the branch on which he was sitting. The people, in fact, their feelings, interests, and ultimate influence, scarcely seemed to enter into their calculations. My father stated, that in his young days to be a popular preacher was rather a matter of reproach and suspicion than otherwise; and Witherspoon

[1] This was either never written, or has fallen aside.—T. S.

lays it down as one of the maxims of Moderatism, that a minister must never on any account be popular. He supposes a case, that a sermon has passed the ordeal of the Presbytery with high approbation, and that afterwards it is approved of by the people; and he declares that in such a case there must be some hidden fault in the sermon, for the Presbyteries are never so uniform in judging right as the people are in judging wrong! This disregard to the interests and feelings of the people is one of the obvious causes which have now brought the Church of Scotland to the verge of ruin. But this ruin, as connected with the separation of the people from the Church, had proceeded rapidly during the old days of Moderatism, after the accession of Principal Robertson to power. It is said that upwards of 100,000 people were driven out of the Church of Scotland in a comparatively short time by the violent settlements, and the number of Dissenters was greatly augmented by the refusal to allow the erection of chapels. It will scarcely be credited that the large chapel in the Cowgate, which now belongs to the Romanists, was offered to the Church of Scotland and refused, and that in all parts of the country the Moderate clergy greatly preferred the erection of Dissenting meeting-houses to the erection of chapels of ease in connection with their own Church. It seems never to have occurred to them, that the carrying out of this policy must ultimately lead to the overthrow of the Establishment. They seem only to have thought of this, that there was no immediate danger to themselves, and that wherever the popular power was admitted their influence was endangered, inasmuch as the people generally preferred evangelical ministers; and their current exclamation was, "Better Dissenters out of the Church than Dissenters in the Church." To us now it may seem almost incredible that the propriety of erecting a chapel at Maxwelltown, for example, should have ever been debated. Here was a large population of several thousands attached to the Established Church, which was removed by some considerable distance, and in which they had no accommodation. What more natural than that they should propose to erect a place of worship for themselves, especially as there were amongst them a number of men both able and willing to support ordinances at their own expense? But this was stoutly resisted, and the first debate that I ever heard in the General Assembly was a debate on this subject. Here was the old parish minister stoutly opposing the erection of the chapel. The tide, however, in favour of more reasonable counsels had begun to turn. The Maxwelltown chapel was sanctioned, and although never dreaming of anything of the kind at the time, I afterwards became its first minister.

In those days the openings into the Established Church for young men who had no patrons, were very few indeed. They were chiefly confined to the seventy chapels of ease which then existed, and to a few other places where popular influence happened to prevail. Although there were several candidates for the Maxwelltown Chapel, the election turned out to be ultimately unanimous. I had now, of course, to pass a new course of examinations, with a view to being ordained by the Presbytery of Dumfries; a body, many of whose members had no special liking for the new arrangement. All, however, passed on well and harmoniously, and I was ordained on the 18th of May 1830. Almost simultaneously with my ordination occurred the death of the Rev. Dr. Scott of St. Michael's Church, Dumfries. Although belonging to the Moderate school in the Church, he had been a very popular minister, and his death produced a profound impression in the town. The Rev. Mr. Wallace, who was assistant to Dr. Lamont of Kirkpatrick Durham, an eminent Moderate minister of those days, officiated at my ordination, and really preached with remarkable power and effect. People said that he had never preached so well before. In the anxiety of the Dumfries congregation lest an unacceptable minister should be appointed to succeed Dr. Scott, a petition was immediately got up in favour of Mr. Wallace. As popular influence had begun to prevail, he was accordingly appointed, and continued for many years a minister of that parish. I was introduced to my new charge on the following Sabbath by Dr. Buchanan of North Leith, whose assistant I had previously been. He preached a very eloquent and powerful sermon on the occasion. I preached of course in the afternoon, and immediately set to work with all my might to build up a congregation in the new and empty church. It is scarcely possible to convey a full impression of the state of ecclesiastical matters, as they at that time existed in the South of Scotland. They were certainly in a very unsatisfactory state. The great and almost paramount influence of the nobility and leading families of the South of Scotland had long been in favour of Moderatism. It was even said that all the great patrons sent the lists of preachers from whom they intended to select the future ministers, to be revised by the Moderate conclave in Edinburgh, lest any single evangelical man should by any means get a pulpit. Notwithstanding this, however, although Moderatism certainly presented an almost unbroken front, there were a few excellent evangelical ministers. Mr. Brydone of Dunscore was an excellent man and most faithful pastor; Mr. M'Whirr of Urr was truly devoted to his great work, and was a good preacher, although with a terrific voice, which he seemed to delight to exert to the uttermost. He sometimes apparently set his back against the pulpit, and shouted as if he would have driven down the opposite wall. It is alleged that Dr. Bruce once said of a preacher about to emigrate, that if he went to Canada he would not require to take any wedges with him, as his voice would serve effectually to split the trees there. I remember that when I was afterwards in Paisley, Mr. Telfer of Johnstone, which is about two miles to the west, had a remarkably strong voice. One day the Presbytery appointed him to preach in the High Church, Paisley, and when he asked what he was to do with his own congregation on that day, one of the ministers, who was rather a wag, quietly said, that if he would only instruct the church-officer to throw open the west door of the Paisley High Church, he would require no substitute, as the people of Johnstone would hear him well enough. Mr. M'Whirr, an excellent man, was certainly most remarkable for power of voice. Mr. Kirkwood of Holywood was an earnest, genial, and popular minister. Crowds attended his communion, dispensed in the open air. But he devoted himself considerably to the practice of medicine, people sometimes coming from great distances to receive his advice, to the considerable annoyance of some of the regular practitioners. Mr. Burnside of Terregles was a man of decided talent, and acted as evening lecturer in Dumfries. Dr. Duncan of Dumfries was a good and worthy man, but certainly no great preacher. His eminent brother at Ruthwell— the inventor of Savings' Banks, and a man of great general philanthropy and intelligence—was a thoroughly evangelical minister. I preached for several of these men during my short ministry at Dumfries, and, in particular, I delivered a charity sermon at Ruthwell on a fine Sabbath evening. There was a large congregation, more than the church would hold, and we conducted the worship in the open air. The grounds about the manse, which had been reclaimed and beautified by Dr. Duncan, afforded an admirable illustration of what an active and skilful minister may accomplish even with a most unpromising subject. For another reason, and at a subsequent period, his excellent son, the late minister of Peebles, sent me the following account of his operations in the way of glebe improvement. It is a beautiful illustration of the way in which things temporal and spiritual were simultaneously promoted by the better class of Scotch ministers :—

"PEEBLES, *Feb.* 23, 1849.

"MY DEAR SIR,—You ask me for an account of the means whereby my father, the late Dr. Henry Duncan of Ruthwell, brought his glebe and pleasure grounds to the state of fertility and loveliness in which you remember to have seen them. This I shall accordingly endeavour, as briefly as possible, to do.

"When my father became incumbent of the parish of Ruthwell, he found the glebe, extending, as it does, over nearly fifty acres, in a deplorably neglected state. The soil consisted for the most part of moor, and the whole was either overgrown with whins, or soaking and sour with a marshy moisture, which little or nothing had been done to drain away. To remedy this state of things, he lost no time in subdividing the land, so as to adapt it to the then new mode of cropping, dug ditches of sufficient depth, planted fences here, threw up dykes there, and drew drains from year to year across the worst parts of the sullen fields, till they became everywhere capable of culture by the plough. The turf, when necessary, he caused to be shaved off to a considerable depth, and after a number of square enclosures had been erected, by means of the most solid of the sods thus obtained, in different parts of the field, the lighter ones, accompanied by masses of thick clay, which abounded in some parts of the glebe, were cast in, and the whole was consumed by means of fire introduced at the openings from below. Never shall I forget the peculiar, and to me now delicious perfume, exhaled from these smoking heaps over the whole district for miles around. The ashes thus formed were afterwards spread over the land, and ploughed in along with lime. I well remember vast accumulations of *compost* which were also turned to good account, nor were there wanting, of course, in the spring season, the ordinary appliances of dunghill manure. Recourse was had to all sorts of experiments in agriculture, the results of which were successively recorded in the *Dumfries Courier*. For ornamental grounds, about five acres were reserved immediately around the manse. These, I have always understood, formed the most unsightly portion of the glebe when my father took possession of the living. Yet, by dint of planting, trenching, top-dressing, tasteful arrangement, and incessant labour, to say nothing of expense, it became at last what you, perhaps somewhat hyperbolically, styled it the other day, 'a perfect paradise.' The garden, covering a space of two English acres, intersected by numerous nicely-trimmed beech hedges, abounding with shady walks and odoriferous bowers, and skirted here and there by clumps of flowery shrubs—such as the lilac, laburnum, and rhododendron—was at first little better than a *cold marsh*. The smooth lawn, now dotted with umbrageous trees, was then a wilderness of stones and gigantic weeds; and the mimic lake, with its promontories and receding bays, adorned with rustic bridges and weeping willows, &c., covers what was once a stagnant and offensive *moss-hag*. The gravel walks, which traversed the pleasure grounds, extended at one time to upwards of a mile. So much labour as all these improvements implied, enabled my father for a considerable period to give constant employment to not a few of his parishioners, who otherwise would have been a burden on the poor's funds; and by this, along with other means, *he contrived to stave off an assessment much longer than, but for this, could have been done.* On the other hand, he was more than rewarded by the satisfaction of watching the gradual development of his plans, and the increasing luxuriance and fertility of his fields and gardens, and still more by the assurance that, in seeking his own advancement and amusement, he was contributing very materially at the same time to the economic well-being of a poverty-stricken and much neglected population.

"Warmly sympathising with you in your views for the amelioration of the miserable condition of so large a portion of our fellow-countrymen, and earnestly desiring for you complete success, I remain, my dear Sir, yours very truly,

"W. W. DUNCAN.

"Rev. James Begg, D.D."

There was also, in addition to these thinly-scattered evangelical ministers, who were as lights shining in a comparatively dark place, the Rev. Mr. Hastie, a probationer who was tutor to a Dr. Laing, and afterwards became a zealous minister at Kirkpatrick Fleming. Mr. Anderson, who afterwards became so zealous and distinguished a missionary at Madras, lived also at that time as a tutor in the family of a Mr. Taylor, one of those who, along with Mr. Stothert of Cargen, founded the Maxwelltown Chapel. Mr. Anderson regularly attended ordinances in the chapel at that time. He was then a most enthusiastic and excellent young man, but scarcely gave promise of the very high eminence to which he afterwards attained. With these excellent ministers and people, however, there was, as we shall immediately see, an overwhelming preponderance of influence on the other side.

I may here remark in passing, that the mode of travelling to Dumfries at that time was very different from what it is now; and as I had occasion to travel frequently when going to Dumfries as a candidate, and afterwards in attending Presbytery, and otherwise during my short residence there, the tedious conveyance of former times has left a deep impression on my memory. The mail-coach started from Edinburgh in the evening from what was then the Black Bull Inn at the top of Leith Walk, but is now a large draper's establishment. We went by Penicuick, Broughton, Tweedsmuir, and Moffat, occupying the whole night, sometimes a cold and stormy night, and arriving in Dumfries next morning in time for breakfast. The people of the present day have in this respect a very great advantage.

The great mass of the ministers of the South of Scotland, and that for a great range, from Berwick to Portpatrick, were at that time decidedly Moderate, having a great horror at anything like stir or energy in religion, which they regarded as fanaticism or righteousness overmuch. They abjured prayer-meetings, classes for the young, and everything distinctively evangelical. But they were again divided into different classes. Some were, upon the whole, respectable men in their own way, and I have reason to believe better preachers and ministers than some in the present day who make much higher pretensions. Others were extremely frivolous and inefficient, card-players, and half-scoffers. Some of them were openly wicked, if reports were true, and anything but an ensample to their flocks. The effect may easily be anticipated. Religion was at a low ebb. The general estimation in which ministers were held was widely different from that to which I had been accustomed in my younger days, and the general tone of religion and morality in the district was very unsatisfactory. There were numerous and frequent proofs of this in the prevailing carelessness and immorality of many of the people. Much debate has lately arisen in regard to the amount of illegitimacy in the north-eastern and southern districts of Scotland, and whilst there are other causes, I am convinced that it has a close connection with the style of preaching which prevailed. At that time I heard some statements in regard to the immorality of the district, which, till then, I could scarcely have believed credible. But the human heart is deceitful above all things and desperately wicked, and where there is no powerful preaching of the Gospel, the whole tone of morality as well as of religion must necessarily sink. The result was not only thus sad and disheartening in as far as the Established Church was concerned, but had a most depressing effect apparently even upon Dissent. A coarse orthodoxy coupled with a servile spirit, seemed to mark some whose ministrations were loudly called for, and who had come to teach higher lessons to the ministers and people of the Established Church. My experience of life has been, that if the Established Church falls low, Dissent does not always compensate for the want, or rise in proportion, and this was at that time strikingly true at Dumfries. Dissent succeeds best where there has been a stirring and evangelical ministry succeeded by one cold and unpopular. Men require a certain measure of life and grace to be prepared for the sacrifices implied in Dissent, but even in that case Dissent does not always maintain the high tone with which it commences. At the time to which I refer, the great mass of the people of the South of Scotland adhered nominally to the Established Church, but they were ready to welcome eagerly evangelical preaching; and if the influential men of the country in Church and State had been prepared to reform and extend the Church of Scotland, according to the advice of Dr. Chalmers and the principles of the Reformation, that Church would probably now have been one of the strongest in the world, a great pillar of the constitution, and of all that is honest, lovely, and of good report. As yet Voluntaryism was mainly a thing of the future.

I lodged during my sojourn at Dumfries with a worthy, quiet bachelor, Mr. John Hair, a draper in the town, and one of the managers of the congregation. His house was situated near what was then "The Windmill," but which is now converted into "The Observatory." The dwelling was quiet and comfortable, and surrounded by an excellent garden and orchard, where I walked and partly studied. My whole time was occupied from week to week in my various duties, in which I delighted. My plan was to spend the whole of Monday and Tuesday in visiting the people, including the sick. Everywhere I met with the greatest kindness. I had in addition two classes, for young men and women respectively, on the Tuesday evenings. On Wednesday and Thursday I wrote my sermons, and on Friday and Saturday I committed them to memory, and again in retirement prepared myself for my Sabbath work. Knowing that the people would very likely, in the circumstances, be specially deficient in the systematic knowledge of theology, I preached a short course of sermons containing a system of theology, beginning with man's state of innocence, and ending with the judgment and its eternal results. At that time I sometimes preached for not less than an hour each end of the day. Some may think this was unreasonably long, but everything depends on circumstances. Length and tediousness are very different things. It is said of a minister that he once said to his beadle, "John, I'm afraid I have been rather long to-day." John answered, "Sir, ye hae been verra teydious." But it is not necessarily so. At other meetings, and dealing with other topics, men are not so easily satisfied if they are only interested; and my Dumfries congregation, I am happy to say, were very far indeed from making any complaint. I believe that this plan of systematic preaching was blessed at the time, and I am sure it has been of advantage to myself during all my subsequent ministry. My work at Dumfries was hard and constant, and in as far as the outward prosperity of the congregation was concerned, I succeeded beyond all my expectations. The church was soon completely filled, although containing upwards of 1000 people—indeed it was crowded—and in the course of six months we had nearly 600 communicants. Upon a scrutiny I discovered that these had previously belonged to various Protestant denominations, and that they came from all the parishes round, within a radius of from eight to twelve miles. This was mainly the result of the comparatively cold and neglected state of things which had previously existed. Everything seemed most prosperous, although one circumstance occurred which tended to damp my enthusiasm, although I afterwards understood the meaning of it more perfectly. Dr. Chalmers visited Dumfries during my ministry there, and was as usual most kind and friendly; but instead of expressing the kind of satisfaction which I felt in this miscellaneous congregation, he rather expressed a regret that the district had not been worked exclusively upon the territorial system. This would have been very well if the circumstances had been different. The best of theories requires to be worked in accordance with what is actually practicable. In the first place, our chapel was not endowed, nor at first free from debt, and therefore had to depend upon the hearers for support. To have turned out all but those in the immediate neighbourhood would have been an act of injustice. Secondly, We had no territorial district in the sense of having a parish, and might have been pulled up by the Presbytery if we had meddled with hearers who did not belong to us or came to us of their own accord. And, thirdly, in the dearth of the Gospel which then prevailed in the district, it would have been found impossible to shut out people who had helped to build the chapel, and who spontaneously attended, so long as the room was not otherwise occupied. Admitting the great value of Dr. Chalmers' territorial theory, it can only be carried into thorough effect in connection with an endowed system, and with public authorised parochial arrangements. Yet I am convinced that nothing else will ever meet the heathenism of our land or of any land, and that the parochial system is at the same time as cheap as it is efficient.

One of the most interesting incidents connected with my residence at Dumfries was my acquaintance with Mrs. Jean Armour or Burns, otherwise called "Bonnie Jean," the widow of the great poet. The grandchildren of Burns were connected with my congregation, and I frequently went to visit his widow in the house near the place where his monument is erected, and in which I presume he died. Mrs. Burns, or "Jean," at the time when I saw her, could not be called "bonnie," although her appearance was well enough. She was rather old and frail in appearance, but extremely interesting and pleasant in conversation. I can quite well imagine that when young she may have been very engaging to an intellectual man. She had beside her always on the table the large family Bible, in which the names of her children were written in the poet's hand. I have not seen this Bible since, although, I presume it is in safe custody somewhere. There were many of the poems of Burns about Dumfries at that time in the bold and marked handwriting of the poet himself, as well as other relics. There were also painful traditions with regard to the latter period of the life of the great poet. It is sad to think of this in the case of a genius so wonderful; but it is a great lesson to all. It was interesting to see the widow of Burns, and I believe she was an excellent Christian woman.

My stay at Dumfries, however, was comparatively short. I received in a few months a call to be colleague and successor to Dr. Jones in Lady Glenorchy's Church, Edinburgh. Taking the whole circumstances into consideration, that I was hardly equal to the heavy and constant work to which I was subjected, and especially that I should have an opportunity as a collegiate minister for more study in consequence of having only one sermon a week, a thing which I felt to be quite necessary, and also that I could have fuller access to men and books, I resolved to accept the new position. I was inducted to Lady Glenorchy's Chapel on the 23d December 1830, being yet scarcely twenty-two years of age. Dr. Jones, to whom I thus became a colleague, was certainly a most able and remarkable man. Originally a Welshman, and with all the characteristic enthusiasm and discrimination in preaching for which the Welsh are distinguished, he had at the same time a powerful and fertile imagination, and to those accustomed to follow him—which certainly required habit—he was a most eloquent and fascinating preacher. Lady Glenorchy's Chapel had long been a centre of evangelical light in Edinburgh. That worthy lady certainly manifested great zeal and discrimination in the efforts and sacrifices which she made for the diffusion of Gospel truth both in England and in Scotland. Dr. Jones himself was a remarkable illustration of the wisdom of her selections, and, as the writer of her biography, he has delineated an admirable model of female sanctified wisdom and zeal in the higher walks of life, without one particle of ostentation or undue forwardness. The volume of sermons which Dr. Jones published, although remarkable in many ways, gives little real idea of the man as we heard him from Sabbath to Sabbath. They are mere skeletons, and it is necessary to have the warm and brilliant filling up by which he made them so attractive, in order to comprehend the real extent of his pulpit power. The semi-prophetic picture which he drew of the probable career of Dr. Chalmers at the very dawn of that great man's popularity, affords an admirable illustration of his discriminating wisdom. He was an extremely agreeable man, and a most profitable and instructive colleague. He preached in the forenoon, and I in the afternoon, and I regularly spent the Sabbath evenings with him in his own house in Hanover Street, at the corner of Thistle Street. My own lodgings were then in Leopold Place. Although a chapel minister, and never admitted to a Presbytery, Dr. Jones was a man in good circumstances, and on intimate terms with all the distinguished ministers of Edinburgh. He was especially intimate with Dr. Andrew Thomson, for whom he cherished a strong affection, and in whose public discussions he took the deepest interest, although not always agreeing with him in his views. He especially differed from him, as I have already said, in regard to Roman Catholic Emancipation, to which Dr. Jones had a rooted aversion. When Dr. Andrew Thomson's sudden death convulsed all Edinburgh, and thousands flocked to manifest their sense of the great loss the Church and country had sustained by his death, no man felt this more keenly than Dr. Jones. His grief, however, was of a deeply solemn and undemonstrative kind. He shut himself up in his room to mourn in solitude over what he believed to be a great public as well as private calamity, and did not reappear in public until we saw him on the following Sabbath forenoon in his own pulpit, where he gave out with the deepest solemnity the psalm—

"Dumb was I, opening not my mouth,
  Because this work was Thine."

Dr. Jones had a peculiar admiration for the Psalms, and had

a knowledge of them probably seldom equalled, and much more seldom surpassed. He cut out even the paraphrases from the pulpit Psalm-book, but he never was at a loss to find an appropriate psalm. He made slight alterations in the psalms; as, for example, in the twenty-fourth, instead of "O Jacob who do seek," he made "O Jacob's God who seek." His sermon on the occasion of Dr. Andrew Thomson's death was an admirable sample of his close textual and yet brilliant style of preaching. It was on the text, "He was a burning and a shining light, and ye were willing for a season to rejoice in his light." He considered, first, "he was a light," that is, he was a minister of truth; this as opposed to the darkness of ignorance or to the distortions of error; second, he was a "burning light," that is, he was a powerful minister, fitted rightly to struggle against error and sin; third, he was a "shining light," that is, he was a brilliant minister, arresting attention and drawing around him all eyes; fourth, "ye rejoiced in his light," that is, the existence of such a minister was the occasion of much gratitude and joy to the people of God; fifth, ye "were willing" to rejoice; it was not mere prejudice or misapprehension, or a hasty or doubtful conclusion. It was a wise and intelligent conviction, founded on the strongest reasons, of what a great blessing God had conferred upon the country by raising up such a man. But, sixth, ye were permitted to do it only "for a season." Andrew Thomson was dead, and a mighty blank created. The sermon was wound up by a very brilliant and effective application. Like most great men, Dr. Jones had a good deal of humour, and a strong apprehension of the ludicrous. Dr. Colquhoun of Leith was a very excellent man. His books are still highly valued. During the comparative dearth of the Gospel many flocked to hear him, and there is reason to believe that his ministry was much blessed. Dr. Jones had been his great ally in the earlier times of his ministry, and he was asked to preach his funeral sermon. It was alleged that if Dr. Colquhoun had a fault, it was that he was a little narrow in dealing with money. We do not know whether there was any truth in this, and people are apt most unjustly to blame ministers for that ordinary prudence which is often with them a necessary virtue. They of all men are bound to do what is sufficient to rescue them from the condemnation of the Apostle, who says, " If any will not provide for his own, and especially for those of his own house, he hath denied the faith, and is worse than an infidel."

Every one knows that no class of men are blamed more unscrupulously than ministers if they cannot pay their just and lawful debts, although the means placed at their disposal are often scandalously inadequate. The treatment which they receive is, in this respect, often like the Scriptural complaint of the children sitting in the market-place, and from either alternative being sure to extort a ground of unreasonable complaint. Still, true or false, such an allegation had been made in regard to worthy Dr. Colquhoun; and it occurred to Dr. Jones after he entered the pulpit to preach his funeral sermon that he had chosen rather an awkward text. The text was, "And the beggar died." Whether it was noticed by others we cannot tell. We have reason to know that the sermon was a very eloquent and appropriate one. Notes of it were preserved and published not very long ago by one who formed part of the audience.

An eminent minister of Edinburgh was anxious to secure the promotion to one of the city churches of Edinburgh of a friend whose talents were more solid than brilliant. With this view he was peculiarly desirous to secure the influence of Dr. Jones, whose congregation was wealthy and influential. The Doctor, however, was a strong Presbyterian, and thoroughly opposed to the use of any undue influence in the appointment of ministers. This eminent man, who called for him, however, was very urgent, and pleaded that if he were to select a minister for himself, his heavy friend would be the very person he would choose. Dr. Jones listened attentively to all he had to say, and then he answered with his usual vivacity, "I have only one remark to make, Dr. So-and-So. What you say may be all very true, but your friend has been weighed in the popular scales and he has been found wanting."

My connection, however, with Dr. Jones as his colleague was very speedily terminated. It lasted only for about a year, although to me it was a time of much enjoyment and advantage, and although, to all outward appearance, the congregation greatly prospered and increased. Indeed, we spoke of enlarging the church, although it was a very capacious building. A number of very excellent men were connected with the congregation, and no congregation could be more united. The great mass of those who formed the membership of Lady Glenorchy's at that time have, however, now passed away, and the church itself, with its schoolhouse and teacher's house standing alongside of it, have been entirely removed to make way for the terminus of the North British Railway. I have a picture both of the exterior and interior of the venerable church, which I greatly value. It was, I have no doubt, the birthplace of many souls. Many ministers and Christian people long regarded it as a place of special Christian privilege. It is hallowed in the recollections of some of the best of the present generation. When I mention the names of such men as Dr. Horatius and Mr. Andrew Bonar, both of whom were brought up under the ministry of Dr. Jones, many will understand what I mean.

CHAPTER IV.

TRANSLATION TO PAISLEY—MINISTER OF A CITY CHARGE.

I RECEIVED a unanimous call to the Middle Church of Paisley, which had become vacant through the death of the Rev. Jonathan Ranken. I was again under the necessity of deciding. New questions of a very serious kind were beginning to arise in the Church and country. The great schemes of reform mooted in the Church were to me deeply interesting; but besides these, a whole host of enemies had simultaneously arisen, and the very existence of Established Churches was denounced as contrary to the spirit of Christianity and the express institutions of Christ Himself. The spirit of reform in the Established Church, which had partly begun with the century, but had received an immense impulse from the accession of Dr. Chalmers to Glasgow and Dr. Thomson to Edinburgh, was beginning to take very definite shape in the Church courts, but chapel ministers were entirely excluded from these courts. And yet I felt strongly that it would be well to have it in my power to take part in the struggle. I had been brought up with very definite views both in regard to the Scriptural lawfulness and practical advantages of Establishments. I had also a strong opinion in regard to the necessity for Church reform; and although most unwilling to leave my present place of comparative ease, great comfort, and many advantages, social and ecclesiastical, yet when called to the full status of a parish minister, in what was at that time one of the most difficult fields in Scotland, I thought it my duty to accept the invitation. Apart from such considerations, I never had the strong feeling of opposition to translations, especially during the earlier period of a man's ministry, which prevails in certain quarters. Setting aside other considerations, as, for example, the advantage of diffusing any gifts which may exist in the Church, so as to make them more available, almost the only way in which a Presbyterian minister can obtain any rest to perfect his studies, recruit his energies, and gather up his strength for a fresh effort, is by means of a translation. Otherwise his work is continuous and increasing, and, taxed beyond his strength, he is apt to sink under the pressure of a heavy round of unvarying work, without having anything like adequate or necessary intervals of rest. This is a matter very little understood. Many of the people imagine that there is enough put into a man at college to serve him for life, and that all that he has now to do is to open his mouth and speak. On the other hand, in passing to a new sphere of labour, he not only secures rest and variety of object, but he carries with him all the fruits of his previous exertions, reading, and experience; and even if he may have made mistakes in his former spheres of labour, he may, if he be a man of sense, avoid them in his new charge. The Wesleyans go to one extreme, and we probably to another.

I was inducted into the Middle Church, Paisley, on the 25th of November 1831, and was introduced to my new charge by Dr. John Bruce of Edinburgh, who preached an admirable and appropriate sermon. Paisley is a place of great intellectual activity, and it had long been exceptionally blessed with good and popular ministers. The names of Dr. Witherspoon, Dr. Snodgrass, Dr. Finlay, and others, were fresh in the recollections of the people. But as popular election had always been the rule, the succession had never ceased. The two other parishes of the town, at the time of my induction, were supplied by Mr. Geddes, minister of the High Church, and Dr. Burns of the Low Church or St. George's, both very able and earnest ministers. Mr. Geddes had a crowded church, and was a very superior preacher. He was afterwards translated to St. Andrew's Church, Glasgow, but died from water on the chest, partly occasioned, I have no doubt, by very hard and earnest work in the promotion of his great Master's cause. The fugitive sermons of his which have been published give little idea of the man. He also was possessed of a pleasant humour, which made his society fresh and agreeable. Being once at a dinner-party, some of the people complained of the length of the Sabbath services, and Mr. Geddes supposed that they might be quietly hitting at him, as his sermons were occasionally long, though never tedious. By and by, after the people had sat at the dinner-table for about two hours, some of them began to propose toasts—a common custom in those days. Mr. Geddes, who had remained quiet during the previous conversation, said, "I'll give you a toast." When silence was proclaimed to receive the minister's toast, he pawkily said, "I'll give ye 'Long dinners and short sermons.'" The rebuke was felt, and the object so far gained. Dr. Burns was a man of extraordinary knowledge and versatility. St. George's was erected in lieu of what was called the Low Church, which is still standing, under the name of the Old Low, and which was too small to contain Dr. Burns' congregation. The new building, however, whilst containing more accommodation, was not anything like so well planned as the older churches. The old churches were square and easily preached in, the Low Church itself being in the form of what was called a Greek cross, namely, three aisles and an area—a very common form of building amongst the Presbyterians both in Scotland and in the North of Ireland. As the result, mainly, I believe, of the faulty construction of St. George's, it was not quite filled during the ministry of Dr. Burns, although he had a large, influential, and deeply attached congregation. He was a peculiar man in some respects, although possessed of great talents and a marvellous memory for facts. But he was not always prudent or judicious, though from his strong personal Christianity, his sheer good-nature and integrity of character, he made few enemies. It is alleged that one of his hearers, who was at the same time a genuine admirer of the Doctor's good qualities, said that he sometimes reminded him of a cow who, "after giving a good deal of milk, ended with putting its foot in the cog." When he gave evidence before the Patronage Committee of the House of Commons, he brought out a large quantity of rare and curious information, delivered with great fluency and fervour. When one of the English officials was asked what was going on in the Committee, "Oh," he replied, "there's a Scotch parson there giving evidence with a forty-horse power." Even to the last, when bent down with the weight of upwards of eighty years, he addressed the Free Assembly with great vigour shortly before his death. It was remarkable to observe how the old spirit and peculiarity of the excellent man remained. He stretched himself up as he warmed in his discourse, and his address to the Assembly, with the old fluency and fervour, seemed very much like the letting on of a mill-race. A rather unfortunate but characteristic incident, illustrative of the Doctor's character and kind Vicar-of-Wakefield simplicity, occurred soon after I went to Paisley. The Doctor had finished his admirable edition of Wodrow's History, interspersed with very valuable notes. He was graciously allowed to present a copy of it to the King, William IV. Delighted with his interview on the occasion, and being swift of pen as well as of tongue, he immediately wrote in the fulness of his heart a true and particular account of what had taken place to "dearest Janet," his truly excellent wife, at Paisley, setting forth in the most characteristic style, and in all the confidence of privacy, the "crack," as he called it, which he had had with his Majesty. Mrs.

Burns was naturally anxious that the honour which had thus been bestowed upon her husband should be known in the place, and she called at one of the newspaper offices with a view to having a paragraph inserted on the subject. With the same view she took the Doctor's letter, and in her innocent simplicity showed it to the editor. What motives may have swayed him we know not; it might have been a dull season in the world of news, and he may have thought the chance too good to be missed. Whatever it was, the simple fact, apart from speculation, is, that the actual document appeared bodily in the Paisley paper next morning. It was a very characteristic and most interesting document; it was read with the greatest avidity by the people, and it flew over the country from paper to paper with a rapidity that defied all attempts to overtake or check its flight, in those days when telegraphs had not been invented. Everybody said it was too bad, and yet the letter was certainly very interesting and characteristic. One passage of it was to the following effect, and every one in Paisley could imagine the scene; we don't profess to give the very words:—"The king asked me if there were any other churches in Paisley besides those connected with the Establishment, to which I replied, 'Please your Majesty, there are a number of other churches in Paisley, and amongst the rest there is an Episcopalian chapel, to which I understand your Majesty contributed, and I have the satisfaction of informing your Majesty that when I left Paisley the building had made very considerable progress, and that it will be a decided ornament to the town.'" The peculiarities of Dr. Burns were, however, well understood by his friends, and were only slight drawbacks to a character of rare excellence, and to talents of peculiar energy and power. He was the great father of colonial missions, and devoted the best of his energies to the promotion of that noble object. He was a most active parish minister, and had a very strong hold of his congregation. He was a most zealous Church reformer, and was always ready to advocate every scriptural method by which the purity and efficiency of the Church might be promoted. He was an earnest advocate of social improvement, wrote intelligently and ably on the poor laws and on other important social questions, and he died at last only recently, full of years and honour. " He rests from his labours, and his works do follow him."

In the Abbey Parish of Paisley, which stretches round the town, there were at that time two ministers. Dr. Macnair was a truly excellent and worthy man, of great simplicity and amiability of character, as well as a painstaking minister. Mr. Brewster, on the other hand, although possessed of very decided talents, was not much distinguished as a parish minister, and held very peculiar views. Amongst other things, it was currently said that he insisted that his children should not be taught the Shorter Catechism at school. He alleged that the true plan was to leave the minds of children without the slightest bias in regard to religious truth, as if there was not a bias already in the wrong direction. He afterwards met with very serious trials, and some people traced them partly to this source. One of his daughters joined the Romish Church, which vexed him exceedingly. He was a very keen politician, and he devoted a large portion of his time to political discussions. He advocated very extreme views and did very eccentric things, as riding into Paisley in the same open carriage with Daniel O'Connell, at a time of great political excitement. There were, indeed, several remarkable characters in the Paisley Presbytery at that time. In addition to those already referred to, there was Mr. Fleming of Neilston, who fought so stout a battle in behalf of church extension, or rather church accommodation, but not in the wisest way, or so as to secure any important result. There was Dr. Macfarlane of Renfrew, a man of great excellence, although very sombre and peculiar; still he was always zealous and active in the cause of truth and righteousness. Mr. Logan of Eastwood was a really witty and lively man. One of the brethren, not remarkable for sense, said to him one day, in the way of complaint, "I am a little hoarse to-day." "I am very glad you are improving," quietly replied Mr. Logan; "when I saw you last you were a great ass." His son Robert inherited a great deal of his father's wit and readiness. After the Burgh Reform Bill had passed, and some very doubtful characters were being chosen to office, he said, "Father, ye have been praying long for *inferior* judges and magistrates, and I'm sure ye've gotten them noo."

End of Autobiography.

Biographical.

CHAPTER V.

DR. BEGG'S FAMILY—HIS CONNECTION WITH GREENOCK.

THE preceding chapters contain all that was ever written of a book, on the composition of which Dr. Begg entered many years ago. It was known to all his most intimate friends that he was engaged in recording his personal reminiscences, with a view to their publication either in his lifetime or after his death. He frequently stated that he found the work more difficult than he had anticipated, and that he was making comparatively little progress in the execution of it. But, while I was well aware that the work was far from completion, it was no small disappointment, when the manuscript was put into my hands, to find that it contains but a brief and fragmentary record of the earliest period of his life, and stops short at a point prior to the commencement of his distinctive work as an ecclesiastic and a social reformer. All readers—and those most who were most familiar with Dr. Begg's sentiments and with his habitual mode of expressing them—will share this disappointment. To have had the judgments of Dr. Begg on the men and the matters with whom and with which he was conversant, and on the important movements in which he took so prominent a part—in promoting some and in opposing others—and these judgments expressed in the racy and honest way which was so characteristic of him, would have been a great gratification to all who knew him, to those who agreed and to those who disagreed with him, and to the more numerous class who partly agreed and partly disagreed; while the book could scarcely have failed to attain the position of a valuable work of information and reference, most useful to those who, in future days, shall study the important history of our times. It has been thought right to produce the fragment precisely as Dr. Begg left it. From the condition of the manuscript as it came into my hands, it is evident that its author had subjected it to frequent revision, and had brought it into the shape in which he would have desired it to be published. This being the case, I have not thought it right in any degree to alter or abridge it. While it must be matter of regret that we have not more of it, we ought to be glad that we have even so much.

Dr. Begg's family for many generations were proprietors, or feuars, or perpetual lessees, of a small piece of land in the parish of Douglas, in the Upper Ward of Lanarkshire. The house in which his father was born, and in which, it is believed, several generations of his ancestors lived, is still standing, and is of a very humble character. But I have no doubt that the owners of even such a "property" occupied a position of no little consideration among the village community of earlier and simpler days. This house and land remained in the possession of the family from a remote period till a quite recent date.

There are still current among the villagers sundry traditions respecting the father and mother of Dr. Begg of New Monkland, the grandfather and grandmother of our Dr. Begg. These traditions concur in indicating them to have been persons of great probity, of great religious earnestness, and of great intelligence and homely wit. The grandmother especially is represented as having possessed these qualities in a large degree; so that when Dr. Begg began, about half a century ago, to occupy a somewhat prominent position, the older villagers, who remembered his grandfather and grandmother, were in the habit of saying that it was chiefly from the latter that he had inherited his powers and gifts. The grandfather and the grandmother both died many years ago, so that none are now alive who were their contemporaries in any sense available for the biographer. Unhappily, too, for this functionary, there were two branches of the Begg family in Douglas, apparently not very closely related to each other; and the traditional anecdotes cannot be authentically apportioned between them. There is a story, for example, of a Mrs. Begg's happily putting to silence a profane scoffer. It befell in this wise. In those days soldiers, moving from one station to another, were frequently "billeted" on the householders. On one occasion Mrs. Begg had two dragoons thus quartered on her. One of them had given her some "chaff," and had acknowledged to his comrade, who had not yet seen his hostess, that he had got the worse in the wordy encounter. The comrade self-confidently boasted that she should not put *him* down. He introduced himself to her in this fashion: "You'll be glad to see me, Mrs. Begg, for I belong to a well-known family. I'm the devil's sister's son." "Very likely," was the reply; "I never saw your uncle, but frae a' I've heard o' him, I sud think there's a strong family likeness." The Mrs. Begg of this story was stated undoubtingly by one informant to have been Dr. Begg's grandmother, but another asserted with equal confidence that it was a certain Elspet Begg, who was only a distant relative. For generations the Begg family were weavers as well as crofters, and evidently occupied a position of great respectability among the village community. As stated in the autobiographic chapters, the Begg family adhered to the Reformed Presbyterian or Cameronian Church; and in fair weather and foul, failed not to worship in the "meeting-house" at Riggside, some three or four miles distant from their home. The minister of New Monkland was the first member of the family that conformed to the Established Church, and his conformity was deemed by his strict parents to be very closely akin to apostasy. One of the floating traditions to which reference has been made is to the effect that when our friend in his boyhood paid occasional visits to his grandparents, he used to compromise the matter by going alternately to the Riggside meeting-house and to the parish church.

The minister of New Monkland was undoubtedly a man of excellent character and of superior ability, although his son's estimate of the latter is very naturally, and very properly, somewhat higher than cotemporary public opinion would have endorsed. His Cameronian education had probably much share in the formation of his character, and of his views with respect both to spiritual and ecclesiastical matters. Many who will regard the latter as unduly strict and narrow, will give him credit for having held fast and held forth the great system of evangelical truth, at a time when too many preached " another Gospel, which was not another," simply because it was in no proper sense a Gospel at all. I remember to have heard him speak on several occasions in the General Assembly. By that time he was generally spoken of as " Begg's father," and the most usual remark was as to the points of resemblance and of contrast between the father and the son. As a speaker he had much logical power; but he had little or none of that grace of manner, of that modulation of manly voice, and absolutely none of that genial humour, which combined to make his son so accomplished an orator, and to call forth the admiration even of those to whom his sentiments were most distasteful. So far as I have been able to ascertain, the chief contribution of the senior Dr. Begg to religious or ecclesiastical literature was a pamphlet which he published in 1808, in connection with the controversy which originated at that time on the introduction of an organ into one of the city churches in Glasgow. This pamphlet was reproduced by his son in 1866, incorporated in a larger treatise by himself. The pamphlet and its author were thus characterised by the late

Dr. Candlish:—"Several [publications], including one by that most strenuous and uncompromising foe of innovation, the late Dr. Begg of New Monkland, are very valuable, and will deserve attention if the fight is to be seriously renewed." Unhappily the fight *has* been renewed, and it is to be feared that the weighty arguments of the foes of innovation have *not* received the attention which they deserve. The following quotation will give a fair idea of the character of this pamphlet:—

"*Arg. 7.*—The music of the organ, well regulated, tends to calm the passions and enliven the affections in the worship of God. It thus assists our devotion, and gives us pleasure in the way of duty.

"*Ans.*—This argument supposes that we may accommodate the worship of God to our own tastes and feelings, and model it in such a way as to enliven our affections and give us pleasure, whereas our worship must be founded upon the Word of God, and our sentiments and feelings, and all our active principles, must be regulated by its authority.

"It has already been proved that instrumental music in Gospel worship is a Judaising and Popish corruption, and however grateful it may be to the feelings of those who are peculiarly alive to the charms of music, and who delight in the pleasures of sense, yet no corrupt addition can give pleasure to those whose consciences are influenced by a regard to Divine authority, and who are desirous to be found 'walking in all the commandments and ordinances of the Lord blameless.' Christ knew what is in man, and if He had judged organs proper to soothe the passions, exalt the affections, and assist the devotions of His people, He would certainly have appointed them. He has made full provision for their comfort, but has nowhere appointed organs for that purpose. His people are to speak to themselves, and to teach and admonish one another, in psalms and hymns and spiritual songs, *singing* with grace in their hearts to the Lord. This is the music appointed in New Testament times to soothe the passions and enliven the affections of the followers of Christ, to assist their devotions, and fill them with pleasure in the way of duty, and none may add to or diminish from the ordinances of the King of Zion."

With another action of Dr. Begg of New Monkland the present biographer has less sympathy than he is quite willing to confess that he has with his resistance to the introduction of instrumental music into the public worship of God. In his zeal against innovations—in this case, I think, excessive—he led a movement with the object of preventing Dr. Chalmers from making a slight change in the position and arrangement of the communion-tables. The following characteristic description of this movement, in Dr. Chalmers' happiest style, is given in his Life, by Dr. Hanna (vol. ii. pp. 393-5). For the information of non-Scottish readers, it may be stated that the minister of New Monkland is specially alluded to as occupying the "Bothwell region," his parish being in the immediate neighbourhood of the battlefield of Bothwell Bridge.

"If there be any geographical distinction between one part of Scotland and another in this respect, I would say that the interesting relics of the older pertinaciousness, and the older zeal for little things, are to be found most abundantly in the West. I am sure I affirm this without the slightest feeling of reproach or even of disrespect. Were there no other principle, indeed, than my love of antiquities, I should feel inclined to regard this peculiarity with the utmost toleration; for, agreeably to the general law which I have just announced to you, I have found it associated in that part of our Establishment with so much of upright and pure and resolute assertion on behalf of great principles, that I, with all my heart, forgive the obstinacy of this adherence to small points, and retain in their favour a very large surplus of high and positive esteem to the bargain. For example, they have been all along the sturdy champions of non-pluralism in the Church, of ministerial residence in the parishes, of sacredness in Sabbath observation, of the cause of Christianity at home by their incessant efforts to enlarge the church accommodation, and of the cause of Christianity abroad by the support which they have ever rendered both to Bible and missionary and colonial societies. After this goodly enumeration of great and noble services, the occasional littlenesses wherewith they at times may be associated are like spots on the sun, and I am sure ought to be viewed in no other light than with the most good-natured indulgence, just as one views the feebleness or peculiarities of some aged friend, for whose substantial worth at the same time we have a just veneration. Accordingly it is not within the limits of the Bothwell region—that land of sturdy principle, signalised by the exploits and the martyrdoms of our covenanting forefathers—where I would attempt the slightest innovation on their ancient forms, however harmless, or even to a certain extent beneficial, seeing there are many there who, on the proposal of any change, however insignificant, will resist you by saying they will never consent to let down even the smallest pin of the tabernacle. There was an attempt some time ago to introduce the organ into the Scottish Kirk—it was the most unwise of all enterprises to attempt it in the West. Since that the abomination of a painted window in one of the churches was obtruded on the public gaze; but it could not be permitted to stand another Sabbath in the West. To read the line in psalm-singing is one of the venerable and antique peculiarities of our land; and the abolition of it met with far the sturdiest resistance in the West.[1] The antipathy to paper in the pulpit, which used to be in force all over Scotland, is still in greatest force and inveteracy in the West. I state this not for the purposes of levity or ridicule, but of presenting to your notice the very peculiar conjunction, which I have just now remarked upon, between a zeal for great principles, mixed up, as it often is in the history of the Church, with a zeal and tena-

---

[1] Having heard this address from the lips of its noble author, I remember very distinctly that at this point he interjected an unwritten account of his own attempt at the abolition of the practice, not in the West, but at Kilmeny in the East. It created much ferment in the parish. The continuance of the old practice was advocated on the ground that there were certain parishioners whose eyesight was so impaired by old age that they could scarcely read. But he heard that there was one worthy woman who stoutly maintained that the change was anti-Scriptural. He took an early occasion of visiting her, and on asking her what was the Scripture of which she regarded the change as a contravention, at once was answered by her citing the text, "Line upon line!"—T. S.

ciousness about the merest bagatelles. The West is the very quarter to which I look most hopefully for the revival of our Church and the maintenance of our highest moral and religious interests; and however amused therefore with the innocent peculiarities to which I have just now adverted, it cannot dispossess the veneration and serious regard wherewith I look at that portion of our Church—very much, in fact, as our General Assembly looked at the question which broke out about the tables, and finally disposed of it;—when our venerable mother, sitting in her collective wisdom, was called on to decide the quarrel that had broken out among her children, she allowed me, the one party, to continue the table-service in the way I had found to be most convenient; but, instead of laying aught like severity or rebuke upon the other, she, while disappointing them of their plea, dismissed them at the same time with a look of the most benignant complacency."

Every one will acknowledge the gracefulness and the geniality of this reference to an opponent, while few will question the soundness of the principle which it enunciates or assumes. But it is quite possible, and not very unusual, to make an erroneous application of a sound principle. In order to the safe application of this one several matters must be taken into consideration; as, for example, with reference to trifling innovations, it must be considered that it is quite as likely that the blame may rest with those who insist upon them as with those who oppose their introduction. It was thus that the English Puritans argued with respect to the "vestments" question; and I venture to think that they argued aright. Then it must be remembered that innovations may be trifling in themselves, yet they may be designed to carry with them important consequences. The posture of the communicant may be very unimportant in itself, but it becomes important if that attitude is insisted on, or even allowed, which owes its original adoption to the doctrine of transubstantiation and the worship of the host. Further, it is a principle in morals, and it is equally applicable to matters of order and ritual, that the magnitude of an offence is not proportional to the magnitude of the matter about which it is committed. The contempt of, or opposition to, authority may be all the more conspicuous by reason of the smallness of the matter involved in obedience or disobedience. I believe that in the actual case Dr. Chalmers was right and Dr. Begg was wrong; but many cases have occurred since then, in which it is by no means certain that those were right who introduced innovations, and vindicated their introduction by the plea that they were matters of indifference, or that those were wrong who resisted their introduction. In view of much that is to follow, all this can scarcely be regarded as a digression. But my object in referring to the matter at present is simply to present a picture of one who is entitled to be noticed in the biography of his son, not merely as his father, but as one who evidently exerted a much more than ordinary influence on the formation of his character.

Respecting Dr. Begg's mother I have very little to add to what he has himself said. The Mathies appear to have been one of the principal families in Greenock, when, of course, Greenock was a very different place from the Greenock of to-day. In an interesting book published five years ago by my friend Mr. Dugald Campbell, formerly chief magistrate of the town, under the title "Historical Sketches of the Town and Harbour of Greenock," is the following paragraph:—

"The only other bank having its headquarters at Greenock, excepting the Provident Bank, to which we will afterwards refer, was the Greenock Union Bank. This bank was established in 1840, and the shares were nearly all held in Greenock or Aberdeen. Its first office was the one at the West Breast, formerly occupied by the Greenock Bank. It was there, however, only for a short time, when having acquired the property in Hamilton Street, now occupied by the Clydesdale Bank, it was removed there. This site was bought from the Rev. Dr. Begg of New Monkland, to whose wife, a Miss Mathie of Greenock, it belonged, she having succeeded to it, and to a two-storey tenement in Manse Lane, which now also belongs to the Clydesdale Bank, through her father. The last-named house was the family residence; and it may not be uninteresting to note that *while Mrs. Begg was on a visit to her friends, her son James, the famous Dr. Begg of the Free Church, was born in this house in the Manse Lane, so that, by the accident of birth, the Doctor is a Greenockian.* Mrs. Begg's brothers were the owners of the smacks which traded regularly between Greenock and Liverpool before the introduction of steam; and one of the brothers, Mr. Hugh Mathie of Liverpool, was the founder of what afterwards came to be known as the Burns & MacIver Line. Mr. Charles MacIver, afterwards the managing partner at Liverpool, was also born in the Manse Lane of Greenock, which, earlier in the century, was a much more respectable place than it is now. The old manse, after which the lane is called, and which was occupied by the ministers of the Mid Parish until about a third part of this century had passed, now belongs to Messrs. Thom & Sons, wine merchants."

With reference to the statement as to Dr. Begg's birthplace, contained in the sentence which I have italicised, I have the following note from Mr. Campbell, the author of the " Historical Sketches."

"The message I got was that you wished to know whether Dr. Begg was born in Greenock or not. I mentioned in my sketches, contributed to a local paper, and afterwards published, that he was born here. I did this on the authority of a Greenock gentleman, who said that Dr. Begg had given him the information. After my first volume was published, the Doctor spoke to me on the subject, and said that Mr. Williamson must have mistaken what he said, as he was born at Monkland.[1] He had frequently, however, been

---

[1] By the kindness of the Rev. Mr. Hutton, clerk of the Presbytery of Hamilton, I have received an extract from the 'Separate Register' of that Presbytery, containing the particulars of the history of the family of New Monkland manse. It shows that there were two sons called James, that the eldest son of the family was born on the 13th August 1803, and died on the following day. The probability is that *this* James was born and died at Greenock, but that *our* James was born, as he himself believed, at New Monkland. I have high authority (female) for asserting that it was by no means unlikely

in his grandfather's house in Greenock with his mother when a boy, and sometimes with his father when he went for his rents before the property was sold. In consequence of his mother's connection with the town, he told me that he always had a warm side to Greenock, and upwards of twenty years ago he came at my request, along with others, and addressed a meeting in the Town Hall on the Forty Shilling Franchise.

"More information might be got about the Doctor's maternal ancestors, but probably what I have mentioned may suit your purpose."

I must acquiesce in Mr. Campbell's concluding statement. The strongest advocate of atavism would scarcely hold me justified in occupying my time with researches into the characteristics of the Mathie family, and filling my pages with instances of the reappearance of these characteristics in their descendant; and all the less because I should have to extend my researches so as to embrace the family of his maternal grandmother, as well as that of the maternal grandfather.

It may be noticed in a sentence that it seems, strange that Mrs. Begg, who was married and "provided for" during the life-time of her parents, should have inherited not only the family residence in Manse Lane, but also the place of business in Hamilton Street, to the exclusion of her brothers who were engaged in the business.

that Mrs. Begg would go for her first "confinement" to her mother's house; but much less likely that she would for a subsequent one, leaving her children at home or taking one or both with her.

The following is the text in full of the extract referred to:—

1. Mr. James Begg settled at New or East Monkland, 13th August 1801.
2. Married 27th April 1802.
3. Had a son named *James*, born 13th August 1803, who died 14th August 1803.
4. Had a son named *John*, 11th February 1805.
5. Had a daughter named *Margaret*, 16th December 1806.
6. Had a son named *James*, 31st October 1808.
7. Had a daughter named *Jane*, 13th October 1810.
8. Had a daughter named *Mary*, 10th December 1812.
9. Had two sons, *Hugh* and *William*, 3d July 1815.
10. Jane died 29th October 1825.
11. Hugh died 9th November 1830.
12. Mrs. Mary Mathie, wife of the said James Begg, died 22d August 1831.
13. Parish became vacant on the 11th day of June 1845.—T. S.

Apart from any extreme views on the subject of heredity, the assertion will find ready acceptance that the sturdy crofters of Douglas, and the enterprising merchants of Greenock and Liverpool, and the faithful minister of New Monkland, and his thrifty and motherly wife, were all fitly and worthily represented in Dr. Begg.

CHAPTER VI.

SCOTTISH PAROCHIAL SCHOOLS.

No Scottish biography can be regarded as complete unless it contain a disquisition on the educational system of Scotland, and a tribute of admiration and gratitude to the memory of John Knox, as the chosen instrument in the hand of our God, for the bestowal of that system, and of innumerable blessings besides, upon our land. In no case could such disquisition and such tribute be more appropriate than in the biography of one who, throughout his life, had no subject nearer his heart, or more frequently upon his lips, than the system and the man. And yet the very frequency with which the subject will recur in the course of this biography might justify the omission of any reference to it in this place, in connection with Dr. Begg's schoolboy days, and not only justifies, but seems to require, that it be treated with unusual brevity.

Although the educational system proposed in the first Book of Discipline was never fully established, yet the most important part of it has been in operation from the Reformation downwards. The institution of parochial schools was at once an essential and most important *result* of the Reformation, and a *means* of rendering the Reformation more thorough in Scotland than in any other European country. These have put within the reach of the whole body of the people the means of acquiring a sound elementary education, which was designed to be, and in general was, so pervaded by Divine truth as to form an important means of grace. One of the most special features of the Scottish system was its comprehension of all ranks and classes of the community. I have heard a late venerable marquis detail with evident delight his recollections of his attendance at the parish school. I suspect that such attendance on the part of young noblemen was exceptional, as they were generally educated by private tutors. But certainly it was usual for the sons and daughters of shepherds and day-labourers, of tradesmen and farmers, of merchants and squires, to sit side by side on the same forms, and receive in common the same elementary instruction, and be subject to the same discipline. There may have been evils connected with this amalgamation of the classes—as with what human arrangement are there not?—but I am persuaded that the good greatly preponderated.

But the weakness of the system in actual practice was dependent on its non-completion according to its original design. The parochial schools were intended for elementary education alone. Alongside of them there ought to have been secondary or grammar schools in the burghs, or in groups of parishes; but these were very partially instituted. The result was, that the schools which were designed to be exclusively elementary assumed in reality a composite character, attempting to combine the primary education of all with the secondary education of some. The teachers were required to be men capable of conducting this secondary education, and were generally selected on the ground of their scholarly attainments, and their ability to teach the Latin and Greek classics. They were generally men who had attended classes in one of the universities for one or more sessions; and a considerable number were probationers of the Church. To these men it was more congenial to impart the higher instruction to the advanced classes than to undertake the drudgery of primary instruction. They could scarcely be expected to resist the temptation of devoting their main energies to their more advanced pupils, and sacrificing the interests of the many to those of the few; especially as their success was estimated by examiners, and by the public, mainly from the proficiency of the few. I have no doubt that many yielded to this temptation, and purchased the credit of being superior teachers, at the price of neglecting or performing very perfunctorily the work which was properly theirs, that of imparting sound instruction to *all* the children of the parish. As in the case of other abuses, this partiality was as injurious to the favoured classes as to the unfavoured. The higher classes were of course recruited from the lower, and the boys entered the higher without proper preparation, and often without the habits of attention which would have made the instruction given in the higher classes really profitable to them. Recent changes have gone far to remedy *this* evil; and of this every one ought to be glad. But they have produced an evil which did not exist before, and for which a remedy must be sought. They have greatly improved the primary education, and so have opened a way to a great improvement of secondary education; but then they have greatly lessened the facilities of acquiring such education. It is to be hoped that this new evil will be remedied, not by an attempt to revert to the annexation of the secondary to the primary, but by the realisation of the original ideal of Knox.

The position of a minister's son in a village school in Scotland used to be a somewhat peculiar, and in some respects a painful one. Accustomed at home to a degree of refinement of manner and language which did not obtain in the homes of his schoolfellows, he was apt to bring on himself ridicule and sarcasm if on any occasion he unconsciously indicated that superiority in school or playground. Considering himself bound by the necessities of his position occasionally to vindicate his rights or his honour *vi et armis*, he fought with the certainty that victory or defeat would equally subject him to disapprobation on the part of the authorities at home, who were sure to regard fighting as in itself an evil, not to be justified, and but little to be palliated, by the plea of provocation received. Then superiority in scholarship, the almost necessary result of a more intellectual heredity and of the breathing of a more intellect-pervaded air, would lead to a kindlier bearing on the part of the master; and this would be imputed to partiality and favouritism, and would lead in turn to suspicions of "sneaking," and might even brand an innocent son of the manse with the most opprobrious epithet in the schoolboy's vocabulary, that of a "tell-tale." I am glad to believe that these and similar evils are lessened now, if they have not altogether disappeared. But in the days of Dr. Begg's boyhood they were a very real drawback to the great advantages which undoubtedly resulted from the noble system of the Scottish parochial schools, and the association of the juvenile population of all ranks on the same forms and in the same playgrounds. *Experto crede.*

Local traditions seem to indicate that these evils were not unfelt by the son of the minister of Monkland, and that he strove to minimise them by various expedients. There is, for example, a reminiscence of his having in summer habitually stripped off his shoes and stockings on his way to school. After spending the day on terms of equality with his barefooted associates, on the way home he would abstract the insignia of his social superiority from the hiding-place to which he had consigned them in the morning, and would appear at home attired, in respect of his feet, in the costume appropriate to civilised life. Whatever may be thought of this and similar incidents, and of whatever evils they may be regarded as indicative, it cannot well be doubted that such a training had in it, associated with these evils, elements not unfavourable to the formation of the character of a Christian minister, whose vocation requires him to associate with people of all ranks and classes and characters, and to regard all men as in some respects—and those the most important of all respects—equal, while giving honour to whom honour is due, whether on the ground of social position and influence, or of intellectual, moral, or spiritual superiority. No man in our day more thoroughly than Dr. Begg realised the ideal of a Christian minister as belonging to no class because he belongs to all; and I have no doubt that this was in good part due to the manner of his upbringing.

The age to which Dr. Begg lived, surviving most of his cotemporaries, makes it very difficult to obtain any definite reminiscences of his youthful days. All the more value will the reader put on the following communication, which I have received from my friend the Rev. W. Gillespie, one of the ministers of the Free Church at Airdrie, a large town within the parish of New Monkland. I give it almost entire:—

"Free West Manse, Airdrie,
10th April 1884.

"My Dear Sir,—Your request to gather anything interesting regarding Dr. Begg's boyhood, came at a time when I was extremely busy. I had just returned from a month's duties at Geneva, and had a great deal of congregational and other work to overtake. I have now got at most that I think is to be had about the Doctor, and I regret to say that it is not much after all. I have 'interviewed' several of his schoolmates, mainly in the landward part of the parish, and the following is the amount of it.

"His father, the minister of New Monkland, was a man of decided characteristics. He had been a powerful preacher. One of my deacons remembers yet the deep and salutary impression made upon him when a young man by a sermon preached by the old Doctor on Eccles. xi. 9, 'Rejoice, O young man,' &c. His emphatic and frequent repetition of the '*but*' seemed sounding in my friend's ears as he narrated the reminiscence at a distance of forty years.[1] The family in the manse were very strictly brought up, and all my

---

[1] The interval was probably longer. Dr. Begg lived indeed till 1845; but he was little able for pulpit work for several years before his death.—T. S.

informants agree that none of them were given to any vice. James is spoken of as having been always honest and truthful. He was a wild, spirited, 'through-ither' boy, always ready for sport, but with nothing low or cruel in it. On New Year's Day there were usually shooting-matches among the country people, and James has been known to stand at a distance and throw his cap in the air as a mark for the shooters, never blenching while the leaden bullets went over his head.

"He was full of lively vigour, and very determined in any project he set his mind on. He and his elder brother John joined frequently in boyish schemes. Once they had watched carefully a partridge's nest in the beautiful plantations of Rochsoles, close to the manse. They were anxious to get the young ones and rear them, as soon as it was advisable to take them from the nest. They had arranged with a shoemaker in Airdrie, a great bird-fancier, to take charge of the young birds when they should lift them. The only suitable time to get the fledglings was in the morning before sunrise, and they were anxious to get hold of them unknown to their father. John declared that the birds were lost to them, but James resolved to carry out his wishes at any risk. The old Doctor always rose at five o'clock, and whatever was to be done must be all over by that hour. Between three and four o'clock the two boys rose from their beds, dressed, and dropped from their bedroom window, which was on the second floor. They got the young partridges all right. James ran into Airdrie, a distance of two miles, to his friend the shoemaker, delivered up the birds, and ran back again to find John waiting in great terror near the manse. Both sought the house to get into their beds before the household stirred. John's heart fell when he saw that they could not climb to the window by which they had got out, but James soon got hold of a tree which was lying at hand. When both had got up the tree and inside the room, James ordered John to strip, while he did the same, and then he cast off the tree, which fell with 'a thud' that roused the old father. In a few minutes he was in the boys' room, but found them sleeping so soundly that he could not get them to awake.

"The schoolmaster of New Monkland, by whom James Begg was taught, was the Rev. Mr. Watt. He was a licentiate of the Church of Scotland, an excellent scholar, and a very successful teacher. He sent a large number of boys straight to College from his school. He was a fine-looking, gentlemanly man, with an unblemished reputation. His old pupils, to be found in all parts of the world, speak of him with great admiration. A son of his is minister of the parish of Shotts. When James Begg was at school there were no pupil-teachers, but the best scholars were made monitors. He was often put to teach the others, and was wont to make fun at the expense of the country dunces. He was never taken off guard himself, and numerous quick-witted replies are current as having been made by him. Indeed, he gets credit for some that were certainly not his. But this shows the reputation he had gained."

Far be it from me to justify any breach of the Game Laws, farther to make light of the deception of a venerable father by simulated sleep. I am not the apologist but the biographer. Without approving of the transaction, one would have liked to ascertain the fate of the infant covey. This, it is to be feared, is now impossible.

With respect to Dr. Begg's panegyrics on his father's compeers, and on the ministers of a still earlier generation, and his somewhat disparaging remarks upon us of the present time, I may be allowed to remind the reader that they were written at a late period of his life, when it was perfectly natural that he should be *laudator temporis acti*. I have no doubt that these our predecessors possessed all the good qualities which he ascribes to them, and that we, their successors, are fairly chargeable with all the faults which he ascribes to us. But then I do not doubt that they had demerits conjoined with their virtues, while I hope that we have some merits combined with our faults; and I venture to think that Dr. Begg gives a one-sided view of them and of us. He is " to *their* faults a little blind, and to their virtues very kind," while he brings his seeing eye to bear upon *our* faults, and turns his blind one towards our virtues. But especially it is to be borne in mind that the men selected by

Dr. Begg for special commendation were confessedly exceptional men, the choicest friends and associates of his confessedly exceptional father, or those who had left an exceptionally good repute. I agree with Dr. Begg in lamenting certain tendencies, doctrinal and ecclesiastical, of some of the younger ministers of our day; and I agree with him in believing that many individuals of the past overtopped the average—what he calls the rank and file—of the present. The most strenuous advocate of the present might well admit that Dr. Balfour and others were greatly superior to the great body of the men of this generation. But were they not greatly superior also to the great body of their cotemporaries? I go farther than this, and doubt whether we have *any* men who are equal to the greatest men of other days. But I believe that the average of the present is higher than the average of the past, of the age of Moderatism. No one can read such a book as "The Fathers of Ross-Shire," by Dr. Begg's special friend and mine, Dr. Kennedy of Dingwall,[1] without being convinced that there were giants in that part of the earth in those days; and there were men of the same breed in the Lowlands. But it is equally evident that their growth was in no small measure due to the existence of dwarfs around them. I do not mean merely that they *seem* great by contrast with their inferior neighbours, but that one of the elements which materially contributed to their growth was the attitude which they were constrained to maintain of opposition to prevalent evil, and the necessity which was ever laid upon them of doing battle for the truth and cause of God. When our Lord prayed that His disciples might not be taken out of the world, it is obvious that He had respect to the need which the world had of them; but had He not respect also to the need which they had of the world?

[1] By one of those coincidences which always seem strange, notwithstanding the frequency of their occurrence, this sentence was written on the 28th of April 1884, within a few hours of Dr. Kennedy's death.—T. S.

CHAPTER VII.

GLASGOW UNIVERSITY.

It was no unusual thing in former days—and unhappily it is not altogether at an end now—for Scottish students to enter College while far too young to enter with profit upon the studies which ought to be prosecuted in a University. The result of this was necessarily a compromise. The standard of University teaching behoved to be lowered; and yet it could not well be lowered to such an extent as to meet the requirements of the youngest students. Thus those who were well prepared found the studies of such a character as not to call forth their energies, while those who were ill prepared found them still beyond their powers, and in many cases ceased to strive after the accomplishment of what they could not fully accomplish. Thus the "profiting" was in very many cases reduced to a minimum. This, at all events, was the tendency of the system. Of course I do not mean to deny that many excellent scholars went out from our Universities; but they would have attained higher excellence under a better system, while many might have attained excellence who did not attain it.

It is very probable—indeed, it is not to be doubted—that the minister's son of New Monkland, under the teaching of Mr. Watt, and the supervision of his intelligent and strict father, attained at a very early age the power of construing a passage in a Latin classic; and so might be able to enter with some measure of intelligence on the academic course. But it is scarcely possible that his mental powers could be so developed as to make the course very profitable to him.

The defect would probably not appear very prominently during the first session, when he would be occupied mainly with the exercises of the Latin and Greek classes. For these exercises he was probably well enough prepared. But the necessary immaturity of his mind must have disqualified him from profiting, in any considerable measure, by the prelections of the Professor of Logic and Metaphysics, whose class he would attend in his second session. It is thus that I account for his very inadequate estimate, as it seems to me, of that Professor. From much intercourse with men who had been Glasgow students, I have been led to regard Professor Jardine as one of the chief ornaments of the Glasgow University, and one of the best educationists of his time. His book on the method of conducting his class[1] indicates this in a very striking way. It confessedly contributed largely to the improvement of educational methods in Scotland, and may be regarded as having been the first systematic and scientific treatise on paideutics, as it has come to be called. It may perhaps be considered to be out of date now; but *that* is only because what were novelties then, are now familiar as commonplaces and first principles. I am glad to be able to confirm the impression which I had formed of the merits of Professor Jardine by reference to what may well be regarded as the highest authority. The following is an extract from Lord Jeffrey's address on assuming the office of Lord Rector of the Glasgow University:—

"I have permitted myself to say thus much of the dead. Of the living, however unwillingly, I believe I should now forbear to say anything. Yet I cannot resist congratulating

---

[1] "Outlines of Philosophical Education, illustrated by the Method of Teaching the Logic Class in the University of Glasgow; together with observations on the expediency of extending the practical system to other academical establishments, and on the propriety of making certain additions to the course of philosophical education in Universities," by George Jardine, A.M., F.R.S.E., Professor of Logic and Rhetoric in that University. Second Edition, enlarged. Glasgow, 1825.

myself, and all this assembly, that I still see beside me one surviving instructor of my early youth—Professor Jardine—the most revered, the most justly valued of all my instructors; the individual of whom I must be allowed to say *here*, what I have never omitted to say in every other place, that it is to him and his most judicious instructions that I owe my taste for letters, and any little literary distinction I may since have been enabled to attain. It is no small part of the gratification of this day to find him here, proceeding with unabated vigour and ardour in the eminently useful career to which his life has been dedicated; and I hope and trust that he will yet communicate, to many generations of pupils, those inestimable benefits to which many may easily do greater honour, but for which no one can be more sincerely grateful than the humble individual who now addresses you."

I have no doubt that Dr. Begg derived advantage from his attendance on Professor Jardine's lectures; but as little doubt that he would have derived much more had he attended them two or three years later. It ought, however, to be stated that when Dr. Begg attended the Logic class, the Professor, as I learn from the volume from which I make the above quotation from Lord Jeffrey's address, had attained the fiftieth year of his professorship and the eightieth of his life. This may account for the under-estimate of his powers as a thinker and a teacher on the part of his young student. I have no apology to make for this digression. The subject is one of vital importance. There is a real evil upon which I can speak with all the more feeling, because I suffered from it myself, and because I have heard very many of my ministerial brethren make the same confession and complaint. In order to the remedy of the evil I would advocate both the institution of an entrance examination, and also the fixing of an age below which students should not be admitted into our Universities. Dr. Begg admits the evil, though he seems to me to under-estimate its magnitude. He seems to regard it as a necessary result—so far as theological students are concerned—of the length of the academical curriculum prescribed by the Presbyterian Churches. Assuming that that curriculum ought not to be shortened, as I believe that it ought not, I think few will question that the years between fifteen and twenty-three are greatly preferable as the years of student life to those between thirteen and twenty-one. But without any curtailment of the curriculum, it might be undertaken in a shorter time by the lengthening of the session. I do not think that either students or professors could reasonably object to this.

Dr. Begg's very brief reference to another of the professors is perhaps less easy to be accounted for. Those who have been familiar, as I have been, with men who were students in Glasgow half a century ago, have been regaled with innumerable anecdotes concerning Mr. James Millar, Professor of Mathematics, but usually designated by the less dignified appellation of "Jamie Millar," or more generally "Jamie." The impression made on my mind by these anecdotes is that "Jamie" had a competent knowledge of mathematics, but that he was utterly incapable of maintaining authority in his class, and that it became a traditional point of honour in each successive class to convert the class-room into a scene of riot and ribaldry. Some of the anecdotes which I have heard are amusing enough; but most of them are simply painful. And the strange thing is that these anecdotes were told by grave and reverend men, apparently without a thought of the unseemliness of the scenes in which they had taken part. If our friend was too young to appreciate the merits of the Professor of Logic, it is all the more to his credit that he did not appreciate, as many of his compeers did, the flagrant demerits of the Professor of Mathematics. It may be that in this respect the boy was the father of the man; for although Dr. Begg had a very genuine turn for humour "within the limits of beseeming mirth," he had no taste for buffoonery; and this latter, it must be confessed, is the predominant element in the current reminiscences of "Jamie."

One result of the extreme youth of Dr. Begg when he entered College was that almost all his cotemporaries were his seniors in age, many of them by several years, and therefore, although he did not himself attain to extreme old age, almost all of them had passed away before him. It was the duty of his biographer to seek access to the rolls of the classes of which he was a member. This access was most kindly granted. The result was disappointing and saddening. The rolls contain the names of many who, but a few years ago, could have given most interesting information concerning the young student, but which is now lost irrecoverably. Among those who were his class-fellows, and whose lifelong friendship he highly prized, and whose death he deeply mourned, it was with melancholy interest that I read the names of James Julius Wood and Robert Smith Candlish. From two only of his surviving cotemporaries I have got in answer to my application a shadow of a reminiscence. The Rev. Dr. Smith, minister of Cathcart, writes as follows:—

"MANSE OF CATHCART, 22d *March* 1884.

"MY DEAR SIR,—I am extremely sorry that it is not in my power to give you any interesting reminiscences of the early life of my late much esteemed friend, Dr. Begg. I left the Divinity Hall the year he entered it, so that our acquaintance as students was very slight. I remember well, however, the high place which he held in the estimation of his fellow-students, both in point of character and scholarship. We were excellent friends all our lives; and although differing widely from the first on many points, there was never any interruption of our mutual affection and esteem. I am most happy that you have undertaken to write his 'Life,' and will look forward to the perusal of it with the deepest interest."

The Rev. Andrew Urquhart, minister of the Free Church

at Portpatrick, gives a very similar reply to the same application:—

"MY DEAR SIR,—It would have given me much pleasure if I had been able to give you any information available for your purpose. But, although at College at the same time with the late Dr. Begg, I had no intimacy with him, and remember him only as a junior student, whom I recognised in the College courts as a brother of one of my class-fellows. I cannot even remember who were his ordinary companions, to whom I might refer you for inquiry. With deep interest in your important undertaking," &c.

The Rev. Robert Wilson, minister *emeritus* of North Ronaldshay, has stated to me verbally that Dr. Begg had the repute of a steady and good student throughout; that during his undergraduate course he was not in any way specially distinguished; but that he took a more prominent place in the theological course, and was especially noted as a proficient in Hebrew.

Such are the meagre gleanings of a harvest which has been reaped and garnered. The gleanings indicate little as to the fulness of the crop or the quality of the grain.

CHAPTER VIII.

GLASGOW DIVINITY HALL.

ALTHOUGH it is probable that in every day and every hour of a young man's life he is subjected to influences which contribute to the formation or modification of his intellectual, moral, and spiritual character—as every ray of light and every drop of dew has its part in the production of the harvest—yet it seems to be a fact that the development of the student's mind is not usually continuous and regular, but rather that it is effected by a succession of upward steps occurring at intervals after periods of advance along a plane. Such an elevation appears to have occurred in Dr. Begg's mental history, cotemporaneously with his entrance upon his properly professional studies. At the close of last chapter it is stated, on the authority of Mr. Wilson, that he was held in higher repute as a theological student than he had been as an undergraduate. This might, of course, be attributable to various causes. His tastes and mental habitudes might be more in the direction of theology than of literature, or science, or philosophy; or it might be because the juvenility to which I referred as necessarily prejudicial to his success in the earlier half of his course had ceased to act so unfavourably during the latter half of it. I have no doubt that both these causes operated to some extent. But I suspect that the main cause of his sudden ascent to a higher level was his being then brought under the influence of Dr. Stevenson MacGill, the Professor of Theology in the Glasgow University. I have no doubt that this constituted a crisis in his mental history. It was impossible to be much in his company in private without perceiving how high was his estimate of Dr. MacGill, while he very often referred to him in public as his *beau ideal* of a theologian and a professor. No one who knows the character of Dr. Begg's sentiments, and the particulars of his career, can read the Life of Dr. MacGill without perceiving that the points of resemblance between the two men were too numerous and too exact to have been undesigned, and therefore that the younger man must, consciously or unconsciously, have formed himself after the model of the elder. The very measures which Dr. MacGill continually advocated in the social department, relating to pauperism, the treatment of prisoners, education, and the economical elevation of the people, were the measures whose advocacy afterwards occupied much of the time and thought of Dr. Begg. On ecclesiastical questions, too, their views were practically identical, although Dr. MacGill was not so thorough an anti-patronage man as Dr. Begg. Even on questions respecting which they differed from the great body of those with whom they generally agreed—as, for example, on the question of "Catholic Emancipation"—they entirely agreed with one another. With secular politics they intermeddled more than earnest ministers of the Gospel generally do, and their political views were identical. They regarded the Revolution Settlement as the real *Magna Charta* of British rights and liberties, and, with an equal abhorrence of Toryism and Radicalism, trod the *via media* of the Whiggism of 1688.

Although it would ordinarily be unwarrantable to occupy any considerable portion of a biographical book with a notice of one of the teachers of the subject of the biography, yet I believe that a brief notice of Dr. MacGill will materially aid the reader in tracing the development of the character of Dr. Begg, and therefore I consider myself justified in presenting such a notice, derived from the Life of Dr. MacGill,[1]

---

[1] "Memoir of the Rev. Stevenson MacGill, D.D., Professor of Theology in the University of Glasgow, and Dean of the Chapel Royal." By Robert Burns, D.D., Minister of St. George's, Paisley. Edinburgh, 1842.

by the late Dr. Robert Burns of Paisley, afterwards of Toronto.

Dr. MacGill began his professional work as minister of the parish of Eastwood, near Glasgow. From the first he was an evangelical preacher, and gave himself faithfully to pulpit preparation, and to diligent study of Biblical truth. Yet the impression made on my mind by the perusal of Dr. Burns' Memoir is that his highest motive at this time was a sense of duty and responsibility, rather than any enthusiastic zeal for his Master's glory, or for the salvation of the souls of his hearers. His conscientiously-prepared discourses were, I suspect, rather devoid of faults in matter or manner than very richly distinguished by fervour, or the fruits of spiritual experience. But if he had no very enthusiastic longing for the spiritual well-being of his flock, he had for their temporal well-being, and their social and economical improvement. And while the former longing waxed stronger and stronger, the latter happily remained in undiminished strength throughout his long life, although I would not say that to the last he was not more of a philanthropist and a social reformer than an evangelist.

"Dr. MacGill" (says his biographer), "while minister of Eastwood, was conspicuous for his diligent attention to pastoral duties. He was careful in his preparations for the pulpit, and he was practically alive to the importance of the more retired parts of the ministerial office. There is one branch of duty to which, as a parochial minister, he was particularly attentive; I refer to the religious and moral education of the youth of his parish. . . . Dr. MacGill entered at once into the spirit of those regulations which the Church of Scotland has laid down on this subject for the guidance of her ministers. Not only did the business of individual examination form part of his ordinary family visitations; he held in addition regular diets of catechising in different districts of the parish, and his affectionate and solemn manner of address rendered these meetings highly agreeable and useful both to old and young. He regularly superintended also the parochial and other schools within the bounds, not satisfying himself with the annual and perhaps formal inspection of them by the members of Presbytery, but frequently looking into the village seminary, affectionately and respectfully encouraging the teacher, speaking in the language of condescending tenderness to the youngest of the pupils, and addressing to them the words of instruction. . . .

"In connection with the education of youth, Dr. MacGill was most assiduous in the general management of the poor of the parish. Eastwood at that time had not become so much a manufacturing locality as it has been of late years, and the number of public works was small. Still it was an extensive and populous parish, and the poor were on the increase. Dissent had drawn away considerable numbers from the parish church, and the weekly collections, thus diminished, required to be augmented by means of assessment. Dr. MacGill, along with a body of faithful elders, paid a very minute attention to the management of the poor, both in principle and in detail, regularly attending the meetings of heritors and session, and guiding their proceedings with that calm dignity and order which ever distinguished him in public matters. . . . Dr. MacGill retained through life his deep impressions of the duty of a clergyman to be peculiarly attentive to the physical and moral wants of the poor. Although properly belonging to a much later period of his history, we may here notice his admirable tract on the subject of 'Public Provision for the Poor,' published in 1820, because it contains an exposition of the principles on which he began to act while minister at Eastwood, and which developed themselves more and more in all his future relations. Competent judges have long ago pronounced this work to be one of the most valuable compends of all that is really useful in principle and in detail on the subject of which it treats. . . . At a time when it was not so common as it is now for clergymen to tell their minds freely from the pulpit or the press on such subjects, Dr. MacGill boldly reminded the affluent and the gay that their idleness and extravagance, irreligion and profligacy, had produced sad 'havoc' among the humbler classes, and that thereby they had contributed both to corrupt the general manners, and to ruin individuals; and he boldly called upon rulers and statesmen, landed proprietors, merchants, manufacturers, and masters of trades, nay, on our literary men and our instructors of youth, who are apt to look on such things as beneath their notice, to consider what example of attention to religious principles, and ordinances, and duties they had for many years given; and he plainly tells them not to be surprised if they should see some portion of the fruit of their own conduct appearing among the people. . . .

"Dr. MacGill was not one of those puling sentimentalists who imagine that a Protestant minister has nothing to do with the great public events of the times, or the influence of civil government on the habits and condition of men. It was during the period of his residence at Eastwood that certain political opinions were extensively circulated among the people, the tendency of which appeared to him, and to many others, unfavourable to the peace and prosperity of the country. His views of the French Revolution had been greatly modified by events; and expectations which he, in common with many intelligent and liberal men, may at one time have formed, were speedily blasted. Anxious for the best interests of his people, he published, in 1792, a small tract entitled 'The Spirit of the Times,' addressed specially to 'the people of Eastwood.' There are seasons when pious and faithful ministers *ought* to depart from their ordinary round; yea, even to leave the retired and peaceful walks of pastoral duty, in order that they may, by methods somewhat unusual, endeavour to do good to their fellow-citizens. Dr. MacGill felt himself so situated, and he lifted up a seasonable warning against prevailing anarchy, infidelity, and crime. While he was far from inculcating passive obedience, or 'the right divine of kings to govern wrong,' he inculcated the lessons of wisdom and brotherly love. It is possible that later events and growing experience may have modified his views on some points; but taking it as a whole, his address abounds in sound maxims on the subject of established government, and the dangers of anarchy and a revolutionary spirit; while the acquaintance it exhibits with the history of the English Constitution, as contrasted with the government of France under the Bourbon dynasty, is exceedingly creditable to his intelligence and his judgment at this early period of his life. There is reason to think that the practical effect of the publication was beneficial; and certainly no man dared to charge its author with the fault of stepping out of his appropriate province in putting it forth. . . . There are great questions of political economy which ought to be viewed apart from all low partisanship, and in connection exclusively with the general social welfare of mankind. A Protestant clergyman ought to be the most enlightened of citizens. In ordinary times, indeed, he may safely leave the details of public measures to those whose habits qualify them better for their development; but at no time should he be ignorant of great principles, or indifferent to their practical application."

If the introduction of these extracts can be justified at all, it can only be on the ground of the personal influence which Dr. MacGill exerted in moulding the character of Dr. Begg; and even on that ground I confess that I am not quite confident of obtaining unanimous acceptance of the plea. But however important it be that we know what men are, it is abundantly more so that we know how they become what they are.

In 1797, Dr. MacGill was "translated" to the Tron Church parish in Glasgow. There he made full proof, in a large city parish, of that ministry which he had begun to exercise in a comparatively small and rural one; although I believe that Eastwood was, even in the days when he was minister of it, neither absolutely small nor strictly rural. *Now* it is embraced in the ever-widening circuit of Glasgow. His ministry in the Tron parish was most faithful and laborious. He wrought under the depressing feeling that the work given him to do was far more than any man could do; but he humbly trusted in God, and faithfully and conscientiously did what he could. In 1814 he was appointed to the Theological chair in the University, his successor in the Tron Church being Dr. Chalmers. By this time Dr. MacGill had become known in the Church as a sound evangelical preacher, and as an advocate in the Church courts of anti-moderate views and measures. His appointment to the chair was therefore hailed by the friends of evangelism as in some sort a triumph, or at all events as an indication of a turn of the tide. It was matter of great rejoicing to such men as Sir Henry Moncreiff and Dr. Andrew Thomson.

I am not aware whether Dr. Begg had been brought in any way into contact with the Professor before he became a member of his class. Most likely he would have been introduced to him by his father, who must have been on terms of intimacy with him. But it was when he became a student of theology, in the technical sense of the term, that he was brought into close relation with one who exerted so potent an influence over him. As to that influence I am disposed to think that it was rather personal than strictly academical. From Dr. Burns' "Memoir" I should infer that this was the case generally; and I have no doubt that it was so in this instance. Indeed, the Professor himself seems to have aimed more at the exercise of a salutary and sanctifying influence over his students, than at turning them out as very profound or erudite theologians.[1] His prelections would certainly be sound, and clear, and candid. But we hear more of his efforts to make his students, with God's help, honest-minded, and upright, and generous, and noble *men*, and faithful *preachers*, and diligent *pastors*, than of any special endeavours to imbue them with very fervent zeal for theological research. He seems to have bestowed very special pains upon the criticism of the exercises which the students were statutorily required to deliver, as well as of other exercises which he prescribed to them. Altogether, the

[1] Dr. Wilson, in his "Memorials of Dr. Candlish," says :—" Of the theological professors, Stevenson MacGill was the one he respected most, and got most good from; but he often spoke of the inadequacy of the theological training of those days. Even MacGill mentioned no books to the students, and so left them quite at sea in the prosecution of their studies." I should suppose that this is an exaggerated statement, but not an unfounded one. —T. S.

impression made on my mind has been that other theological professors may have been better *instructors* than he was, but that he was eminently an *educator* of those under his charge. I need not say that instruction and education are by no means identical, although the former is certainly an important means towards the latter. It will not be disputed that a combination of the two is greatly preferable to either of them singly, and, indeed, that they must always be combined in some proportion or other. But as perfection of proportion is, like all other perfection, unattainable so long as men are imperfect, it will probably be admitted that a larger proportion of the latter with a smaller of the former is much preferable to the converse. Dr. Begg's complaint, however, that the "art of preaching" was not taught—a complaint which he constantly reiterated in public and in private—is not to be carried too far. The elaborate teaching of the "art of preaching" is too apt to degenerate into the regarding of preaching simply as an art. Certainly, the ordinary books on homiletics do not seem to indicate that such teaching is capable of doing much good to the learner. The art of preaching consists essentially in having something to say, and in saying it naturally and unaffectedly, under a deep sense of the awful responsibility of delivering a message from God to men. In my student days in Edinburgh, Dr. Welsh gave us every Friday a lecture on preaching. The lectures, it needs not be said since the lecturer has been named, were most admirable. I remember little of them except the following sentence, a priceless gem, "When you write a particularly fine passage—draw your pen through it!"

Without question, however, the state of theological education in our Scottish Colleges, in Dr. Begg's student days, was very unsatisfactory. The great evil was that more was given to the Professor of Theology to do than it was possible for any man to do efficiently. In my time in Edinburgh the

Theological Faculty consisted of the Professors of Systematic Theology, Church History, and Hebrew : I believe it was the same in Glasgow in Dr. Begg's day. The three professors had, in all, five classes each day. Since that time the Theological Faculties have been increased by the foundation of professorships of Biblical Criticism. But the greatest improvement has been made in the Theological Schools outside the University. The Free Church College in Edinburgh has six professors, who have eleven classes each day, while a seventh has two classes during a portion of the session. The Glasgow and Aberdeen Colleges, each with a professor fewer, have as many classes. The United Presbyterians also have a fully equipped hall, and a long session, instead of a session of six weeks conducted by professors who were also ministers of congregations. The Congregationalists also have materially extended their course. Certainly the means and appliances for theological study are greatly extended. The valley is made full of ditches (2 Kings iii. 16); would that the heaven-sent rain might fill the pools (Ps. lxxxiv. 6).

Of Dr. Begg's residence as tutor in the family of Mrs. Neilson (see p. 59), I have received the following interesting account from Mr. Stuart Neilson, W.S., who was not himself under Dr. Begg's tutorship, but who was at home in his mother's house while Dr. Begg was an inmate of it.

"1 North Charlotte Street, Edinburgh,
5th July 1884.

"Dear Sir,—In compliance with your request, I shall now, with the aid of my brothers, note down some reminiscences of the late Dr. Begg while residing in our family at Millbank, near Edinburgh, about fifty-five years ago; but I regret that I can communicate very little.

"Mr. Begg was licensed, I believe, by the Presbytery of Paisley, when he was only twenty years of age, on condition that he should not preach till he had completed his twenty-first year.[1] It was arranged that during that year he should reside with us as tutor to my youngest brother, who died many years ago, that he might have the opportunity of attending Dr. Chalmers' Theological Lectures; and as he was only occupied with my brother for part of the evening, he had the whole day at his disposal. He attended Dr. Chalmers' class, where he became acquainted with the late Principal Cunningham, commonly known among the students as 'clever Cunningham.'

"Mr. Begg generally spent his forenoon in town, or in walking in the country with some of the students. In the afternoon he was generally occupied with his theological studies. He was especially fond of Jeremy Taylor, 'Pearson on the Creed,' and the old Fathers, and, having an excellent memory, often introduced quotations from them in conversation, but without any ostentation. He was very intelligent and fond of argument, but very good-tempered. I remember an instance of his enthusiasm. A military friend of ours who had been in India and was in delicate health paid us a visit. He went to bed early, but could seldom fall asleep for a considerable time, and after he was in bed Begg generally entered with 'Pearson on the Creed' under his arm, and then there would be at least an hour of reading and discussion, though our friend acknowledged that his eyes were sometimes closed in slumber before the end of it.

"Mr. Begg conducted family worship morning and evening. During his residence with us one of my sisters who had long been delicate became dangerously ill. She was a very devoted and consistent Christian, intimate with the late Dr. Gordon, and a member of his congregation, but of a very retiring and timid disposition, so that she shrank from expressing her opinions. On the night when she died, the family were around her bed, Begg being present, and her natural timidity disappeared, and she gave a bold and striking testimony to the truth. Begg told a friend that his experience of that night first gave him an adequate sense of the power of the Gospel.

"My brothers and I were fond of leaping, vaulting, quoits,

---

[1] This is not strictly accurate; he was not licensed when he came to Edinburgh; and he was licensed by the Presbytery of Hamilton.—T. S.

throwing the hammer, &c., and Begg always joined in these sports with great enjoyment, and excelled in them all. He had then a spare sinewy figure, and gave the impression of a man who could undergo a great amount of work without being fatigued, and he entered heartily into merriment. He had a great fund of humour, and an unlimited stock of comic anecdotes. He was not impulsive, but had a cool persistency which fitted him for overcoming difficulties and accomplishing what he designed. This manifested itself in a short pedestrian tour in the Highlands, which my three brothers and their friend, Mr. George Ross, afterwards a legal professor in the University of Edinburgh, had arranged. Begg gladly joined the party, and being the senior, was made guardian of the purse.

"At that time 'a natural' walked on the slopes of Stirling Castle, having always in his hand a large iron key. He was famed for his great memory in connection with the Bible, so that if any chapter and verse were mentioned he could at once repeat the text. Begg made a point of seeing him and putting him to the test, and was much impressed with the astonishing memory of the man. From Stirling the party walked to Callander. Having dined, they went up the Pass of Leny, and when they reached the road to the Trossachs on their return, heavy rain was falling, and the hills were covered with mist, and it was proposed that they should return to the inn at Callander, but Begg would not hear of that. He said they must go through with their day's work of thirty miles as arranged, and if they were prevented by the mist from seeing the hills, he said, 'So much the better, for you can fancy them any height you please.' My brothers still persisted that they would return to Callander, when he said, 'Well, of course, you may do as you please, but I have the purse, you know;' and that was conclusive; so during their walk of nine miles they had the pleasure of becoming acquainted with a Highland shower. That night they slept at the old small hotel at the Trossachs, and next day, there being then no steamer on the Loch, they were rowed up Loch Katrine to Stronachlacher. On landing, some 'sma' still whisky' was brought out, but Begg would have none of it, being a strict abstainer, which was a rare thing in those days. In fact, cold water was a hobby of his, so that there would be a general smile when he enlarged, as he frequently did, on the virtues of pure cold water.

"On arriving at Glasgow my brothers thought that he guarded the purse too conscientiously, for he took them to a third-rate hotel, and when they grumbled at the shabby entertainment, he, in his pleasant way, consoled them with the assurance that they might have been worse off.

"From Glasgow he took them to his father's manse, where they spent two pleasant days with the family. Some time before this a coloured window representing a figure had been introduced in a church in Glasgow, which roused the indignation of Begg's father, who published two pamphlets on 'The Painted Image.' Begg not being impressed with this innovation as indicating 'the thin end of the wedge,' used to joke in a mild way about the 'Painted Image,' but not in any spirit of disrespect to his father.

"The first time that Begg was a member of Assembly his father made a speech to which some one replied in rather a free way, on which Begg rose and defended his father so ably that the late Lord Moncreiff came forward and shook hands with him, and congratulated him on the success of his first appearance.

"On the first Sabbath after completing his twenty-first year, he preached three times in Edinburgh, his evening service being in Lady Glenorchy's Chapel, where he afterwards became the popular assistant of the late highly esteemed Dr. Jones.—I am, dear sir, yours truly,
"STUART NEILSON."

In days when the distance between the east and the west was practically much greater than it is now, Dr. Begg's sojourn in the eastern capital brought him into contact with many men and many minds which else would have been unknown to him. And it was a grand privilege to be a member of Dr. Chalmers' class for even a single session. I only repeat what has been said hundreds of times before, when I state that his students received from their great teacher an impulse and a quickening which they could not have received otherwise, and for the bestowal of which, as a precious gift from the Father of lights, he was specially raised up. I have no doubt that Dr. Begg received it to a far greater extent than it would appear from his narrative that he was conscious of. Or perhaps it was that he shrank from the "ridiculous excess of gilding refined gold, or painting the lily, or adding a lustre to the diamond." It has become common to speak slightingly of Dr. Chalmers as a theologian and a theological teacher. It is no doubt true that he had not a great amount of scholarship or erudition; and I have no wish to deny that this was a drawback. But even in this respect his deficiency is commonly exaggerated. The truth is, that he had a habit of unduly depreciating his own scholarship; and, however it may be with those who form too high an estimate of their own attainments, those who follow the opposite course are generally taken at their own valuation. And then his deficiency was precisely of the kind which is most conspicuous. Whether it was from defect of musical ear, or from lack of early training, I do not know, but he could scarcely quote a Greek or Latin sentence without a "false quantity;" and most amusing was his humility when a titter intimated to him that he had thus stumbled. But this was not incompatible with the ability to apprehend the meaning of the passage and its argumentative bearing. And then it is to be remembered that a very small portion of the theological system is dependent on the nice distinction of Greek particles, or the explication of doubtful phrases in Greek or Latin fathers. I am confident that an intelligent reader of Dr. Chalmers' lectures on the Romans will conclude that he had powers which compensated for his lack of nice scholarship, even in those departments in which that is most brought into play. We all know how, in conversing with a very intimate friend, with whose train of thought and form of speech we have become familiar, we seize upon his meaning before his sentences are fully uttered, or when they are not very clearly expressed. Now Dr. Chalmers had that intimate familiarity—the old writers called it *inwardness*—and that entire sympathy with the fervent apostle, and that apprehension of the spirit of his writings and the substance of his arguments, which put him into a far better position for apprehending and interpreting the epistle, than the position occupied by many accurate scholars who have been without this sympathy. It is a sound institute of critisism—

> "A perfect judge will read each work of wit
> With the same spirit that its author writ,
> Survey the whole;"

and hence the first essential to interpretative criticism is sympathy with the spirit of the author. Given this, and the more of scholarship the better; without this, no amount of mere scholarship will be of much avail. If interpretation must generally proceed from multitudinous parts to a well-constructed whole, it will lose nothing by frequently viewing the parts in the light of the whole.

I believe that I speak the common sentiment of my *quondam* fellow-students, when I say that we do not feel our obligation to Dr. Chalmers so much for the theology he taught us, as for his inculcation and exemplification of the right methods of theological study, and the lines and limits of theological research—what I may be allowed to call the philosophy of theology. His lectures on Hume's "Argument on Miracles," and his examinations on Butler's "Analogy," no one of us has forgotten or will ever forget. None the less logical because they were so rhetorical, they were at once the rein and the spur; and I am sure that all of us, in our subsequent studies, have often reverted to them, and have been led to self-questioning as to the manner and the spirit in which we were prosecuting these studies. If Chalmers may not occupy the position of a theological Newton, I am sure that his disciples revere him as a theological Bacon, whose "Organon" contained the germ whence many a goodly harvest was to spring.

It does not appear that Dr. Begg attended any class in the Edinburgh University besides that of Dr. Chalmers. If he attended any other, it would presumably be the Church History class; and it was before the day when the chair was occupied by Dr. Welsh, who first made the class memorable for aught but weariness. We have therefore no such reminiscences of the Edinburgh as we have of the Glasgow University. But indeed, when Dr. Chalmers and Professor Wilson have been named, the celebrities of the College have been well-nigh exhausted. There were indeed many most respectable men and painstaking teachers, whose memories, as such, their students cherish; and there were a few men more widely known, as Sir John Leslie and Professor Wallace. The Medical Faculty, too, had its Munro, and its Hope, and its Alison, and its Christison, the last-named destined subsequently to acquire world-wide fame. But the University had not then attained the unification which now pertains to it, and the theological and the medical portions of it were more widely separated than they happily are now.

It is more remarkable, and more regrettable, that Dr. Begg notices none of his fellow-students excepting him to whom we shall often have to refer in the sequel, Dr. Cunningham.[1] It is almost strange that he has not a word to say of one

[1] Dr. Begg's earliest remembrance of Dr. Cunningham is given in the "Life" of the latter in similar terms to those in p. 73. "James Begg came to Edinburgh that winter to enjoy a closing session under Chalmers. He joined a debating society connected with the University. It was the hot time of the Row heresy, and the subject of debate one evening was, Whether assurance is, or is not, of the essence of faith. The debate was opened for the affirmative by one student. Then a very tall and thin young man rose and delivered a speech on the other side, of astonishing power, and showing a wonderful command of language. This was William Cunningham; and Dr. Begg says that, magnificently as he spoke in after years, he perhaps never surpassed this speech in the debating society."—*Life of William Cunningham, D.D., by Robert Rainy, D.D., and the late Rev. James Mackenzie.*

with whom he must have been cotemporary, of whom all Edinburgh students are proud, as perhaps the most distinguished as a student of all her thousands of *alumni* in the three hundred years of her existence—John Brown Paterson.

To an Edinburgh student it seems strange that Dr. Begg should have passed over without note or notice two men who in those days occupied a unique position in the College. The prominence which he gives to "Blind Alick" (p. 53), who, after all, does not seem to have had any special relation to the Glasgow University or its students,—to have been, in fact, a mere townsman, and in no sense a gownsman,—makes it all the more remarkable that he takes no note of Dr. Syntax and Sir Peter Nimmo. The former of these, whose real name was Sherriff, and whose academical prefix, like the knightly one of his *confrère*, belonged to the courtesy class, was said to have been at one time a medical student. He had considerable ability as a sketcher of portraits, and it was understood that he maintained himself by taking likenesses of the professors in their classes, and of ministers in their pulpits, and selling them to them or their friends. Sir Peter had no talent of any kind, and depended for support on simple charity. He had been a fellow-student of my father in the divinity classes, as he was mine after an interval of some forty years. The Doctor did not come very often to the theological classes, giving his preference to the Faculties of Arts and Medicine, while the knight was generally found browsing on his old theological pastures. They seemed to have undisputed right of entrance into all the classes. They must have caused considerable annoyance to the professors; but I never heard of any proposal to exclude them; and, indeed, their exclusion would have been seriously regretted by the students. After all, they did no great harm, as they always comported themselves with perfect decorum in the classes; and it was only at the beginning of a session, before the new-comers had learned to realise their position, that in the corridors and the quadrangle one or other of them might occasionally be made the object of a somewhat too boisterous fun. The seniors would certainly have repressed the carrying even of this to excess; and ere two or three weeks had passed, the *genius loci* constrained the juniors to respect the traditions of the University, and to regard Sir Peter and the Doctor as indispensable adjuncts of the institution. I suppose that such characters would not be tolerated in any educational institution now, and probably it is right that they should not; but I am sure that the tolerance of them then has furnished to those who were students in the former half of the century one pleasant memory the more of the dear bountiful mother;—for bountiful she was, and dear she is to us all, however Mrs. Oliphant (see p. 45) and other outsiders may sneer.

CHAPTER IX.

LICENSE AS A PREACHER—ASSISTANT AT NORTH LEITH—CHARACTER OF HIS PREACHING.

As I hope to have some readers outside of Scotland, and as some of these may probably be partially ignorant of Presbyterian habitudes, I must say a few words for their information concerning what, in the Presbyterian Churches, is called licensing. All the Presbyterian bodies in Scotland require of aspirants to the ministry attendance on the undergraduate course of a University. The student is then, after examination, admitted to the Theological School or Divinity Hall, which, for the Established Church, is a department of the University, while the other Churches have separate Colleges of their own. Ordinarily the undergraduate or arts course in the University occupies four years. But students who pass an entrance examination are exempted from attendance on the junior or first year's classes, and so they can complete their course in three years. The theological course used to occupy four years in the Established Church, and five years in the United Presbyterian Church, the sessions in the latter, however, being much shorter than in the former. Since the Disruption, the theological course in the Established and United Presbyterian Churches has been reduced to three years, while in the Free Church it is still four years, the sessions in all the denominations being now of the same length, viz., about six months in each year. At the end of that course the student is subjected to a strict examination, conducted by a Board of Examiners appointed by the General Assembly.

He is then taken on "trials for license" by the Presbytery within whose bounds he is resident. Those trials consist of examinations on the subjects taught in the theological school, and the delivery of certain discourses on subjects prescribed by the Presbytery. On his passing these trials satisfactorily, and expressing verbally and by signature his adherence to the doctrinal and ecclesiastical tenets of the Church, he is licensed by the Presbytery to "preach the Gospel as a probationer within their bounds, or wheresoever, in the providence of God, his lot may be cast."

Although the position of the probationer is in some respects similar to that of the deacon in Episcopal Churches, yet it is essentially different. He is still a layman, and is not permitted to dispense either of the sacraments, or to do any of the acts which are regarded as strictly ministerial, with the one exception of that act for which he is licensed, preaching the Gospel, and conducting the ordinary public worship. While the probationer is technically a layman, he is in social usage very properly treated with the respect and "reverence" due to one who is invested with the right of discharging one of the most important functions of the ministry; and all the Churches hold the body of their licentiates in much honour, as their destined future ministry, and the hope of the Church for the future.

In Dr. Begg's time, and in mine, it was generally considered that it was this license alone that entitled a man to preach; and I believe that a student preaching without license would have been regarded as guilty of something of the nature of ecclesiastical insubordination. In point of fact, none of us ever did preach till we were licensed. *Now* I think it is generally understood that the license is not to *preach*, but to preach *as a probationer*. At all events, almost all—probably all—of our students do preach more or less frequently, especially during their last session at College, and during the long summer recess. There are advantages and disadvantages pertaining to each of the systems. The later one is probably the better of the two, if used judiciously; but it is more liable to abuse. It is apt to lead to superficiality of study. It is apt to lower the estimate of the solemnity and responsibility of preaching. It only to a very limited extent corrects the evil which Dr. Begg deplores as pertaining to the former system, because, instead of the experienced and kindly counsel which he so earnestly desiderated, the student, preaching in a village congregation in absence of the minister, much more frequently receives indiscriminate commendation and flattery. Certainly the receiving of license was a more important epoch and a more solemn crisis in a man's life in former days than it is likely to be now, when, in many cases, it makes little material difference in the habits or the employment of the licentiates.

It has been seen that Dr. Begg spent the whole period of his probationership—which in his case was very brief—as assistant to Dr. Buchanan of North Leith, whom I remember that the late Dr. Candlish, in the course of conversation with me, characterised as the best preacher at that time in Scotland. It was a trying position for a young man to occupy. To have been minister of one of the largest and most intelligent congregations in Scotland would have taxed to the uttermost, and overtaxed, the powers of any man. To minister to such a congregation without the *prestige* naturally attaching to its stated ministry, and the sense of duty imposed on the people by the formation of the pastoral tie, and to be almost necessarily brought into comparison with such a preacher and pastor as Dr. Buchanan, constituted an ordeal through which not one young man in a hundred could have passed without damage. That Dr. Begg passed through it, and that at the very beginning of his career, I regard as one of the most creditable parts of his life. I have before me a few notes, accidentally preserved, which the assistant had occasion to write to his principal. They refer to merely trivial matters of every day occurrence, and have no interest so far as their contents are concerned. But the cordial familiarity which their manner indicates as having subsisted between the two men—a cordiality which remained unimpaired when in later years they occupied other positions, and stood in different relations to each other—is equally creditable to both. There has also been kindly put at my disposal a draft letter by Dr. Buchanan, addressed to Mr. Stothert of Cargen, who was one of the leading men connected with the chapel at Maxwelltown. The draft bears marks of careful revision and correction by its author. I subjoin it in full, although I am not aware whether it be an exact copy of the letter actually sent. No doubt it is substantially identical:—

"CATHERINE BANK, NEWHAVEN.

"DEAR SIR,—I received your esteemed favour of   , and hasten to reply. Having been myself a minister of a Chapel of Ease, I am deeply interested in the erection of such places of worship throughout the country, and regard them as the fittest direct effort, as well as, in the present case, the most practicable means of supplying the great lack of church accommodation which has more or less been felt in every populous neighbourhood.

"In compliance with your request, permit me to recommend to you and the other managers of the chapel at Maxwelltown, Mr. James Begg, preacher of the Gospel. Being the son of a worthy minister in the west, he had the best means of acquiring in early life that knowledge and those habits which were necessary to qualify him for the sacred profession; and his public appearances since he obtained license have given ample proof that the means of improvement were not in his case given in vain. Being indisposed at the beginning of the year, I was advised to employ a temporary assistant, especially in the more private duties of the parish, and have much reason to be thankful that I was able to secure the services of Mr. Begg. Although very recently licensed to preach the Gospel, the discourses which he delivered in North Leith during my absence were universally acceptable, and such of them as I heard manifested the very rare combination of a plain but nervous style, with a simple, unaffected, and often impressive delivery, and were equally adapted to the comprehension of the poor and the taste of the higher classes of his hearers. In the discharge of his week-day duties among the families of the sick and the poor, I have reason to know that he was equally acceptable; and from all that I know, whether of his talents and attainments, or of his disposition and habits, I shall regard any congregation as peculiarly fortunate who may be the first to secure the benefit of his services.

"I have reason to believe that he will receive an ample certificate from Dr. Chalmers and other divines, who, from their standing in the Church, are much better qualified to recommend a pastor to you than I can be. But this recommendation, which is the first I have ever granted, was due from me, owing to my intimate connection with Mr. Begg as my own assistant.

"May I request that you will take the trouble of communicating this, with my best respects, to Mr. Taylor, whom I have had the pleasure of meeting, and to the rest of the managers.

"Mr. Begg's address is M'Queen's Lodgings, Newhaven, by Edinburgh."

It scarcely needs be said that Dr. Buchanan's giving of this recommendation at the request of his correspondent was a thing as different as possible from the practice denounced by Dr. Begg, and which, indeed, he was never weary of denouncing and ridiculing, the practice of soliciting testimonials on the part of probationers from men supposed to be influential. With such action as the former I do not see how any one can reasonably find fault; against such as the latter every man of honourable mind ought resolutely to set his face. So far as my knowledge or information goes, I do not think that the practice is so common as Dr. Begg believed it to be. It ought to cease absolutely. It is a plausible but invalid apology that it is done in self-defence, that if one competitor has recourse to it, others must also, or submit to be beaten. I do not believe that this would generally be the result of high-minded abstinence, for God favours the right. But if it were so, let not evil be done that good may come.

While no terms were too strong to express the sense in which I hold the evil of the practice in question, I would say two things concerning it. First, that, so far as my observation goes, the practice is not regular, but so exceptional, and so decreasing, that it may be fairly hoped it will soon cease altogether. Secondly, that of the three parties—the givers of such certificates, those in whose favour they are given, and the congregations or congregational committees to whom they are submitted—the blame rests upon the first and third much more than the second. If any "leading man"—a minister or professor, for example—had an intimate knowledge of *all* the probationers, and had undoubting confidence in his own power of judgment, he might very well arrange them in a classified or graduated series, and might give to each or to any of them a testimonial statement of the place which he occupied in the graduated leet. But for a man who has various degrees of acquaintance with some probationers, and none at all with most, to give to any one a certificate, whose value will depend upon its being understood as indicating its holder's superiority in the judgment of the certifier to others, is to do what ought not to be done. For it is to be borne in mind that certificates are evil only when they are used competitively. There is nothing more pleasant, as there is nothing more proper, than for a professor to bear frank testimony to the merits of a former student, or a minister to commend the ability and the faithfulness of his assistant, when the competition is at an end, and the question with the electors is no longer, *Whether this man or another?* and has come to be, *Whether this man or no?* This was the state of matters at Maxwelltown when Dr. Buchanan intervened, not at the request of Dr. Begg, and probably without his knowledge, but on the earnest application of those who were satisfied that in other respects this was the best man for them, but who earnestly desired the opinion of such a man as Dr. Buchanan respecting points on which he had better means of judging than any other.

I said that in the apportionment of the blame of the competitive-certificate offence, no small share lies at the door of those to whom they are to be presented. If there were no demand, the supply would dwindle and ere long cease. And if those on whom devolves the solemn duty of choosing a pastor for a congregation would seriously consider what is the most that such a certificate can possibly amount to, they would not be disposed to attach much value to it. I presume that no man ever certifies that he to whom the certificate is granted is the most eligible of all the probationers, or even that he is in every respect the best of all that the certifier knows. It ought to be considered that he who certifies that a particular probationer is possessed of certain good qualities would probably, with equal conscientiousness and equal truth, give the same attestation to a dozen others; while of course he has no doubt that there are many of whom he knows nothing, regarding whom it would be equally true. From the very nature of the case then, it follows that such certificates ought to have absolutely no competitive value assigned to them.

It was not to be expected that the young assistant to such a minister should exercise any very powerful influence over the large congregation, or over the inhabitants of the large parish. One who afterwards occupied the same position thus writes in familiar style:—" Any *sough* I might have heard, had I followed him immediately, had ceased to be audible ere I came on the field. None of us were much spoken of or thought of, or much more than tolerated, when filling the place which nobody almost was thought worthy to fill or fit to occupy but the minister himself, whose preaching in those days, when he was at all able, was certainly A 1."

Still, even to this later time there does come a *sough*, not altogether inaudible, though necessarily faint. There are, of course, but few survivors among Dr. Begg's North Leith hearers, and their recollection of his ministrations is but the recalling of childish impressions. But there are many who remember to have heard from their parents and other seniors that even his incipient ministry gave good guarantee of his attaining a high rank among preachers and pastors. From all that I have learned, I infer that his early preaching had much of the same character which distinguished his later; and this I should have expected. As it was characteristic of his mind that in advanced years he gave no token of senility, so it would appear that in his early days he exhibited less than an average amount of juvenility. The absence of the one and of the other was probably due mainly to the calmness of his temperament, and to the self-restraint which was in part constitutional, and was partly due to early discipline. I shall have many occasions to speak of his mental characteristics, and of his peculiarities as a preacher, a public speaker, and debater. But it may not be inappropriate here, in connection with his entrance upon his public career, to say a word on the subject. To me it always appeared that his success depended very much on his knowledge of the extent and the character of his own powers, and on his never attempting aught that was above these powers or outside of their range. His mind was one of great force, but of comparatively little subtlety. He seemed instinctively to know this, and therefore he confined himself to a forcible statement of the general scope and bearing of his subject, leaving minute details and nice distinctions to others who had more ability or more taste for them. Thus his preaching and his speaking were thoroughly popular. In his preaching was manifest his apprehension of the condition of *man* as a state of sin and misery, and his glorying in the gospel as the divine remedy for this condition. But he did not analyse so skilfully as others might the specially besetting sins and the specially poignant sorrows of particular *men*, and the special adaptation of the gospel in its infinitely various phases to these peculiarities. And so as an ecclesiastical debater his power lay—and he knew it—in advocating or in opposing the general principles of a proposal, and in refusing to be led into the discussion of minute points. This almost of necessity led to repetition and a lack of variety in his debating; and it would have occasioned a similar defect in his preaching, but for his almost unequalled knowledge of the Bible, and his rare power in quoting scriptural passages. It were too much to say that his quotations were always strictly apposite. But they were always interesting, and relieved by their variety what would have been the sameness of his own thought. Some one has said that preaching, to be effective, must resemble the art of the fresco, rather than that of the miniature painter. And the effectiveness of Dr. Begg's preaching was largely due to its fulfilment of this requirement.

CHAPTER X.

CHAPELS OF EASE—CALL TO MAXWELLTOWN—MINISTRY THERE.

It was certainly a somewhat remarkable coincidence that Dr. Begg's first visit to the General Assembly was during the discussion as to the sanctioning of the chapel of which he was to be the first minister. I suspect that in those days—however it may be in these—the first entrance of a young provincial into the General Assembly had a "disillusioning" effect. A country minister's son especially, accustomed from his childhood to hear the Assembly spoken of as a most venerable body, whose proceedings related to the most solemn and important events that can occupy the thoughts of men, was not likely to form a very accurate estimate of the way in which these proceedings were frequently, if not generally, conducted. I remember my own first entrance into the gallery of the General Assembly. It must have been, I think, in 1834. It was a "cause day," and Mr. Patrick Robertson was pleading at the bar. His speech, full of rough jokes, bitter sarcasm, and fierce invective, and the hearty laughter which it called forth, alike from "house" and gallery, were not in accordance with what I had expected when, with solemnised thoughts, I took my place for the first time in the students' gallery, prepared, if not to tread on holy ground, at least to gaze reverently upon a hallowed and hallowing scene. But there were occasions on which grave matters were discussed with gravity, and solemn subjects were treated with solemnity. I have no doubt that the discussion as to the Maxwelltown Chapel of Ease was grave enough.

It seems impossible to account for the undoubted fact of the opposition offered by the dominant party in the Church to the foundation of "Chapels of Ease." Of one thing there can be no doubt, that the erection and sanctioning of such chapels were recognised by the Church of Scotland in its best days as perfectly constitutional. The opposition offered by the Moderate party seems to have been intended mainly as a buttress to patronage; while yet it would appear that there was no way in which the evils of that system could more effectually have been made intolerable, than by depriving the parishioners of an unacceptable presentee of any relief within the bounds of the Established Church. The existence of a chapel in a parish did not, of course, interfere with the patronage of the parish. But it seems to have been feared—and probably with good reason—that the existence of such a chapel, whose members would have the right to elect their own minister, would lead to invidious and unfavourable comparisons between the people-elected and the patron-presented ministers, and so public opinion would be gradually formed in favour of election and in opposition to presentation. With a short-sighted policy, almost every proposal to erect a chapel was opposed by the minister of the parish to which the proposal referred, and in most cases the opposition was supported by the Moderate leaders. When this opposition could not be successful, care was taken to minimise the influence of the chapel minister. He was made merely a curate or assistant to the minister of the parish, with no separate kirk-session, no right to administer sealing ordinances except by arrangement with the minister and kirk-session of the parish, and with no right to a place in the Presbytery or higher Church courts. It was not until 1834 that these anomalies were rectified by the passing of an Act of Assembly which will come under our notice at a subsequent stage of this history, as its disallowance by the civil court in the deciding of the "Stewarton case" was one of the matters—and not the least important of them—which led to the Disruption in 1843.

As indicating the spirit of the opposition to the institution of chapels, I may refer to an Act of Assembly passed in 1798, which gave Presbyteries power to *refuse* an application for the institution of a chapel, but reserved to the General Assembly the power to *grant* such an application. From a pamphlet now before me,[1] published while the passing of this Act was under discussion, it appears that chapels were objected to on the following grounds, viz., (1) that they were a novelty, and (2) that their congregations were likely to be assemblies of narrow-minded and enthusiastic persons, whose opinions ought to be prevented from spreading. It was even argued that the chapel services would be occasions of propagating disloyal and revolutionary sentiments! In opposition to these objections the author of the pamphlet has no difficulty in showing that chapels were no novelty, but had existed and been recognised all through the history of the Church. In this connection he cites an Act of Assembly, 1647, for "pressing and furthering the plantation of kirks," the preamble of which is as follows:—

"The General Assembly, considering how the work of provision, plantation, convenient dividing, dismembering, better uniting, and enlarging of parish kirks as hitherto foreshowed, to the great prejudice of many ministers, many good people, and hindrance of the work of reformation, do ordain that all Presbyteries have special care that the present opportunity be diligently improved."

As to the strange charge of disloyalty, the author of the pamphlet of course declares that there was not a shadow of a foundation for it. He goes on to say:—

[1] "Address to the Members of the Church of Scotland on the subject of the Overtures and Regulations respecting Chapels of Ease. By a Moderate Clergyman of the Synod of Aberdeen. 1797." In the catalogue of the library of the New College, the author is stated to have been the Rev. Mr. Skene, Keith.

"Owing to some of the causes which shall be afterwards mentioned, a certain number of people wish to have a chapel of ease erected at their own expense. The minister of this chapel must be regularly educated, and first a licensed probationer, and afterwards an ordained clergyman of the Church of Scotland. Even after his ordination he must be subject to its discipline. As the livings of these chapels are, in many respects, inferior to those of the Establishment, the clergyman is generally in the expectation of being promoted to an Established Church; and in this he is often successful. Can it be supposed that such a man is not preferable, in the eyes of the Church of Scotland, to a Relief, an Antiburgher, a Burgher, or an Independent clergyman? Are not his people more to be favoured, as they wish to continue in the communion of the Church, than if they had left that communion? .... Such is the nature of all chapels of ease, so far as the Church is concerned with them.

"But are they disloyal meetings? In general, I certainly know that they are not disloyal. And indeed I do not approve of confounding political with religious opinions. The people of this country, of all descriptions, are loyal. Is not Dr. Young, whose essays[1] have been so generally read, a Seceder clergyman? From whom needs this country dread any harm to its constitution? Not surely from any description of Christians, but from the disciples of Thomas Payne, and men who have no religion at all. . . .

"The Church of Relief and the Seceders should contribute for a piece of plate to be presented to the framer of this overture. If it pass into a law, it will be a most beneficial law for these dissenters."

Dr. Begg's subsequent connection with chapels and with the chapel question was such as, independently of the coincidence of his first entrance into the Assembly with the dis-

---

[1] I presume that the work referred to is the following :—

"Essays on the following interesting subjects: viz. I. Government; II. Revolution; III. The British Constitution; IV. Kingly Government; V. Parliamentary Representation and Reform; VI. Liberty and Equality; VII. Taxation; VIII. The Present War and the Stagnation of Credit as connected with it. By John Young, Minister of the Gospel at Hawick." Glasgow, 1794.—T. S.

cussion of that question, to justify the transference to these pages, from the newspapers of the day, of the report of that discussion. The following is the report given in the *Edinburgh Evening Courant* of 1st June 1828. It may be proper to explain that Mr. Cockburn spoke from the bar as counsel for the petitioners, Mr. Turnbull for himself as minister of the parish, and Mr. Yorston for the Presbytery of Dumfries. These were the parties at the bar. The subsequent speakers were members of the House.

"The Assembly then proceeded to consider the case of the Maxwelltown Chapel of Ease. This question was an appeal against a sentence of the Presbytery of Dumfries[1] delaying to give judgment on an application for a chapel of ease, as to whether it was expedient or inexpedient.

"Mr. Cockburn, in explaining this case, would not enter into any large discussion of the principle on which chapels of ease were established. He considered that matter to resolve into a narrow point; but as it was necessary to look at the broad end of the case as well as the narrow point, he must lay before them a short view of the circumstances with which it originated. He repeated it would be short, for he considered the principle established by the Act of Assembly, 1798. He considered, according to that Act, that it might be taken for granted that if the Assembly wished to save the Church from being drowned by the encroaching tide of dissent on all sides, they must sanction the establishment of chapels of ease where the church could no longer accommodate the wants of the population. The learned gentleman proceeded to detail the facts and circumstances under which the application was made. From these it appeared that Maxwelltown, or Bridgeton of Dumfries, as it was wont to be named, is situated in the parish of Troqueer, and that the parish church, which only affords accommodation for 704 persons, is situated at a considerable distance from the town. The population of the parish by last census was 4654. Of these, 3187 were examinable persons, and the law requires that Church accommodation should be

---

[1] That is, an *appeal* on the part of the petitioners. There does not seem to have been any *dissent* by members of Presbytery.—T. S.

provided for two-thirds of that number, or 2124. But by recent decisions heritors are not bound to take down or rebuild a church unless that church is ruinous. The church had recently been examined, and a report made up, setting forth that it was not in a ruinous or dilapidated condition, though some portions of it required repairs. In the parish, exclusive of Roman Catholics, Episcopalians, and Dissenters, there were 3123 persons. Of those above twelve years of age there were 2138, consequently 1424 were beyond question entitled to church accommodation. The Presbytery, founding on the state of disrepair, had ordered the heritors to build a church that would accommodate 1500. But that judgment had been suspended and brought before the civil court, on the ground that while they were willing to repair the old, they would not build a new church; and according to the view of the law as it now stood, these heritors could not be compelled to build a new church. He next adverted to the application for the chapel of ease, and argued that the Presbytery was bound to decide upon its expediency or inexpediency, and ought not to have delayed the consideration of the petition. They had no right to found on their own act, decerning that a new church should be built, especially as they knew that a suspension had been taken out against their decision. The Presbytery being thus in the court, no man could anticipate when the action would terminate. Would his clients consent to remain shut out from the gospel till the question was decided, which may undergo a quinquennial discussion in the Court of Session, be appealed to the House of Lords, remitted back by an English Chancellor to the Court of Session, sent by that court to a jury on some matter of fact, against whose finding a bill of exceptions may be taken? Back it goes to the Court of Session, and the judges differ in opinion as to the meaning of the unanimous verdict of twelve honest men. He wished that his clients would wait all that time; but was it to be expected that they would? Would they not join the Secession, and be justified in doing so? And he maintained that if a history of the rise and progress of the Secession was prepared, it would show that in nine cases out of ten Secession churches had arisen from want of accommodation in parish churches.

"Mr. Turnbull, the minister of Troqueer, followed Mr.

Cockburn, arguing that the Presbytery could not have acted otherwise than as it had done. That court had given a judgment ordaining that church accommodation should be provided for 1500 persons, which finding was suspended, and, as he understood, that suspension just left matters as they were, but did not prevent subsequent arrangement. When the petition for the chapel of ease was presented, the question came to be, whether it was preferable that church accommodation should be given in the parish church or in a chapel of ease? The Presbytery could not proceed to consider the one until the other was disposed of. Besides, there were many persons interested. The kirk-session, who pay a large portion of the stipend,[1] were anxious that the new church proposed to be built should be in Maxwelltown, and implored the Presbytery to use means to accomplish that wish, but held that one church was sufficient. A body of the heritors were also desirous that the new church should be built in the burgh, and subscriptions to a considerable amount were obtained in a few days with that view. Matters seemed to be going on to an amicable arrangement, until some members of Presbytery turned round and insisted on having a church capable of holding 2200 persons. The consequence was that the heritors broke off the treaty. But he had still hopes of such an arrangement being effected as would obtain the building of a church sufficient to contain 1500, which, in the peculiar circumstances of the parish, would be ample accommodation for all that belonged to the Establishment. In these circumstances, the Presbytery had no other course but to vote for delay, for if a new church was built, there would be no occasion for a chapel of ease, and still less for both.

"Mr. John Yorston, for the Presbytery, followed in nearly a similar line of argument.

"Dr. Chalmers was disposed to treat this question on its broad and general merits. He considered the propriety of granting constitutions to chapels of ease as entirely a question of arithmetic—a question to be solved by numbers, and by no other consideration. Give me, said the Rev. Professor, a

[1] This must mean that individual members of the kirk-session, being also heritors, paid a large portion of the stipend. The kirk-session, as such, could have no such obligation.—T. S.

population where, after deducting two-thirds of the aggregate number of examinable persons who may be accommodated in the church, and if there be an excess sufficient to fill the chapel, then I would give it a constitution. He would hold that a parish in that situation had established a full ecclesiastical right to the erections claimed. . . . The law now declared that however populous a parish may be, and however small the church, if in repair, a new one need not be built. There was no relief but in a chapel of ease. It was physically impossible to compress a dense population into a house that would not contain a small fraction of the whole; yet the people were not to be suffered to expand themselves at the door and hear the gospel under the canopy of heaven. This he considered as an anomaly, and likely to prove deadly in its effects. He did not dread consequences from the outfields of sectarianism, but he feared a far more practical evil from the people being driven to the wilds of heathenism. He was convinced that in cases of this nature greater numbers go nowhere than go to dissenting places of worship, having uniformly observed that where accommodation cannot be procured in the Established Church, the Dissenters seldom pick up one-half of the surplus; and thus, from a want of religious instruction, a great proportion throw off the decencies of a Christian land. If the Assembly refused to sanction the erection of this chapel, Government would have good ground to refuse that in the gross which the Assembly refused in detail. It would therefore paralyse the efforts of the committee for obtaining additional church accommodation were they to refuse the offer now made, and it would look as if they were not sincere in the declaration made on a preceding day. How could they ask aid from Government, which was not bound to give anything, and refuse from the people, who offered to pay for all? The previous votes and opinions of that Assembly he held to be quite decisive of the point of the expediency of chapels of ease; and having supported the Glasgow overture, he could not vote for the chapel being refused without feeling that he was playing fast and loose with the same principle. He concluded by moving, in substance, that the Assembly should sustain the complaint and appeal, approve of the report of the committee, and find that in the case the Presbytery ought not to have delayed judging of the expediency; and remit to them to proceed in the subject according the laws of the Church, reserving the civil rights of all parties.

"After considerable discussion, Dr. Chalmers stated that he was satisfied that the Presbytery had acted rightly. He therefore withdrew that portion of the motion which implied a reflection on them. Thus modified, the motion was unanimously agreed to."

Dr. Begg's ministry at Maxwelltown was a brief one, but not unimportant. In addition to what is stated by himself in the autobiographic chapter, I have pleasure in inserting the following "memoranda," furnished to me, at my request, by Mr. George Henderson of Dumfries, an influential citizen of Dumfries, and a consistent promoter of all good objects:—

"In an address at his ministerial jubilee, Dr. Begg stated that the first time he was in the old Assembly they were discussing a question about whether a chapel should be built in a suburb of Dumfries which contained 2000 people. The minister was there, arguing strongly at the bar that no place of worship was needed in this suburb. It was, however, carried against him. The reference was to a 'chapel of ease' proposed to be built in Maxwelltown, a populous suburb of Dumfries, but situated in the parish of Troqueer—the parish from which Mr. John Blackadder was extruded in 1662. The late William Stothert, Esq. of Cargen, and other evangelical laymen in the parish, were the promoters of this movement. The chapel was built in 1829, and opened on the 13th December of that year by one of the evangelical ministers of the Presbytery of Dumfries. There was a large congregation on the occasion. The prospect of the people getting evangelical preaching, and of their having the choice of their minister, made the chapel quite popular from the first. It was a large building, capable of accommodating 1200 sitters. Seven probationers of the Church had been appointed to preach with a view to the election of a minister. The first of these preached on the Sabbath after the opening, 20th December 1829. There was a large congregation assembled, and a deep impression was produced by the young preacher, Mr. James Begg, who had never been heard of in this quarter, he being then a youth of little more than twenty-one. His text was Hebrews ii. 9, chiefly the words, 'Christ crowned with glory and honour.' After the seven had been heard, a short leet of three preached a second time in February 1830. The appointment of the first minister was in the hands of the shareholders, consisting of contributors to the building of the chapel to the amount of £10 and upwards. But a memorial was got up and signed by nearly all the sitters, anxiously requesting them to appoint Mr. Begg. This memorial was cordially complied with, and Mr. Begg was unanimously chosen as the first minister of Maxwelltown chapel. His ordination took place on the 18th of May following.[1] The

---

[1] The following "cutting" from the *Dumfries Courier* of May 25, 1830, has been kindly forwarded by Mr. Henderson :—

"ORDINATION.—On Tuesday last, the 18th current, the Rev. Mr. Begg, whose talents as a preacher and qualities as a man are best attested by the respectability of the parties who signed the call, and the formidable opposition he encountered and overcame, was formally ordained to the pastoral charge of the new chapel of ease, Maxwelltown. Large as this place of worship is, it was densely crowded in every part; and of the hundreds or thousands that approached its gates, many went away grievously disappointed that, after all their exertions, they could not possibly obtain admission. The services of the day were conducted by Rev. Mr. Wallace, Kirkpatrick-Durham, with a degree of earnestness, fervour, and eloquence which excited, we may safely say, the highest admiration. After the usual questions had been put by the preacher, and answered to the satisfaction of the Presbytery, the brethren present proceeded to the 'laying-on of hands,' a very beautiful and imposing ceremony, which very seldom fails to excite in the most callous minds feelings alike solemn and soul-subduing. As is customary on all similar occasions, Mr. Begg, previous to the dismissal of the congregation, repaired to the principal gate of the chapel, and, as the worshippers withdrew, received the cordial greetings, not only of his own people, but, we believe, of every individual who had the happiness to witness his ordination.

"On Sunday Mr. Begg was introduced to his flock by the Rev. Mr. Buchanan, minister of North Leith. The character and acquirements of this reverend gentleman are well known; and as his name has gone abroad among the Churches, he requires no eulogy of ours. His sermon was at once impressive and appropriate. He preached from 2 Cor. v. 20, and in the course of a truly eloquent discourse did every justice to his young friend, without overstepping the modesty of nature, or violating in the smallest tittle that propriety which so well befits the dignity of the pulpit. In the afternoon Mr. Begg himself addressed the congregation in a manner that confirmed, deepened, and strengthened the lively impression he had previously made on them."—T. S.

novelty of the occasion and the popularity of the young minister attracted a large congregation. On the following Sabbath Mr. Begg was introduced by Rev. James Buchanan of North Leith, to whom he had previously been assistant. In the afternoon Mr. Begg commenced his ministry, and preached from the text Luke xv. 7. The crowd was again very great. A series of discourses was at once commenced by the young minister, intended to illustrate in a systematic way the great facts and doctrines of the Bible, very much in the order of the Shorter Catechism.

"It is well known that Dumfries and the district around, like many other parts of Scotland, had long suffered under the blighting influence of Moderatism. There were a few evangelical ministers who preached the gospel faithfully, but the preaching of the great majority was of that dry and sapless or merely moral kind which was characteristic of that system. In the dearth of evangelical preaching, the fluency and fervour with which the eloquent young minister declared the great doctrines of the gospel in their simplicity and fulness produced a great impression, and drew many to hear him, not only from the town, but from the surrounding parishes also. So much was this the case, that at times not only were the pews occupied, but the window-sills and pulpit-stairs were also filled.

"Mr. Begg's work was not confined to the pulpit. He immediately began classes for young people, which met on week-nights, the young women meeting at seven o'clock, the young men at eight. These classes were largely attended, each numbering about sixty. The subject taken up was the Shorter Catechism, and the whole of it was gone over during the six months of his ministry in Maxwelltown. Mr. Begg was also most diligent in the visitation of his large and widely-scattered flock, sometimes walking many miles a day in overtaking this work. His first communion was dispensed in the month of November, and nearly 500 became members of the congregation, of whom a large proportion of those who had attended his classes were admitted as 'young communicants.' The number would have been much larger if a rumour had not arisen, some weeks before, of the likelihood of his removal to Edinburgh. This produced a depressing effect on the congregation, who had become very much attached to their young minister, and were much cast-down at the prospect of losing him. This prospect was, unfortunately, too speedily realised, as, on the Sabbath after the communion, the pulpit was occupied by a stranger, the late Dr. Gemmel of Fairlie, while Mr. Begg occupied the minister's pew, both forenoon and afternoon. Mr. Begg left for Edinburgh on the following day. This was a great disappointment, not only to the congregation, but to the general community, and much feeling was shown and regret expressed at so unexpectedly losing such an earnest and useful minister. In the following summer Mr. Begg revisited Dumfries, and preached in his former place of worship, when seats and passages were filled, and numbers could not gain admittance. His text on that occasion was 1 Cor. xv. 1–3, and his discourse was listened to with great attention by the crowded congregation."

The manner of the termination of Dr. Begg's ministry in Maxwelltown must excite surprise in the minds of all who have an idea of the perfection of the ecclesiastical arrangements of the Presbyterian Church in earlier days. To me the statement of Mr. Henderson as to the close of Dr. Begg's connection with the Maxwelltown Chapel was utterly unintelligible. It appeared that there was no presbyterial action in the matter; that the Presbytery had no part in the dissolution of the pastoral tie which they had so recently formed; that there was neither a "resignation" accepted by the Presbytery, nor a "translation" agreed to by the Presbytery of Dumfries at the instance of the Presbytery of Edinburgh. An application to Mr. Henderson brought the reply that he was as little able as I to give any account of the *rationale* of the proceeding, but that the facts were as he had stated them. Through the kindness of the Rev. Mr. Gillespie of Kirkgunzeon, clerk of the Presbytery of Dumfries, I am able to state more definitely what really took place. On learning that he had been elected as assistant and successor to Dr. Jones, Mr. Begg addressed to the "managers" of the Maxwelltown Chapel his resignation of that charge, which was accepted *by them*. A week after his induction to Lady Glenorchy's, the

Presbytery of Edinburgh intimated to the Presbytery of Dumfries that he had been so inducted; and it was only then and thus that the latter Presbytery became officially cognisant of the transaction! This certainly indicates that I have not exaggerated the anomaly of the relations of chapels of ease in those days to the Church of Scotland. It shows that the minister of such a chapel was merely the *employé* of the managers. I do not suppose that they could dismiss their servant; but it is manifest that they had the irresponsible power to negotiate with him respecting his resignation, and this would not differ widely in practice from the power of dismissal.

As Mr. Gillespie's letter contains a reference to a subject to which I have only alluded—the relation of the Maxwelltown congregation to the kirk-session of Troqueer—it may be well to quote the letter in full:—

"THE MANSE, KIRKGUNZEON,
26th August 1884.

"REV. AND DEAR SIR,—I am sorry I have been unable to reply sooner to your letter of the 15th. I find from the Presbytery Records that on the 1st December 1829 the 'managers' of the chapel of ease at Maxwelltown obtained the sanction of the Presbytery to hear the following candidates:—Mr. James Begg, Dr. James Gardiner, Mr. Henry Gordon, Mr. W. M'Lean, Mr. Henry Riddel, and Mr. John Clugston. On the 17th March 1830 there was laid before the Presbytery a minute of election by the 'shareholders' of the chapel in favour of Mr. Begg to be minister, which was sustained, along with other relative documents. Mr. Begg's call was moderated on the 23d of April, his ordination trials were taken on the 4th May, and he was ordained on the 18th May 1830. Mr. Wallace of St. Michael's, Dumfries, preached and presided at the ordination, and among the ministers present I find the name of the Rev. Dr. Begg of New Monkland. The record states that Mr. Begg was ordained 'to be minister of the chapel of ease at Maxwelltown, and statedly to labour and officiate in said chapel.'

"By the constitution of the chapel the sacrament of the

Lord's Supper was to be dispensed twice a year, at the same time as in the parish church. The members of the kirk-session being all required at Troqueer, the Presbytery authorised Mr. Begg to ordain *deacons* to assist in dispensing the sacrament.

"The only other reference to Mr. Begg is on the 5th of January 1831, when his letter of resignation was read. The following are the terms of the minute referring to the matter:—'There was produced and read a letter from Mr. Begg, stating his resignation of the chapel of ease in Maxwelltown. There was also produced a certified extract from the Records of the Presbytery of Edinburgh, testifying that on the 25th[1] December 1830 they had admitted Mr. Begg to be assistant and successor to the Rev. Dr. Jones, as minister of Lady Glenorchy's Chapel. The Presbytery sustained Mr. Begg's resignation of the chapel of ease in Maxwelltown.' It would appear from the terms of the constitution of Maxwelltown Chapel, which was approved by the General Assembly of 1829, that the minister's resignation to the managers became valid without the intervention of the Presbytery.—I am," &c.

[1] 24th?—T. S.

CHAPTER XI.

LADY GLENORCHY'S CHAPEL, EDINBURGH.

THE chapel of Lady Glenorchy, to the joint-pastorate of which Dr. Begg was now removed, had a constitution which, so far as I know, was unique in Scotland. Its relation to the Church of Scotland was not very clearly defined. That relation was closely connected with its history, and in order to make the former intelligible, some attention must be given to the latter—a history which in itself is deeply interesting. The facts of that history I gather from the Life of Lady Glenorchy by the Rev. Dr. Jones.[1]

Willielma Maxwell was one of the two daughters of William Maxwell, Esq. of Preston in Kirkcudbrightshire. She was a posthumous child, and was born on the 2d of September 1741. Mrs. Maxwell, twelve years after the death of her husband, became the wife of Lord Alva, one of the Judges of the Court of Session, who afterwards became Lord Justice-Clerk; and the two young ladies grew to womanhood as members of the family of their stepfather. "The Misses Maxwell," says Lady Glenorchy's biographer, "were in their day celebrated for their beauty, accomplishments, and amiable manners, as well as for their fortune. Their mother, lofty and ambitious, had from their infancy destined them, in her own mind, to the attainment, by

---

[1] "The Life of the Right Honourable Willielma, Viscountess Glenorchy, containing Extracts from her Diary and Correspondence. By T. S. Jones, D.D., Minister of her Chapel, Edinburgh. Second edition. Edinburgh, 1824."

marriage, of high rank." The ambitious mamma was more successful than matchmaking mammas sometimes are. The elder daughter became Countess of Sutherland, and the second, in 1761, became Viscountess Glenorchy, her husband being the only son and heir-apparent of the proud title and immense estates of the Earl of Breadalbane. In the year following the marriage Lord Glenorchy became, through the death of his mother, the actual owner of a good estate in Staffordshire. A year after Lord Glenorchy's marriage, from the time of Lady Breadalbane's death, the Earl virtually made over to his son and daughter-in-law his house in Edinburgh and his noble castle of Taymouth, and for the remainder of his son's life lived with them as their guest rather than their host.

At the time of her marriage Lady Glenorchy was entirely a woman of the world, a lover of pleasure more than of God; but feeble health and a severe illness led her to reflection, and occasional residence in Staffordshire brought her into intimate association with the family of Sir Rowland Hill. Her intercourse with this family, and especially with Miss Hill, a young lady of her own age, was the means of her conversion to God. From this time she lived a life of much devotedness, setting herself very strenuously in opposition to the vanities of the world, and especially to the gaieties of the fashionable portion of it, exercising a constant, painful jealousy over her own heart, and striving to relieve the sufferings and promote the temporal and spiritual welfare of all around her. Her diaries, of which large portions are given in her biography, are full of bitter self-condemnation, and of lamentation over her lack of joy, and even of peace, in believing. It must be confessed that these diaries do not give the idea of Christian healthfulness. The want of it was probably due, in some measure, to constitutional physical causes, and partly also to a particular abiding sorrow, to which there are none but the vaguest allusions, but whose nature it is not difficult to perceive. Probably, however, her Ladyship was far more cheerful through all the hours of the day than she was during the hour or half-hour which she spent in self-censorious introspection, and in recording her estimate of the result. It is to state the matter very mildly to say that her husband had no sympathy with the mode of life to which she was led by her religious views; and it is quite conceivable that, without any unfaithfulness or sinful compromise, she might have been somewhat more conciliatory, with a better hope that he might be "won by the conversation of the wife." This, however, is manifest, that he ever regarded her with great respect, and seldom or never attempted to oppose her efforts to do good in her own way, although he made no secret of it that that way was not his. It would appear, however, that he gradually came to take some interest in these efforts, and ultimately was willing to render them an aid as little strenuous as had been his original opposition. This would appear, at all events, from his will, to which I shall have to refer ere long. It should be mentioned, too, that the fine old chieftain, Lord Breadalbane, uniformly treated his daughter-in-law, not only with the noblest and highest-toned courtesy, but also with fatherly tenderness. All through Lord Glenorchy's life, and perhaps still more after his death, the Earl took care in countless ways to make Lady Glenorchy feel that she was his own beloved daughter, and none the less although she was not destined to prevent the extinction of his noble line.

In various works of well-doing, in unceasing endeavours to induce her relatives, her dependents, and her neighbours of every class to give heed to the things belonging to their peace, and in the exercise of bountiful but judicious liberality to the poor—but frequently in bitterness of spirit, from a sense of unworthiness and a morbid jealousy of her motives and affections,—Lady Glenorchy spent some six years from the time of her conversion (1765-71). In November of the latter year Lord Glenorchy died. "His last days and hours," says her biographer, "showed that the religious sentiments with which Lady Glenorchy had endeavoured to impress his mind were not altogether lost." The biographer goes on to say:—

"Lady Glenorchy's feelings on this trying occasion may be better conceived than expressed. In the prime of her life and noonday of her prosperity, to be deprived of one who, with all his failings, stood in the near relation of her husband, to whom she had been united for a period of ten years, who undoubtedly had a high esteem and ardent affection for her, and with whose life was connected the continuance and increase of her wealth and honours, must to any woman have been a very great and afflicting bereavement. And although Lady Glenorchy, as became an exemplary Christian, summoned up all her religious principles to her support on this occasion, she felt deeply her loss, and, as is usual in such cases, forgot the failings of her deceased lord, while the instances of his kindness and affection were recalled to memory with peculiar interest. There were seasons, indeed, when these recollections came more forcibly into her mind than others; but even on such occasions, when her heart was under the overwhelming influence of grief, she became gradually calm and serene by the mild and consoling influences of true religion. In short, it is to her pure and elevated piety that we are to attribute that firmness and composure which she endeavoured to exhibit in circumstances which, even taking everything into account, would have overset the mind of a person in her situation, under so painful and unexpected a bereavement, who was a stranger to the views and principles and feelings which Christianity alone can inspire and maintain. This stroke was unquestionably the severest which Lady Glenorchy ever felt."

It may not be out of place to remark in passing, by way of annotation to this extract, that it seems to be in questionable taste to represent the climax of the widow's grief as consisting in the consideration that her husband's death put an end to her prospect of becoming Countess of Breadalbane. But let that pass.

I have already referred to Lord Glenorchy's will. It was entirely in favour of his wife. He bequeathed to her unreservedly the estate of Barnton, near Edinburgh, having previously sold his Staffordshire property, and invested the proceeds, and a good deal more, in the purchase of this estate. Besides this he assigned to her, "for the favour and affection which he bore to her, all his plate, furniture, linen, pictures, prints and books, and everything over which he had a disposing power, making her his sole executrix and legatee." It is specially interesting to note, as indicating the sympathy with which he had begun to regard her evangelistic zeal, that he gave "full power to the said Willielma, Viscountess Glenorchy, upon [his] decease, to convert the whole of [his] said estate, means, and effects hereby conveyed into money, and to employ or bestow the whole, or such part thereof as she shall see cause, for encouraging the preaching of the gospel, and promoting the knowledge of the Protestant religion, erecting schools, and civilising the inhabitants of Breadalbane, Glenorchy, Nether Lorn and other parts of the Highlands of Scotland, in such a way and manner as she shall judge proper and expedient."

Lady Glenorchy had thus become a rich woman. Dr. Jones speaks of the "fortune" of Miss Maxwell as contributing, with her "beauty, accomplishments, and amiable manners," to make her an eligible bride for a man of "high rank." What the amount of this fortune was I do not know. It may be presumed that it would be "settled on herself" by a marriage contract. Then I find an incidental reference to a jointure of £1000 a year, which would, I suppose, be a burden on the Breadalbane estates. Lastly, Barnton was sold for £28,000, which, invested at 4 per cent., would yield her £1120 a year. Thus she must have had an annual income of about £3000, which was a large income in those days. Then her personal expenditure must have been but small, as the old Earl more and more, with advancing years, clung to her, and almost demanded that she should be with him in one or other of his splendid mansions.

Before this time, while her income was smaller and less under her own control, Lady Glenorchy had already spent considerable sums of money in providing church accommodation and the supply of Christian ordinances to the poor of Edinburgh. Thus in 1770 she had rented Mary's Chapel—once a Romish place of worship—in Niddry's Wynd, and had arranged for services—apparently daily—to be conducted by ministers of all evangelical denominations. From this she was dissuaded by some of her chiefest friends, ministers of the Established Church, but was as warmly supported by others. Of the former class, the most strenuous was Mr. Walker, her own pastor and her most valued friend. On the other hand was Dr. Webster, who was all for "Evangelical Alliance," and who frequently conducted the services, while Mr. Walker decidedly refused to have aught to do with them. His objection, and that of other friends, was to co-operation with Wesleyans. Lady Glenorchy herself was strongly Calvinistic; but Lady Maxwell—probably a relative—her life-long friend and chief coadjutrix, was herself a Wesleyan; and for a time Lady Glenorchy consented to admit "Mr. Wesley's preachers" into the pulpit of Mary's Chapel.

In the course of 1772, only a few months after the death of her husband, Lady Glenorchy resolved to erect a church in Edinburgh, which should be in connection with the Established Church, but which should not, like the chapels of ease previously referred to, be connected with, or subordinate to, the church of the parish within whose bounds it might be situated. She set about the execution of her resolution with great energy. A site was purchased in what was then called the Orphan Park, overlooked by the North Bridge, and now forming part of the Waverley Station of the North British Railway. On the 11th of August 1772 she was able to give orders that the work should be proceeded with, and on the

8th of May 1774 the church was opened for public worship. It was a plain substantial structure, void of ornament, but comfortably seated for 2000 people, while it could, without any great pressure, hold some 500 more. It is necessary that I should dwell at some little length on the relation in which the chapel was to stand towards the Established Church.

When the building was nearly completed, as Lady Glenorchy had intended that her chapel should be in full communion with the Established Church, she wrote to the Presbytery of Edinburgh in the following terms:—

To the Rev. the Moderator of the Presbytery of Edinburgh.

"REV. SIR,—It is a general complaint that the churches of this city that belong to the Establishment are not proportionate to the number of its inhabitants. Many who are willing to pay rent for seats cannot obtain them, and no space is left for the poor but the remoter areas, where few of those who find room to stand can get within hearing of an ordinary voice. I have thought it my duty to employ part of that substance with which God has been pleased to intrust me in building a chapel within the Orphan House Park, in which a considerable number of our communion, who at present are altogether unprovided, may enjoy the comfort and benefit of the same ordinances that are dispensed in their parish churches, and where I hope to have the pleasure of accommodating some hundreds of poor people who have long been shut out from one of the best, and to some of them the only, means of being instructed in the principles of our holy religion. The chapel will soon be ready to receive a congregation, and it is my intention to have it supplied with a minister of approved character and abilities, who shall give security for his soundness in the faith and his loyalty to Government. It will give me pleasure to be informed that the Presbytery approve of my general design, and that it will be agreeable to them that I ask occasional supply from such ministers and probationers as I am acquainted with till a congregation be formed and supplied with a stated minister; and I beg you will do me the favour to present this letter, with my respectful compliments, to the Rev. Presbytery of Edinburgh at their first meeting.—I am, Rev. Sir, your most humble servant, W. GLENORCHY."

The answer of the Presbytery, through their clerk, was as follows:—

"The Presbytery unanimously approved of Lady Glenorchy's general design, and desired that she might be informed that her asking occasional supply from such ministers and probationers as her Ladyship is acquainted with till a congregation is formed and supplied with a stated minister will be agreeable to the Presbytery."

The opening services were conducted by Dr. John Erskine and Mr. Walker, who preached respectively from Prov. viii. 33, 34, and from Gal. vi. 15. "The few persons who survive," says Dr. Jones, "speak of this day with much satisfaction and delight. Fervent prayers for the usefulness of this institution were offered up to Almighty God, which we have every reason to hope and believe have already been heard and answered, and will be answered for ages and generations yet to come."

At this time there was serene weather and plain sailing, but a storm was brewing, and there were rocks ahead. While the Presbytery had, after a sort, accepted the chapel as a gift to the Church, and were proverbially precluded from a critical examination of the gift-horse's mouth, it was natural that they should inquire whether it were really a gift at all, or, if a gift it were, on what terms or with what conditions it was given. There was nothing determined as yet respecting the constitution which was to be given to the chapel, or the relation which it, its ministers, and its people, were to sustain to the Established Church. Looking back, after the lapse of more than a century, I cannot but think that the controversy which was soon to ensue between Lady Glenorchy and the Presbytery of Edinburgh was the natural and inevitable result of the indefiniteness of the proposal which her Ladyship made, and which the Presbytery accepted. Lady Glenorchy's letter, which I have quoted, gives really no information on these points. The chapel was to supply ordinances to a considerable number of *our* "communion," and the Presbytery was asked to "approve of the general design," and did express approbation of it. But the "general design" might be carried out in many ways, and the Presbytery did not ask, and, if they had asked, I doubt if Lady Glenorchy could have given, any information as to the details; for I do not think she had as yet formed any very distinct conception of the constitution and character of the chapel. It might be Presbyterian, or it might be Congregationalist, or it might be Episcopal. Probably her ideal was a mixture of the three. Well, that may be the very highest and the very best ideal of Christian unity; but it was not an ideal that could be grafted on the Presbyterian Church of Scotland. It might have been foreseen that "the little rift within the lute" would widen and become manifest under the vibration which must ensue in connection with the appointment of a minister; and so it did. Mr. Groves, an English Nonconformist, officiated in the chapel, at Lady Glenorchy's request, for the last three months of 1774, and again for the last three of 1775. The congregation generally were very desirous that he should be their permanent minister, and Lady Glenorchy did not think it right to oppose their wish. But when she intimated his nomination to the Presbytery, they desired to have some better security than was actually forthcoming for his doctrinal and ecclesiastical soundness. Mr. Groves, who held strongly anti-Establishment views, and who knew that these would not pass muster with the Presbytery, proposed that the connection, such as it was, between the chapel and the Established Church should be broken, and that he should enter upon its ministry as an Independent. To this Lady Glenorchy would not assent, and Mr. Groves returned to England.

Lady Glenorchy next attempted to obtain the services of a minister of the Church of Scotland, apparently in the expectation that the Presbytery would recognise him simply as a minister of the Church, over whom they could exercise control as living within their bounds, without seeking to define the power which they should have over him as minister of the chapel, or over the chapel itself. Amongst the ministers of the Established Church, or of any other Church, a happier choice could not have been made than of Mr. Robert Balfour, who was then minister of the parish of Lecropt, in the Presbytery of Dunblane. Mr. Balfour agreed to resign his charge and to accept Lady Glenorchy's nomination to her chapel. Lady Glenorchy intimated this to the Presbytery, and requested them to "countenance his admission to the chapel by appointing one of their number to preach on the occasion." The Presbytery expressed their hearty approbation of the choice of Mr. Balfour, but requested further information respecting several matters. On the report of a committee appointed to confer with Lady Glenorchy on these matters, a majority of the Presbytery agreed that as soon as they should be certified of Mr. Balfour's resignation of his charge of Lecropt having been accepted, they would appoint Dr. Webster to preach on the occasion of his admission to Lady Glenorchy's Chapel. A minority, however, dissented and complained to the Synod. As this involved delay and suspense to both the congregations, Mr. Balfour thought it best to withdraw his acceptance of the nomination, and withdrew it accordingly. Shortly after he accepted a call to one of the churches in Glasgow, where he soon became, and long continued, one of the most noted and the most influential ministers of his day.

It might have been expected that in these new circumstances the dissentients would have fallen from their complaint. But they did not do so; and on the motion of the celebrated Dr. Carlyle of Inveresk, the Synod sustained the dissent and complaint, reversed the judgment of the Presbytery, and further discharged all the ministers and probationers within their bounds from officiating in the said chapel, and further discharged the ministers of the Church from employing the minister of the said chapel to officiate for them. The reversal of the Presbytery's resolution to appoint Dr. Webster to preach at the admission of Mr. Balfour was, of course, of no consequence, as it had become a dead letter through Mr. Balfour's having declined to be admitted; but the gratuitous addition to the reversal of the judgment was felt to be intolerable, and an appeal was taken to the General Assembly. After two days' discussion, in which the leading men on both sides of the Church took part—for it had become really a party question—the Assembly pronounced the following judgment:—

"The Assembly, waiving the consideration of the first part of the Synod's sentence, disapproving of the Presbytery's appointing Dr. Webster to introduce Mr. Balfour to the chapel by preaching on that occasion, agreed, without a vote, to reverse, and hereby do reverse, the second part of the Synod's sentence, prohibiting all the ministers and probationers within their bounds to officiate in the said chapel, and discharging the ministers of this Church to employ any minister of the said chapel to officiate for them; and in case the matter shall again be brought before the Presbytery, the Assembly recommend to them to take proper care that the person to be admitted to the said chapel conform himself to the standards of the Church."

Thus the storm had spent itself, and a blink of fair weather supervened. But it did not last. Lady Glenorchy's attention had been directed to Mr. Sheriff, who had been licensed by the Presbytery of Haddington, and ordained by them to the chaplaincy of a Scottish regiment. The regiment was on active service in Holland, and Mr. Sheriff's physical strength was not adequate to the roughing of a campaign. He was therefore invalided, and accepted the offer which

Lady Glenorchy made him of temporary or probational service in her chapel. It was evident that he was unfit for the two services in so large a church; but so favourable was the impression which he made, that it was earnestly desired to obtain so much service as he was able to render. Lady Glenorchy therefore proposed that he should accept the appointment, and that she should provide him with an assistant. He did accept. But his race was run. He preached only twice in the chapel after his appointment, and the commandment came, "Go up higher."

After a somewhat protracted and eventually unsuccessful negotiation with Mr. Hodgson, minister of Carmunnock, Lady Glenorchy's eyes were again turned southward. One of the trustees of the chapel, Mr. Dickie, went at her request to London to confer with Mr. Clayton, who had just begun a ministry in one of the Nonconformist congregations in the metropolis,—a ministry destined to be a long and an eminent one. Lady Glenorchy also wrote to Mr. Jones, with whom she had become acquainted in England, and of whom she had formed a very favourable opinion, requesting him to co-operate with Mr. Dickie in endeavouring to persuade Mr. Clayton to come to Edinburgh. Mr. Clayton declined the invitation, but Lady Glenorchy's correspondence with Mr. Jones suggested her addressing the same invitation to him, and he accepted it. Mr. Jones was a Congregational minister in Devonshire; but he received Presbyterial ordination in London, and entered upon the ministry of the chapel, apparently without any recognition on the part of the Presbytery. But a year after he presented himself before the Presbytery of Edinburgh, signed the formula in their presence, and "expressed, in proper terms, that though he did not enjoy the emoluments of the Establishment, it would always give him the highest satisfaction to be in communion with the ministers and members of this Church." Thus endeth this Iliad.

I do not anticipate a *consensus* of judgment on the part of readers and critics as to the propriety of introducing this long statement, as preliminary to a very brief account of Dr. Begg's very brief ministry in Lady Glenorchy's Chapel. I can only say that without some knowledge of the previous history of the constitution of the chapel, and its anomalous and indefinite relation to the Established Church, it would be impossible to form a right estimate of Dr. Begg's action, either in coming to it or so soon leaving it.

The ministry of Dr. Jones was long and successful. During a period when in many—indeed, in most—of the Edinburgh churches there was a "famine of the word," many of the most earnest Christians in the city found in Lady Glenorchy's a supply of that "pure milk of the word" which was denied them elsewhere. The result was that there was probably no congregation in Scotland which contained so large a number of intelligent and zealous Christians; while it may be freely admitted that the position of semi-antagonism and of virtual protest which they were constrained to occupy was unfavourable to the development of large-heartedness or catholicity of spirit. So far as I can judge from Dr. Jones's published sermons,[1] he was a man of more than average ability, with much power of clear exposition of Christian doctrine, and of earnest inculcation of Christian duty. The preface or dedication of this volume appears to me to be an exceptionally elegant and excellent specimen of a peculiarly difficult department of literature; and on this account, rather than on account of any germaneness to the matter in hand, beyond the desirableness of casting some measure of light on the position occupied by his assistant, I take the liberty of transferring it bodily to these pages. It is as follows:—

---

[1] "Sermons by Thomas Snell Jones, D.D., Minister of Lady Glenorchy's Chapel, Edinburgh. Printed at the desire of the Congregation, to whom they were originally preached. Edinburgh, 1816."

"To the Trustees and Gentlemen of the Vestry, and to the Individual Members of the Congregation of Lady Glenorchy's Chapel, Edinburgh.—Thirty-seven years ago, by the instrumentality of the foundress of your chapel, the good providence of the Almighty brought me to minister in your place of worship; and, having obtained help of God, I continue unto this day. In the prospect, however, of the period when my ministry among you must cease, you have requested me to put a volume of my sermons into your hands, that you may give them to your children, as a memorial of what you have heard. Take, then, this volume, and let it be the memorial you desire. When the records of eternity shall be revealed, it will appear that these sermons were composed and delivered with a sincere and ardent desire to speak, and to speak only, the truth of Christ, and by that truth to promote your edification and salvation. If I shall obtain this important object with respect to you, and if you, by presenting these to your children, shall obtain a similar object with respect to them, I shall, on this head, have but one desire more, which is, that if any copies of this book shall find their way beyond the limits of your congregation, the same design may also be accomplished in those who shall thus receive them. In this event, I shall certainly be more disposed to say, at my departure, that I go in peace.

T. S. Jones."

"Edinburgh, *July* 25, 1816."

Dr. Jones lived for many years after this, and for ten of these years he discharged unaided the laborious duties of his large and important congregation. But while his eye was not dim, and his mental and bodily strength was little abated, I have learned from those who in those now distant years were juvenile attendants in the chapel, that his enunciation became very indistinct, and that it was with difficulty that they were able to follow him, while their seniors with sadness missed the ring of the voice which they loved so well to hear. Not too soon, therefore, did he give ear to the warning voice—

> "Solve senescentem mature sanus equum, ne
> Peccet ad extremum ridendus, et ilia ducat."

In 1826 he consented to the appointment of an assistant and successor. Mr. John Purves was accordingly appointed, and laboured with much acceptance until he was removed to Jedburgh, where he died a few years ago, after a distinguished ministry in the Established and the Free Church of more than half a century's duration.

Mr. Begg was elected to succeed Mr. Purves in Lady Glenorchy's, and was inducted by the Presbytery on the 24th of December 1830. The following brief paragraph must have been "communicated" to the newspapers, as I find it *verbatim* in the *Courant* and the *Scotsman* of the following day :—"Thursday, the Presbytery of Edinburgh met in Lady Glenorchy's Chapel for the purpose of inducting the Rev. Mr. Begg, of Maxwelltown Chapel of Ease, as assistant and successor to the Rev. Dr. Jones, in room of the Rev. J. Purves, removed to Jedburgh. The Rev. Dr. Lee, of Lady Yester's Church, presided on the occasion, and preached an excellent and appropriate discourse from Romans i. 14, 15, 16."

From this it appears that the Presbytery had now no scruple in recognising the chapel as having some sort of connection with the Church of Scotland, and their interest in it was manifested by their appointing Dr. Lee, one of the most eminent of their members, to conduct the service. But I believe that the precise nature of the relation between the chapel and its ministers on the one hand, and the Presbytery and the Church of Scotland on the other, had never been properly defined, and that, indefinite as it was, it was unsatisfactory to both parties. It may have been noticed, for example, that in the dedication which I have quoted, Dr. Jones designates a certain class of men in the congregation by the un-Scottish and un-Presbyterian term, "gentlemen of the vestry." I presume that this was because it might have given offence to the High Church section of the Presbytery had he called them "elders," or represented them as unitedly constituting a "kirk-session"!

Thus Dr. Begg's ministry in Lady Glenorchy's began with the year 1831, and with this, it may be said, began his life as a public man. From this time onward, to the close of his life in 1883, he occupied a prominent position in the public view, exercising a potent influence over the sentiments of his countrymen, and taking a considerable part in the discussions and in the events of that most notable half-century. It was well for him that at the outset of his career he had no temptation to turn aside from pastoral work into the devious paths of ecclesiasticism. We have seen that as a chapel minister, first at Maxwelltown, and now in Edinburgh, he had no proper ecclesiastical standing, and so was for the time excluded from a department which would certainly have had a seductive attraction for him, while yet he was not prepared to take part in it with safety to himself. He was all the better ecclesiastic in due time, because he was at first constrained to give his mind without distraction to his work as a preacher and a pastor. His experience gained in the study and the pulpit, and in the sick-rooms and by the death-beds of his people, shielded him from the dangers which beset the path of the mere ecclesiastic, habituating him to the consideration that the ecclesiastical department is of importance, mainly or solely, as subordinate and subsidiary to the pastoral and the spiritual. I do not say that this conviction abode always with him, or that it can be expected to abide always with any man who is much occupied with the discussion of ecclesiastical questions, or the making or regulating of ecclesiastical arrangements. But I can testify of him, more than of many "Church leaders" with whom I have been brought into contact, that in the thick of many an ecclesiastical fray, the paramount consideration with him was as to the bearing of this or that decision on the spiritual interests of our people. I may be permitted to say in passing that the principle which I have ventured to lay down with reference to this matter is capable of indefinite extension, and of application to all the legitimate pursuits of ministers of the gospel. The most laborious researches, historical or critical, or the most extensive acquaintance with science, literature, history, poetry, or whatever else, are right or wrong, safe or unsafe, for our ministers, according as they are, or are not, kept in subordination to the great work of the ministry, the converting of sinners to God, the edifying of the body of Christ. It were well, let me say, that our ministers, in the earlier years of their ministry, should give themselves undividedly and undistractedly to this work. When once their minds and their hearts have been thoroughly imbued with the pastoral habit, and experience has shown them at once the responsibility and the blessedness of the pastoral work, then that which would else have been a snare will be a help, and all acquisitions in whatever field will contribute to their efficiency in their proper work.

> "Quo semel est imbuta recens, servabit odorem
> Testa diu."

And not only does the jar retain the flavour of its first contents; it imparts it also to what is afterwards put into it.

It is therefore chiefly, or almost exclusively, as a preacher that we have to do with Dr. Begg at this stage of his career. And as at previous stages, so at this, we find among surviving members of the congregation little more than a general impression of great earnestness, and of remarkable fecundity of scriptural quotation. In the Autobiography reference is made to the Bonars as having been worshippers in the chapel during his incumbency. On application to Drs. Horatius and Andrew A. Bonar, I have received the following notes.

Dr. Andrew writes from his holiday retreat as follows:—

"Isle of Mull, 28th August 1884.

"My dear Dr. Smith,—I remember the days when I sat

in Lady Glenorchy's listening to Dr. Begg pouring out Scripture upon Scripture in full flood. But there is nothing definite to tell beyond the fact that he kept his hearers interested, young as well as old, throughout the whole service. My brother Horatius may probably recall those days better than I can. At that time we scarcely knew him in private, and little did we think what his influence was to be in after days. How strange to be obliged to remember that he is no more with us!"

Dr. Horatius writes somewhat more at length:—

"10 PALMERSTON ROAD, GRANGE, EDINBURGH,
26th August 1884.

"MY DEAR DR. SMITH,—You ask me for some reminiscences of Dr. Begg during the short period of his Edinburgh ministry in Lady Glenorchy's Chapel as assistant to Dr. Jones, who was then my minister, and under whom for many years my father was an elder.

"Fifty-four years have elapsed since that time, and my impressions are not very vivid now; not only because of this intervening half-century, but because I had almost no private acquaintance with him. It was chiefly in the pulpit that I saw and heard him. Once or twice I met him at a friend's house; as, for instance, when I breakfasted with him at Dr. Chalmers's some short time after Edward Irving had lectured in town and had published his work on baptism, which I remember formed the subject of conversation at the breakfast-table. I had read the volume; Dr. Chalmers and Dr. Begg had not, and so the burden of stating some of its views fell on me. Dr. Chalmers wanted to know its drift and contents. He was, as usual, singularly candid and fair in listening and judging. Dr. Begg inclined to summary condemnation of the man and his book. I do not remember the details or the issue of the conversation, nor the parts taken by the different speakers, but I carried away the deep impression of Dr. Chalmers's remarkable fairness in dealing with controversial subjects, as also of his affection for Irving, and his desire to know exactly what he held and what he did not hold. I was but a student then, but I learned a lesson of candour in judging of men and books which a young man was not likely to forget when thus exemplified by his Professor.

"Dr. Begg's ministry at that time proved very attractive. His manner in the pulpit was impressive and his style clear. He did not overshoot his audience, so that 'the common people heard him gladly.' I cannot speak as to spiritual results, but the crowded church, Sabbath after Sabbath, showed how he was appreciated by the public. His 'popularity' at that time was great in Edinburgh, and 'calls,' or intimations of calls, from several places reached him. His utterance was energetic, though his tones were not musical, and his gestures not elegant or oratorical. His power lay in direct Scriptural appeal. His sermons and prayers were filled—some thought overfilled—with texts which flowed out from a retentive memory, stored in youth with Bible knowledge and language.

"He and his venerable colleague Dr. Jones worked well together, and the old minister found a congenial friend in his young assistant. One of the secrets of Dr. Begg's attractiveness was his freedom of delivery. He used no notes, many or few, but spoke with that apparently extemporaneous fluency which carries the hearer along with the speaker in full sympathy. He was the only one of Dr. Jones's assistants who did not 'read.' The aged pastor himself only used brief notes, jotted down in shorthand. The free delivery of Dr. Begg told all the more upon the Edinburgh public because the other ministers, such as Dr. Grey, Dr. Thomson, Dr. Gordon, and others, all 'read.' The novelty of non-reading produced a most favourable effect, though I do not know that it was at all followed for some years after.

"I cannot recall any special incidents in the Edinburgh ministry of Dr. Begg which might illustrate his life and assist you in delineating his character. The 'Apocrypha' controversy was just over, the 'Row' movement was just beginning. In neither did Dr. Begg take part; and the 'Voluntary' controversy had not begun."

I need not point out that, by dwelling upon the extreme candour of Dr. Chalmers, Dr. Bonar implies that Dr. Begg exhibited some measure of dogmatism. It needs not be said that it is no disparagement to so young a man that he was found wanting when weighed in the balance with Dr. Chalmers, especially when the holder of the scales was one of Dr.

Chalmers's best students and most enthusiastic admirers; and then we are to take into account the strong personal attachment between Chalmers and Irving, which must have made the former unconsciously more lenient towards the vagaries of the latter than he would have been towards those of a man whom he did not know. I know not whether it will be regarded as an extenuation or an aggravation of Dr. Begg's dogmatism if I point out that the meeting in question must have taken place, not in 1831, when Dr. Begg was minister of Lady Glenorchy's, but in 1829, when he was still unlicensed, and when he was tutor in Mrs. Neilson's family. It was, as we have seen, during Dr. Begg's residence there that Irving lectured in Edinburgh; and I find by reference to a library catalogue that his book on baptism was published in 1828. Moreover, the "Row movement" could not be said to be "just beginning" in 1831. Rather it was just ending then, for Mr. Campbell was deposed by the General Assembly of that year.

I have said that I leave undetermined the question whether dogmatism is more culpable in the inexperienced student, or in the minister with more age and with some measure of experience. It is one of those questions to which the Addisonian maxim is applicable, that "much may be said on both sides." On the one hand, it may be argued that consciousness of ignorance and inexperience ought to inculcate modesty and caution; on the other hand, that dogmatism being the result of ignorance, he is the more to blame in whom a larger experience has operated ineffectually. At the same time, I ought frankly to admit that all through his life the character of Dr. Begg's mind and his habit of thought imparted to him a dogmatic tendency. He had little or no power of nice analysis, or of appreciating minute distinctions. With him a view was either simply right or simply wrong; and the rightness or wrongness he judged with reference to its general character; while a subtler intellect with equal honesty might have seen some good in that which was on the whole worthy of condemnation, and some defect or positive evil in that which was worthy of commendation in its totality. In controversy the strength and sterling honesty of his mind secured that he was generally right in condemning what he did condemn, and approving what he did approve. But an opponent could generally point out that there was something good in what he condemned, or something not good in what he approved, and so could produce the impression that Dr. Begg was condemning the good or approving the evil. Dr. Begg had no eye to see thorns upon rose-trees, or roses upon thorny bushes.

From two correspondents I have accounts of an incident which seems to have made much impression on them. On one occasion whilst preaching in Lady Glenorchy's, Dr. Begg was seized with a violent bleeding at the nose. Dr. Jones was in the church, and he mounted the pulpit and continued the service. The matter would not be worthy of record were it not that it indicates the intensity of Dr. Begg's earnestness in preaching. To those who heard him he appeared to be perfectly cool, and to be speaking without any considerable effort. In reality he was "nervous"—sometimes to an almost feverish degree. When he occasionally preached for me, I noticed that when he came from the pulpit his clothes were literally soaked with sweat, while he had certainly made no extraordinary physical exertion, nor had seemed to tax, to any great extent, his mental powers. I have seen the same in the case of others who appeared to speak as easily as he did. I have no doubt that the nose-bleeding in Lady Glenorchy's was just an extreme instance of the same overstraining of the mental energy. Without being a Materialist, I believe that every mental effort is accompanied by an expenditure of material energy—call it brain-power, or nerve-force, or vital energy, or what you will—and that there can be no effective oratory without such expenditure.

I conclude this chapter with a note from the wife of an eminent man, whose name I do not give, as she marked her note "private:"—

"*11th August* 1884.

"REV. AND DEAR SIR,—My sister and I have been thinking over what might be interesting to you respecting Dr. Begg's short connection with Lady Glenorchy's chapel; but I regret that we recollect but little that can be of any value for his Biography. We well remember that he was very rapid in his utterances; that his prayers were full of Scripture references; that he was very popular; that the church was always crowded when he preached; and that steps were taken for enlarging the chapel to accommodate the increasing number of worshippers. But we do not remember any salient fact likely to illustrate his character or mode of preaching at the time. All we can say is, that he left a deep impression of his powers and capacity. From the record of a member of the church we find that on Saturday, November 5, 1831, before a communion service, he preached in the afternoon from 1 Cor. xi. 26; that on the following Sunday he was prevented through indisposition from attending the duties of the day; and that on Sabbath, November 13, he took leave of Lady Glenorchy's, to become pastor of the Middle Church, Paisley, the text on that occasion being Daniel xii. 3. Hoping these few particulars may be of some use to you, I remain," &c.

CHAPTER XII.

TRANSLATION TO PAISLEY AND MINISTRY THERE.

DR. BEGG's leaving Lady Genorchy's was confessedly a protest against the policy which excluded chapel ministers from any share in the government of the Church. He was conscious of powers which might find appropriate exercise in the discussion of questions of Church polity, which could be discussed effectively only in the Church courts. His enthusiastic admiration of the leaders of the liberal or popular party made him long for the opportunity of standing side by side with them in the chivalrous and apparently almost desperate struggle on which they had entered. And they too were desirous of having the aid of one in whom they saw fair promise of "yeoman service." Moreover, Dr. Begg had a conviction, which he retained throughout his life, that the position of a chapel-minister, such as it then was in the Church of Scotland, was not only unfavourable, but positively unscriptural. He regarded it as a putting asunder of what God has joined together; a virtual supersession of the scriptural office of the teaching ruler, and an unauthorised substitution of a non-ruling teacher. Holding these views, the position of a chapel minister—and the minister of Lady Glenorchy's was scarcely even that—was peculiarly distasteful to him; and he would have been willing to exchange it for the ministry of the humblest and remotest parish in Scotland. As it happened, the acceptance of the call to Paisley involved no such sacrifice. It meant, indeed, the imposition on him of double the amount of pulpit-work which fell to him in Lady Glenorchy's, for Dr. Jones was still generally able for the forenoon service. But it would have been strange if he, in the full vigour of early manhood, had shrunk from the performance of an amount of work which hundreds of his brethren all over the country were constantly performing. No doubt he had felt the work at Maxwelltown heavy, but in one respect the work at Paisley would be lighter, as the pastoral supervision of a large congregation, whose members were scattered over a large and indefinite territory, required a great amount of walking; whereas in Paisley his charge would be confined to a comparatively small section of the town.

In point of fact, the population of the Middle parish in 1831 was 9884,—a number, of course, hopelessly beyond the possibility of any effective pastoral superintendence on the part of the minister. Thus from the period of his going to Paisley Dr. Begg had an experience, which made an indelible impression on his mind, of the utter inadequacy of the provision made in the Established ecclesiastical system of Scotland for exercising a real influence over the population of our large towns. In such a town the minister was constrained, with the name of parochial minister, to occupy the position of a congregational minister; and Dr. Begg never ceased to regard this necessity as a great evil. I need not say that there is a large portion of our population who conscientiously dissent from the doctrines of the Established Church; and another large portion who, regarding an Established Church as an unwarranted innovation, refuse to belong to it simply because it is established; and it is right that all facilities should be afforded to all of these for obtaining the ministrations of pastors who represent their several views. But beyond these there are multitudes, in all our cities and larger towns, who are altogether neglected, and whom neither the Established Church nor the Dissenting bodies have been able to reach and to reclaim. How they are to be evangelised is a problem that urgently demands solution; and the devoutest hope that can be cherished is, that when the present period of ecclesiastical unrest shall have come to an end, men will gird themselves for its solution under an adequate sense of its unspeakable importance—an importance which ought to outweigh all personal and all denominational interests.

For nearly a century after the Reformation, the whole inhabitants of Paisley were under the pastoral care of the one minister of the Abbey Church. In 1641 that church was made a collegiate charge, and such it has since continued to be. In 1736 the Burgh was separated from the Abbey, and was constituted a distinct parish. Twenty years later the Burgh parish was divided into the High Church and the Low Church parishes; and in 1781 it was further divided, and the Middle Church parish was formed. Afterwards, as we shall see, there were added five *quoad sacra* churches and a Gaelic chapel. Still, even then, all the provision of church accommodation in connection with the Established Church was for 12,744 out of a population of 57,880. The Dissenting bodies, viz., the Reformed Presbyterians, the Burghers, the United Secession, the Relief, Independents of different classes (including Baptists and Methodists), the Episcopalians, and the Romanists, provided 16,130 sittings more; making in all 28,874, or almost exactly one for every two of the population, which, I believe, is generally regarded as an adequate provision. Dr. Begg's predecessors in the ministry of the Middle parish from its formation in 1781 were Dr. John Snodgrass, 1781-97, and Mr. Jonathan Ranken, 1798-1831. In the other charges in Paisley some notable names occur. The following may be mentioned. Robert Boyd, of Trochrig, was minister of the Abbey Church, 1626-27.[1] Alexander Dunlop was minister of the second charge of the Abbey parish from 1644 to 1653,

---

[1] There is a confusion among the authorities as to the order in which Boyd of Trochrig held his several offices—the Principalship of the University of Glasgow, the ministry of Paisley, and the Principalship of the

and of the first charge from the latter date to 1663, when he was summoned before the Lords of the Council, and, on refusing to take the oath, was ordained to be "banished forth of his Majesty's dominions." It does not appear that he ever actually left the kingdom; but he was silenced. He died in 1667. James Stirling, who succeeded Dunlop in the second charge when he was promoted to the first, was one of the authors of "Naphtali," the other being Sir James Stewart of Goodtrees.

But the most noted and most influential man among the ministers of earlier days in Scotland was Dr. Witherspoon, who, after being successively minister of Yester in East Lothian, and of Beith in Ayrshire, became minister of the Low Church parish of Paisley in 1757. There he remained till 1768, when he became President of the great American College of Princeton, and was a prominent man in the events which issued in the formation of the great Western Republic. His writings are voluminous. They relate to a wide range of subjects, theological, religious, ecclesiastical, and political, and are worthy of all commendation. I shall mention only his book on Regeneration, and his Ecclesiastical

---

University of Edinburgh. He had been minister at Vertali, in France, and afterwards minister and Professor of Theology at Saumur. Thence, according to "Memorable Characteristics," by Mr. John Livingstone, he returned to Scotland, and became "Principal of the College of Glasgow and minister at Govan." Livingstone studied under him in the College, and attended his church at Govan from 1618 to 1622. He writes thus:—"Being filled with anxiety, and finding that he could not peaceably continue in that station, he left the College at Glasgow, and having a call to be minister at Paisley, some popishly and profanely affected threw out his goods and stopped his entry; yea, when he had been received minister in Edinburgh, and the greatest part of all the well-affected leaving the rest of the kirks and constantly hearing him, the rest of the ministers, being prelatically affected and moved with envy, dealt with the King that he should be put from that employment." Here it seems to be intimated that he went from Glasgow to Paisley, and from Paisley to Edinburgh. But the "Statistical Account of Paisley" gives the date of his abortive ministry there as 1626-27; while the "Edinburgh University Calendar" makes him Principal there in 1622.

Characteristics. The former is one of our most esteemed religious classics, and the latter is almost worthy of taking rank with the immortal "Provincial Letters," which it resembles so much, that it can hardly be doubted that it was Pascal who suggested to its author the idea of employing sarcasm and irony in the cause of truth. I do not know whether Witherspoon's writings are much read now. I am sure they may be read with pleasure and profit.

The Middle Church became a separate charge, as has been stated, in 1781, and in the fifty years of its separate existence Dr. Begg had only two predecessors in its ministry. Dr. Snodgrass, who was minister for sixteen years (1781-97), was a man of considerable note in his day. The following is the conclusion of the notice given of him by the celebrated Dr. Balfour of Glasgow, in preaching his funeral sermon; and commendation by Dr. Balfour meant something very different from indiscriminate eulogy:—

"As he began, so he uniformly conducted his ministry, by preaching 'not himself, but Christ Jesus the Lord, and himself your servant for Jesus' sake.' This was not only his subject and solemn profession when he first addressed you from the place where I now stand, but it was the unvarying aim of all his ministrations; and what should endear him to your memory is, that his only desire of life was to secure this grandest and most interesting theme, and with his best powers of health and voice to press it upon your hearts in all its importance and influence. Of these things you will recollect striking proofs, not only in all his sermons, but in his prevailing temper and uniform conduct. Did he not learn of his Divine Master to be meek and lowly in heart and manners? Though he was continually adding to his stock of mental endowments, he was not wise in his own conceit, nor puffed up with his superior and growing knowledge. So far was he from the pride of ostentation and boasting, that public duty alone brought him into view; and that discharged, he was glad to return to the quiet retreats and humble walks of private study and domestic life. This, however, was not the unwilling modesty of a feeble, irresolute, or timid mind. For none acted with more decision and courage, independence and energy. When any object possessed real magnitude and importance, of which he was a ready and accurate judge, he shrank not from the acknowledgment and pursuit of it on account of any difficulty or danger. With equal firmness, and zeal, and wisdom, he maintained it against all opposition. There can be no doubt that he was fonder of home and of his study than of any public appearance; but if it was difficult to draw him forth, when convinced it was his duty he cheerfully obeyed the call, and then appeared with greater advantage and more effect.

"While he yielded to conviction, he detested the suppleness of temporising compliance. In the cause of truth, especially evangelical truth, he never flinched. He fought the good fight, he kept the faith; and, warmly attached to the sterling principles of civil and religious liberty, he abhorred every encroachment upon them, while he was equally a zealous and a steady friend of lawful authority and good order. While animated with the purest patriotism, he was not less animated with universal benevolence. His great and good mind wished and sought salvation to those who were far off, as well as to those who were nigh. The honour and applause, the pleasures and riches, of this world made but a slight impression on his mind. Though able to fill any station in the Church with personal credit and public honour, he never sought great things for himself. While others of much inferior talents pressed forward to hold the pre-eminence, he delighted in the enjoyment of the shade. He loved the place of his fathers; he was attached to Paisley; he was attached to *you* of this congregation. To improve his own mind in private, and be useful to you in public, in promoting your best, your eternal interests, seemed to be the height of his ambition here. But his great Lord found use for him in a better world. He is entered into his Master's joy. *We* are left in the vale of tears, to lament our loss, to pursue our journey, and to prepare for a happy and eternal re-union in the heavenly mansions."

Dr. Snodgrass was the author of "A Commentary, with Notes, on a Part of the Book of the Revelation of John," which was well received at the time of its publication, but which has shared the lot which seems to be the heritage of almost all Apocalyptic commentaries.

The successor of Dr. Snodgrass, and the immediate predecessor of Dr. Begg, was Mr. Jonathan Ranken, who was minister of the Middle parish for thirty-three years (1798-1831). He seems to have been an excellent man, a sound evangelical preacher, and a diligent and faithful pastor.

In those days, ere railroads and penny newspapers had annihilated individual and local characteristics, the people of Paisley had a distinctive character of their own. Good-naturedly designated by their Glasgow neighbours the "Paisley bodies," they were distinguished by the possession of a peculiarly large amount of those qualities which are commonly regarded as possessed by the Scottish people generally in comparison with other peoples;—sagacity and shrewdness, a quiet observation of the circumstances which might make for or against their own interests, and unwearying patience in turning these circumstances to the best account. Their manufactures, though on a very small scale as compared with their subsequent development, had already attained a great repute, and Paisley shawls were known and worn and admired in all the continents of the world. Dr. Begg's residence in Paisley was in the transition period, midway between the days when the "Paisley bodies" were a distinct community, with but little in common with the rest of the world,—excepting in so far as the rest of the world purchased the shawls which they wove,—and the time when Paisley was to become virtually a suburb of Glasgow,—or, as the "bodies" would perhaps express it, Glasgow a suburb of Paisley. He came at a most fortunate time, precisely when the tide was beginning to flow; and he was precisely the man to take advantage of the opportunity. To what extent he contributed towards the immense advance which the town has made during the past half-century, and how far he influenced the direction of that advance, it is of course impossible to estimate with any precision. But no one who knew him will doubt that he was "the right man in the right place," and that he must have exerted a potent influence over that spirit of enterprise which has wrought so mightily in the extension of the town and the increase of its wealth.

The patronage of the Middle Church was vested in the Town Council of Paisley. But on the death of Mr. Ranken it was intimated that, if the congregation could agree in recommending a successor, the Council were willing to appoint him. The Middle Parish had, from its first formation, had an evangelical ministry; and it might have been predicted that the man whom the people would choose would be the man who most earnestly and powerfully preached the simple gospel of the grace of God. In keeping with this anticipation was their choice of Dr. Begg. He was accordingly presented by the Council, and all the ordinary steps were taken for his translation from Lady Glenorchy's and his induction into the Middle Church, which took place on the 25th of November 1831.

From many quarters I have testimony borne to the power of Dr. Begg's ministry in Paisley, and to the affection with which he was regarded by all classes in his congregation, as well as to the high position which he held in the estimation of the whole community. Of these I shall present a single specimen.

Among the few letters which Dr. Begg had preserved, I found one addressed to him on occasion of the celebration of the completion of the fiftieth year of his ministry. I applied to its writer, Mr. George Dobie, and received from him the following letter, which is interesting as showing the friendly feeling which subsisted between Dr. Begg and the congregation of the Middle Church, not only while he was their minister, but all through his subsequent life. Such feeling is creditable both to minister and people:—

"CASTLEHEAD, PAISLEY, *9th September* 1884.

"DEAR SIR,—I duly received your letter of 6th inst. regarding our late friend Dr. Begg. My time in various capacities is much occupied; but I hasten to reply, that I am afraid that I cannot be of much service to you, but what I can do shall be done cheerfully. There are a few people here who sat under his ministry. Those who occur to me are mostly females, from whom I may gather something that might to a certain extent prove interesting. . . . I am old enough to remember as a boy Dr. Begg's tall, slight, handsome figure marching along our streets. He was very popular here as a preacher, and I have frequently been one of a crowded audience who listened with rapt attention to his earnest, eloquent, and impressive expositions of God's Word. He came here, I think, in 1832, and I have occasion to remember—from a family incident—that he preached his farewell sermon—and an impressive sermon it was—in June 1835.

"I presume you are aware that he came for many years to assist his friend Dr. Fraser at our October communion. His appearance was always hailed with pleasure; and his evening sermons on these occasions never failed to fill the church with an attentive and admiring crowd, many of whom remained behind to shake hands with their old friend.

"On the occasion of the death of our loved and lamented pastor Dr. Fraser, Dr. Begg was at once fixed on as the proper person to preach his funeral sermon, which he did in a very able and feeling manner in the month of September 1879. A considerable portion of this sermon was published in the *Glasgow Herald*, a copy of which I enclose, in case you may not have it. I do this, of course, with the view of illustrating the character of Dr. Begg, and of showing the high value he attached to the principles and conduct he praises so highly in his departed friend. . . .

"During Dr. Begg's ministry here the Voluntary controversy was at its height; and he and his youthful contemporary, the Rev. John Macnaughton, played an important part in these stirring times. They were both powerful platform speakers, and many a public meeting they addressed of a very exciting character. In my opinion, notwithstanding Dr. Begg's ability as a preacher, he was even more powerful as a platform speaker, and he had many opportunities of testing his powers during his sojourn in Paisley. . . .—Yours very sincerely, GEO. DOBIE.

"Rev. THOMAS SMITH, D.D."

CHAPTER XIII.

PAISLEY MINISTRY CONTINUED—CHURCH EXTENSION.

DR. BEGG's ministry in Paisley began under most trying circumstances, as much so as any with which a young minister ever had to contend. In 1832 there was a fearful outbreak of cholera, which visited many parts of the country, carried off many of all classes, and produced terror in the hearts of multitudes who escaped its actual attack. Probably on account of overcrowding and the want of sanitary arrangements, Paisley was one of the places which suffered most severely. The greater portion of the victims were of the destitute, enfeebled, and dissipated classes. But not all. The mansions of the higher classes were not exempt from the visitation. The strong and the fair were among the victims. The virtuous and the pious did not escape. In all faces were traces of deepest sorrow, mingled with the expression of anxiety and alarm. And there was more than simple sorrow, comfortless weeping for the dead because they were not. A strange madness took hold of the minds of the most ignorant portion of the people, and in some cases extended even to some of whom better things might have been expected. The medical men, who battled with the fell disease with all the courage and energy which are nobly characteristic of their profession, were regarded as its abettors. Every case which baffled their skill was regarded as a murder perpetrated by them. This strange and wicked delusion was, unhappily, not confined to Paisley, but it seems to have found there a peculiarly congenial soil. It seems probable that the wretched class of body-lifters, or resurrectionists, as they were called, did take advantage of the extra-mural burying, and exercised their vocation in the secluded and unwatched cemeteries. The medical practitioners were supposed to incite them to the spoliation of the grave, or at least to furnish them with the inducement by purchasing the spoil. Hence such scenes as the following, described by a correspondent of a Glasgow newspaper of the day:[1]

"Paisley is at this moment in a state of greater commotion than it has been since the period still known as the 'Radical times.' Yesterday some idle persons wandering about the Moss, the place allotted for the reception of the bodies of those who have died of cholera, found a short spade, hook, and bag, and some other of the known implements of the resurrectionist. Immediately the report got abroad that the exhumators had been at work in the cholera burying-ground; and had it not been Sunday, the scenes exhibited to-day would in all likelihood have taken place yesterday. This morning crowds were assembled about the Cross discussing the affair, and expressing their determination to inspect the burying-ground if the authorities did not set about it immediately. There being no appearance of any public authorised inspection, the populace went down about ten o'clock to the ground, and commenced operations. So many discordant rumours are afloat respecting the result of the inspection, that it would be improper to state positively what it may have been. There is no doubt, however, that the resurrectionists have been at work, though to go the length of saying that all the bodies of the victims of cholera, with the exception of six or seven, have been taken away (the popular rumour) would be the greatest exaggeration. About two o'clock a considerable body of the crowd left the Moss, bearing along with them one of the empty coffins, and armed with the stobs that surrounded the burying-place. Their first act of violence was the demolition of the windows of Drs. Vessie, W. Young, and A. K. Young. At this time we saw the crowd, and can declare that it did not consist of

[1] *Scottish Guardian*, March 30, 1832.

more than 200 grown-up boys[1] altogether, and had the authorities made any show of resistance, it could have been easily dispersed. No attempt, however, was made to obstruct its progress, and the shout was now raised 'To the hospital!' There the windows were partly broken, and the cholera van seized and brought down the Pend triumphantly. Dr. Kerr's windows were next demolished, and the windows of all, or almost all, the medical men in the town followed. The van was next broken to pieces, and its wreck was borne along with the populace as a token of their power and success. So determined were the mob that, finding in one instance that a druggist had put on his window-shutters to save his panes of glass, they broke the panels. . . . About three o'clock part of the depot of the 25th regiment and the staff of the Renfrewshire militia were called out, when the mob in a great measure dispersed; and at present (half-past four o'clock) all is comparatively quiet. . . . Some of the police were considerably injured by stones, but not one of them seriously. A great many gentlemen were likewise pretty severely pelted by the mob. One or two of the medical gentlemen found shelter during the riot in the Police Office. The shops in town were all shut during the disturbance."

Three days later, on Thursday the 26th of March, the same correspondent writes:

"Ever since the riot on Monday, the town has remained tranquil. There was indeed on Tuesday a slight disturbance in the west end of the town, and the cholera hearse and its drivers were pelted with stones, but the respectable part of the neighbourhood turned out and quelled the proceedings. A minute investigation is going on into the whole affair, many parts of which are still involved in mystery. There is reason to believe that a conspiracy has been formed in order to excite the disturbance, and those who are best acquainted with the history of the matter as at present developed, scruple not to declare that the resurrection-men have never been at work in the burying-ground at all. Fifteen persons have been committed to prison as accessories to this disgraceful riot."

[1] Qu. "Grown-up men and boys?"—T. S.

The sequel is told in the *Guardian* of next week:[1]—

"Many painful scenes have been exhibited in Paisley last week, resulting from the riotous proceedings of Monday. The Board of Health and the district surgeons deemed it necessary to discontinue in a great measure their invaluable services, in order that the public might learn from experience how unpleasantly they would be situated without their assistance. The hospital was shut up, the ordinary aid given in interments was withdrawn, except in peculiar circumstances, and the people were thrown on their own resources. On Friday the streets were crowded by an assemblage collected to witness the harrowing spectacle of a poor man hurling, on a common barrow, the body of a girl, a relation of his own, and followed by her sobbing mother carrying a spade wherewith to dig a grave for the body of her child. The procession was stopped by a gentleman, who generously secured for the corpse a burying-place. The wreck of the cholera hearse cannot be obtained unless forty neighbours promise to protect it and its drivers from injury; several times lately has it passed along the streets surrounded by individuals armed with sticks, who have come under the required obligation. In despite even of this guard, some foolish persons have more than once attempted, and succeded too in the attempt, to turn the hearse, and leave the body in the house from which it has been taken. No less than four bodies on Saturday remained unburied till long after the time considered prudent. In consequence of this shameful interference, one of the bodies was so corrupted that the smell of it was felt even by persons passing along the street; and it was judged right to summon out, on Saturday, the constabulary force in order to secure the interment of these victims of cholera. Their services, however, were happily not required, as the ignorant part of the public desisted from their opposition."

It is very difficult to estimate, and almost impossible to over-estimate, the delicacy of a minister's position when such a state of feeling exists among the people of his charge, as these extracts show to have existed in Paisley at this

[1] *Scottish Guardian*, April 3, 1832.

time. No doubt the number of the actual rioters was small. But as undoubtedly, as in all such cases, the feeling which prompted a few to riot rankled bitterly in the hearts of many. The minister could not but reprobate the action of the misguided rioters, and express his sympathy with the ill-used doctors. Thus he would give offence to many, who would regard him as the partizan of the rich in their attempts to injure and trample upon the poor; and so for a long time their hearts would be steeled against him, and their ears closed to his ministrations. On the other hand, the well-to-do community would cherish, along with a righteous condemnation of the crime, a bitter feeling of resentment against the criminals. The minister, while equally reprobating the crime, would almost certainly make more allowance for the ignorance of the criminals, and for the excitement caused in their hearts by sorrow and terror. Any expression of such a sentiment would cause him to be regarded as an apologist for disorder, or as one courting the favour of the rabble, or as one afraid to incur their hatred. In such cases, as it is simply impossible to please both parties, perhaps the highest commendation that can be given to a minister is to say that he displeased both; and that commendation is Dr. Begg's due.

Coincident, in point of time, with the visitation of cholera, was an extreme depression of the Paisley trade, and this seems always to exasperate class-feeling. The employers and the employed alike have their income reduced. But the former have their capital to fall back upon, while the latter are brought to absolute penury. The employed consider that the employers are indebted to them for that capital, and that they are injured when that capital enables its possessors to live with scarcely diminished expenditure, while its earners are reduced to almost intolerable straits. It is not my part to attempt the solution of the many politico-economical problems, hitherto unsolved, as to the relations of capital and labour. I refer to the matter only to call attention to the fact that a minister in a manufacturing town occupies a peculiarly delicate and difficult position at a period of great depression. He desires to be, and is, and in ordinary times is acknowledged to be, the friend of all. But in evil times, when class-bitterness prevails, each class will regard the friend of the other class as its own enemy. Here again, in the absence of a possibility of pleasing both parties, the highest attainable merit is to displease both.

Further, 1832 was the year of the Reform Act. In the earlier months of it, while the passing of the Act was delayed, there was tremendous bitterness; and when it was actually passed, there was intense excitement among the newly enfranchised electors. I have not a word to say in disparagement of political earnestness. Every citizen of a free country *ought* to take an intelligent and earnest interest in all matters bearing upon its well-being, and therefore in political matters; nor have I much sympathy with the denunciations, which one sometimes hears, of *party* politics. As long as there are independently thinking men, there will be different views on political questions. And while there is some truth in the adage, *Quot homines, tot sententiæ*, yet the sentiments of men will generally tend to range themselves on one or the other of two sides. And it is by the resultant of the two forces thus originating that the best government is to be secured. It is not, therefore, political agitation that is to be deprecated; not the use, but the abuse of it. Such abuse is sure to occur in periods when important changes are imminent, and when they have just been effected. I have some recollection of the excitement and the animosities of the era of the first Reform Bill, when I was a very young student, and I do not think that these have been equalled during the half century which has elapsed since then. Nowhere was this excitement more intense, or these animosities more bitter, than in Paisley; there again it was a war of class against class, and a man could not exercise his judgment in supporting a particular candidate without being regarded as almost a personal foe of every man who supported another. Dr. Begg took no part in the fierce agitation, but quietly gave his vote in favour of the candidate whose views accorded with his own; for all through his life, rightly or wrongly, he was a thorough Whig, or what is now called a Liberal Conservative, and a very strong opponent of Radicalism, or what is now denominated advanced Liberalism. The result of the election showed that among the Paisley electorate Constitutionalism was in the ascendant, but Radicalism was strong in the non-electoral section of the community;[1] and every man—especially every minister—who voted with the majority was subjected to obloquy and misrepresentation.

Yet further, it was in 1832 that the Voluntary controversy began. It did not originate in Paisley, but Paisley soon became one of its hottest foci. In this controversy every minister of the Established Church necessarily took a more or less prominent part; and Dr. Begg's was a somewhat prominent one. I am not aware that he issued any publication on the subject, but he took no unimportant part in the contest by speeches and lectures. His actings in this protracted controversy will come frequently before us in the sequel.

It would appear from the notices (in the *Scottish Guardian*)

---

[1] As indicative of the prevalent Radicalism I find the following paragraph in the *Scottish Guardian* of 29th May 1832.—T. S.

"At the last celebration of the King's birthday, Paisley presented more the appearance of a flower-garden than of a dull, dingy, smoky town. Yesterday a stranger could not have discovered, except by the ringing of the bells, that it was a day appointed to commemorate the birth of our sovereign. Hardly a flower was to be seen in any window; not a branch appeared in the trappings of a horse. The absence of the usual manifestation of loyal feeling may, in part, be attributed to the bustle occasioned by the 'flittings' (the 28th being term-day); but it arises also from the unpopularity of the King, produced by an unfounded suspicion of His Majesty not being hearty in the cause of Reform."

of the local church courts—the Presbytery of Paisley and the Synod of Glasgow and Ayr—that Dr. Begg did not, in the early days of his Paisley ministry, take a prominent part in their discussions. It is true that the reports, in those days of weekly and semi-weekly papers, were much briefer than they are now. I suppose that Dr. Begg modestly kept in the background, and willingly gave place to the "potent, grave, and reverend seniors." I find only sententious notices, such as the following.

In the Synod of Glasgow and Ayr, at its spring meeting in 1832, Mr. Macfarlane of Renfrew moved that the Synod should petition Parliament in opposition to the scheme of education for Ireland, which was then a burning question all over the land. This was seconded by Dr. Burns of Paisley in a long speech. (All his speeches were long.) A counter-motion was made and seconded, and discussion ensued, which is very briefly reported. In the middle of the report are the following paragraphs:—

"Dr. Hill of Dailly, in a very solemn and impressive manner, pleaded for the overture, while he did not approve of all its sentiments, nor of the language in which it was expressed. He proposed a committee to draw up a petition and report.

"Mr. Wood of Newton-upon-Ayr seconded the proposal, and ably defended the principle of the overture; as did Mr. Begg of Paisley, who said that two things had struck him in the debate as rather strange. The one was that some gentlemen opposed the petition because it was premature, while others did so because it was too late. The other was that a member had eulogised the Kildare Place Society, and with the same breath had praised the Government which had done what it could to put it down."

Then at a public meeting held in Paisley to petition Parliament on the subject of Sabbath observance, I find the following:—"Mr. M'Dermid and Mr. Begg entered at great length into the subject of Sabbath profanation."

We find him somewhat more fully reported in the meeting of the Synod of Glasgow and Ayr on the 10th of October 1832. His father, Dr. Begg of New Monkland, moved that the Synod should overture the Assembly "for a modification of the law for the disjunction of overgrown parishes and the erection of new churches." This was opposed by the Moderate party, on the ground that it would give offence to the heritors; and it was suggested by Dr. Patrick Macfarlane, who was no Moderate, that as this was likely to be the case, and as there was no prospect of success, "that it would well become them not to arrive at any hasty conclusion. He would not make any motion on the subject, but he earnestly suggested that Dr. Begg should withdraw the motion for the present, and reproduce it at the meeting in April."

"Dr. Begg was not sanguine of success; but the measure was necessary, and the step must be taken some time, and the sooner it was laid before the Assembly the better. Perhaps other Synods would take up the subject immediately; whereas, were it postponed to the next meeting, their concurrence would be too late.

"Mr. Begg could not see that delay would be detrimental to the question. It was notorious that the Church of Scotland had been labouring under great disadvantages; particularly in the west of Scotland, where parishes of 20, 30, 40, 60, and even 80,000 were under the superintendence of one individual, and where there were teinds unavailable.[1] It was their duty to assert their rights; and if they were united in this they would bring the world to a sense of their grievances. If after this the Church were called inefficient, the assertion would be estimated at its proper value. The statement of Mr. Macfarlane regarding the ignorance abroad on this subject, was one of great importance, and should stimulate them to adopt the course he suggested. He had no objection to the question being set aside till April, but he would have the Synod record their strong approbation of the overture, and instruct their Presbyteries to furnish them with such statistical information as Mr. Macfarlane had referred to."

[1] Qu. "Available?"—T. S.

It will be seen that the son was not less solicitous than the father as to the matter proposed, although he differed with him as to the necessity of immediate action. Indeed, this was one of the subjects nearest to the heart of the son, and all through his life he was continually referring to it as one of Scotland's chief *desiderata*. It must have afforded a good deal of amusement to see the son opposing the father even on this question of immediate action or six months' delay.

But whilst the minister of the Paisley Middle Parish was lamenting the inadequacy of the means at the disposal of the Church of Scotland for overtaking the work which was considered to belong to it, he was most energetic in employing the means which were available, and in stirring up others to employ them energetically. It has been incidentally stated that near the beginning of the present century the "Low Church" parish became "St. George's" parish, and a new church was erected for it. How the old Low Church, or Laigh Kirk, was occupied during the interval I do not know. But when Dr. Begg went to Paisley, he found that it could be rented, and he took it at an annual rent of £30. In this a probationer was appointed to officiate, and there was soon gathered a large congregation. The *Scottish Guardian* of 26th June gives the following account, extracted from the *Paisley Advertiser*, of the opening of this place of worship:—

"Low Church.—This church was opened for public worship on Sunday last by the Rev. Mr. Begg. The text which he chose was very appropriate, Mark xvi. 15, 'Go ye into all the world, and preach the gospel to every creature.' At the conclusion of a most impressive discourse, he stated that when he first came to the town, he was surprised to find, amidst so dense a population, a church standing empty, and so many poor people wandering about on Sunday without the means of religious instruction. He had therefore considered it his duty to make exertions to have this place opened for public worship, and he had never rested until he had succeeded in having a clergyman appointed to preach every Sabbath, and he hoped that it would continue open until it crumbled into ruins. He trusted they would receive Mr. Steel gladly, and treat him with kindness, for he was every way well qualified to instruct them in the important truths of Christianity, and he was certain that Mr. S. would take a deep interest in their welfare. He felt averse to speak of the contributions which would be necessary to support this church; but what he had himself given to aid them, he had given cheerfully, and he hoped that others would act on the same principle. The attendance was numerous and respectable."

The last sentence of this extract indicates what was the weak point of all these earlier efforts for church extension, and it is not altogether eliminated even now. The new churches afforded accommodation to those who had some desire for Christian ordinances, but scarcely touched a multitude who had no such desire, and a considerable number who had a positive aversion to the gospel and its ordinances. I have no disposition to despise the day of small things, or to make little of the good that was done, or of the evil that was prevented, by these efforts. They did some good, and they prevented not a little evil. That they did not do more of the one and prevent more of the other, was not merely due, I suspect, to their inadequacy in point of extent, but also to some defects in their modes of operation. Dr. Begg always maintained strenuously—and I, with more experience in this department than he ever had, am disposed to agree with him to a considerable extent—that endowments, and authoritatively defined parochial and territorial boundaries, are essential to complete success. But these, if essential, are not sufficient; and they are capable of such abuse that they may become a hindrance and not a help. The great problem of the "evangelisation of the masses" is still unsolved. It is high commendation that is due to Dr. Begg, who was one of the first to apprehend its importance, and earnestly to grapple with it. Of one thing I am confident, that its solution will not be effected by desultory efforts, however strenuous these may be, but by the persistent and prayerful concentration of the energies of the Church of Christ. And in this work there surely might be, there surely ought to be, cordial co-operation among all the sections of the Evangelical Church.

In the next issue of the *Guardian* I find the following paragraph from its Paisley correspondent, referring to the same matter:—

"The opening of the Low Church, Paisley, has most decidedly proved that the neglect of the public ordinances of religion so lamentably prevalent in our large towns, springs at least as much from the want of *cheap* church accommodation as from the apathy and unconcern of the population in reference to sacred things. When that place of public worship was about to be opened, it was pretty generally said, that though a few individuals from the various congregations of the town might be induced, from the low price of the sittings, to assemble there, yet that the number of church-going people would not be increased, for that it was in vain to look for an accession of worshippers from those who had long given up attending any church. These prognostications have happily not been realised. A congregation of from 700 to 1000 individuals has actually been collected from among those who hitherto, from poverty or other causes, have rarely or never entered a place of public worship. The proof of this is just the fact that such a number regularly assemble in the Low Church, and that the attendance in the other churches is not sensibly diminished. The result of this experiment of the Rev. Mr. Begg affords great encouragement to such philanthropists as may be disposed to bestir themselves in providing additional *cheap* church accommodation for the population. Their efforts stand every chance of being seconded and appreciated by those for whose benefit they are made. At Charleston, which has long been the exclusive seat of the exertions of one of the agents of the Paisley Town Mission, where, of course, a sermon was regularly preached every Sabbath evening, a strong desire has been awakened to enjoy the benefits of public worship more frequently. To meet this desire, the Rev. Mr. M'Nair, the minister of the parish, has agreed to preach in a large room every fortnight, and the inhabitants of that district themselves, poor though they generally are, and peculiarly heedless with respect to religion though they are esteemed, have raised voluntarily a fund sufficient to remunerate any minister whom they may obtain to preach on the Sabbath on which Mr. M'Nair does not officiate. Thus, in that destitute quarter, public worship is now regularly celebrated twice every Lord's-day."

I have no doubt that the experiment was successful, although I am not convinced that the success was so thoroughly as is here represented among the class which it was mainly designed to benefit. It might be quite true that the attendance at the other churches was "not sensibly diminished," but neither, I fear, was the number of loiterers and mischief-makers on the streets, or of the customers of the public-houses, for there was no Forbes M'Kenzie Act in those days.

Be this as it may, it is gratifying to find that Dr. Begg's zeal in the Home Mission cause was not exhausted, but rather stimulated, by this experiment. If he could not do all that he desired, he was ever ready to do with energy the best that he could. His second experiment in this direction is detailed in the following paragraph, which appears in the *Scottish Guardian* of the 11th of September:—

"When the Old Low Church was lately opened for public worship, the Court Hall, the place where Mr. Steel had formerly preached, was shut up. Mr. Begg, however, finding that his missionary, Mr. Steel, had obtained something like a regular congregation, and that the watching over it would demand all his labours, and finding also that a considerable part of the Middle Church parish still required to be attended to, determined to secure the services of another missionary, and to re-open the Court Hall for public worship. In this place the Rev. Mr. Wood preached for the first time last Sabbath, to an attentive and respectable congregation, composed chiefly of the young and the aged. Thus there have been added within these few months no fewer than 1500 sittings to the ordinary church accommodation of the town of Paisley, and this great good has been accomplished chiefly through the zeal of one reverend gentleman. Another place of public worship is being fitted up in the west end of the town, for the benefit of such of the High Church parishioners as are unable to pay for accommodation in the other churches of the place; but we have not yet heard the name of the rev. gentleman whom Mr. M'Naughton intends to labour in this part of his parish. It is, we believe, intended to have a third parochial missionary in Paisley, besides the two town missionaries, so that opportunities of obtaining religious knowledge, and of joining in religious worship, will no longer be awanting here. The funds for accomplishing these great objects are derived in part from the collections made at the Sabbath evening sermons delivered in the High Church, and in part from the direct contributions of the ministers of Paisley themselves."

I may perhaps be excused for mentioning that it was in connection with the appointment of Mr. Wood that I was first introduced to Dr. Begg. Mr. Wood was the son of the minister of Wiston, the next parish to that of which my father was minister. Dr. Begg was, I believe, on a visit to his relations in Douglas, which is quite near to Wiston. He had been on terms with Mr. Wood about the assistantship, and had agreed to come to Wiston and take part in the sacramental services. The report went abroad that a distinguished preacher was to conduct the service on the Monday, and many went from the neighbouring parishes. I was a very young student, at home during the summer after my first session in Edinburgh. I went with others to church, and was asked to dine at the manse. I confess that I have no remembrance of the sermon, or of any other of the services. But I have—to use an expression which occurs again and again in the autobiographical chapters in this volume— a "vivid remembrance" of the fine physique, the handsome face, and the earnest and impressive manner of the preacher, and of the kindly notice which he took of me when I was introduced to him. I did not come in contact with him again for some half-dozen years, and although he did not recognise me at first, when I told him who I was he at once recalled the conversation we had had at Wiston Manse on the subject of my predilections in the matter of studies.

Mr. Wood had been assisting his father for some time, and had an immense reputation, locally, as a preacher. With good powers and many advantages, his career was not a happy one. I am not aware that there was anything very flagrantly amiss in his conduct while his connection with Dr. Begg subsisted; but there could be little cordiality between them.

Once more; in the *Scottish Guardian* of the 26th December, 1832, is the following notice:—

"The Rev. Mr. Begg, on Sabbath last, brought before his congregation the wants of his parish with regard to church accommodation. He stated that the parish contains 15,000 inhabitants, and that his church could only contain 1500 persons. With a view to afford to the people generally an opportunity of attending upon public ordinances, he has devised a scheme for raising as much money as will enable him to build a plain place of worship, capable of holding a few hundred individuals. The leading features of the scheme are, that the elders shall immediately wait upon all the members of the church, in order to induce them to subscribe from a penny to sixpence weekly, for the purpose of affording their poorer brethren, at a trifling rate, or without charge, an opportunity of enjoying the public ordinances of the sanctuary. Mr. Begg is very sanguine of success, and we heartily wish he may prosper. Some idea is likewise entertained of building a chapel of ease, of a similar kind, in the western extremities of the High Church parish. Should this be done, then all the parishes of Paisley will have a chapel within their bounds; and something will have been accomplished with regard to what has been long felt to be a great desideratum, namely, cheap and ample church accommodation."

These notes, fragmentary as they are, all relating to the first year of Dr. Begg's ministry in Paisley, indicate that he set about the work of pastor and evangelist with characteristic ardour, and did with his might what his hand found to do. They make it manifest, too, that his zeal was infectious; for it must have been due, in large measure, to his influence and example that his co-presbyters, the ministers of the other Paisley parishes, began precisely at that time to undertake evangelistic work in their several districts. Of course there were those who said, and those who insinuated, that the animating motive of all this zeal was a desire to "smash the Dissenters;" and I believe that he did, on one occasion, give utterance to this unguarded and unseemly expression. But I can testify that few men were ever readier to acknowledge the invaluable services rendered by the Dissenters to the cause of God in Scotland. His ideal, doubtless, was, and continued all through his life to be, an Established Church so good that Dissent should be unnecessary, and so adequate in extent to the wants of the people that there should be no need for Dissenters to supply its lack of service. He did not consider that the Establishment to which he belonged, and to which he was so warmly attached, was actually possessed of either of these characteristics; and he devoted himself to strenuous and unceasing efforts for its purification and its extension. He apprehended that in proportion as these efforts were successful, Dissent would be lessened; but his object was not the weakening of Dissent, but the removal of the evils which had originally caused it, an object with which many seceders—such, for example, as Dr. M'Crie—very cordially sympathised.

CHAPTER XIV.

FIRST SPEECH IN THE GENERAL ASSEMBLY.

WE have seen that the minister of the Middle Church of Paisley, during the first year of his ministry there, took no very prominent part in the proceedings of the local church courts of which he was a member, the Presbytery of Paisley and the Synod of Glasgow and Ayr. His appearance in the General Assembly of that year, and the speech which he delivered on the most important subject that came before it, excited a good deal of surprise, both in the "house" and in the galleries. The Assembly of 1832 was an epoch-making Assembly. In it began that "Ten Years' Conflict," which has exerted, is exerting, and is destined still to exert, an immense influence on the ecclesiastical and spiritual history, not of Scotland only, but of the world. Dr. Begg was, accidentally, as some would say, but providentially, as I believe, one of the representatives of his Presbytery in that memorable Assembly. Dr. Chalmers was its Moderator, and this of itself would have made it memorable, though the business transacted in it had been less important than it was.

Eleven overtures—eight from Presbyteries and three from Synods—had been sent to the Assembly on the subject of "calls." The overtures differed materially from one another, but they all agreed in setting forth the indefiniteness of the law and the unsatisfactoriness of the practice in respect of the part that the members of a congregation were entitled to take in order to the settlement of a minister among them. By the law of the land, acquiesced in by the Church courts during the "Moderate" ascendancy, the patron—who might be the Crown, an individual subject, a corporation, or a voluntary association which might have purchased the patronage—had the unquestioned right of presentation. But the same Acts of Parliament acknowledged indefinite rights of the parishioners to "concur," and these rights had always been conceded by the Church in their insistence upon a "call" addressed to the presentee by the members of the congregation. I am not aware that this call was ever dispensed with, but it came to be regarded as merely an opportunity afforded to the congregation of expressing their cordial acceptance of the presentee as their minister. If they expressed their acceptance by signing the call, it was well. If they declined to express it—at all events if half-a-dozen, or three, or even one of them expressed it—it was still well. The presentee was inducted by the Presbytery simply on the ground of the patron's nomination. Yet in the very act of induction the whole proceeding was made to rest on the call of the congregation. No reference was made to the *presentation*, but the question was solemnly put to the presentee whether he "closed with this *call*."[1]

Such a state of things was tolerated, yea, professed and vindicated, by the ecclesiastical authorities during the Moderate ascendancy; with this result, among others, that thousands of the best and most intelligent of the people had left the Church of their fathers, and, beginning with dissatisfaction with such abuses, had gradually become displeased

---

[1] I believe it has been argued that the term *call* in this connection was not to be understood as referring to the call of the people which had been put into his hand, but to the whole transaction, including both the presentation by the patron and the call by the people, the two together constituting what is often designated as a "call in Providence." This explanation is utterly untenable. But at all events it has never been denied that the call by the people was an essential and indispensable element of this providential call.—T. S.

with her very existence. It is freely admitted that the evils complained of were not constant or invariable in their atrocity. For a long time there had been no instance of a "forcible settlement," that is, an induction effected by a Presbytery acting under the protection of an armed force. But it was held even in our own day that this might still be resorted to if it should be necessary. This comparative peace was partly due to the secession of many of the representatives of those who in former days had stood up strenuously for the rights of the Christian people:—

"Solitudinem faciunt, pacem appellant."

Many of those who remained, under the influence of Moderate preaching and worldly associations, had become indifferent to what their more pious fathers regarded as all-important. Others were contented to acquiesce with silent and sullen dissatisfaction in an evil which they had no power to redress. And it ought to be stated that many of the patrons were exercising their powers in a more conciliatory spirit than that which had previously obtained. It had become no unusual thing for a patron to intimate to a congregation that if they could agree in their choice of a man, that man should be presented. Still more frequently they gave the people "a leet" of three or four men, and engaged to present the one of them who should be most acceptable to the people. But these were concessions, made, and represented as made, as acts of special grace, while the right to refuse them was maintained as being as inviolable as the right to grant them. And of course every such concession that was made in one case went to embitter the feeling of wrong inflicted in every case where a similar concession was refused.

It was this state of matters that gave rise to the discussion on "calls" in the Assembly of 1832. The debate was animated. It was before the days of *Blue-Books*, but a special report of it was published in a pamphlet.[1] The speeches are said to have been revised by their authors, but they are very briefly reported, and altogether the report represents very imperfectly the power and the interest of the debate. The first speakers were the Rev. William Clugston of Forfar, the Rev. Alexander Cameron of Edderton, and the Rev. Duncan Macfarlan of Renfrew. These three spoke from the bar, presenting the overtures to the Assembly. Then the discussion began, and the following took part in it:—The Rev. John Cook, Rev. Professor R. J. Brown, the Right Honourable the Lord Justice-Clerk (Boyle), the Rev. Alexander Maxtone, the Rev. Dr. Henry Duncan, the Rev. Principal Macfarlan, the Rev. James Begg, the Rev. Alexander Stewart, the Rev. Dr. John Brown, Robert Whigham, Esq., Advocate, and the Honourable Lord Moncreiff. The motions were (1.) by Professor Brown, "That the General Assembly, having considered and deliberated on these overtures, and finding that they relate to a subject of great importance, on which various opinions appear to be entertained, remit the said overtures to a committee, with instructions to consider the same, and report to next Assembly;" and (2.) by Principal Macfarlan, "That the Assembly judge it unnecessary and inexpedient to adopt the measures recommended in the overtures now before it."

It will be seen that formally Dr. Brown's motion expressed no approval of the contents of the overtures, and might have been supported even by those who were opposed to them, while Principal Macfarlan's was of the nature of "the previous question." But in point of fact the discussion and the vote were simply for approval or rejection of the overtures.

Dr. Begg's first appearance in the General Assembly was so important an event in his life as to require the transcrip-

[1] "Report of the Debate in the General Assembly of the Church of Scotland on the Overtures anent Calls, 24th May 1832. Edinburgh, 1832."

tion of his speech in its entireness, and this involves the additional necessity of transcribing that of the Lord Justice-Clerk, against which that of Dr. Begg was mainly directed, and without which it would scarcely be intelligible:—

"THE RIGHT HONOURABLE THE LORD JUSTICE-CLERK, one of the Commissioners from the Presbytery of Irvine, said that this question appeared to him to be one of gigantic importance, and that for a period of thirty-eight[1] years during which he had sat as a member, no question of greater moment than that which was raised by these overtures had occupied the attention of the House; and although he was of opinion that it was one which would be much better and more ably discussed by his clerical friends, yet he considered it his duty as a lay member to take an early opportunity of declaring his most determined opposition to the motion which was laid on the table by the reverend professor. It appeared to him that before a proposition of such a nature should be entertained, a necessity for some new measure must be shown, as it was impossible to deny that the tendency of these overtures went to introduce one of the greatest innovations into the Church. Before the proposition could be entertained, it should be made out to the satisfaction of the House that there existed a great evil in the present system which called for its interference. It should have been shown that the table was groaning under the load of overtures, and of cases of disputed settlements. Had there been a series of these disputed settlements in the country, there might be some reason for the overtures on the table of the Assembly; but in place of this, with a few exceptions, there had been a long period of calm tranquillity throughout the Church, showing that not only the members but the people were fully satisfied with the system as it now existed. He had heard no evils stated as resulting from the law of patronage, and he would desire those gentlemen who called upon the House to remedy an

---

[1] Thus his first Assembly must have been that of 1796. Dr. Buchanan ("Ten Years' Conflict") takes notice of the fact that he took part in the famous "Rax me the Bible" debate of that year. It need not be stated on which side he spoke and voted. It is interesting to think that the same man contended against Dr. John Erskine in 1796 and against Dr. James Begg in 1832. Dr. Erskine was born in 1721 and Dr. Begg died in 1883.—T. S.

evil to point out in distinct and intelligible terms what that evil was. If the House were to accede to the proposition contained in some of these overtures, it would declare that by the law of this Church, before a Presbytery could settle any presentee, he should have a concurrence of the majority of heads of families. In this there would be an open violation of the rights of patrons. In every settlement the candidates would consider it necessary to canvass the parish, and it was well known how canvasses of that kind were carried on to secure a majority. No man could honestly say that this would not be a direct blow at the rights of all patrons, from the king down to the lowest of his subjects. Instead of going forward in a manly manner to Parliament, and praying that the law of the land should be altered, which would be the straightforward course to adopt, a few overtures were laid upon the table, whose tendency was to injure, by a sidewind, the rights of patrons, and to deprive them of that power which was vested in them by the law of the land, and he would beg to say that the speech of the reverend gentleman who had opposed these overtures (Mr. Cook of Lawrencekirk) was by no means liable to the imputations that were cast upon it by the last speaker (Prof. Brown). That speech reminded him of the best periods of this House, when they were enlightened by the eloquence and the knowledge of the distinguished ancestor of this gentleman (Principal Hill of St. Andrews), than whom no man was more conversant with or had a more thorough knowledge of the laws and constitution of this Church, and whose sentiments the reverend gentleman may be considered to have spoken. The charge made against him was that in the course of his speech he had imputed improper motives to those who supported the overtures. His lordship appealed to the judgment of the House that the reverend gentleman had uttered no such thing. His lordship would, on that gentleman's part, disclaim any such sentiments. On the contrary, admitting that the movers of the overtures had been actuated by the most fair and honourable motives, he merely contended that the adoption of the overtures had a tendency to produce the evils stated, and therefore his lordship held it to be his duty to state that the speech of the reverend gentleman did not appear to him to be liable to such imputations as had been cast upon it. Of the evils resulting from extension of the right of election, his lordship stated that he had happened to have some experience, and he trusted he would be pardoned in stating those cases that came under his observation where the right of election was in the heritors. In one of them the parish was so completely divided that the court in which he presided had to discuss a question and decide as to the right of an individual to give a casting vote. Whether the minister was duly elected depended entirely on a casting vote, and the point was litigated with an obstinacy which he had seldom witnessed, and it was carried to the House of Lords. What was the melancholy sequel? It was this, that after the decision in the House of Lords on this disputed election, there arose a most foul and abominable conspiracy against the character of the reverend gentleman who was appointed to the living, involving charges of the most flagitious nature, and the result was that a solemn trial took place before the High Court of Justiciary, when a person convicted of that conspiracy was sentenced to transportation. The other case, which had likewise come before him in his judicial capacity, was that of a parish, upon the heritors of a part of whose territory the right of patronage had been conferred by a former proprietor, and in which, a vacancy having occurred, measures were resorted to for carving out of that territory a multitude of nominal and fictitious qualifications, composed of the smallest pendicles of land, to enable the holders to vote as heritors, but which, on investigation, was pronounced to be wholly illegal, and the presentation in favour of the opposite candidate sustained. But had the matter terminated there? Certainly not, as there has arisen out of the same contest a question which actually abides the decision of this very Assembly. These were instances of the evils arising from the right of patronage being widely extended in parishes. There were no doubt many honourable exceptions to these cases, and where the people acted as one man. But he would say that if there was an evil that they wished to introduce into the church, it would be the carrying a proposition that in all cases a majority of the heads of families must agree in the settlement of a minister. It must be consistent with the knowledge of all that in all human probability such a measure would introduce an universal confusion in the land, instead of that genuine harmony and peace which have hitherto so generally prevailed throughout the Church. To the proposition contained in these overtures he could not give his concurrence. Being convinced, likewise, that it would have the effect of depriving patrons of their undoubted privilege, he would give it most decided opposition."

It is obvious to remark that his lordship's instances have not even the remotest bearing upon the question at issue. They were both instances of disputes between joint patrons as between themselves, and did not touch the question as between patrons, joint or individual, and the members of congregations. Such disputes would occur, neither oftener nor seldomer, if the prayers of the overtures were granted. The only way by which they could have been prevented would have been that which many of the authors of the overtures most earnestly desired, but which neither the overtures nor the motion of Professor Brown ventured to propose, even the abolition of patronage. Of course his lordship's contention was that a multiplicity of interests in an election is an evil—in other words, that irresponsible monarchy is preferable to limited.

$$\text{Οὐκ ἀγαθον πολυκοιρανιη · εἰς κοιρανος ἐστω}$$
$$\text{Εἰς βασιλευς.}$$

But where then were the British Constitution? Above all, where were Presbytery? But I have introduced his lordship's speech, not with the view of answering it, but merely with the view of making Dr. Begg's answer to it intelligible.

After a speech by Mr. Maxtone of Fowlis in opposition to the overtures, and one by Dr. Duncan of Ruthwell in favour of them, Principal Macfarlan spoke, and concluded with the motion which I have already quoted. Then—

"The REV. JAMES BEGG OF PAISLEY said: Moderator—I knew before I entered this House—and the sneering with which this debate has in certain quarters been accompanied has abundantly confirmed me in the knowledge of it—that a certain obloquy would attach, in the minds of many members of this Assembly, to those who stood up in defence of these overtures. But yet, in the face of all this, I feel it to be only justice to myself, to the Presbytery of which I am a member, and to what I believe to be the cause of truth, to make a few statements in reply to the arguments to which you have just listened.

"It appears to me that there is no force in the objection which has just been urged by the rev. principal against the motion of Professor Brown, upon the ground that were that motion adopted the Assembly would sanction the measures proposed in these overtures. All that that motion asserts is merely that 'the General Assembly, having considered these overtures, regard the subject to which they refer as of great importance.' Now, its importance has, I think, been admitted by every member who has spoken. Even the right honourable judge (the Lord Justice-Clerk) who lately addressed you, although violently opposed to these overtures, declared that the subject was of great importance—nay, of 'gigantic importance,' of greater importance than any question which had been agitated in this House during all the period of his membership—a period of thirty-eight years. And all that we wish the Assembly to do is simply, under a conviction of the truth of these assertions, to transmit these overtures to a committee, that the subject may be gravely considered, and that the law of the Church may be declared, and hereafter strictly acted upon. In decreeing, therefore, in terms of the rev. professor's motion, it appears to me that the Assembly by no means pledges itself to any ultimate decision, and that this objection is unfounded.

"Of the four speeches which were delivered on the opposite side of the question, only three were audible in this part of the house. The first was delivered by a young reverend gentleman (Mr. Cook) who came nobly forth as a knight-errant in defence of absolute patronage, of which he seemed greatly enamoured; and who, after expending what appeared to me a very unnecessary quantity of pathos in deprecating the evils which, in his opinion, would result from departing from it in the least degree, spoke of clinging to the ruins of the present system, and gravely announced to the Assembly what I must call his heroic resolution, if it was doomed to perish, of burying himself amidst its ruins. I trust, sir, that that gentleman has seriously considered the nature of that resolution, for it is my firm conviction that if his opposition, and that of his friends, to the satisfactory settlement of this question be persisted in, his courage will soon be put to the proof. But I do trust that, if that gentleman shall ever perish, it will be in defending a nobler cause!

"Next came the arguments of the learned judge (the Lord Justice-Clerk), for whom all of us, I am sure, entertain the most profound respect; but I must say that most of his statements on this occasion seemed to be totally inapplicable to the question before us. His lordship set out by asserting, what we all admit, that it is necessary to show the existence of an evil before a remedy should be sought for; but he proceeded to assert that no evil had in this case been shown sufficient to call for our interference. Now it appears to me that the very existence of so many overtures upon your table from so many Presbyteries proves clearly that in the opinion of many ministers of this Church there does exist an evil. To prove the existence of an evil it is not necessary, as the honourable judge seemed to require, that our table should be literally '*groaning under the weight of overtures, and of cases of disputed settlements.*' The experienced opinions of so many ministers of this Church, both in this House and without, proves that dissatisfaction with the present arbitrary mode of settling ministers widely prevails; and, therefore, the propriety of immediately examining the subject. The learned judge next enlarged on the monstrous evils of popular elections, and told us of two cases which he had himself decided in his official capacity, to prove that they were fraught with danger. Now, all this may be true. I am not disposed at present to dispute it. But no man in this Assembly, so far as I have heard, has maintained the propriety of popular elections. All the supporters of these overtures have admitted that patronage should continue to exist—that at least it is not in the power of this court to put an end to it—and have only contended that this Church should prevent its becoming an instrument of evil to our population, by the exercise of her legitimate authority.

"Last of all, we had the speech of the rev. principal at your right hand, full of ingenuity, and, no doubt, of law also, but from every part of its conclusion I take the liberty firmly to dissent, and for the following reasons: First of all, we had the oft-repeated allegation that we are intending to invade the rights of patrons. At all events the rev. doctor declared that in his opinion it was impossible to concede to the people the right of expressing their approbation or disapprobation without virtually abolishing patronage. Now, instead of this, it is our opinion that were the object which we have in view secured, it would confirm patrons in the exercise of their rights; only their power would be undoubtedly limited, and they would no longer be allowed, under the name of patronage, to exercise an arbitrary authority which they ought never to have possessed. It has been demonstrated to be the law of the Church that no minister should ever be placed in any parish without the *consent* of at least some portion of its inhabitants. No reply has ever been attempted to the legal statement on this subject, and the reasonableness of the requirement will not, I think, be disputed. There is an express Act of this[1] Assembly 'against intrusions,' specially providing 'that no minister shall ever be settled in any parish against the decided wishes of the people;' and all that we contend for is, not that patrons should be deprived of the just exercise of their rights, but that, *according to the law*, they should be prevented from intruding into parishes those who, in all likelihood, will not discharge satisfactorily and with success the ministerial duties. If any man shall hereafter maintain that we contend for more, we shall expect at least to hear the statements accompanied with something like proof. No more is contended for in these overtures; no more has been contended for by those who have spoken in support of them; no more is contended for in the motion of

---

[1] The expression, "*this* Assembly" does not here mean, as it usually does, the Assembly actually sitting. The Act referred to seems to be that of 1736, though the quotation is not verbally accurate. Its words are: "The General Assembly, considering that it is, and has been since the Reformation, the principle of this Church that no minister shall be intruded into any church contrary to the will of the congregation," &c. This is substantially the same. But it is quite possible that there may be another Act of Assembly containing the words given in the text.—T. S.

Professor Brown. We believe that patronage and a substantial call may subsist together, and all that we wish is simply that, leaving patrons to discharge their duties as to them may seem meet, the Church should rise and exercise her own power also, which has long been dormant, of preventing persons unfit for discharging the duties of parishes from being *intruded* into them.

"But it was next contended by the rev. principal that this could not be done without violating the law of the land. Now, sir, what does this amount to? To this, that the Church has made laws which she is unable to execute—that the Church has been acting in the face of the law of the land all along, in making the Acts to which we have already referred, in vesting in Presbyteries the power of rejecting unqualified presentees. But I have no fear of civil interference. *Indeed, if such interference were attempted, it would then become a question for every honest man to determine how long he could consistently remain a member of a Church thus rendered unable to enforce its most salutary laws.*[1] But how then came it to pass that this very Assembly lately rejected a presentation from the highest patron in the land to a licentiate of our Church, and that for a cause not inferring deposition, without question on the part of that patron?[2] Does that prove that the civil power is ready in such cases to interfere? But the very law of the land itself, as just quoted by the rev. principal, expressly states, that although patrons have the right of presenting, it remains with Presbyteries in every case to determine the qualifications of presentees, and that the decision of the Church courts shall in every case be final. And all that we wish is simply that this element shall hereafter be reckoned necessary to constitute a full qualification—the satisfaction of those among whom the minister is to labour. There is in this no interference with the law of the land; there is in it a perfect conformity with the oft-repeated requirements of the law of the Church; in addition to which, you have just been assured by the rev. principal himself,

---

[1] I have italicised this sentence, on account of its vital bearing on subsequent events. So far as I know, it is the first foreboding of the action of the patrons and the civil courts—then regarded only as a possibility—and the first indication of what would be the duty of the Church if that action were taken.—T. S.

[2] "King; case of Dunkeld."

that one reason why so much peace and tranquillity prevail in the midst of us is, that patrons have lately in their appointments consulted very much the feelings of the people; in other words, they have done that in many instances with salutary effect, which we are anxious that this Assembly should require to be done throughout every part of the Church.

"We were next told that these overtures called upon this Assembly to legislate anew upon this subject; nay, we were defied from another quarter to prove that we did not aim at innovation. Now, in opposition to this, I have only again firmly to assert, that we only wish this Assembly to declare that the laws to which we have referred on the subject of calls do exist, are still in force, and ought in every case to be observed. We wish no new law, and if the committee which we are desirous to have appointed shall find that no such laws exist at all, our arguing shall cease. Our simple desire is to return to the original constitution and practice of the Church, and we wish the committee simply to make evident what that constitution requires, and what that practice ought always to have been.

"The rev. principal next contended, with considerable indignation, that it was absurd to call the mode in which 'calls' are now conducted 'a solemn mockery.' Now, sir, notwithstanding all that has been said on the subject, I fearlessly give it as my opinion that that ceremony often at present deserves no better name. On such occasions mockeries have been practised—are practised—and unless this Assembly shall interfere, will no doubt continue to be practised. Let us only conceive a frequent case. A parish becomes vacant. The patron looks round—not for the person best qualified for discharging the duties of the situation—he does not, as his name implies, exercise the office of a father towards the parishioners—but he presents simply one of his own friends, some one for whom he is bound to provide, and many of whom he may have in reserve, without at all considering what the feelings of the people towards him may be. A day is appointed for moderating in his call, and although it is not subscribed by six of the inhabitants of the parish, he is forthwith ordained. Nay, instances are on record of calls subscribed by only one inhabitant of the parish, and Presbyteries have connived at all this, and they now turn round and say to the people who remonstrate, 'We have been exceedingly generous to you; we have given you, by moderating in a call, an opportunity of welcoming your future minister,'—a minister whom no one wished to welcome, whom all the inhabitants of the parish despised. What is this but mockery? What is it but adding insult to injury? I would much rather that calls were altogether and for ever abolished, than that such farces as these should any longer be tolerated.

"Then came that part of the rev. principal's speech which related to the peace and contentment which now prevail in our great towns in the settlement of ministers. Now, so far is this from proving anything in favour of his argument, that it proves a great deal in favour of our motion. This peace has, by his own admission, arisen from consulting the feelings of congregations in the appointment of their ministers. And what is the conclusion? Is it, as seemed to be inferred if the argument was good, that the feelings of the people should no longer be consulted? Undoubtedly not; but that we should do all over the Church what has been done in these cases with such admirable effect. And this is all that we contend for.

"Last of all, the rev. principal reminded us that all over Europe the present is a period of great political excitement; that a very universal feeling of hostility prevails against established churches, and that a question of that nature would be better settled in times of calmness and peace. Now, sir, it is an unquestionable fact, and it is not to be forgotten, because it accounts for much of the contentment of which our opponents have boasted, that when there was no excitement in the country—no feeling against established churches—this court did discard with contempt this important question. In the midst of tranquillity the subject was neglected; and now, when there is a storm and confusion without, it is proposed to neglect it still. When, sir, I ask, shall the time arrive for settling this question, if it is neither a time of peace nor a time of agitation? The subject cannot be avoided; sooner or later you must give it due consideration. I say more. Let no member of this House suppose that by endeavouring to hush up the question and to silence discussion, his object will be secured. That will only cause it the more to be sifted to the bottom. And as to the feeling said to exist against established churches, my firm conviction is that the only way to strengthen the Church, and to make it stand secure amidst all the efforts of its enemies, is to base it firmly on the affections of the people. If all the inhabitants of this country were members of the Church of Scotland, no Government that ever existed, or that ever will exist, could overturn it, and we might laugh at all our enemies! Though all the other Churches in the world should fall, ours would stand secure. But, on the other hand, if the people shall abandon it and leave it to stand alone, how can it remain? And they have undoubtedly in many instances adopted the natural remedy for the evil of which we have complained. As soon as a minister has been thrust into a parish contrary to their wishes, they have at once abandoned the Church, and procured a minister for themselves; and the result has been that Dissenters have gradually increased, are now exceedingly numerous, and in general very hostile to the Church. It is evident, however, that a very limited declaration of this court would restore at once the confidence of the people, and arrest the progress of Dissenterism. But if the present system is recklessly persevered in, for aught I know, the result may be that the governors of this country, without consulting us, may reckon it sound policy, as they formerly transferred the funds which supported Popery to the support of the Protestant Church, to transfer the property of our establishment, because inefficient, to the support of those who really are spiritual instructors to the inhabitants of the country.[1]

"But all this is away from the question before you, although necessary in reply to the statements which you have just heard. The motion on your table is, that a committee be appointed to examine into this important subject, that so the laws of the Church respecting 'calls' may be distinctly declared, and hereafter firmly acted upon; and there is, I think, abundant reason to induce us to adopt such a measure.

---

[1] It is difficult to assign a precise meaning to this sentence. To whom did he refer as possibly being the real spiritual instructors of the people? One thing is obvious, that he did not then contemplate the possibility of its ever being proposed that the property of the establishment should be applied to other than spiritual purposes.—T. S.

We have all heard from an authority which none of us are disposed to question, that this subject is of 'gigantic importance.' All of us believe that it is; and I can see no reason why some of the able and learned men of the Church should not be appointed to examine it, that the members of every Presbytery may in all time coming know in every case how they ought to act. I would ask what reason any man can give why this subject should not be examined. The cause of truth and justice can never thus be injured. Are those who have opposed us afraid of the results of inquiry? Are they afraid that the laws of the Church and of the land shall be found beyond all doubt to be exactly what we have stated them to be? This indeed seemed to be the case. But does any one suppose that one adverse decision of this court can arrest the progress of investigation and set the question at rest? The evil cannot be smothered up. And I trust that those members who think as I do, that the very existence of the Church depends upon the satisfactory settlement of this question, if they are left in a minority, will not suffer themselves to be baffled. They may meet and form a committee of their own, fully and fairly to investigate the subject. And be assured, that it will in many ways force itself upon the consideration of this House, whether it will or not, and that it is infinitely better to proceed at once to the examination of it, than after long delay to have justice reluctantly wrested from our hands. I do therefore sincerely trust that the Assembly will adopt the motion of Professor Brown."

This is manifestly a pretty full report of a "maiden speech." But incidentally I have evidence that it must be materially abbreviated. A newspaper of the day, commenting editorially on the proceedings of the Assembly, adverts to the failure of Dr. Chalmers in every case to merge the *man* in the *Moderator*. In this leader occurs the following passage:—"He has acquired a reputation as solid as it is brilliant, and by the force of his genius, the soundness of his opinions, and the moral elevation of his character, he has placed himself in the proudest position in Scotland—a position which he could never have occupied in this country, had he been nothing more than an orator, had not the most comprehensive and enlightened views of any man of his age been the foundation of his oratory; and had he not crowned all with a consistent life, a spotless integrity of character, and that Christian meekness with which he bears his honours. It is not to be denied, however, that in the little things of form and order, Dr. Chalmers, as Moderator, sometimes appeared ridiculous enough. His want of taste and ready perception of what ought to be done, might have presented him to a stranger under great disadvantage, and were it not that he blunders with so much good-humour and *naïveté*, they might wonder if this were the man who did great things so well. Yet there was interest in his very blunders, *and during the sitting of the Assembly, nothing occurred half so delightful as the manner in which the Moderator, in listening to a successful stroke in the speech of the Rev. Mr. Begg, actually fell from his dignity into a hearty laugh, and for an instant clapped his hands with delight.*" That Dr. Chalmers showed a deficiency of "taste," or that he made himself "ridiculous," I do not believe; but I can easily imagine the things—to the "blundering" with "much good-humour" I do not very strongly object—which gave the occasion to a somewhat pedantic editor to make these statements. But I have to do at present only with the sentence which I have italicised, and with it only as showing that the report of Dr. Begg's speech must be but meagre; for there is nothing in the speech as reported which could possibly have moved any hearer to hearty laughter.

It must be extremely difficult, if not simply impossible, for any one unacquainted with the oligarchical habitudes of the Assemblies of those days to estimate the "pluck" of the young man who, in the first Assembly of which he was a member, and before he had completed his twenty-fourth year, took up the gauntlets of two such champions as the Lord Justice-Clerk and Principal Macfarlan. According to the result, it must have been attributed to the insolence of youthful self-conceit, or to the consciousness of innate power. In the present case the result necessitates the latter ascription.

The "intrusion" of the youthful combatant into the inner ring of debate could not fail to take the Assembly by surprise. That it did so I have the testimony of my venerable friend, as I must now call him, the Rev. Donald Ferguson of Leven, who in the Assembly of 1832 occupied a position similar to that which Dr. Begg himself had occupied three years earlier. Mr. Ferguson writes thus:—

"After the lapse of more than fifty years, they are but broken reminiscences that remain to me of the scene of Dr. Begg's appearance in the General Assembly of 1832. I think that it must have been his first Assembly speech, but I am not sure. I know that I witnessed Dr. Cunningham's first Assembly appearance in West St. Giles', which was certainly not less striking and successful.

"The Assembly of 1832 met in the Tron Church. I had not witnessed an Assembly field-day before, and I had got a seat in the front gallery, along with some of my fellow-students, being deeply interested in the debate that was to take place upon the 'Overtures on Calls.'

"After the bar had spoken, Mr. John Cook of Lawrencekirk, one of the rising hopes of his party, opened the debate upon the Moderate side of the House. I think that he also was making his first Assembly appearance. He spoke with considerable ability and great fluency. Among those who followed on the same side was Lord Justice-Clerk Boyle, who addressed the House in his usual pompous style, his speech being distinguished more by its pretentiousness than by its argument. Shortly after, a young man, seated far back under the gallery opposite to where I was sitting, caught the eye of the Moderator. He began to speak with a slightly nasal twang, which in after life almost left him. After two or three sharp hits at the previous speakers, curiosity was aroused. 'Who is he?—who is he?' was whispered right and left, and it was some time before I heard a person say, 'It is Mr. Begg of Paisley.' His good-humoured but pungent sarcasms were immensely relished by us youngsters; and when he turned upon the Lord Justice-Clerk, dealing with him and his speech in a style in which the House was little accustomed to hear the speeches of the judges handled in those days, the Assembly became considerably excited and amused. The unfortunate dignitary, who winced under every fresh infliction of the lash, was, however, far from amused. His face, flamed with passion and indignation at the plain truths that he was hearing about the oration which he had so recently delivered, is at this moment before me, for though I have but little recollection of the argument, what was present to the eye is well remembered.

" After having disposed, in a few effective sentences, of his opponents who had preceded him in the debate, he directed his attention to the overtures under discussion, which he supported warmly. He had the good sense not to detain the House. The speech was short; but he sat down, having established his reputation as a fearless and formidable and withal a prompt debater."

I am confident that the speech, even as thus imperfectly reported, will be regarded as a remarkable phenomenon. It is manifest, from the fact that it is entirely occupied with answering the preceding speakers, that it was perfectly extemporaneous. There is not a point in the speeches of the Lord Justice-Clerk and Principal Macfarlan which is not met and satisfactorily answered. Moreover, there is no appearance of juvenility in the speech, no straining after effect, no rhetorical flourishes, no carrying of the argument to extremes; but a calm exposition of principle, and an earnest insistance on truth and righteousness in opposition to lifeless form and virtual injustice.

A question of much importance is suggested by this speech. The speaker repeatedly intimates that he does not seek to interfere with the rights of patrons, and argues that what was proposed was not inconsistent with these rights. It is well known that among those who advocated the requirement of a real call, and among those who afterwards advocated the *veto*, there were some who held that patronage should be abolished, and others who desired only that it should be restricted. I had always understood that Dr. Begg belonged to the former class from the outset of his career, as he certainly did from an early stage of it. But there are some passages in the speech that are scarcely consistent with this belief. It is true that he might have meant no more than this, that *in supporting the motion of Professor Brown* he was not asking the abolition of patronage, or aught that was incompatible with its continued subsistence. But I confess to a suspicion that he had not then that intense horror of " the Act of 1712," which afterwards he felt so strongly and expressed so frequently.

It is in this speech that I find the first use of the argument which afterwards became a commonplace in the discussions. It was argued that the law gave to the patron the right of presentation, and to the Presbytery—with the right of appeal to the Synod and General Assembly—the right of judging of the qualifications of the presentee; but that there was no recognition of any right of the people to express either concurrence or dissent. The main answer to this argument was that it is an essential principle in the constitution of the Church that a minister be not intruded on an unwilling congregation. But a subsidiary argument, and a perfectly tenable one, was, that acceptability to the people was an essential "qualification" of which the Presbytery must judge. I have not noticed that this argument was used by any one before it was used by Dr. Begg in the speech before us.

As it was in the Assembly of 1832 that Dr. Begg began his career as an Assembly speaker, so I believe that it was with reference to that Assembly that he first came out as a contributor to the press. In the *Scottish Guardian* of June 8, 1832, there is an article entitled "List of the Division of Ministers and Elders in the Recent General Assembly on the subject of the Overtures regarding Calls. (From a Correspondent.)" That correspondent I happen to know to have been Dr. Begg; and I have not been able to identify him as the author of any earlier production. Assuming, therefore, that this is the first-fruit of his authorship, I give it *in extenso*, as I have already given his earliest speech. It is as follows:—

"We subjoin a list of the division in the General Assembly on the question of Calls, from which the people of this country may learn how their ministers and elders defend their undoubted rights in that venerable court. To every impartial person the result must appear very strange, especially when it is remembered that the motion carried was not a *counter* motion. It was declared to be 'unnecessary and inexpedient to adopt the measures proposed in the overtures on the Assembly's table.' But no one had asked them to adopt these measures. Indeed, they were so various that to adopt them all was impossible. All that was asked was simply that the Assembly should appoint a committee to examine the whole subject, that so the laws of the Church and of the land, in regard to calls, might be fully declared, and that question, about which so much has been said, might be calmly and satisfactorily set to rest. No demand could have been more reasonable, and none, we should have supposed, but those who feared the result of such an examination, would have shrunk from it, and yet a majority of the members of the Assembly did shrink from it, and by an evasive motion set aside the question.

"It is instructive to observe that the majority of ministers against Professor Brown's motion is only ten, whilst that of elders is twenty-nine. How comes it to pass that these worthies are so afraid of examination? Do they fear that it would hasten on the time when many of them will be ejected from that court as altogether unfit to represent an order of men so sacred? How comes it to pass that amongst them are found the names of the former and present Lord Provost of Edinburgh, who have *all along, in their official capacities,* been 'adopting the measures proposed in these overtures'? Indeed, if they did not, how long would the Church in Edinburgh remain? Why do we see the name of a cotemporary of our own (Peterkin), who has all along been forward to defend the rights of the people, and whose blundering apology, since published, only convinces us the more that his conscience was accusing him of inconsistency? Why is Dr. William Muir of Edinburgh's name to be found among the majority? Or why did he not at least condescend to tell the Assembly the particular reasons on account of which he objected to the investigation of this subject? Above all, why were so many ministers, who would undoubtedly have voted for the appointment of a committee, absent at the vote? It is thus that many a great question is lost. Ministers should remember that they represent the feelings of others as well as their own, and that it is shameful to prefer their enjoyment to the cause of justice. But let not those who are the friends of the Church of Scotland, and of the inhabitants of the country, for a moment imagine that this question is lost on account of the Assembly's decision. Most of those who supported the overtures expected even a greater majority against them, and are more firmly convinced than ever that their success is certain at no distant day. They observed with much pleasure that most of the patrons voted with them, as Sir James Colquhoun of Luss, one of the magistrates of Edinburgh, and both those from Glasgow. The question will come before the next Assembly with a force and an urgency which the dominant party in the Church will be unable to withstand. And before many years it will be the declared law of the Church, that no minister shall in any case, by whomsoever presented, be intruded into a parish. Nay, men will wonder that any other law should ever have been recognised. In despite of the efforts of those who should be the warmest friends of the Church to bring her into disgrace, she will yet shake off her abuses, and extend herself over the length and breadth of the land; including again in her wide embrace those who, because of forced settlements, 'went out from her,' and then, defended on every side by her thousands of devoted sons, she shall, in defiance of all her enemies, remain the glory of the land."

This is followed by a full list of the vote, the numbers being—

For Professor Brown's motion . . .	85
For Principal Macfarlan's	127
Majority for the latter	42

CHAPTER XV.

THE YEAR 1833.

IN the immediately preceding chapter, I stated a doubt whether in his maiden speech Dr. Begg meant to express a personal desire for the continuance of patronage, with the limitation which would be put upon it by the requirement of a real call on the part of the people, or whether he only took that ground argumentatively, as the common ground which he could occupy with his opponents. I have no doubt that at a later period of his life he would honestly have said that he had always been opposed to patronage, because his opposition to it grew so steadily that he could not have specified a time when he began to disapprove of it. And yet I suspect that at this time—the Assembly of 1832—he held, with Dr. Chalmers and many others, that, with an efficient call, patronage, if not altogether a good thing, was at all events tolerable. It is thus that I account for his standing aloof, as he seems to have done, from a violent anti-patronage agitation, which was straightway set agoing all over the country, and especially in the West. In the newspapers of the day I find long reports of anti-patronage meetings held at Greenock, Paisley, Port-Glasgow, and Glasgow. At these meetings two other Paisley ministers, Dr. Burns and Mr. MacNaughton, were generally the chief speakers, and very ably and eloquently they spoke; but I do not find Dr. Begg mentioned as taking any part in any of the meetings.

But in the same newspapers I do find most gratifying testimonies to the faithfulness with which he discharged his pastoral duties, and the efforts which he made for bringing Christian ordinances within the reach of all the inhabitants of his parish, and of the town of which that parish was a part. A few extracts from the *Scottish Guardian* of 1833, some of them contributed by " our corespondent," and others extracted from a local paper, the *Paisley Advertiser*, will enable the reader to estimate the position which he had then attained, and the influence which he was exerting.

I have already spoken of the employment of Mr. Steel and Mr. Wood as assistants, or curates, to Dr. Begg. The following extract shows that this good work was still further extended:—

"PARISH MISSIONS.—The Rev. Thomas Wilson has been unanimously appointed by the Middle Church session to preach regularly in the Court Hall, with a salary of £60 per annum. His resignation as agent for the Town Mission Society was received on Monday evening with deep regret, and it was resolved, at a very full meeting, 'unanimously to record their most unqualified approbation of Mr. Wilson's whole conduct while acting as their missionary.' The people of Charleston, we understand, many of whom have been induced to attend public worship owing to his efforts, deeply regret his departure."[1]

The same column of the *Scottish Guardian* contains another extract from the *Paisley Advertiser*. In reading it we must bear in mind that a testimonial or presentation meant a great deal more half a century ago than it does now. In making this statement, I should be sorry to be understood as depreciating such presentations now. Only, they were much more unusual then, and therefore had a higher value attached to them:—

[1] *Scottish Guardian*, April 30, 1833.

"On Tuesday evening the young men and women who form the classes for religious instruction under the Rev. Mr. Begg, met in the Middle Church, and presented that gentleman with a very elegant gold watch and appendages. The following inscription, tastefully engraved by Mr. Blaikie, will sufficiently explain the object for which it was given:— 'Presented to the Rev. James Begg, by the young men and women attending his weekly classes, in testimony of their gratitude for his religious instructions.—*Paisley, 23d April,* 1833.' It is gratifying to observe such excellent feelings subsisting between pastors and the young people of their congregations. Next to the pleasure of sowing the seeds of religious instruction in the minds of their juvenile hearers, must be that of knowing that their labours are duly appreciated. The rev. gentleman returned thanks for the splendid present in an appropriate and affectionate address, which made a deep impression on those present, and will not soon be forgotten."[1]

In the report of the proceedings of the Synod of Glasgow and Ayr, there is reference to a curious case which came up from the Presbytery of Paisley. So far as I can make out, it was in this wise. Mr. MacNaughton had been elected and presented to the charge of the High Church of Paisley. A day had been appointed for his induction. The Presbytery met, and the preliminary services were gone through. But Mr. MacNaughton had not arrived. How he was detained, and how, in those ante-telegraphic days, he managed to make it known that he might be expected in the evening, I do not know. But it was the last day of the half-year, and if the induction were postponed, Mr. MacNaughton would have forfeited a half-year's stipend. The Presbytery therefore adjourned, to meet in the evening for the induction. The public dinner, which was to have followed the induction, preceded it, and the induction took place in the evening. It was certainly an irregular proceeding, scarcely justified, I think, by the necessities of the case. The matter was

[1] *Scottish Guardian*, April 30, 1833.

brought before the Synod at their meeting in April. The following is the report of the proceedings:—

"Mr. James M'Lean, in a very long speech, called the attention of the Synod to certain informalities in the induction of the Rev. Mr. MacNaughton to the High Church of Paisley;—among others, unconstitutional precipitancy in the induction, the *pro re nata* meeting, the delivery of the discourse on the occasion when Mr. MacNaughton was not present, the subsequent adjournment of the meeting till his arrival, and the division of the duties of the presiding clergyman;—on which grounds Mr. M'Lean called upon the rev. court to pass a vote of censure on the Presbytery of Paisley.

. . . . . .

"Mr. Begg defended the Presbytery's proceedings in an eloquent speech, and was followed by Dr. Lawrie, Dr. Begg (!), Dr. Hill, Dr. Stewart, Mr. Henderson, and Principal Macfarlan on the other side. The Synod agreed to express their disapprobation of the unconstitutional and irregular conduct of the Presbytery in some of the proceedings alluded to, and ordered the clerk to record the deliverance in the Synod books."

Well done, the brave old minister of New Monkland! who is ready to unite for once with the Moderates in censuring irregularity, and cannot be charmed by the voice of his own son, charm he ever so "eloquently."

In the *Scottish Guardian* of the 30th of July we find the following paragraph, extracted from the *Paisley Advertiser*. It indicates how patiently and energetically, and successfully, Dr. Begg was labouring for the accomplishment of the great end on which he had manifestly set his heart, that the Gospel might be preached to every creature:—

"CHURCH ACCOMMODATION.—It is gratifying to observe that an additional place of worship belonging to the establishment has been opened in the Middle Parish by Mr. M'Coll, who has the advantage of knowing both the Gaelic and English languages. It is to be hoped that the situation of the place (the chapel formerly occupied by the Episcopalians), and the visitations of Mr. M'Coll from house to house, will induce many who have not been in the habit of attending church to wait upon religious worship, and thus be made better members of society, and be filled with the hopes and the faith of the Christian. It is also to be hoped that the efforts of Mr. Begg, in thus encouraging so many places of worship, will be seconded by the efforts of those who may be managers of public works, or whose influence over others, from their worldly circumstances, might avail in directing their dependants to the great duty of public worship. In addition to his more sacred duties, Mr. M'Coll proposes, we understand, to commence a class for the purpose of teaching English reading, writing, and arithmetic, on the week-day evenings, between 8 and 10, to young people whose education may have been defective, and whose opportunities of instruction may have been neglected in their younger days. The importance of such a seminary can be estimated from the fact that many young people are too soon abstracted from school to the business of life, and are afterwards so occupied that they have not time for mental culture. The terms of education are to be exceedingly small, that the advantages may be the more widely extended, and the time of meeting is intended to suit those of both sexes who may be otherwise employed at an earlier hour."

It is one of the blessed results of good work well done that it stirs up others to imitation and emulation. I think I am safe in saying that Dr. Begg was the originator of the "Church Extension movement" in connection with the Established Church. Not that he was the originator of "church extension." That had always been recognised as incumbent on the Church. It had been carried out by the founding of a not inconsiderable number of chapels of ease, and it had received a mighty impulse from Dr. Chalmers during his Glasgow ministry. Indeed, I do not doubt that it was from the torch of Dr. Chalmers that that of Dr. Begg was lighted. But none the less was it Dr. Begg that undertook church extension in a systematic method; and so I think he is entitled to the high credit of the origination of the *movement.* He seems to have been generally recognised as its originator; and, therefore, his aid was sought in pushing it on elsewhere than in Paisley. Thus we find in the *Scottish Guardian* the following extract from the *Aberdeen Journal*:—

"CHURCH ACCOMMODATION.—In accordance with intimations read in the different churches of the city, a sermon was preached on the evening of Monday last by the Rev. James Begg, one of the ministers of Paisley, in Greyfriars' Church, in behalf of the Home Mission department of the association in that parish. The wants of Aberdeen in these respects were adverted to, and a sermon full of Scriptural truth, embodied in the most eloquent language, and delivered with the most powerful effect, was concluded by an appeal to the people for support to a proposed place of worship in Greyfriars' parish, where, though there was a population of about 5000, many of whom, it has been ascertained, never enter any place of worship, the church afforded accommodation for only between 800 and 900. The congregation, as had also been previously intimated, then resolved themselves into a meeting with a view to home missionary exertions on a more extended scale. The Rev. Principal Dewar was called to the chair, and opened the meeting with prayer, and with a statement of the fearful destitution in Glasgow, Paisley, Kilmarnock, and other large towns in the West of Scotland. He also referred to the state of Aberdeen as loudly demanding the vigorous efforts of the ministers and members of the Established Church; since, he declared, there was little hope of Government making any further provision for the spiritual wants of the population, unless they, in the first instance, exerted themselves individually.

"He was succeeded by the Rev. A. L. Gordon, who urged upon the meeting the importance of this object, particularly in regard to the parish where they stood, and called upon them, from various considerations, to assist in accomplishing it. The Rev. A. Gray, and Mr. Brown of Anderston, Glasgow, also stated many most striking facts as to the necessity for such efforts, and the success which had already attended them wherever they had been made, and obviated convincingly the frivolous objections stated against these measures. The Rev.

Mr. Begg detailed especially the results attending them in his own parish, which were so striking and important as to arrest the attention, and, we trust, create a deep and salutary impression upon the audience. The Rev. Mr. Duncan, Glasgow, concluded with prayer. The collection was very great—amounting to nearly £30. The church was literally crammed with people in every part, and the elders believe that not fewer than 1000 went away, unable to procure admission. We understand that these measures are immediately to be followed up, and subscriptions solicited for the place of worship referred to, which is to be erected either in the Porthill, in the Gallowgate, or at Causewayend."

This extract, although it is barely fifty years old, may be almost said to possess an antiquarian interest, for it brings us into contact with a state of matters which has as much passed away as have the habitudes of our antediluvian fathers. Mighty efforts had evidently been put forth to make the meeting a great success. Dr. Dewar was Principal of one of the Aberdeen Universities—for, like England, she then had two (I think the joke was Sir Robert Peel's). Messrs. Abercromby L. Gordon and Andrew Gray were the most eloquent and the most popular of the local clergy, Messrs. Brown and Duncan, though Glasgow clergymen, were natives of Aberdeen, the former being the son of a Lord Provost of the city; and Dr. Begg was brought as a "bright occidental star" to shine for one night only in the northern sky. The church was literally crammed, and a number estimated at 1000, and therefore probably not much less than 500, could not find admission; and "the collection was very great, amounting to nearly £30!" We have changed all this, and surely, in some respects at least, for the better.

The growing reputation of Dr. Begg prepares us for the next notice which we find in the *Guardian* relating to him:—

"GLASGOW: ST. ANDREW'S CHURCH.—We learn that the Rev. James Begg, of the Middle Church, Paisley, has received the presentation to the charge of the vacant church and parish of St. Andrew's in this city."[1]

I do not think that this statement is accurate. I have not been able to ascertain the exact truth regarding it, but conjecture that Dr. Begg received the *offer* of the presentation, and declined the acceptance of it, so as to prevent its actual offer. The statement is a proof that already—and it is to be remembered that he was yet but in his twenty-sixth year—he was marked in public estimation for an important city charge. In point of fact, the charge of St. Andrew's became the subject of a protracted and somewhat bitter controversy. Several men of eminence were proposed for it—Dr. Cunningham for one. It was eventually filled by my late venerable friend Dr. Nathanael Paterson, a man whose name no one who knew him can mention, even incidentally, without staying to pay a passing tribute to his immense information and his most attractive kindliness.

Four days later we find the following notice of one of Dr. Begg's sermons, reported by a "Correspondent of *Paisley Advertiser*." It justifies what has been already said regarding the early formation and permanence of Dr. Begg's mode of preaching. It is just such a sermon as he might have preached in Newington in the last year of his life:—

"THE CHOICE OF MAGISTRATES.—On Sabbath afternoon last, a most eloquent and impressive sermon was delivered by the Rev. Mr. Begg on this subject. The text, a very appropriate one, was Exod. xviii. 21, 'Moreover, thou shalt provide out of all the people able men,' &c. After stating the privilege of living under a well-organised government, where peace and justice reign, in opposition to a state of anarchy, where every one does that which is right in his own eyes, he adverted to the solemn duty soon to be discharged by many of our citizens, of appointing magistrates for themselves;[2]

---

[1] *Scottish Guardian*, September 27, 1833.

[2] I suppose that this was the first popular election of town councillors under the Burgh Reform Act.—T. S.

and stated that the four different classes alluded to in the text were placed in plain opposition to four different kinds of characters, to be found in every age, in every sect and community, endeavouring to push their way into seats of authority, who ought to be most carefully shunned. The truly 'able man,' whom the people shall respect, is placed in opposition to the vain noisy talker, who is merely wise in his own conceit. The man 'fearing God' is placed in opposition to him who acts merely under the fear of man, which bringeth a snare. The 'man of truth' is opposed to him who, like Absalom of old, and many of the present day, will tell abundance of lies, and make promises which they never intend to perform, and who, to gratify their ambitious views, will exclaim, 'Oh that I were made judge in the land, that every man which hath any suit or cause might come unto me, and I would do him justice.' The man 'hating covetousness' is in opposition to him who would take bribes, that he might pervert the course of justice, or squander, as has often been done, upon himself or his own friends, the funds of the community placed at his disposal. The similes used in illustration, and the inferences drawn, were peculiarly appropriate, *and, as is usual on all such occasions, were applied by every man, not to himself, but to his neighbour.* The sermon was particularly well-timed, and would, if published, do much good in turning the public attention to the necessity of electing men of respectability, influence, intelligence, sound judgment, and patriotic views, rather than ambitious, bustling intriguers, who have nothing to recommend them but their ambition and their volubility."

In the sentence which I have italicised, the author of this paragraph puts his finger on the weak point of this "preaching to the times." The Gospel ought to be so preached as to exert a potent influence on men's conduct in all the relations of life, and not least in their civic relations. But this should be rather by aiming at a general or universal elevation of the moral and Christian standard, than by special sermons at particular times. It would be almost impossible for any man to preach on such a subject *at the time of a disputed election* without giving rise to a suspicion on the part of some of his hearers that he was acting the part of a canvasser for a candidate or a section of the candidates; and this although no thought might be farther from the preacher's mind. I should be sorry to be understood as recommending a timid reserve on the subject of the duty of men as electors, or in any other capacity; but instead of thinking that a sermon on such a theme was "particularly well-timed" on the eve of a contested election, I should regard that as precisely the least appropriate time for it. Our next extract is particularly gratifying, inasmuch as it shows that Dr. Begg's zeal for church extension was infecting the community, and that his appeals were calling forth a hearty response.

"As a proof of the interest taken in the erection of a chapel in the Middle Parish, Paisley, and as an example worthy of imitation by many in more opulent circumstances, a very few young females who have associated themselves for prayer, in addition to former subscriptions, sent one guinea, and the following interesting letter, addressed to Mr. Begg:—

"'We unite in sending you this small sum in aid of the chapel to be built in the parish. This is but a small sum to what we would desire to give; but the widow's mite was not despised; and our united and sincere desire is that the Lord may bless your many holy exertions, and forward the building, so that many may be brought from darkness to light, and from the power of Satan unto God. May the pleasure of the Lord prosper in your hands.
(Signed) FEMALE FELLOWSHIP MEETING.'"

The next extract I confess that I do not quite understand. I should suppose that the *Evening Post* may have satirised what he regarded as the boastfulness of the Edinburgh people, by recommending them to send some of their superfluity to help the destitute Paisley, and that Dr. Begg professed to take it seriously, and said that they could not do better. It is possible that a file of the long defunct *Post* may exist, and that a reference to it might cast light on the subject. But I doubt if the play would be worth the candle. The following is the extract:—

"NEW MANIFESTATION OF MISSIONARY ZEAL.—We understand that the Rev. Mr. Begg is most anxious that the religious population of Edinburgh should immediately take the hint of the *Edinburgh Evening Post*, and send a few missionaries to Paisley. He will welcome them most cordially, and give them every encouragement in his parish. Perhaps, however, if they will inquire, they will find that the Grassmarket would also be vastly the better of a few; and that some of the zeal, at present expended very unnecessarily, would be better devoted to the support of parish ministers, who are left everywhere to struggle almost alone amidst a headlong torrent of atheism and profanity, which is threatening to sweep away before their eyes every appearance of religion. At the same time, it is a fact universally admitted in the West of Scotland, that the Established Church was never more vigorous in Paisley in the memory of man than it is at this moment. One chapel is now building in connection with it, and two more are just about to be built."

I have already submitted to the reader Dr. Begg's first speech in the General Assembly, and am tempted to insert here the first platform speech of which I have found a full report. But it would occupy a disproportionate amount of space. But it is not to be supposed that this was the first by many of his public speeches. The occasion of its delivery was this; a public meeting was held in Glasgow "for the purpose of forming a society for increasing the means of church accommodation in connection with the Church of Scotland, within the bounds of the Synod of Glasgow and Ayr." The meeting was presided over by Mr. Smith of Jordanhill. The first motion was proposed, in a long and eloquent speech, by Dr. Begg of New Monkland. His son moved the third resolution in a speech highly characteristic. The main drift of it is an exposition of the obstacles which stood in the way of providing adequate church accommodation for the ever-increasing population of such a city as Glasgow. First was the Act of 1706, which arrested the progress of subdividing parishes, and so greatly crippled the Church. This is the Act to which reference has been made already, which required the heritors to provide accommodation for a certain proportion of the inhabitants of the parish, *only when the church was so ruinous that it had to be taken down.* The church might have been built for the population of a village. That village might have become a large town. If the church had fallen into a ruinous condition and was incapable of repair, then the heritors were under obligation to build a new one, and to make it sufficiently large for the population. But as long as there was a church standing, however inadequate it might be, they were not required to provide another. And, if I mistake not, each individual heritor was entitled to stand upon this right. A great majority of the proprietors of a parish might be willing, and even desirous, to do what the law did not require them to do; but if a single proprietor objected, there was no power to compel him. Not only so, but I believe that if any other of the heritors, or the body of them, had in such a case engaged to bear the objector's share of the expense, he would have been entitled to prevent them, on the ground that a larger church imposed on him and his heirs liabilities for larger cost of maintenance and repairs. Of course a Voluntary would say, "Let the people build churches for themselves, and set the heritors free from all obligation to provide them with church accommodation." But grant the principle of a church establishment, and it is utterly impossible to vindicate this law. This, then, was Dr. Begg's first appeal to his Glasgow audience, that they should demand its repeal. "What you must therefore do in the first place is, petition for the total abolition of this Act. Raise such a shout that the ears of the members of Parliament shall tingle. Tell them that in all country parishes it is the birthright privilege of every Scotsman to hear the Gospel without money and without price. Urge the General Assembly to petition Parliament on the subject. Let every minister speak to his people. Let every newspaper advocate the good cause. Let us all join heart and hand, and many months shall not pass until a law is repealed which mocks our people, by professing to provide them with religious instruction out of money of which heritors are trustees, whilst in reality it gives them nothing, and is in every respect, I am bold to say, a disgrace to the statute-book of a Christian nation."

The next obstacle was that to which I have had occasion to refer so often, the disabilities of chapel ministers, their exclusion from a place in the Church courts, and their virtual subjection to the ministers and kirk-sessions of the parishes in which their chapels were situated. On this subject the speech contains one important statement of the greatest interest, as indicating how early Dr. Begg grasped the principle of the spiritual independence of the Church.

"Now, why is it that this state of things is suffered to continue a single instant longer? Why is it that the Assembly turns a deaf ear to the prayers of this noble band of ministers, who stand upon the threshold, backed by their congregations, demanding admittance in the name of self-evident consistency? Is it because the court has not power to admit them in one moment? My motto shall always be, THE OMNIPOTENCE OF THE CHURCH OF SCOTLAND. No power on earth can dictate who shall be admitted into her courts, or what shall be done there. In this city of Glasgow, where sat, two hundred years ago, a glorious Assembly,[1] which set at defiance the representative of majesty itself, when he endeavoured to overrule its proceedings, and for nearly a whole month enacted the most manly feats with a noble independence, I hold it unnecessary to say more in defence of the truth, that in such a matter as that referred to, our Church is omnipotent, and that the opposite opinion is only maintained by knaves or fools, for party

[1] The Assembly of 1638.—T. S.

purposes. Is it then because these men are unworthy of admission? Were I only to refer to my highly talented, eloquent, and most excellent father, Dr. Jones, with many more, some of them on this platform, who are at once the most determined supporters and the noblest ornaments of our Church, it were enough to repel for ever the insinuation. Is it then inexpedient? The highest of all expediency demands their admission; justice demands it; their usefulness demands it. The increase of such ministers, that our perishing population may be overtaken, and our Church made strong as in the days of old, can only be accomplished in consequence of it."

The third grievance was the obstruction thrown in the way of the erection of chapels of ease, already referred to in connection with the Maxwelltown case, by the Act of Assembly which gave to Presbyteries the power to prevent the erection of such chapels, but reserved to the Assembly the power to allow it. The peroration of the speech is as follows :—

"I rejoice that such a society as the one on whose account we have met has been formed. I hail it as the dawn of a brighter day, and I trust that out from this city a mighty spirit of reformation shall proceed. I wonder not, though I bitterly regret to hear, that our countrymen in distant lands are now becoming notorious for their profligacy. I see the cause of it in our monstrous overgrown parishes, in those pent-up receptacles of sin into which no messenger of peace ever penetrates, those dens of deep depravity to be found in all our cities. To you we appeal for assistance in carrying to all these the glad tidings of salvation. And we trust that we shall soon be cheered by beholding similar societies to this springing up on every hand, increasing, and gathering into one glorious whole all the scattered elements of moral greatness, hushing the sound of factious discord, and spreading holiness and peace far and wide over all the land, until Presbyterian Scotland shall stand forth again before the world—no longer rent and torn into sects and parties, but nearly as a whole unanimous in religion, and that religion the pure and undefiled Gospel of Jesus Christ."

From these fragmentary details of the work of a year it is manifest that Dr. Begg had already assumed the position which he was to occupy so long and so honourably, as an energetic and faithful pastor, and a constant and unflinching champion of the claims of God and the rights of man. It is interesting to note that he began as he was to continue and to end, animated by the same conviction that the Gospel of Christ is the only remedy for the moral and social maladies of men, and that as it is indispensable, so it is sufficient. Thus early, too, he had the conviction that the parochial arrangements of our fathers have in them the elements of the best and fittest means for the ministration of that remedy. And although he was afterwards constrained by conscience to put himself outside of these arrangements, he never ceased to pray that in the future it might be possible for him, or for others like-minded with himself, to occupy a position similar to that which was occupied by the fathers of the first and those of the second Scottish Reformation. For this he hoped even against hope, and it was with extreme reluctance that he was at last compelled to relinquish the hope, while the desire remained in all its strength.

CHAPTER XVI.

THE YEAR 1834.

THE references to Dr. Begg in the *Scottish Guardian* throughout the year 1834 are as numerous as those in the preceding year, and are very similar in character. Of these I shall present some specimens. But first I would remark, that nothing could show more clearly how prominent a position he occupied in the Church, than the frequency of these references. And this, I have occasion to know, was not due to any special connection between him and that important journal, or any special intimacy subsisting between him and its conductors. Some of them, no doubt, are in the form of extracts from a local paper, and I know not what may have been the relations between him and that paper—very probably its editor may have been a member of the Middle Church. But the *Guardian* contains abundant extracts from other local papers published all over the country; and yet, on looking over its file, I do not find the name of any minister occurring so frequently as that of Dr. Begg. My first extract is as follows:—

"PAISLEY.—On Monday night a numerous and respectable meeting took place in the Old Low Church, of those friendly to the formation of a society, similar to one recently formed in Glasgow, for the reformation and defence of the Church of Scotland. . . . Every one of the speakers spoke in strong terms of the evils of the disgraceful system of patronage, and of the imperious necessity of its instant abolition, which was warmly responded to by the meeting; and it was pointed out as one of the chief objects of the intended society to arouse the country to send petitions to the General Assembly, the Parliament, and the King, for this purpose. A committee, of which the Rev. Mr. Begg of the Middle Church is to act as secretary, were appointed to carry the resolution for forming the society into effect, and a resolution was passed calling on the ministers and elders of the town to attend a meeting on the 31st inst. in furtherance of the cause."

The meeting was accordingly held on the 31st of January, and its proceedings are reported in the *Guardian* of the 4th of February. The report is evidently by no means a full one; and Dr. Begg's speech is so compressed that it may be reproduced as it is given. I need not say that my design in transferring it to these pages is not to revive the controversy which was then waged, nor is it my part to justify or to condemn the strong language in which Dr. Begg characterises the views of his opponents. At a later time it was frequently said, by some who had used as strong language as he ever did, that they had misapprehended these views. I am not aware that Dr. Begg was ever convinced of this; and therefore I have not thought myself entitled to soften or modify the terms in which he reprobated these views. At all events my duty is to represent fairly his sentiments in the several stages of his public career. The report of his speech is as follows:—

"The Rev. Mr. Begg, in rising to second the resolution, said it was unnecessary, and would be unpardonable, in him to detain the meeting by his remarks, after the very able and eloquent addresses to which they had just listened. Referring to the slight opposition manifested, he would say, that though it had been greater, it would not have astonished him; for, said he—It must gall the enemies of our Church to see this immense crowded assembly, voluntarily congregated for her defence; to hear the loud shouts of applause with

[1] *Scottish Guardian*, January 24, 1834.

which every honourable mention of her has been accompanied; to know that there are so many now fully determined to resist, even to the death, every attempt to wrest from us privileges which were purchased by our fathers' blood. They know that when it shall be told all over Scotland that 3000 this night assembled together, and carried, amidst acclamation, such resolutions as have been submitted to you, it will fill our enemies with terror, and the hearts of all churchmen with joy, and that, could they have upset our proceedings, the victory would have been great. But they cannot do it, and the attempt will only teach us what manner of spirit animates them, and will only, I trust, make us more determined, come what will, to defend with our whole might what I believe to be the cause of everlasting truth. — The rev. speaker then alluded to similar opposition to all measures for the improvement of the Church—to the building of chapels, the appointment of missionaries, to every manifestation of voluntary benevolence within the establishment; and said his opinion had always been that the people of the establishment, now that she was rousing herself so mightily from her slumbers, were not jealous or afraid of the Dissenters, that the Dissenters were rather afraid of them. On no other principle could he account for their inconsistencies. He referred to a statement made by one of the councillors, who professed himself an enemy to the Established Church, that the three ministers of the town, if they would only trust to their seat-rents, would, instead of £300 a year, get £600. This, perhaps, was true, and he took advantage of the admission to prove that every statement he made at that meeting proceeded at least from one disinterested; for in this view, his arguments lay directly in the face of his worldly interests. But he begged once for all to say that it was not for money they were contending, but for everlasting indestructible principles; and he hoped that he expressed the sentiments of both his fellow-labourers, when he declared that he would rather receive only a tithe of his present income than maintain the detestable opinions which have lately been avowed; rather live by the labour of his hands than be instrumental in depriving the poor inhabitants of the glens and the hills of his native land of that dear-bought inheritance of glorious blessings conferred upon them by our

Church, in time and throughout eternity. He referred to the case of America, especially to the fact that there were in it 2,500,000 slaves, besides much infidelity and profligacy; as many slaves as the whole inhabitants of Scotland, kept in the most grinding bondage, by those very Voluntary Christians whom we are called upon to imitate!—A voice comes, said he, from this new association, 'Only look across the sea, and you will behold that there is no necessity for an Established Church; see what a moral Paradise, what a land of universal Christianity is there!' I look, but the picture of iniquity which shocks me here, is there heightened into greater enormity, and 'behold the tears of such as are oppressed, and they have no comforter, and on the side of their oppressor there is power, but there is no comforter.' I turn again with joy to my native land, and I see it spread out into its peaceful parishes, and sending forth its educated sons to climb to the highest places of rank and influence in every nation under heaven, and I trust that the glorious machinery by which these results have been effected, may not merely be preserved, but strengthened and extended, that generations yet unborn may rejoice, and Scotland maintain her high moral position amongst the nations of the earth.—Mr. Begg referred to the great body of the inhabitants of Scotland as those by whom the Church of Scotland was established at first, as those by whom her standard has been 'kept flying upon the mountains' in the midst of every persecution. And now that enemies had started, assailing the citadel, when he looked round on that large assembly, and especially on that platform, he saw that it was the same class of men that were springing forward to the rescue, seizing the glorious blood-stained banner of our Church with strong hands, that they may bear it aloft in triumph above all her foes,—who were bringing out the old weapons of war from the Church's armoury, now that the days of peace have passed away, pointing the eyes of their children to the noble device upon her shield, and, above all, to her imperishable motto—burning, persecuted, but never, never consumed. The speaker proceeded to recommend union, activity, determination amongst all the members of the Church, declared that he regarded it as the highest honour under heaven to be a minister of our venerable establishment, and trusted that every year would see her extend her limits, and increase in the purity and vigour of her ministrations. The rev. gentleman sat down amidst loud and long-continued cheering, by seconding the second resolution."

Our next extract is of great interest, as showing what a strong hold the chapel question had taken of Dr. Begg's mind. He shrank not from grappling with a man for whom he, and all good men, had the profoundest respect and veneration, a man with whom he generally agreed, and whom he regarded as his leader on most questions, Dr. Patrick Macfarlane of Greenock.[1] A committee of the General Assembly had sent down to Presbyteries a schedule of queries respecting the chapels within their respective bounds. When these queries came to be considered by the Paisley Presbytery, the following discussion took place:—

"Dr. Macfarlane moved, in answer to the twelfth query circulated by the Assembly Committee on chapels of ease, that it should be suggested to the committee to use their utmost efforts to obtain for the chapels of ease such a permanent endowment as would warrant the said chapels being erected into parish churches. The rev. doctor expressed his conviction that it would be altogether improper to give the privileges of parish ministers, unless the permanence of their situations could be secured.

"Mr. Begg reckoned it of great importance in settling this question, that, as ordained ministers of our Church, having a cure of souls, the ministers of chapels ought to have a seat in our Presbytery, and in all Church courts. His opinion was, that the grand fundamental principle of Presbyterian parity was flagrantly violated by keeping these ministers for one instant in their present condition, and he would defy any man to prove that it was not. If you have two orders of ordained clergymen, why not twenty? He was sorry that

---

[1] It should be explained that there was at that time no separate Presbytery of Greenock. That Presbytery was formed by the disjunction of certain charges from the Presbytery of Paisley, and certain others from the Presbytery of Irvine.—T. S.

the queries of the Assembly referred merely to temporal matters; holding, as he did, that the first duty of a Church was to act consistently, and at all hazards, to fill the land with ministers; the second, and a far inferior one, was to make these ministers secure and comfortable. He feared that the Assembly were disposed to place the last before the first, and to reckon it of so much importance as for its sake to violate justice and Presbyterian consistency. His opinion was, that the Assembly ought immediately to admit to all ecclesiastical privileges all the ministers of chapels of ease, and *then* endeavour to secure their comfort.

After some further discussion—

"Dr. Macfarlane did not understand the doctrine which had been maintained in regard to Presbyterian parity. Was it meant that every ordained minister, every chaplain of a regiment, for example, was entitled, simply in consequence of ordination, to sit in Church courts? He hoped, as his friend was only a young man, he would examine the subject more fully. He knew his candour, and was persuaded that he would then think as he did.

"Mr. Begg was not in the least moved by all that had been said. He was not ashamed of his youth. He was old enough to have read a little of the history of Presbyterianism, and to have discovered that the doctrines which he had maintained were those of the purest days of our Church, those which every minister present had bound himself by a solemn oath to maintain, and which it was wholly impossible for any consistent Presbyterian to upset. The case of chaplains was not in point; though Dr. Macfarlane would find that the first free Presbytery held in Ulster was composed of ordained chaplains of Scottish regiments, who, upon receiving congregations there, instantly proceeded to exercise all the power that ordination had conferred upon them. There was no such insecurity in chapels as was imagined. It was all very well to speak of endowments. No one admired them more than he did; but there was not the slightest prospect of securing these for the chapels within our bounds, and if there was, it would not be diminished by admitting these ministers. He was sorry to differ from so many of his brethren, but he would move as an amendment, 'That the committee be instructed to recommend that the General Assembly shall immediately admit all the ministers of chapels of ease to all the ecclesiastical powers and privileges of parish ministers, and at the same time adopt every means by which to secure their comfort and the permanence of their charges.'"

Dr. Macfarlane's motion was carried against the amendment by a majority of 9: 12 to 3. But we shall see in a little that the General Assembly took the opposite view, and legislated substantially on the line of Dr. Begg's amendment—legislation from which, as I had occasion to hint before, issues accrued which probably no one anticipated.

The *Scottish Guardian* of the 18th February contains the following brief statement, extracted from the *Paisley Advertiser*:—"The following inscription is to be placed on the front of the new chapel in Love Street. 'NEW NORTH CHURCH.—This church was erected by voluntary contributions, in the year 1834, during the ministry of the Rev. James Begg, and will remain in perpetual connection with the Established Church of Scotland.'"

On the 7th of March we find two statements with reference to this church extension movement, the one to the effect that "a powerful sermon was preached in the parish church of Dumbarton, to a numerous and attentive audience, by the Rev. Mr. Dow of Largs, on behalf of the Paisley Middle Parish Church Accommodation Society." The other statement is the following:—

"On the 4th inst. a most harmonious and almost unanimous call was given to Mr. J. Steel to be minister to the North Church, erecting in Love Street, Paisley, in connection with the Church of Scotland. The subscribers towards its erection most honourably extended the right of voting to seatholders in general, and the votes were, for one candidate 7, for another 2, and for Mr. Steel 128, exclusive of numerous votes by proxies. We understand Mr. Steel is a pious and highly talented preacher, and the circumstance of his collecting, in a very short period, when employed as one of the

Rev. Mr. Begg's assistants, a large congregation in the Old Low Church, some time occupied by Dissenters, affords satisfactory evidence of his well-merited popularity.—*From a Correspondent.*"

We next find our friend taking part in a large and enthusiastic *soirée*, held in the Assembly Rooms, Glasgow, " to testify attachment to our National Church, and to the parochial system of Scotland." Many of the speeches are very fully reported, but of Dr. Begg's—I presume because he spoke late in the evening—only the following summary is given:—

"The Rev. Mr. Begg of Paisley rose, and was greeted with deafening applause. In an eloquent and energetic address he urged the great importance of *extending* the Church, so as to embrace the entire population, as the only means by which it can be made efficient and enduring as the island on which it stands. He exposed the gross hypocrisy of the Voluntary party, and of some of the heritors, in their recent outcry against Mr. Colquhoun's Bill, and with great effect pressed upon the friends of the Church the necessity of determination, union, and activity. The rev. gentleman was enthusiastically applauded throughout his address."

Again:—

"At the close of the meeting the Rev. Mr. Begg rose, and said that the General Assembly of our National Church had, from time immemorial,[1] closed its sederunts by all the members rising and singing the 122d Psalm. He would now propose that this interesting meeting should be closed by all present rising and joining in singing the last four verses of that psalm, beginning, 'Pray that Jerusalem may have peace and felicity.' The whole audience joined with one voice and one heart. The Rev. Mr. Begg then concluded with a short prayer."

It is interesting to note how thoroughly Dr. Begg, at this

[1] This is a mistake. From the older records it appears that, till a comparatively recent date, various psalms were sung, selected, I presume, by the Moderator. I trust that the present practice of always singing Psalm cxxii. shall never be departed from.—T. S.

comparatively early stage of his career, was the same man that he continued to be till its close. A few years ago the expression was frequent, in the mouths alike of sympathising friends and of kindly opponents, that "Begg has got" this or that subject "on the brain." I do not know whether the phrase was in vogue in the earlier time; but it is manifest that at that time he was wholly engrossed with the idea of church extension, and that he regarded that as the means best fitted, with God's blessing, to remedy the "thousand numerous ills" which he saw and deplored. For this he laboured, he gave, he spoke, he prayed, "instant in season, out of season."

Hitherto the Voluntary controversy had been conducted with decency, each party holding their own meetings, and claiming that all truth was on their side, and all error on the side of their opponents. But at last they came into open and violent collision. A meeting was held at Dundee in defence of the Church of Scotland. Two representatives attended from Paisley, Messrs. Begg and MacNaughton. An organised opposition was determined on by "certain lewd fellows of the baser sort." The proceedings of the meeting were interrupted by profane and blasphemous shouts. Cries of "Burn the Bible!" and of the most obscene ribaldry, were mingled with cheers for some—especially one—of the clerical advocates of Voluntaryism, and a scene ensued which is described as "a picture of pandemonium." It cannot be necessary to say that no Christian men had any part in, or any responsibility for, these riotous and blasphemous proceedings; and Christian Voluntaries lamented and reprobated them quite as much as Christian advocates of the Established Church. It could scarcely have been expected, however, that these advocates, when they met on the following evening, should not have made something of the fact, which was made patent at the abortive meeting, that the atheistic and the lewd parties were on the side of the enemies of the Establishment. To a certain extent, doubtless, this fact had an argumentative value; but it was scarcely in human nature to refrain from deducing from it more than it would legitimately yield. Thus we read in the same issue of the *Scottish Guardian* which contains the account of the "Demoniacal Exhibition of Blasphemy and Voluntaryism:"—

"On Thursday evening, at seven o'clock, we understand that a second large meeting of churchmen was held—one of the magistrates in the chair. After prayer by the Rev. Mr. Brodie of Monimail, the Rev. Mr. Roxburgh spoke in strong and eloquent terms of the diabolical spirit displayed on the previous evening by the enemies of the Church, and of the absolute necessity for union and vigour among her friends. His address was much cheered. He was followed, in the same style, amidst much applause, by the Rev. Messrs. Mac-Naughton and Begg, from Paisley, who both with great emphasis expressed their disgust and surprise at such an exhibition on the part of the professed friends of liberty, as also their conviction of the utter wretchedness of the Voluntary cause, when such means were employed for its defence, now that all their arguments had been torn to pieces and given to the winds; and, above all, the necessity of banding together in a solemn covenant to defend our dear-bought privileges against clamour and violence, blasphemers and Voluntaries, if necessary, to the death. The rev. gentlemen said they were determined not to be driven from the town until their object was secured, and announced their resolution to preach thrice on Sabbath, and to address any other meetings that might be held on the important subjects in which they were all so deeply interested."

A full report of the speeches is given in a subsequent issue of the *Guardian*.

The following paragraph (*Scottish Guardian*, 20th May) shows him still doing with his might what his hand found to do; this time in his own Paisley :—

"THE ESTABLISHED CHURCH.—On Thursday evening the Rev. Mr. Begg delivered a long address on the great principles upon which the Established Church rests, in the High Church, to a large audience. The Church, he said, was rousing in every direction, and the zeal would spread and fill all the land. Mighty interests were at stake—interests committed to us by a thousand martyrs; and he hoped that multitudes would stand forward in the glorious cause, saying, 'For my brethren and companions' sake I will still pray that peace may be in thee; for the house of God our Lord I will always seek thy good.' We have heard that such lectures will be continued, and we have no doubt they will be attended with the best results.—*Paisley Advertiser*."

We have already seen the success that attended Dr. Begg's efforts for the erection of an additional church in Paisley. On the 26th of August it is announced that the church was to be opened on the following Friday, and after a statement of the need of additional church accommodation, it is added, "We hope the exertions of Mr. Begg in the erection of this church will be crowned by a very substantial proof of public favour at its opening." On the 7th September we find that "the Rev. Mr. Begg delivered three sermons here (Glasgow), in which he eloquently pleaded the cause of the Paisley Middle Parish Church Accommodation Society. The churches were all crowded, and in the evening many were unable to gain admittance." In a subsequent issue we find that the collections at these services amounted to more than thirty guineas, which was raised to above forty guineas by subscriptions, "two gentlemen on the list of subscribers to the church fund being members of the Roman Catholic faith!"

It may be remembered that Mr. George Henderson (p. 177) refers to a visit paid by Dr. Begg to Dumfries after he had ceased to be minister at Maxwelltown. I presume that the reference is to a visit paid in September 1834, as described in the following extract from the *Dumfries Times*, which I give at length, because it affords an insight into the progress of Dr. Begg's mind, and into the order in which he took up the various subjects to whose discussion he contributed:—

"A meeting of fifty or sixty gentlemen, called by special notice, took place in the Academy on Thursday evening. Mr. Stothert of Cargen having taken the chair, the Rev. Mr. Begg of Paisley opened the meeting with an impressive prayer. The rev. gentleman afterwards described the purpose for which it had been summoned. It had been called in order to form a society for promoting the interests of the Established Church of Scotland, a resolution as to which it was not necessary for him to say much to secure its adoption. He would therefore only make a few remarks in support of it. There were three things which demanded their attention. 1st. The indifference of the members of the Church to her interests; 2d. The removal of the errors which had crept into the Church; 3d. The attacks of her enemies. It was matter of exceeding regret to see the members of the Church so heedless of the interests of the Church which our forefathers had shed their blood to establish, which was not only an ornament to our land, but which was of such vast importance to the spiritual welfare of the people. He earnestly entreated them to throw off their indifference, to be up and doing in support of the Church of their fathers, and not to treat it with silent neglect, as had been done at a late dinner.[1] Even the proceedings of Parliament argued ill for the Church. Almost all the Irish members were opposed to it; and of our own representatives also, who were returned on what was called the pure system, forty, if they did not oppose, were at least heedless and indifferent to the interests of the Church. He had said that errors had crept into the Church. They certainly had, but they were trivial; indeed, he might say they were almost entirely comprehended in the matter of patronage, the evils of which had, by the late Act of the General Assembly, been removed for ever.[2] The last point

---

[1] I presume that the reference is to a great demonstration held at Edinburgh, a few weeks before, in honour of Earl Grey.—T. S.

[2] At a public meeting held a few days later, Dr. Begg repudiated this statement. He said: "While on this point, I beg to correct a misstatement which has been put forth in a newspaper. . . . That paper, in a notice of a meeting which I attended, sets me down as saying that the evils of patronage had been cured by the Act of the last General Assembly. Now, it so happens that what I stated was exactly the reverse. I then stated as my opinion that the evil would not be cured till it was cut up by the roots."—T. S.

to which he begged to draw their attention was the attacks of the enemies of their Church; but these attacks were of little importance were the members of the Church true to themselves, and zealous in its support. The troops of the enemy were hardly worthy of notice; and as for their arguments, they were as threadbare as they were idle and useless.

"The rev. gentleman then went on to consider the evils of a legal poor assessment, which he denounced as one of the greatest curses that had ever afflicted Dumfries. He maintained that that evil might be mitigated, if not altogether removed, were it not for the large sums drawn by Dissenting congregations for the support of their ministers.[1] After some statistical details, he concluded by moving that the meeting do form themselves into a 'Society for the Support of the Church of Scotland.'"

As intimated in a footnote, a public meeting was held, at which Dr. Begg was one of the chief speakers, and also replied to some objections which were offered by a professed Voluntary, and supported by a member of the Established Church, who seems to have argued that the Church ought not to be extended till she were reformed by the abolition of patronage. With reference to this meeting we find the following short paragraph:—"We understand that £36, 10s. will be added to the funds of the North Church, in consequence of the visit of the Rev. Messrs. Begg and Macmorland to Dumfries. A meeting was also held in one of the churches there on Tuesday evening last week, which was crowded to excess, the Provost in the chair, when it was unanimously resolved to form a society for giving increased extension and energy to the Established Church, and especially to appoint immediately two additional preachers for Dumfries and the

---

[1] By all that is said in this speech, Dr. Begg would, I believe, have stood to the last of his days, with the exception of this last statement. He never ceased to deplore the introduction into Scotland of a compulsory assessment for the poor; but he would certainly have seen and acknowledged that no portion of the blame was attributable to the Dissenters, who applied their weekly offerings in whole or in part to their congregational purposes, and not to providing for the poor.—T. S.

neighbourhood, with a view to building more places of worship."

At no period of his life did Dr. Begg take any prominent part in secular politics, but at this time the question of the day—the great question of "practical politics"—was the question of Disestablishment, and almost all earnest ministers, established and non-established, exerted their influence in favour of politicians according as they were unfavourable or favourable to the Voluntary movement. The ecclesiastical and the political lines which separated parties were not indeed coincident. It may be taken for granted that the Conservative party were almost, if not absolutely, unanimous in desiring the continuance of the Establishment. But there were many Liberal politicians who were equally zealous in its advocacy. Two men of this class in the west of Scotland were especially prominent—Sir Daniel Sandford, member for Paisley, and Mr. Campbell Colquhoun of Killermont, member for Dumbartonshire. The latter was a special friend of Dr. Begg, although he ultimately adopted a course with respect to ecclesiastical matters which Dr. Begg and his earlier friends regarded with disapproval and regret. At this time, at all events, he was a powerful champion of the Church, and had introduced a bill into Parliament which would have been a great boon to her if it had become law. The Paisley Church Society agreed to present him with an address of thanks "for his talented and indefatigable exertions in behalf of the parochial churches and schools of Scotland." Dr. Begg took a leading part in promoting this movement, and was one of three who were appointed to proceed to Killermont and present the address.

About this time a matter of great moment was beginning to take practical shape. I refer to the return to the Church of Scotland of some of the representatives of those who had left it, or rather had been driven out of it, a century before. Even if I knew much more accurately and minutely than I do the details of the separations and reunions of the seceding communities, I should probably deem it suitable in this place to confine myself to a very general outline. I would say, then, that the followers of the founders of the Secession divided into two parties, under the designations of Burghers and Anti-burghers. The main bodies of these were reunited under the title of the United Associate Synod. But there was a residuum of each of the parties who remained apart, and were designated respectively the Original Burghers and the Original Anti-burghers. The "United Associates" had very largely adopted Voluntary sentiments, but both the "Originals" held fast by the Establishment principle. The object of the movement to which I am now referring was to reunite these two "Original" bodies to the Established Church. It may be convenient to anticipate the chronological order so far as to state that the movement was successful so far as the Original Burghers were concerned, but the Anti-burghers remained apart until a large portion of them were united to the Free Church after the Disruption, and after the passing away of their most distinguished representative, Dr. Thomas M'Crie, a man whom all the branches of the Scottish Church would have felt it a high privilege to be able to call specially their own.

This movement was introduced into the Synod of Glasgow and Ayr at their autumn meeting, when Mr. MacNaughton moved the following overture :—"It is humbly overtured to the very reverend the Synod of Glasgow and Ayr, that they transmit to the venerable the General Assembly the following overture : Whereas it is a matter of deep importance, in aiming at the extension of our Church, to promote the return to her bosom of all who have conscientiously left her communion; it is humbly overtured that the General Assembly do forthwith hold communication with those bodies who may be anxious to return to the Church of their fathers;[1] adopting

---

[1] I presume that it was *per incuriam* that this expression was introduced. Certainly the first Seceders did not consider that they had ever left "the

such means as shall invite and facilitate their honourable and early return to the bosom of our Church on sound and constitutional principles." Dr. Begg's speech, as reported, is as follows:—

"Mr. Begg rejoiced that they were to have no opposition from the rev. doctor who had now spoken,[1] which he accepted as a token that neither would they be opposed in the General Assembly, where he hoped the subject would be received not only without opposition but with cordiality. He would now only express his own decided desire to have a union with these most admirable and estimable men. With regard to what the rev. doctor had said about the Assembly being left to itself, he held that it was alike the duty and the privilege of the inferior courts to record their opinions to the Assembly on all important questions; and if ever there was a subject more than another in behalf of which the table of the General Assembly should be loaded with overtures and petitions poured in from all quarters of the land, this was one. Besides, it was to be remembered that many of them would not be present in the Assembly to speak for themselves, and this was the only method which they could adopt for making it acquainted with the sentiments they held on this important subject. But the rev. doctor had deprecated the application of strong language to those who had set themselves in array against the Church.[2] Now, he confessed that he had himself frequently spoken strongly of the conduct of these individuals. He had characterised it as impious and unscriptural. He had openly charged them with attempting to rob the people of Scotland of their birthright; and he was glad to hear such strong expressions of disapprobation of the conduct of these parties by his fathers and brethren of this Synod. If it was the duty of the magistrate to exercise his

Church of their fathers." Of course the Established Church held that they had; but it does seem offensive to put this assumption so prominently forward on this occasion.—T. S.

[1] Dr. Hill of Dailly, afterwards Dr. M'Gill's successor in the Glasgow Theological Chair, who, along with Principal Macfarlane, led the Moderate party in the west.—T. S.

[2] It seems to have been especially Dr. Begg of New Monkland that Dr. Hill referred to as applying language of undue severity to the Voluntaries.—T. S.

influence in every possible way for the support and dissemination of religion, were they to remain silent when a class of men calling themselves churchmen, but who were in reality doing the work of Satan, threw themselves forward to intercept him in the performance of that high duty? Hard language we found employed in Scripture in the reprobation of wickedness, for there things were called by their right names. Even the Saviour Himself was accustomed to rebuke the enemies of religion in strong language,[1] and, much as I love charity, added the rev. gentleman, I love truth more. The rev. doctor had also referred to the possibility of their brethren in the Secession being exacting in their demands; but were he (Mr. Begg) a Seceder, he would not consent, for instance, to return to the Church under such disabilities as had too long been allowed to obtain in the chapel of ease system. He held that they had a most perfect right to exact, as a condition of their returning to the communion of the Establishment, that their ministers, elders, and congregations should be admitted, as the members of a sister Church, to an equal participation in all the rights and privileges of the ministers, elders, and congregations of the Establishment. And, moreover, he trusted to see the day when they would receive accessions from the United Secession and the Relief also; the effect of which upon our venerable Church would be, to use the language of Scripture, as life from the dead."

Further on in the discussion there occurred a scene which afforded intense amusement to the Synod. Dr. Patrick Macfarlane, after expressing his cordial approbation of the overture, felt it his duty to warn the brethren not to commit themselves to any promises as to the conditions on which

---

[1] However reluctantly, I am constrained to state my disapproval of this citation of our Lord's example. He, who knew what was in man, pronounced terrible woes upon those scribes and Pharisees, whom He certainly knew to be hypocrites, who devoured widows' houses, and for a pretence made long prayers. His terrible denunciations might be very fairly applicable to the section of Voluntaries represented by the Bible-burning rioters of Dundee, but certainly not to the Heughs and the Wardlaws, and others, who sincerely, however erroneously, believed that Voluntaryism was fitted to promote God's glory and man's good. As an honest chronicler I record these statements, but I cannot vindicate them.—T. S.

the proposed union might be effected. "If the members of the Synod allowed themselves to be carried away by their feelings, and pledged themselves in the meantime to a particular course, they would only find at last that they had been cutting before the point. Without committing themselves at all to any one point, let them stand calmly aside, and ascertain what is to be solicited on the one hand, and what can consistently be granted on the other. What he would deprecate was the excitement of any such agitation on this subject as had been raised on some others before the meeting of the Assembly, thus leading members to prejudge the case, and defeating the object for the present. . . . He thought it would be highly proper and becoming in them to leave to the Assembly the grounds of their union, and to say nothing to prejudge the matter. Send up the overture without conditions, and leave the question wholly in their hands."

"Mr. Begg rose to explain. He had stated that the ministers, elders, and congregations of the Seceders should be admitted to all the rights and privileges of the ministers, elders, and members of the Established Church, and that they should come in upon no other terms. Dr. Macfarlane perhaps thought an endowment a pre-requisite, and one minister in the Presbytery of Perth had wished them to come in on the footing on which the ministers of chapels formerly stood—a most shameful proposal as he thought. He stated his opinion in this Synod, because he would have no opportunity of doing so in the General Assembly.

"Dr. Macfarlane admired the straightforwardness and honesty of his young friend. Few men admired him so much, and he wished that all the ministers of the Church were in many respects like him; but he wished the members of the Synod not to commit themselves respecting the particular terms on which the Seceders were to be re-admitted. Whilst they approved generally of the measure, his young friend went rather *too fast*. (Loud laughter.)

"Mr. Begg—And I, with all respect and reverence for the rev. doctor, think that he moves rather *too slow*—(continued laughter)—and it so happens, that when we last differed about the admission of chapel ministers, though I was left in a minority in the Paisley Presbytery, the General Assembly, by a majority of fifty, confirmed the view of the question I then took, and not that of the rev. doctor. (Continued laughter.)"

On Friday the 7th of November a great meeting was held in Edinburgh in connection with "the Edinburgh Young Men's Association for Promoting the Interests of the Church of Scotland." Dr. Cunningham was chairman, and Dr. Begg was one of the speakers. In a long and eloquent speech he moved: "That this meeting resolve that, notwithstanding all the endeavours of the enemies of the Church of Scotland, there are many encouraging circumstances in the present day, warranting the confident hope that this Church will not only retain its stability, but soon become purer and more efficient than ever." I content myself with extracting a single passage from his speech.

"It seems plausible to say, Oh! you are not such spiritual men as we are. You are fighting for churches and manses, and not for the spiritualities of Christianity. But let us suppose that attempts were made to collect together and destroy all the Bibles throughout the land, and that there was to be a vast conflagration of them, and that many had already collected together to assist in consuming them, and in raising a shout of triumph over their ashes, would not hundreds issue forth in haste, with anxious looks, from every street of every city and village, to arrest the progress of this fearful calamity? And yet might not some wise head be found saying, 'Citizens, what means all this zeal and anxiety? You are fighting only for pasteboard, and paper, and printing. These are not the spiritualities of religion. Religion will last though all the Bibles in the world were consumed.' The cases are precisely the same. Both are only means for advancing Christianity, but as such they must be defended with all our might."

Dr. Cunningham, in acknowledging the usual vote of thanks to the chairman, referred to the strangers who had come from a distance to address them. These were Dr. Willis of Glasgow, a minister of one of the bodies whose union with the Church of Scotland was in contemplation, and Dr. Begg. Referring to the latter, he said—"Of Mr. Begg he would merely say that, young at he was, he might well be designated, in reference to the cause of the Church of Scotland, 'the hero of many a fight;' and he was sure, therefore, it would be the pleasure of the meeting to express their warmest acknowledgments to these gentlemen." It needs not be said that such *was* the pleasure of the meeting.

The following short paragraph is important as containing, so far as I know, the first indication of that interest in the Highlands and the Highlanders, which ultimately attained the potency of a passion, and which was destined to be productive of important consequences. "The Rev. Mr. Begg, of Paisley, preached an eloquent sermon in Hope Street Church (Glasgow) on Sabbath evening last, when a handsome collection was made in aid of the funds of the 'Highland Strangers' Society.' The church was filled,[1] and many went away disappointed at not getting admittance." The same paper states that in the Presbytery of Paisley "Mr. Begg read a petition from the sitters in the North Church, praying that measures might be taken to have it duly constituted, which was laid on the table, and ordered to be taken into consideration at next meeting. Mr. Begg stated that this church was in a prosperous condition. It contained 1000 sittings, more than 800 of which had been let. There were 200 communicants last Sunday; and he had no doubt that the erection of this church would tend greatly to the increase of sound religious knowledge."

We have had many specimens of Dr. Begg's eloquence in the pulpit, the public meeting, and the Church court. But we have not yet heard his voice attuned to post-prandial oratory. And, indeed, all through his life he avoided attend-

[1] And it is a very large one.—T. S.

ance at public dinners. But at the close of 1834, a banquet was held in Paisley in honour of Sir Daniel Sandford, who had been elected member of Parliament for the burgh, mainly as a defender of the Church, and who was compelled to resign his seat on account of the failure of his health. Dr. Begg was present, and proposed the toast, " The cause of Protestantism in Ireland." Not merely as the first specimen of the species of oratory to which I have referred, but as being his earliest statement of views which he retained to the last, and which he often propounded in the midst of much obloquy, I feel that I ought to give his speech entire.

"The Rev. Mr. BEGG.—I believe the only reason why my name has been coupled with this toast is, that, whatever I may be in myself, I have the honour to be immediately descended from a good old stock—the Covenanters of Scotland; and I am persuaded that somewhat of the iron nerve, the brazen energy of purpose, by which these noble men were characterised, will be necessary for us, who are, I fear, about to live in times not dissimilar to theirs—men whose characters, ignorantly and foully slandered, have this evening been nobly vindicated by our most eloquent and admirable representative. The reunion of seceders with the Established Church places the present controversy with the Dissenters in a most striking light. The old walls of the citadel are still strong as adamant. Not a stone, not a turret has been moved; and the men of war are all still at their posts, more prepared than ever for the fight, not to be taken by surprise, not to be beaten off by violence, whilst all the guns of the enemy have been spiked, or turned round upon themselves. Their last arguments, the American argument, the Constantine argument, and many more, have been all found to be in favour of a church establishment, and their troops are, in wild confusion, falling back into the arms of the Revolutionists, whilst a detachment of 50,000 at once, to whom they perhaps looked at first as their best troops, are in full march to join the old citadel. Even now their advanced guard is knocking for admission at the gate below. Let us all be down to meet them with joy on the threshold, to grasp them with a warm and friendly hand, and let all Scotland re-echo the shout of exultation. For more than a hundred years they have been absent, but still their love is unchanged. More than two whole generations have gone down to their graves, and still their children are staunch to ancient principles. Let us welcome them back with joy, and perhaps the example will become infectious, and the old Covenanters may seize the banner of the Covenant, and march to join us also; and we may yet, before we die, have the satisfaction of seeing Dr. Symington and Dr. M'Crie presiding over the highest ecclesiastical deliberations of a nation again unanimous in religion.[1] I have said that the controversy in regard to our Scottish Church appears to be nearly settled. Till all the present generation are in their graves, men will scarcely venture to insult us by producing the miserable, threadbare arguments which have been torn into a thousand tatters, and scattered to all the winds of heaven. But to Ireland they are now directing their designs, and the dark cloud for whose elements of mischief we found a safe conductor here, is beginning to settle, and is threatening to discharge its destructive contents on the Protestant institutions of that unhappy island. But you will say, 'Oh! you are a Presbyterian, and you are about to stand up for Episcopacy; and especially such an Episcopacy as exists in Ireland!' I am not afraid to meet the challenge; I stand up for no abuses. But I am, and I trust ever will be, a Protestant, and the question in Ireland is not between Presbytery and Episcopacy, but between Protestantism and Popery. It is the device of the enemy to perpetuate divisions among Protestants, that he may destroy us both; but I will not be deceived by names. I can discover sound principle and admire it under an Episcopalian dress; and I can discover and detect false principle under a Presbyterian dress. And when Popery comes forth with all its horrors claiming the

---

[1] Dr. Symington and Dr. M'Crie had both passed away before the unions hinted at took place. But Dr. Begg did "before he died have the satisfaction of seeing" Dr. Thomas M'Crie, the son of the latter, in 1856, and Dr. W. H. Goold, the son-in-law of the former, in 1877, "presiding over the highest ecclesiastical deliberations" of that branch of the Church which he regarded as the proper representative of the National Church of Scotland. The expectation of a religiously unanimous nation has not yet been realised.—T. S.

ascendancy, all these inferior questions appear to me to sink into nothing. 'But would you really,' it may be asked, 'establish the religion of a minority?' Most undoubtedly, I answer, if it be true in itself. Truth can never be determined by majorities. If it can, let us bring in all the inhabitants of the world to the vote, the unnumbered millions of pagans, and they will vote all Christianity false, Popish as well as Protestant. Would it be false on that account? Nay, though only one man stood up under the whole canopy of heaven, with the Word of God in his hand, and professed himself a Christian, all the rest of the world having gone away to idols, that man would be right, and all the millions wrong. The religion to be supported by our Government in Ireland must not therefore be tried by numbers, but by Scripture and history. And Popery is condemned by both. Even civil liberty was never known till it was abolished. It drew a mighty gloom over the world, and in the midst of that it maintained its dark dominion, the chained millions of Europe bowing before its shrine. Protestantism came forth at the Reformation, dispelling the awful darkness, making the scales fall from men's eyes, and the fetters from their arms. The millions of Europe were free. But Ireland still remained partly under the dark cruel bondage, under more than half an eclipse; and beneath the darkness every form of superstition is practised, and more than seven hundred murders are annually committed. And what I most earnestly wish is, not that the cloud should be drawn over the entire surface of the island, but that the light which gilds its northern regions should be made to penetrate and pervade the whole, that Ireland may emerge before our eyes 'great and glorious,' because morally and spiritually 'free.' Our gracious king has been pleased to say that he will stand by this noble cause, and aim at the destruction of Popish domination throughout all his kingdom. 'I heard his speech to the bishops,' said one of these prelates lately in Bath. 'His Majesty's words were, *If I desert the cause of Protestantism, may God desert me.*' Let the enlightened sentiment be re-echoed by millions of voices; let it ring from shore to shore, and to the latest generation."

Dr. Begg was not a member of either of the Assemblies of

1833 or 1834. It seems necessary, therefore, to state, in the briefest compass possible, the chief of the important proceedings of these two Assemblies.

It has been already seen that in the Assembly of 1832 a motion for the appointment of a committee to consider certain overtures designed to give validity to the call of the congregation in order to the settlement of a minister over them was defeated by a not very large majority. In 1833 the VETO law was proposed by Dr. Chalmers. His motion was as follows:—"That the General Assembly, having maturely weighed and considered the various overtures now before them,[1] do find and declare that it is and has ever been since the Reformation, a fixed principle in the law of this Church, that no minister shall be intruded into any pastoral charge contrary to the will of the congregation; and considering that doubts and misapprehensions have existed on this important subject, whereby the great and salutary operation of the said principle has been impeded, and in many cases defeated, the General Assembly further declare it to be their opinion that the dissent of a majority of the male heads of families, resident within the parish, being members of the congregation, and in communion with the church at least two years previous to the day of moderation of the call, whether such dissent shall be expressed with or without the assignment of reasons, ought to be of conclusive effect in setting aside the presentee under the patron's nomination, save and except where it is clearly established by the patron, presentee, or any of the minority, that the said dissent is founded in corrupt and malicious combination, or not truly founded on any objection personal to the presentee in regard to his ministerial gifts and qualifications, either in general or with reference to that particular parish; and in order that this declaration may be carried into full effect, that a committee shall be appointed to propose the best measure for

[1] They were forty-two in number.—T. S.

carrying it into effect, and to report to next Assembly." This motion was opposed by Dr. Cook, the main difference between his motion and that of Dr. Chalmers being that the former allowed a *veto* with reasons whose validity was to be judged of by the Presbytery, whereas the latter admitted a veto with or without the assignment of reasons. Much is very properly made by the historian of the "Ten Years' Conflict" of the fact that Dr. Cook's motion was as liable as that of Dr. Chalmers to the objections on the ground of which the Veto Law was afterwards disallowed by the civil courts. Dr. Cook's amendment was carried against Dr. Chalmers' motion by the narrow majority of 12—the vote being, for the motion 137, and for the amendment 149.

By the still smaller majority of 4, Dr. Cook carried a motion with reference to the applications of chapel ministers in the following terms: "The General Assembly, taking a deep interest in whatever can promote more effectually the spiritual instruction of the people, and increase the comfort of members of chapels of ease, and approving of the overture, appoint a committee to consider by what means these may be most extensively obtained." This may seem to be substantially all that Dr. Begg and others contended for, and Dr. Cook contended against, in 1832. But it is to be noticed that this motion of Dr. Cook was in opposition to one by Dr Robert Brown, which founded on an essential right of all ministers to an equal place in the government of the Church.

Both these decisions were reversed by the Assembly of 1834, the Veto Act, proposed by Lord Moncreiff, being carried against a motion proposed by Dr. Mearns of Aberdeen, by a majority of 184 to 138; and the motion of Dr. Robert Brown for the admission of the chapel ministers being carried against Dr. Cook by 152 to 103. The former was sent through the Barrier Act, but was made an Interim Act. Although in the judgment of some who were decidedly in favour of the latter—notably Dr. Patrick Macfarlane—it also ought to have been subjected to the operation of the Barrier Act, the Assembly decided otherwise, and passed it at once into a standing law.

This Assembly, as already stated, separated the parishes in the lower part of Renfrewshire from the Presbytery of Paisley, and constituted them, with the addition of certain presbyteries in Ayrshire, into the new Presbytery of Greenock.

CHAPTER XVII.

PRESENTATION TO THE PARISH OF LIBERTON.

WITH the exception of some short paragraphs stating that Dr. Begg occupied the chair at various meetings and *soirées* held in connection with the Paisley Church Defence Association, of which he was president, I find nothing in the *Scottish Guardian* of 1835 until the 3d of February, when there appears the following quotation from the official *London Gazette*:—

"WHITEHALL, *January* 29.—The King has been pleased to present the Rev. James Begg, of Paisley, to the church and parish of Liberton, in the Presbytery and county of Edinburgh, in the room of Mr. Wm. Purdie, deceased.—*London Gazette of Friday.*"

In the same issue of the *Guardian* there is the following "leader," commenting on this announcement:—

" The *London Gazette* of Friday announces the appointment of the Rev. Mr. Begg, of Paisley, to the church of Liberton. The parish of Liberton has always been reckoned one of the most desirable in Scotland, being beautifully situated about a mile from Edinburgh, and possessing many advantages. Of course when it became vacant lately there were a vast number of applications, but the present appointment reflects the highest honour both on the heritors and the Government. It so happens, rather curiously, that this church was the first that became vacant after the admission to office of the late Whig Ministers; and they, with admirable consistency, after all their outcry about jobs and corruption, appointed a minister at once—an excellent man, as it turned out—but only the tutor of Mr. Cockburn, and therefore appointed without consulting a single individual in the parish. The same church was the first to become vacant also after the appointment of the present Ministry; and the heritors, with the full concurrence of the parishioners, having made application for one of the ministers of our Church to whom they were personally utter strangers, and whom they knew only by reputation—the Ministry, with a liberality for which in former times they were ever distinguished, have sent down to him the presentation. This fact should be proclaimed all over Scotland. It illustrates strikingly the difference between *profession* and *practice;* and along with the case of Mr. Dale, recently appointed by Sir Robert Peel, under similar circumstances, to an important and valuable living in London, proves how much the members and friends of the Established Church may justly expect from their upright and honourable exercise of trust."

While it is one of the things which have come to "go without saying" that the Whigs have always been more alive than the Tories to party and family interest in the exercise of their patronage, the two appointments to Liberton are not very strong cases in point. First, as to Mr. Purdie's appointment by the Whigs. It is true that Mr. Purdie had been for ten years tutor in the Solicitor-General's family, and that it was in consequence of the high opinion he had formed of him in that relation that Mr. Cockburn was anxious to bring about his appointment to Liberton. Now it was understood that the patron of Liberton was Wauchope of Niddry. He was a minor, and his guardians had agreed to present Mr. Purdie. After the presentation was actually made, but before it was made public, a doubt was raised whether the patronage was not exclusively, or alternately, vested in the Crown. This could only be determined by a legal process which was sure to be tedious, and which would have caused a long vacancy. It was at this point that Mr. Cockburn interposed, and urged Lord Melbourne to grant a presentation in favour of the same man, so that he might be immediately inducted, leaving it to the law courts to determine at their leisure which was the valid presentation and which the superfluous one. This was done. Of course there are several points in the transaction of which I have no knowledge. I do not know, for example, whether the presentation by the Niddrie curators was obtained at Mr. Cockburn's instance, nor whether he would, or would not, have made application on Mr. Purdie's behalf with the same urgency had it been understood from the first that the presentation was in the hands of the Crown. Very likely he would; but the argument which he actually used would in that case have been invalid.

Granted patronage, the appointment of Mr. Purdie by the Whig Government was not a very flagrant instance of the abuse of it. And then, during his short life and ministry, he justified Lord Cockburn's estimate of him, and his early death was sincerely mourned by the whole parish, to whom he had endeared himself by personal and professional qualities of a high order.

And then, as to Dr. Begg's appointment by the Tory Government, we have his own testimony that the motives which led to it were not specially commendable. In his jubilee speech (18th May 1880) is the following passage:—

"His transference from Paisley to Liberton was in connection with a somewhat singular event. His excellent friend Dr. Jones lived at Liberton Tower, and he (Dr. Begg) went there to spend the Sabbath with him. It so happened that the minister of Liberton, a young man, only one year there, became unwell, and the people, hearing that he was at Dr. Jones's house, came and asked him to preach, which he readily did. That worthy minister died immediately after. The people determined to do what they could to get him as their minister. In those days, however, patronage was paramount; but it so happened that there was a political election going on at the time, and the people of Liberton having it very much in their power to turn the election, they went to Sir John Clerk and said, 'Get this man appointed for us as our minister; if not, we'll not vote for you.' That was the way he came to be minister of Liberton."

It does not appear, then, that, in the matter of the successive presentations to Liberton, either political party was in a position to throw a stone at the other. If the one was smeared with the colour of the pot, the other bore no faint trace of the hue of the kettle.

"Iliacos intra muros peccatur et extra."

Of more consequence than any attempt to apportion the blame betwixt the rival parties in the State, is the consideration how much better it would have been if the power of evil had never been in the hands of either, or that it had been removed long ago. How different might the ecclesiastical and social history of Scotland have been if patronage had been abolished half a century sooner. Alas, that its abolition came too late to modify that history so materially as it would have done had it been effected earlier!

It was not to be expected that the "Paisley bodies" would tacitly acquiesce in the removal of such a minister from the midst of them. Nor did they. Accordingly, the issue of the *Guardian* immediately following contains the following letter:—

"Mr. EDITOR,—I was surprised to find in your excellent paper of Tuesday, which announced the Rev. Mr. Begg's appointment to Liberton, your *approbation* of his removal to that parish. As I have always regarded you to be a Church Reformer, and one zealous for treading again in the old paths, I expected, when you announced such an appointment, you would have spoken plainly out your mind as to the monstrous evil of frequent translations. It is not enough, as you seem to think, that a parish should be '*desirable*,' and should have many rural and picturesque attractions, to justify the removal of a minister from a charge where he is labouring with acceptance and usefulness. Mr. Begg, by the consent of all thinking men, is already in the very *niche* he was designed to fill. He has energy, and hardihood, and readiness of mind, for contending with the infidel and Voluntary population of Paisley, beyond most men; and during the three past years, he has contended not unsuccessfully. According to his own frequently reiterated accounts, Paisley is the most destitute of all the towns of Scotland, and lies under the double shade of irreligion and voluntaryism. Why should he withdraw his light from its horizon ere it has well arisen? I would advise you, Mr. Editor, to say nothing favourable of such a translation, and Mr. Begg, with all respect, to reject the temptation (if temptation it be) now offered to loose him from his present charge, reminding him of the old Scotch proverb, 'a rolling stone gathers no fog.' The Church acknowledges Mr. Begg at present as one of her stars. Let him beware, lest, by his frequent translations, he provoke her to change the designation, and to call him henceforth, 'the wandering star.'—I am, Sir, yours,

"A LOVER OF CONSISTENCY AND CONSTANCY."

The *Guardian* comments upon this letter in a leader, from which I can only extract a few sentences. "The approbation of the conduct of the Ministry, in thus consulting the feelings of the parishioners, implies no sort of opinion, favourable or otherwise, to the removal of Mr. Begg from his present sphere of usefulness. This question we leave to Mr. Begg's own high sense of ministerial duty, so frequently expressed in his speeches, and so strongly signified in his zeal for the defence, purity, and extension of the Church. That gentleman's admiration of the ancient worthies of the Scottish Church, his praises of the 'old paths,' his longings for the return of the spirit of disinterestedness and singleness of heart, as opposed to the self-seeking and mercenary spirit of modern ecclesiastics, forbid the idea that Mr. Begg can avail himself of any presentation which his well-deserved popularity may have obtained for him, for any other purpose than to give fresh proof to the Church of his determination to act in the spirit of the olden time, and to join high practice to high profession."

Although this leader professes to maintain absolute neutrality, and expresses the conviction that Dr. Begg might be trusted to act conscientiously in the matter, yet it is not difficult to "read between the lines" the writer's belief that it would be better for Dr. Begg to remain in Paisley. And, no doubt, there was strong reason for a presumption that that would be the better course. He went to Maxwelltown in May 1830, and the presentation to Liberton was dated in the first month of 1835, and it was—and is—probably without example that a man should leave his third charge after being a minister for only four years and a half. But it is impossible to formulate general rules or laws with respect to such a matter. Every case must be judged on its own merits, and on a consideration of its own circumstances. Very naturally, and very properly, we all respect the man who faithfully and perseveringly has laboured in a remote and obscure parish,

"Nor e'er has changed, or wished to change, his place;"

and every book of ecclesiastical anecdotes contains witty and sneering jests, of which the point is that the "call of the Lord" is always from the smaller to the larger stipend, and never from the larger to the smaller. But there are cases in which men are bound to set their faces as flints against such jeers, and to break the ties that bind them to loving and loved congregations, if they will be faithful to the Church, and to her living Head. Such a case, I honestly think, was that before us. The Middle Church of Paisley needed, and well deserved, the whole energies of an energetic man. Such a man, above most, was their minister. But at that particular time it was absolutely necessary that some of the ministers of the Church should give a very considerable amount of their time and energies to other than parochial work, and just *because* Liberton was an easier, and in some respects a less important charge than Paisley, it was more fitting—*ad magno bonum ecclesiæ*—that *it* should have the man on whom the general voice of the Church imposed a large share of extra parochial work.

It was very much on this ground that his old and dear friend, and former co-presbyter, Dr. Cunningham, pleaded for the translation. Dr. Cunningham had been translated from Greenock to the College Church in Edinburgh, and was sent as a commissioner from the Edinburgh Presbytery to prosecute the translation. The proceedings are recorded, very briefly, as follows:—

"The Rev. Mr. Cunningham, as one of the commissioners from the Presbytery of Edinburgh for prosecuting Mr. Begg's translation to the church of Liberton, laid upon the table of the Presbytery the various necessary documents, and especially a call signed by 500 males, heritors, elders, and communicants in the parish of Liberton, praying Mr. Begg to become their minister; and reasons of translation, signed by Mr. Bruce and Mr. Cunningham of Edinburgh, Mr. Buchanan of North Leith, and Mr. Torrance, elder.

"Mr. Cunningham was heard at some length in support of these reasons, and stated strongly his conviction that the proposed translation would greatly promote the interests of the Established Church. He paid a high compliment to Mr. Begg, and expressed his great desire to see him translated to the Presbytery and neighbourhood of Edinburgh, as the centre of Scotland, and the great headquarters of ecclesiastical influence. He knew no man, he honestly declared, all things considered, more eminently qualified for such an important station.

"Dr. Burns could not give a final opinion on this important subject, but thought there was enough of evidence to warrant the Presbytery in proceeding to take the usual steps. He was delighted to see such a harmonious, he might say unexampled, call, and whilst he should regret exceedingly Mr. Begg's removal, he was convinced that, in a parish so important in itself, and situated at the very centre of Scottish influence, more ample scope would be afforded for Mr. Begg's talents and exertions.

"Mr. MacNaughtan was then appointed to preach in the Middle Church on the third Sabbath of April, and intimate the call to Mr. Begg's congregation."

It is probable that Dr. Begg explained to his congregation his reasons for accepting the Liberton call, and requested them to offer no opposition to it. Accordingly, at next meeting of Presbytery, "after some preliminary business it was agreed, after summoning all parties, and considering the reasons of translation assigned by the Presbytery of Edinburgh, to loose Mr. Begg from the Middle Parish of Paisley, with a view to his induction to the parish of Liberton." The deliverance would of course contain the customary clause that he should continue minister of Paisley until the date of his actual induction by the Presbytery of Edinburgh; for, as the king never dies, so a minister translated from one charge to another does not cease to be minister of the one till the instant of his becoming minister of the other.

I find no notice of his "farewell sermons;" but it may be safely assumed that they were characterised by the faithfulness and the tenderness which were ever characteristic of his ministrations. But I do find a notice of a farewell *soirée* held in his honour on the eve of his quitting Paisley; and of this I find among his papers a full report of the proceedings on that occasion, transcribed from the local paper, manifestly with the intention of its being incorporated in his "Autobiography." Considering myself pledged to present that autobiography in all the fulness that it ever attained, I insert the paper without the abridgment to which I should certainly have subjected it had it come into my hands otherwise, or with less distinct intimation of the purpose to which it was destined:—

"On Tuesday evening a *soirée* was given in the Renfrewshire Tontine Assembly Rooms by the friends of the Church, in honour of the Rev. James Begg, previous to his departure for Liberton. A. H. Simpson, Esq., was in the chair, supported on the right by Mr. Begg and Mr. Macnair; and on his left by the Rev. Mr. Gibson and Mr. M'Corkle, from Glasgow. A blessing was asked by Mr. Macnair, and thanks returned by Mr. Stevenson. After the customary services of tea and its accompaniments,

"The Chairman shortly addressed the audience. He believed it would be thought by most of those who were present that he should hardly congratulate them on the occasion of their present meeting, originating, as it did, in an event which they had all so many reasons to regret, namely, the removal from Paisley of their talented guest, Mr. Begg. They must be aware, however, that they had not assembled this evening to mourn over Mr. Begg's departure, but for the express purpose of doing him honour for his unwearied and strenuous exertions on behalf of the Church of Scotland.

"They might well then be happy for an hour or two in the grateful recollection that the star which was about to become fixed in the east had shone for a time with such benign and gladdening influence in the west, and instead of sorrowing that the luminary was now to leave them, they should rather rejoice in the belief that it would only be to shine with increasing brightness in another region—in that constellation of Chalmerses and Gordons, and other radiant lights, whose glories shed a lustre over the whole land. He did not intend to occupy their time with any statement of the grounds on which it had been deemed proper to offer this public testimony of their affectionate regard for their respected friend. His great merits were perfectly known to every individual present, and the fact of their assembling here this evening was a sufficient acknowledgment that they recognised in Mr. Begg not only an eloquent preacher and a sound divine, but a most zealous and intrepid churchman— an able and courageous defender of that venerable establishment whose ministrations in days of old rendered the people of Scotland the praise and renown of Christendom, and in whose reviving strength and greatly enlarged efficiency we shall find the surest guarantee for their happiness and welfare in time to come. He could not doubt that such a meeting as the present must be highly gratifying to Mr. Begg; but he felt convinced that this gratification would arise much less from anything in the meeting that was personal towards himself, than in the persuasion that by assembling here to-night in such large numbers they were expressing their devoted attachment to the Church of Scotland; and that while they were breathing forth the most ardent wishes for his future happiness, they were at the same time resolving to exert all their energies to accelerate her coming greatness and future glory.

"In conclusion, he apologised shortly for the absence of Sir D. K. Sandford and Mr. Colquhoun of Killermont, both of whom had been expected, but had, from indisposition, been unable to attend.

"Mr. Gibson expressed his regret at the unavoidable absence of Sir D. K. Sandford and Mr. Colquhoun of Killermont, both of whom had been expected, and both of whom, he was sure, would have entertained them better than he could do. He found himself pretty much in the same predicament as the Waterloo sergeant, who, when asked to describe the scene, said he would rather fight the battle over again than give a history of it. In like manner, he felt that he would rather fight his battle over again with the Voluntaries, than make a speech on the present occasion. The rev. gentleman, after a handsome eulogium on Mr. Begg, and after alluding to the mixed feelings with which he, in common with the assemblage present, contemplated his removal, proceeded at considerable length to show the claims which the Established Church had on the affections of the people of Scotland. He conceived that the extinction of the Established Church involved the extinction of religion itself, and strongly deprecated the principle which would deprive men in their collective capacity from having anything to do with religion. Their opponents attempted, in their endeavours to sever the Church from the State, to set aside the authority of the Old Testament when it militated against their cause; but he held that all Scripture was given by inspiration, and that we were not at liberty to set it aside as it suited our purpose. If the authority of the Old Testament might be set aside, so might the authority of the New, which was founded on it. If the Old Testament could thus be set aside, what rule could those have had for their guidance who lived between the Old Testament dispensation and the time when the New Testament was written? He could not avoid expressing his satisfaction in seeing such a number present on the occasion, expressive of their attachment, not to their guest alone, but to that Church of which he was so able a supporter. He conceived that Voluntaryism was by no means the greatest enemy the Church had to fear. The religious men who ranged under its banners were cheered and urged onwards by other agents who had other and more dangerous designs in view. They were placed in the front rank by infidels and Papists, whose object was to undermine the Protestant religion altogether. But the Voluntaries, should their object prove successful, would very soon find themselves overwhelmed by the torrent which they had helped to swell. He adverted to the great increase of Popery, both in this country and in America, of which he gave several proofs, and adduced from this various arguments to show how necessary it was for Protestants to be on the alert. He was happy to see such favourable symptoms abroad. In Scotland alone, £70,000 had been raised in the course of one year for the purpose of extending the benefits of religion in connection with the Established Church. He concluded by reading and commenting on a few passages of a book published recently in America, and sent to this country by Mr. Thomson, in which the working of the Voluntary system was depicted in the most fearful colours.

"Mr. M'Corkle afterwards addressed the meeting in a speech imbued with good humour and good feeling, in which he took occasion to eulogise Mr. Begg for the great zeal, intrepidity, and candour with which he had stood up in defence of the Church, and trusted that his exertions would be still more conspicuous when exerted in a more influential sphere.

"Mr. Begg said he was not vain enough to think himself deserving of the flattering testimonies of respect that had been paid him by his friends. Considerable allowance must be made for the colouring of friendship, though he did not think that one of them had advanced what they themselves did not fully believe to be true. For his own part, he felt conscious of his deficiencies. He had done nothing but what he had felt it his duty to do; or rather, he had done much less. He was convinced that he ought to have exerted himself still more on behalf of a cause on which the temporal and everlasting happiness of so many depended. He acknowledged with gratitude the kindness shown him by so many assembled on such an occasion, and would ever bear it in warm remembrance. He conceived that it was not to do him a kindness merely that they had assembled, but to testify their love to that Church of which they were members, and which in times past had proved a praise and a glory on the earth;—to testify their willingness to defend her, and to express their hopes that she would continue with increasing usefulness and increasing extension, to be a blessing and praise to the latest generations.

"It was their duty to unite for this purpose, for it was by the benefits of union that great actions could be achieved. In no cause more honourably or more extensively useful could they combine, it being to stem the current of infidelity and atheism that had been threatening such devastations. From the whole tenor of Scripture, and from the lessons of ancient and modern history, they might learn how beneficial it was that religion, the most important of all subjects in the destinies of men, should be acknowledged, and protected, and encouraged by the State; and no Church had ever had the hardihood to put upon their records that kings, as such, should abjure God. Whatever outcry the Voluntaries might raise against an endowed church, he was not aware that they had ever refused money when offered them. The acceptance of the 'Regium Donum' in Ireland was a proof that they would accept of it when placed within their reach. To what better use, he would ask, could money be applied than in educating a nation on religious principles? He would appeal to the considerate reason of every man whether the most advantageous way of doing so was not to divide the land into districts, and place an able and efficient minister in each.

"Were a thousand cultivators let loose upon an island at once and at random, could we, even on the supposition that the number was sufficient, expect that the whole island would be well cultivated? No. We would expect that they would crowd to the banks of rivers, and to the fertile plains, where the greatest crops could be reaped with the least exertion; while the distant rugged glens, where it would be almost banishment to live, the barren uplands and the shaggy wilds, would all be left in an uncultivated and barren waste. So with spiritual labourers. They would crowd to the busy towns and the populous cities, while the great extent over which a thinly scattered agricultural population was extended, would be left to all the destitution of moral and spiritual barrenness. He contended, therefore, that it was one of the brightest ideas that had ever entered the mind of man to divide a country intended to be brought under the influence of religion into distinctly defined portions, and to appoint a schoolmaster and a minister of religion to each. It was a system on which any true lover of his country was bound to look with admiration, and exert his time, and talents, and influence in its preservation and extension. The attacks on the Established Church were precisely the same as had taken place in France when men's principles and practice were boiling up in angry ebullition against religion and government. It was the duty of men to learn wisdom and take warning from experience, and resist the beginning to prevent the end. He was bound to consider how much good the Church of Scotland had done, and to respect her accordingly. She was a Church that had proved most beneficial to the nation, and that was enough for him. If the boat carry us safely across the ocean of life, and bring us to our harbour, that was the principal consideration; and he was not to be driven to abandon her on complaint of her not being accurately trimmed, nor scientifically balanced, nor so well rigged as speculators require. He would pity the man having the blood of a Scotchman in him that did not reverence this Church, when he considered that she had been the means of securing religious liberty to those who now aimed at her downfall, and use the liberty she had procured them in reviling her. When he considered the close connection of religion and education with the Established Church, and considered the high rank to which Scotland in former times had been raised by their joint influence, he could not but think that the man had a cold heart and a reckless hand who should attempt her overthrow. He believed, however, that the controversy was now settled, settled beyond a doubt; all the cavilling of their opponents had been met and refuted over and over again, and what they had advanced in the shape of argument had been turned against them. In the parish he was about to go to there were no seat-rents charged whatever. The parishioners had their seats free, and they had the spot to which they were to be consigned as their last resting-place free, and this was just the privilege which he wished to see extended. Therefore it was that he wished endowments. Not certainly that ministers might live in idleness, because he would scorn the man that would eat of her bread and refuse to do her work; but that the poor might have free access to the temple in which they were to offer up their prayer and their praise. Their opponents could bear with speeches, and with writings, and with refutations, but they could not bear with the building of churches. This was the point which most galled them, and which they regarded with the most bitter dislike, and of course it was the point to which the friends of the Church should give most attention. The great object of all should be to place the benefits of religious instruction within reach of the poorest in the land; and this was the grand practical issue which the friends of church extension had in view; and until this was accomplished, the Church was not what she ought to be. Her enemies, no doubt, thought they had deprived her of power, that they had shorn her locks, and, after making her the sport of her enemies, cried out, 'The Philistines be upon thee!' but she had risen with vigour from her apparent apathy, and totally discomfited her enemies. It gladdened his heart to see so many hopeful symptoms to the Church of Scotland, and it gladdened his heart to see so many kind looks from so many of her friends.

"He did not wish to look on those who were enemies of the Church as his enemies, though, perhaps, he could not altogether avoid looking at them with a sidelong glance. He did not wish to hate them, but he wished to wring out of their degenerate bosoms that awful hatred to a Church to which they were so much indebted, and to render abortive their efforts in rendering the Church of Scotland from becoming co-extensive with the population. Allusion had been made to his driving the Church of Scotland with steam: he would certainly endeavour to give her more power. When beset with adverse currents, he would strive to increase the power of the engine that she might make headway against them, and be enabled with her crew of immortal souls to reach in safety the haven of rest. He wished them all a most cordial farewell. He would hear from them often through various channels, and would always delight to hear of their prosperity. He would rejoice to hear in the extension of their schools—in the extension of their churches—and in the prosperity of their religious societies. He trusted the young men would persevere in their attachment to the Church of their fathers, and that many of them who had now united for her defence would become her office-bearers, and that some of them might be honoured to minister at her altars, and that the Church among them might increase in usefulness a thousand-fold."

[During the delivery of his speech, of which the above is but an imperfect outline, the rev. gentleman was often warmly cheered, and at its close the cheering was enthusiastic.]

"The meeting was afterwards addressed by Mr. M'Rae and Mr. M'Kay, two young gentlemen from Glasgow, and by the Rev. Mr. M'Nair, but our limits do not admit of going into detail. Mr. M'Nair stated that three different reasons had induced him that evening to attend; the first was, that the meeting was in honour of the Church of which he professed himself a warm friend; the second, to do honour to their guest, whose talents he admired, and whose friendship he highly valued; and in the third place, out of respect to the congregation, for whom, on account of several circumstances enumerated, he entertained much regard. The rev. gentleman spoke with great satisfaction of the friendship which had existed between them since the commencement of their acquaintance, and of the intrepidity, zeal, and ardour which his friend had ever shown in the cause of the Church. In allusion to some remarks by foregoing speakers relative to a star shifting its sphere, he jocosely remarked that Mr. Begg was not going to be a completely fixed star in the east, for he intended, like a comet, to visit us occasionally—(cheers)—and he was happy to say that one of these visits would be soon to preach on behalf of the infant schools. He hoped many now present would attend on that day, and assist them to shake off the incumbrance of a little debt that had been contracted in the erection of the school. They would at least have seats that day without money and without price. He concluded by warmly desiring the welfare of his friend and of the congregation he was leaving, and his prayer was, that they might all meet together hereafter in peace.

"Besides Mr. Bennie's band, which exhibited its usual ability, the choir of the Middle Church was in attendance, and sung some sacred airs in excellent style. The services were managed with much skill, and the company seemed highly delighted. We never on any occasion witnessed the room more densely crowded. About half-past eleven the meeting was closed with prayer by Mr. Gibson, and the company (with the exception of great numbers who lingered to take farewell of their pastor) retired, to the air of the King's Anthem.

"The numbers present on this occasion, the agreeable manner in which everything was conducted, the eulogiums bestowed on the principal guest for his zealous exertions in defending and extending the Church, the solicitude displayed by so many to get a parting word with him, and a parting shake of his hand, could not but prove highly gratifying to Mr. Begg, evincing, as it did, that he was leaving behind him many warmly attached friends."

For the sake of connection it ought to be stated that the General Assembly of this year passed the interim Acts of 1834 on calls (the Veto Act), and on chapel ministers into standing laws of the Church; and pronounced the famous decision in the Auchterarder case which was so fruitful of consequences. Dr. Begg was not a member of that Assembly.

CHAPTER XVIII.

MINISTRY AT LIBERTON.

THE parish of Liberton, to which Dr. Begg was now translated, was in many respects one of the most desirable in Scotland. It had all the advantages of a city charge, and all those of a rural parish, without the disadvantages of either. Within two miles of Edinburgh, it was as completely rural as if it had been situated in the remotest Highlands. From the manse is one of the finest views of our incomparable metropolis, while conversely the church and manse themselves constitute one of the most picturesque objects seen from the southern side of the city. It was no exception to the rule of Scottish parishes in the respect that its "living" was no bait to avarice; and, indeed, in accepting it the Paisley minister did not materially increase his income. Still, it was sufficient to enable its holder to live in perfect comfort.

The population was mainly agricultural, but with an important element of colliers and lime-quarriers. At that time, or till very near that time, the coal proprietors of Gilmerton and Niddry, both in the parish, had almost a monopoly of the supply of coals to Edinburgh, while as yet railroads had not given more distant proprietors the power of competition with them. There was thus a large mining population in the parish, and also a special community of "Gilmerton carters," who are often referred to in descriptions of old Edinburgh, and who constituted a distinct race, marked by peculiar characteristics.

The agriculture was probably the best in Scotland, and

therefore not inferior to any in the world. I understand that the soil is not naturally very good. But by a long course of judicious culture, and with the facilities which the proximity of Edinburgh affords for procuring manure, it is made to produce abundant crops of the highest quality. The farms were not large as compared with those of East Lothian and Berwickshire, but the rents were much higher per acre, and in some cases the farmer rented more farms than one. It is mentioned in the statistical account of the parish, written by Dr. Begg in 1839, that the average value of the "gross raw produce of the parish," agricultural and mineral, "as nearly as can be ascertained," was upwards of £56,000. The population was about 4000.

"The number of families in the parish in 1831 . 922
    Chiefly employed in agriculture . . . 145
    In trade, manufactures, or handicraft . . 201."

I should suppose that there must be a misprint here, as the balance, of 576 families, is surely too large to represent the miners and others employed in connection with the mines.

When Dr. Begg went to Liberton, the parish church was the only place of public worship in the parish; but during his incumbency, in 1837, Gilmerton, a village containing 800 inhabitants, was constituted into a parish *quoad sacra*, and a very handsome church was erected. The parish church was capable of accommodating 1430 persons. I believe I am correct in stating that the erection of the church at Gilmerton was due mainly to Dr. Begg's zeal in the cause of church extension, although in his statistical account of the parish he makes no reference to his having had anything to do with it. His account of the religious condition of the people is characteristic:—

"*Dissenters.*—There is no dissenting place of worship in the parish, and the great mass of the people profess to belong to the Established Church. In 1836, 2873 persons professed to belong to the Established Church, and 689 to be Dissenters of all denominations. But the number of Dissenters has diminished since then, and although some of them are most excellent persons, a few who call themselves Dissenters are in fact heathens, as is also the case with some who say they belong to the Established Church; nor will it be otherwise until the parish is considerably subdivided. There are no Papists in the parish."

The statement that a further subdivision of the parish was necessary in order to the proper pastoral supervision of the people might be true positively; but the state of things in Liberton was vastly better than in very many parishes. After the assignment of a district with 1100 inhabitants to the minister of Gilmerton, Dr. Begg would have considerably fewer than 3000 under his pastoral care, just about twice as many as his church would hold; and of these nearly 700 professed, at least, to belong to other denominations. This might not be altogether a "manageable parish," but it approached, within measurable distance, a little to that designation. Dr. Begg was the nineteenth Protestant minister of Liberton. Among his predecessors there were no such notable men as were some of those who had preceded him in Paisley. The most distinguished was Mr. Andrew Cant, who was minister of the parish for fourteen years (1659–1673). He ultimately became Principal of the University of Edinburgh. The seventeenth minister was Mr. James Grant (1789–1831). He was a man of great respectability, and was held in much esteem by the parishioners. But he was not a man of much energy. His views were thoroughly Moderate; and after a ministry of forty-two years he left behind him the repute of an intelligent gentleman, rather than that of an able or faithful minister of the New Testament, and his ministry, which had at no time been very energetic, had gradually become less so with the advance of his years. He was succeeded by Mr. William Purdie, to whose fair promise, and the frustration, by his early death, of the hopes entertained regarding him, reference has already been made. Dr. Begg's notice of his own appointment in the statistical account is as follow: "Mr. James Begg was translated from the Middle Parish of Paisley to this parish, June 25, 1835. He was presented by the Crown in consequence of a petition from the heritors, elders, and parishioners, and is the nineteenth minister since the Reformation, and the ninth since the Revolution." It has been already stated, also on Dr. Begg's own authority, that it was the backing of Sir George Clerk that gave its efficacy to this petition. He was inducted by the Presbytery of Edinburgh on the 25th of June, Dr. John Paul officiating on the occasion, as substitute for Dr. Runciman, who was prevented by indisposition from discharging the duty. On the following Sabbath he was "introduced" to his new flock by his early and life-long friend Dr. Cunningham.

Dr. Begg immediately entered on the discharge of his pastoral duties with characteristic energy. To say that he preached evangelically and energetically were superfluous; for he could not preach otherwise. The impression made on the people generally was that expressed by one of them: "We ne'er kenned what preachin' was, till he cam amang us." And he did not confine himself to preaching and preparation for the pulpit; I have information from one of his parishioners that she remembers his visiting her mother on every day of the week at the close of which she died; and my informant evidently regarded this as his regular habit. He instituted a Sabbath morning school, which was attended by about 300 children, of whom my informant was one. He conducted a weekly service in one of the villages in an outlying district of the parish; and it was largely attended, some attending regularly who had previously lived in the total neglect of religious observances. Upon the whole, the good work prospered in his hand; and it was a work specially to his taste. All through his life his ideal of the happiness and blessedness of the ministerial life had in it more or less of the distinctive element of the country parish minister and his relation to the people of his charge. Before this, as a town minister in Paisley, and after this as a city minister in Edinburgh, he did with his might what his hand found to do, and did it not merely as a cold duty but as a work of love; and his people in both these charges knew well the intensity of his interest in them, and his readiness to spend and be spent in efforts to promote their well-being. But it often occurred to me that he spoke as if the circumstances of his Liberton life and ministry were specially congenial to his natural tastes. He entered with great zest into the cultivation of the manse garden, working in it himself almost every morning. Even in his very brief statistical account of the parish, he cannot resist the temptation to record the weight of a monster cabbage of his own growth. And then he took intense delight in the agricultural and the horticultural operations of his parishioners; and not less in the mining and lime-quarrying operations, in so far as these could be observed above ground. Moreover, the rural relations of landlord, and farmer, and farm-servant were entirely in accord with his patriarchal tastes.

But there were serious drawbacks to his enjoyment, sufficient to guard him against the danger of lapsing into idle contentment. There were evils to the cure of which he must energetically devote himself. When he went to Liberton there were 32 public-houses for a population under 4000, or 1 to every 125 of the people, or every 30 of the families.[1] This was a miserable state of things, and Dr. Begg succeeded in creating a public opinion against it, and in lessening the evil to a very considerable extent.

[1] Probably two or three of these houses were on the sides of the public roads, and were supported in part by carters and others passing along. But then a large number of these carters were themselves Liberton parishioners, and it may be presumed that they were as good customers to extra-parochial houses as the extra-parochial travellers were to the Liberton houses.—T. S.

He found also that funerals on Sabbath were the rule rather than the exception, and that the attendants constantly adjourned from the churchyard to one or other of the public-houses, all of which were in those times allowed to be open, with no restriction as to days, and little as to hours. Being the only minister in the parish, he could without much difficulty put his hand on this evil, as the people would have been most unwilling to forego the presence of the minister at the burials of their friends. But all the more hardly and heavily the iron hand was to be laid upon the abuse, did it behove that hand to be cased in the velvet glove. There is probably no part of a minister's duty that requires more to be done with all delicacy than one which comes into collision with the funeral customs of the people. I do not know precisely the details of his procedure; but I know that, without giving serious offence to any, he managed nearly to abolish the usage of Sabbath funerals, excepting in such cases as they were manifestly "works of necessity and mercy."

There was another crying evil, over which he could exercise no direct control, but on which he brought all his influence to bear. The houses of the farm and mine labourers were in an extremely bad condition, utterly incompatible, in many cases, with health, comfort, or even decency. Now, this was a matter on which he was always insistent to the extent of enthusiasm. By bringing the matter constantly under the notice of proprietors and farmers, he succeeded in many cases in having most wretched huts superseded by neat and comfortable cottages. To few things did he point with greater satisfaction than to a framed drawing on his study wall of a range of those huts, and side by side with it a photograph of the corresponding range of model cottages. The former were more picturesque than the latter; but as places for human habitation, the latter were infinitely preferable. This matter of the housing of the rural population was always very near his heart; and I shall have occasion to advert, at a later stage, to his exertions towards its improvement.

It was not in this way only that he sought to promote the temporal comfort of the poor. He came too late to withstand the imposition of a compulsory assessment for the poor. But he endeavoured to minimise its deleterious influence, and to revive the better way of voluntary contributions in the form of church-door collections. To such an extent did he carry this, that when the Gilmerton church was opened, and while the provision secured for the support of the minister was of the scantiest, and while the church-door collections did not exceed £35 or £40 a year, he took care that a portion of this sum should be devoted to the support of the poor, under the direction of the kirk-session. Not only so; but in the weekly village service, to which I referred a few pages back, he occasionally had a soup-plate placed at the door for a collection, the proceeds of which were distributed among the poorest of the villagers by the most trusted and most trustworthy of the attendants. A biography of Dr. Begg would be sadly incomplete if it did not make prominent reference to his Chalmerian enthusiasm for the charitable as opposed to the compulsory, the ecclesiastical as distinguished from the civil, provision for the support of the poor. He watched with intense anxiety the gradual but constant increase of the assessment after it was legalised, and mourned over the departed days when venerable elders administered the love-gifts of Christian sympathy, and it was esteemed blessed to receive, and more blessed to give—days of which it were vain to sigh for the return.

But it is not only the pauper for whose temporal wellbeing the faithful minister cares. Such an one is still the counsellor and the friend of all; and it was more so when a simpler order of things prevailed in our rural parishes. If it be the duty of all Christians to bear one another's burdens, and *so fulfil the law of Christ*, it is of course that no small portion of these burdens must be borne by him who is officially an administrator of the spiritual comfort which best enables the Christian to bear and profit by earthly sorrows; and every faithful and large-hearted minister realises that while there is blessing to himself both in rejoicing with them who do rejoice and in weeping with them who weep, it is better to go to the house of mourning than to the house of feasting. And it is not only the darkened dwelling of bereavement and mourning that it is good for the pastor to visit, not merely the tear of great and bitter sorrow that it is good for him to wipe away; but there is a blessing also in smoothing the rough way of daily life, and by hearty sympathy and prudent counsel, and sometimes by timely help, heartening the toiler to persevere in the maintenance of his integrity. There is perhaps no higher ministerial quality than the power to do all this judiciously and efficiently. And Dr. Begg had this power in more than usual degree. The secret of it lay in the thoroughness of his humanity. *Homo sum* might have been his motto; *humani nil a me alienum puto.* All this might have been introduced without irrelevancy at any stage of my task. But I suspect that it was in his Liberton ministry that he found the most appropriate outlets for that genuine humanity which was one of his grandest characteristics. And with reference to his sympathy and his helpfulness, I may take occasion to say, once for all, that, while he prided himself rather on carefulness than on profusion, and while he ever regarded indiscriminate money-giving as one of the worst forms of mistaken charity, instances have been brought under my notice for which I was not prepared, of the liberality with which he expended his own means, not so much to help others, as to put them in the way of helping themselves. My informants have been those who were the recipients of his aid; and they have agreed in attesting the delicacy with which the aid was proffered, and the anxiety which he displayed that his left hand might not know what his right hand did. As to the frequency with which such acts were performed, I have, of course, no means of judging. I can only conclude that as the instances which have been brought to my knowledge had nothing about them that would indicate them to have been exceptional, they were probably only a few instances indicating a habit.

I have hitherto made no reference to the fact that in all this good work Dr. Begg was not without "an help meet for him." I must now make another extract from that *Scottish Guardian*, on which I have already drawn so freely. The issue of 25th September 1835 contains the following brief but important notice:—

"At Barnhill, Dumbartonshire, on the 23d instant, the Rev. James Begg, minister of Liberton, to Margaret, daughter of Alexander Campbell, Esq., Sheriff-Substitute of Renfrewshire."

Thus within three months of his taking possession of Liberton manse he brought to it one who, according to all testimony, was its chiefest ornament as long as he and she remained in it. It is no part of my assigned and chosen task to be the biographer of Mrs. Begg, and from all that I have learned of her I believe that she would have sensitively shrunk from the idea of having her life made public : I shall, therefore, say only this respecting her, that her memory is cherished with great tenderness by the Liberton parishioners, who agree in representing her as having been all that a minister's wife should be. They dwell especially on the assiduity with which she visited the sick when ecclesiastical affairs called her husband away, perhaps too frequently, from home. I shall scarcely have occasion to say more of Mrs. Begg until I shall have to record her premature removal.

CHAPTER XIX.

CHURCH CONTROVERSIES.

THE controversy within the Church itself, and that between the Church and the Government, were by this time being carried on with a determination which clearly indicated that they must be fought out "to the bitter end." It has been stated already that a declaratory Act against intrusion, and a legislative Act allowing a *veto*, without reasons assigned, to a majority of the communicants, or a *veto* to a minority of them on reasons which could be substantiated to the satisfaction of the Presbytery, were passed as an interim Act in 1834, and became a standing law of the Church in 1835. It is very noteworthy that the ecclesiastics who opposed the passing of this Act did not in their reasons of dissent impugn the power of the Assembly to pass it. They treated it not as an assumption of power which did not pertain to the Church, but as an injudicious use of the power of which they admitted the Church's possession, both *de facto* and *de jure*. A leading member of the Scottish bar, who afterwards was professionally employed in the lawsuits which arose out of the legislation, did indeed dissent, on the ground that the Act of Assembly might be held to be incompetent to the extent that a presentee rejected under it might still have a claim to the stipend. But no one denied the competence of the Assembly to prescribe the qualifications without which presentees might not be inducted, or its competence to prescribe that the assent of the people should be one of these indispensable qualifications. But in the course of 1834, while the veto law was still only an interim Act, the "Auchterarder case" was instituted, a *cause célèbre* which has strangely modified the history of our country. The Earl of Kinnoull presented Mr. Robert Young to the vacant church of Auchterarder. The call was signed by two persons entitled to sign it, and was objected to by substantially the whole of those entitled to object—the male heads of families in full communion with the Church. The Presbytery, of course, rejected the presentee. Appeals regarding some points of procedure were taken to the Synod of Perth and Stirling, and thence to the General Assembly. The Assembly dismissed the appeals, and ordered the Presbytery to proceed according to the laws of the Church. The Presbytery accordingly found that in accordance with these laws Mr. Young could not be inducted. This finding was also appealed to the Synod, but the appeal was fallen from, as before the meeting of the Synod the presentee had resolved to have recourse to the civil court. Mr. Charles Hope, who, in his capacity of elder and member of Assembly, had dissented from the passing of the veto law, was retained as leading counsel for the presentee.[1] Mr. Hope at first framed his plea in accordance with his own reasons of dissent, claiming compensation for Mr. Young for the loss of the benefice, and *solatium* for the damage to his feelings and character by the action of the Presbytery. This was a perfectly legitimate plea, as the Church has always acknowledged the right of every man who conceives that he has been wronged, by whomsoever, to seek redress at the hand of the civil court. The Presbytery would, of course, have pleaded that Mr. Young had sustained no *wrong*, because he had no *right* to the benefice apart from his ordination, and that he had no *right* to claim ordination at their hands save on conditions

---

[1] Nominally the patron and the presentee; but it was understood at the time that Lord Kinnoull merely lent his name, and that Mr. Young was really the only plaintiff.—T. S.

which had not been fulfilled. If this plea had not been sustained by the civil courts the Church would certainly have been in an awkward position, as a precedent would have been constituted, in virtue of which any amount of the endowments of the Church might have been alienated from the support of the ministry. Still the spiritual independence of the Church would have been intact, and the cases would probably not have been numerous of rejected presentees braving public opinion by claiming the stipend of the ministry while they were prohibited from performing the functions of the ministry.

But before the case actually came before the Court of Session Mr. Hope changed his ground, and claimed that the court should declare that the Presbytery were bound to proceed to the examination of the presentee, and to his induction, without reference to the call or the veto of the people, if he should be found otherwise qualified. The historian of the "Ten Years' Conflict" shows admirably how this shifting of the ground tended to complicate the case. At one point the pleading was relevant enough—whether sufficient or not—for the maintenance of the plea originally instituted, and it was carefully concealed that *that* plea was non-existent. The actual plea asked for a different conclusion altogether. The only relevant contentions betwixt the Dean of Faculty Hope for the patron and presentee, and the Solicitor-General Rutherford for the Presbytery, were these two— Had the Assembly, or had it not, the right to pass the veto law? and on the supposition that it had not that right, had the Court of Session the right to correct its error? Mr. Rutherford answered the former question affirmatively, and the latter negatively, and supported his answers with consummate ability. But the court, by a majority of eight judges to five, decided against the Presbytery, and in favour of Mr. Young. This decision was given on the 8th March 1838. Having thus got judgment in his favour, Mr. Young presented himself to the Presbytery, demanding that they should proceed with the steps in order to his induction, in terms of the judgment of the Court of Session, and in opposition to the Act of Assembly, which that judgment virtually declared to be incompetent and illegal. The Presbytery very naturally shrank from a responsibility of unprecedented magnitude, and resolved to send up the whole case, by "reference," to the Synod. Thereupon Mr. Young tendered a notarial protest, intimating that he held the Presbytery and its individual members liable to him in damages for such loss as might accrue to him for their delaying to implement the judgment of the Court of Session. The Assembly of 1838 resolved to appeal to the House of Lords against this judgment, "first giving forth such a declaration of its own views and intentions in regard to the great cardinal principles which had been brought into dispute as would prevent any subsequent misconstruction of the Church's conduct. It had become altogether indispensable that there should be no pretence left at any after period for insinuating that she had put herself into the hands of the courts of law, and then refused to abide by their sentence when it was found to have gone against her."[1]

In point of fact, such insinuations were made at after periods, and are occasionally made still. I must therefore, in a sentence or two, point out that in point of fact the Church never "put herself into the hands of the courts of law." She was not plaintiff, but defendant. The courts of law had laid violent hands upon her. The judgment of the Court of Session was not final unless it was confirmed by the House of Lords. It was essential that she must have a final judgment, in order to enable her to decide what her future course of action should be. The very fact that she did not mean to obtemper the judgment of the inferior court made it imperative on her

[1] "Ten Years' Conflict," vol. i. p. 470.

to have that judgment either affirmed or reversed by the supreme court.

The judgment of the House of Lords was given by Lords Brougham and Cottenham on the 2d of May 1839, confirming that of the Court of Session. This is not the place to criticise the speeches of the noble and learned lords. This has been admirably done by the late Dr. Buchanan in the "Ten Years' Conflict." It is difficult to conceive how, even without that trenchant criticism, any one can read these speeches without perceiving that the principle on which they proceed is sufficient to justify every act of aggression and persecution that has ever been perpetrated, and to require that a Christian man living in a heathen state should renounce his Christianity at the bidding of the civil ruler. It is Cæsarism of the most unmitigated kind.

In the Assembly which met three weeks after was one of the greatest debates ever conducted in any Church court. Three motions were made—by Dr. Chalmers, Dr. Cook, and Dr. Muir respectively. It was said at the time that Dr. Chalmers had never before made so magnificent a speech. Dr. Candlish appeared for the first time as an Assembly speaker, and at once was acknowledged as *the* destined leader of the Church in a future which could not be far distant, when Dr. Chalmers should cease from his noble labours. The motion of Dr. Chalmers was as follows :—

"The General Assembly, having heard the report of the Procurator on the Auchterarder case, and considered the judgment of the House of Lords affirming the decision of the Court of Session, and being satisfied that, by the said judgment, all questions of civil right, so far as the Presbytery of Auchterarder is concerned, are substantially decided, do now, in conformity with the uniform practice of this Church, and with the resolution of last General Assembly ever to give and inculcate implicit obedience to the decisions of civil courts in regard to the civil rights and emoluments secured by law to the Church, instruct the said Presbytery to offer no further resistance to the claims of Mr. Young or of the patron, to the emoluments of the benefice of Auchterarder, and to refrain from claiming the *jus devolutum*, or any other civil right or privilege connected with the said benefice.

"And whereas the principle of non-intrusion is one coeval with the Reformed Kirk of Scotland, and forms an integral part of its constitution, embodied in its standards and declared in various Acts of Assembly, the General Assembly resolve that this principle cannot be abandoned, and that no presentee shall be forced upon any parish contrary to the will of the congregation.

"And whereas, by the decision above referred to, it appears that where this principle is carried into effect in any parish, the legal provision for the sustentation of the ministry in that parish may be thereby suspended, the General Assembly being deeply impressed with the unhappy consequences which must arise from any collision between the civil and ecclesiastical authorities, and holding it to be their duty to use every means in their power, not involving any dereliction of the principles and fundamental laws of their constitution, to prevent such unfortunate results, do therefore appoint a committee for the purpose of considering in what way the privileges of the National Establishment and the harmony between Church and State may remain unimpaired, with instructions to confer with the Government of the country if they see cause."

The motion of Dr. Chalmers was carried against that of Dr. Muir by a majority of 36—(197 to 161), and against that of Dr. Cook by a majority of 49—(204 to 155). It is not without interest to note that six more voted for Dr. Muir's motion than for Dr. Cook's, indicating that some who could not go fully with Dr. Chalmers, could as little stop short with Dr. Cook.

While the Assembly, by adopting this resolution, consented to the severance of the stipend from the ministerial function in this particular case, it was manifest that the Establishment could not long subsist under the operation of a law which, as now interpreted by the highest legal authority, would gradually alienate the endowments from those whom the Church held to be entitled to them. But the judgment of the Court of Session, now confirmed by the House of Lords, went much further than even thus far. It had not, indeed, ordered the Presbytery of Auchterarder to proceed to the ordination of Mr. Young, but it had declared that they were bound to do so.

It is true that in all these proceedings Dr. Begg had no direct part, but it seemed necessary to give an account of the state of matters when he came to Liberton, professedly on the ground that there he would occupy a more favourable position than in Paisley for taking an active part in the conduct of ecclesiastical affairs. It is not necessary, however, to trace the course of these affairs further at present, or to make special reference to them, except in connection with Dr. Begg's action from time to time. It may be said generally that the subsequent legal proceedings—the second Auchterarder case, the Stewarton case, the Lethendy case, and the Marnoch case—were legitimate and necessary corollaries from the principles laid down as the basis of the judgment in the first Auchterarder case. When I include the Marnoch case in the list, I refer only to what I may call its civil side. In the other cases the dispute was between interested parties on the one side and the Church on the other. But in the Marnoch case the gauntlet was thrown down to the Church by her own sons. Her authority was defied, and her most sacred ordinances desecrated, by those who had in the most solemn manner vowed allegiance to her; and the action of these rebellious and unnatural children was probably prompted, certainly vindicated, by a minority indeed, but a numerous and influential minority, of the members of her supreme court. The scene at the so-called ordination of Mr. Edwards at Marnoch is one of the most interesting, and on its one side one of the grandest, ever enacted in our national history. I shall have occasion to notice this case further on.

The attempts to mend matters by legislation eventually failed. When the committee appointed by the Assembly of 1839 sent a deputation to the Government, they found them subsisting only by the forbearance of their political opponents. It was not to be expected that in these circumstances they should enter on so great and difficult a task. And there is no reason to believe that a Government whose Lord Chancellors were successively Lords Brougham and Cottenham would in any circumstances have promoted legislation which would have been satisfactory to the Church. Lord Melbourne had recourse to his usual tactics of doing nothing, or letting well alone. Lord John Russell was more energetic and more reasonable. "He admitted that the intervention of the Legislature had become indispensable—that things could not go on as they were, and he engaged to give, on the part of the Cabinet, a definite answer as to the intentions of Government by the middle of March. His lordship further expressed his hope that they would be able by that time to propose a satisfactory measure, and authorised this statement to be communicated to the Assembly's committee."[1] The middle of March came and went; and it was only after repeated applications that on the 26th of March Lord John made the following statement, verbally, to the deputation. "They thought," his lordship said, "that they could frame a measure fitted to serve the object the Church had in view, and which ought to be satisfactory; but he did not see any reasonable prospect of their being able to carry it through the Legislature. There was so much division on the subject in the Church itself, in the country, and in Parliament, that they despaired of being able to obtain at present the necessary support for such a measure as they would be disposed to introduce. By and by, perhaps, there might come to exist a greater unanimity on the subject, and then it might be in their power to effect what could not be attempted now."[2]

[1] "Ten Years' Conflict," vol. ii. pp. 154, 155.   [2] Ibid. pp. 159, 160.

The Government having thus declined to interfere, there ensued a great deal of negotiation, of misunderstandings, and explanations between the Earl of Aberdeen and the committee. It is evident that the earl, as a Scotchman, had a much clearer perception than Lord Melbourne or Lord John Russell had, of the gravity of the crisis, the substantial reasonableness of the claims of the Church, and their accordance with the laws of the country, rightly interpreted. His party also had a clear majority in the House of Lords, while parties were pretty equally balanced in the Commons. Thus it happened that he, although in opposition, might move in the matter with greater hope of success than the Government could have done. That he had a sincere and earnest desire to succeed seems to be beyond question. Yet there does seem to have been a great deal of vacillation in his proposals and actions, probably to be accounted for by the supposition that he himself was in favour of a measure such as the Church would have welcomed, but that he found from time to time that he could not carry along with him those without whose support he could not carry any measure. Lord Aberdeen's bill was introduced into the House of Lords on the 5th of May 1840. It may be described in brief as proposing to give legal sanction to a presbyterial veto, as distinguished from a congregational. The congregation were to dissent *with reasons assigned*, and the Presbytery were to decide upon the whole merits of the case, and the circumstances of the parish, these reasons being of course an important element for their consideration. Without entering into any detailed consideration of the merits and demerits of Lord Aberdeen's bill, I may say that it appears to me that the refusal of the General Assembly to accept it is highly creditable to the majority of that Assembly. In the first place, it gave promise of a settlement which would probably have wrought smoothly enough for a considerable length of time. *Then* it proposed to give to the *Church* all that the Church claimed, the right to subject to conditions the claims of presentees to ordination and induction. But then it proposed to misplace its gift, bestowing upon the *Church courts* what belonged of right to the *people*. Had the leaders of the Non-Intrusion party been the ambitious ecclesiastics that some have represented them as having been, it is scarcely conceivable that they should have received Lord Aberdeen's bill otherwise than jubilantly. It gave them a victory over those who had shown their disposition to harass them by ceaseless litigation; it put a power into their hands, as ecclesiastics, which they had never claimed. But then the concession made to ecclesiastics was at the expense of the Christian people of the land—it was to their honour that they would have none of it.

The bill of Lord Aberdeen was considered by the General Assembly on the 27th and 28th of May 1840. The debate was one of the most notable that ever took place in the Assembly. It was not a mere battle of skirmishing. It was a critical action in the course of a great war. All the leading members of the Assembly appear to have taken part in the debate, which was opened by Dr. Chalmers in a three hours' speech. Dr. Begg was a member of this Assembly. The part which he took in this momentous debate is summarised as follows in Dr. Buchanan's "Ten Years' Conflict:"—

"The Rev. Mr. Begg of Liberton, in a singularly effective speech, reminded the Assembly of the consequences to which they must make up their minds in the event of their accepting this bill—they must be prepared to intrude ministers against reclaiming congregations, and that, if need were, at the point of the bayonet. Not, of course, that even their Moderate friends would do this wantonly and gratuitously. He read an extract from Dr. Cook's evidence before the Patronage Committee of the House of Commons, with reference to the parish of Shotts, in which he (Dr. Cook) stated that he would not have recourse to the assistance of the military, *if he could help it*. Even Principal Robertson would have gone as far as that admission, for he probably was not an *amateur* of dragoons. But then the thing must be done if that bill was to be made law. It had been done before when there was no civil compulsion in the case; and it would become a matter, not of simple choice, but of stern necessity under the Act of Lord Aberdeen.[1] The rev. gentleman then referred, in illustration, to the case of Jedburgh, in which all the parishioners, except five, were in arms against Mr. Douglas, the presentee, in consequence of whose settlement 2000 left the church in one day; to the case of Biggar, in which it was objected, and admitted by the Presbytery, that the voice of the presentee could not be heard in the church, notwithstanding which he was settled; and to the case of Kirkcudbright, in which the presentee was stone blind. In this last case it was very amusing to see the extent of clerical ingenuity; for it had been specifically stated by the court who sustained the presentation of the blind man, that the objection to his want of sight would have been all very well in Popish times, when there were so many *hocus pocus* ceremonies that it was impossible such a presentee could see how to perform them; but that now the objection was totally inapplicable and irrelevant where the Gospel was administered in all its simplicity. He had brought forward these instances for the sake of those on the other side of the house, and in the expectation that they would be brought to look upon and contemplate them in the same way as the wanderers referred to by the Rev. Dr. Macleod were brought to view the bones of the Macdonalds."[2]

---

[1] That is, if I understand it, that a case might have occurred in which a Presbytery could not take the responsibility of declaring that the reasons assigned by the people were valid for the rejection of a presentee. In that case they would have been not only entitled, but bound, to proceed with his admission, and so to have recourse to all the means at their disposal for accomplishing that admission, including even the employment of military force. It would have been said, of course, that that force was not used for effecting the settlement, but only for opposing unlawful resistance. But then, if non-intrusion were the *right* of the people, resistance to intrusion would not be *wrong*, and ought not to be *unlawful*.—T. S.

[2] The allusion is to the following passage in Dr. Macleod's speech:— "Suppose, for instance, if I, Norman Macleod, was presented to the parish of Eigg, inhabited by the clan Macdonald, an island in which, among its other curiosities, is shown a cave in which are still to be found the dry bones of the clan Macdonald, cruelly massacred long since by the Macleods; and that

From so brief a summary it is difficult to perceive precisely what was the point of the speech. I take it to have been this. In all these cases the Presbytery decided regarding reasons assigned by the people, and decided wrongly; in the first case settling a man whose settlement drove the parish into dissent; in the second case, one who could not preach so as to be heard in the church; and in the third case, one whose blindness must have lessened his usefulness. The conclusion, as I understand it, is, that the Presbytery is not a safe court to which to commit a practically discretionary power, as would have been done by Lord Aberdeen's measure. The bill was condemned by a majority of 87—(221 to 134). The Earl still proceeded with his bill in the House of Lords. On the 16th of June the second reading was carried by a majority of 47—(74 to 27), against a motion for its rejection by the Marquis of Breadalbane. But on the 10th of July, Lord Aberdeen stated that "he had come to the conclusion, although very reluctantly, that it would not be expedient for him to press the third reading of the bill during the present session."

The Marnoch case, which had broadened into the Strathbogie case, also came up to this Assembly of 1840, and Dr. Begg took a somewhat prominent part in its discussion. For the sake of connection, I must give some account—but it shall be a brief one—of this case, in some respects the most important, at once from the nature of the issues involved, and from its bearing upon subsequent events, that have occurred in our times.

In 1837 a vacancy occurred in the parish of Marnoch, in the Presbytery of Strathbogie. Mr. John Edwards, who had

---

an objection was raised against my presentation simply on the ground that I was a Macleod, I would consider myself entitled to protection from a sentence on such causeless prejudice as this." The obvious answer to such an argument as this is that even such prejudices might very possibly have been an insuperable obstacle to the forming of a right pastoral relation between a Macleod and a congregation of Macdonalds.—T. S.

at one time officiated as assistant to the former minister, and with so little acceptance that his employer, though a Moderate of the purest type, had removed him from that office, was now presented by the trustees of the Earl of Fife to the vacant charge. The presentation was of course sustained, and the day came for the moderation in the call. The call was signed by one parishioner, and three out of thirteen heritors, while 261 out of about 300 male heads of families in full communion dissented. The case came up to the Assembly of 1838, which ordered the Presbytery to reject the presentee, and he was rejected accordingly. He carried his case to the Court of Session, and obtained a judgment holding the Presbytery bound to proceed with the steps towards his admission. A majority of the Presbytery agreed to obtemper this judgment. The Commission of Assembly, at its ordinary meeting in November, enjoined them to desist from their purpose, and ordered them to appear, personally or by procurator, before a special meeting of the Commission, which was appointed to be held on the 11th December for further consideration of the whole case. This injunction was adopted unanimously. "The conduct of the Presbytery did not find in the Commission even one solitary defender." On the day appointed the parties appeared at the bar by advocates. After pleadings at the bar, and after an offer virtually made to the seven ministers that they should be most leniently dealt with if they would now express regret for their past acting—which offer they declined to accept—the judgment of the Commission was moved by Dr. Candlish in a speech equally remarkable for moderation and for power. The judgment, after a long preamble, concluded thus:—"The Commission therefore did, and hereby do, suspend the said seven ministers from the office and function of the holy ministry, aye and until they shall be reponed by the General Assembly, or otherwise as after-mentioned; prohibiting and discharging them from the exercise of any of their functions till reponed, as aforesaid; and declaring all acts, ministerial and judicial, performed or attempted to be performed by them, or any of them, from and after the date hereof, and until reponed, to be void and null; reserving to the Commission at their stated meeting in March, and also to the unsuspended ministers of the said Presbytery, in Presbytery assembled, to repone any of the parties suspended as above who may appear personally and subscribe an assurance that they will submit themselves to the judicatories of the Church in this and in all other matters, but not otherwise."

A few days afterwards the seven suspended ministers met in what they still held to be a Presbytery, and resolved to disown the authority of the Commission, and to apply to the Court of Session to set aside its finding. Their application to the court was simply monstrous. Even that court was not prepared to accede to their demands. But it did grant an interdict, prohibiting the minority of the Presbytery, and all others, from using the church, churchyard, or school-house, in executing the sentence which the Commission had pronounced. This action of the Court of Session was not *right*, but the court had a *right* to take it. It was within their competency to consider and to declare who had, and who had not, right of entrance into the churches, schools, and churchyards of Scotland. That was a civil question which they were entitled to consider. In the consideration of it they were not infallible; but they were not only entitled, but bound, on application made to them, to consider it. Accordingly no violation of the interdict occurred. Those appointed to intimate the sentence of the Commission discharged the duty elsewhere than in the interdicted places, and preached the Gospel as it probably had never been preached in Strathbogie before. This was very galling to the seven. They therefore applied afresh to the court, and obtained a much more extensive interdiction. The Commission which had suspended the seven ministers had of course taken measures, as they were bound to do, for the supply of ordinances in the parishes thus rendered practically vacant. This second interdict prohibited the entrance of the men appointed for this purpose into the parishes. This was absolute persecution. The interdict could not be obeyed. Public opinion pronounced that the court had gone too far. And so the interdict was served on several ministers each week. In every case it was treated with contempt, and no attempt was made to impose penalties for its breach. Dr. Begg was one of the interdicted ministers. It was to him and to all his brethren a matter of intense suffering to be obliged to occupy a position of antagonism to the supreme civil court of the country; but in his case the suffering was considerably mitigated by the power which, more than many others, he possessed of apprehending the ludicrous aspect of the matter. Many a time in after years it afforded him great amusement. Further on I shall give his own account of his visit on this occasion to the Strathbogie district.

I must not follow the details of this sad case, but only note the prominent facts of its progress, referring the reader to the clear and admirable account of it in the "Ten Years' Conflict." The General Assembly of 1840 approved of the action of the Commission in suspending the seven ministers, and after appointing a committee to confer with them and receiving its report, agreed "that the sentence of suspension be continued; that they be cited personally to appear before the Commission in August; and if they then continue contumacious, and refuse submission to the Church courts, that they be served with a libel for that contumacy, and that the Commission shall proceed until the case be ripe for the next General Assembly." Mr. Edwards next raised a friendly process against the Presbytery of Strathbogie, craving that the Court of Session should order the Presbytery to admit and receive him as minister of Marnoch, and claiming damages of £10,000 in the event of their refusing. This was, of course, a stroke of policy on the part of the suspended seven, being designed to furnish them with the plea that in defying the Church courts, to which they had vowed subjection, they were only obeying a positive order of the supreme civil court. I cannot imagine that any Scotchman, be his ecclesiastical position what it may, can fail to regard the day on which the court lent itself to the furtherance of this ignoble design as one of the most humiliating in his country's history. On the 21st of January 1841 the pretended ordination of Mr. Edwards took place. The proceedings of the actors in the disgraceful proceedings were worthy of themselves. Those of the people of Marnoch were dignified and solemn. They asked the seven ministers in what capacity they were in the Marnoch church, refused to acknowledge them as a Presbytery, and, with tearful eyes and swelling hearts, and almost in solemn silence, walked in orderly procession from the church, with the stern determination never again to cross its threshold.

> "A babe will weep a bramble's smart,
> A maid to see her sparrow part,
> A stripling for that maiden's heart;
> But woe betides a nation when
> It sees the tears of bearded men."

CHAPTER XX.

CHURCH EXTENSION MOVEMENT.

WHEN Dr. Begg became minister of Liberton it is evident that it was understood that he should render efficient aid to Dr. Chalmers in the great movement for Church Extension. It was a difficult problem in his experience, as it has been in that of many others, to apportion his time between the sedulous performance of his parochial duties, and taking an active and prominent part in the general work of the Church. That he always succeeded in this apportionment I will not assert. The love and esteem with which the people of Liberton regarded him acted in a twofold direction. The parishioners regretted his frequent absence all the more in consequence of their delight in his presence, and for the same reason acquiesced in it more cheerfully than they would otherwise have done. I am not aware that the minister of Liberton had any official relation to the Church Extension movement, but Dr. Chalmers evidently regarded him as his most efficient ally. Happily, through Dr. Chalmers' habit of preserving the letters addressed to him, I possess several in which the subaltern reports his proceedings to his noble commander-in-chief; and thus, with reference to this period more than any other, I have it in my power to make Dr. Begg, in the ordinary phrase, "his own biographer." Unhappily, a considerable number of the letters bear such dates as "Liberton, Monday," or "Liberton Manse, Tuesday;" but the more important ones are properly dated. In quoting the letters I shall omit names of private persons in all cases in which their publication might give pain to any.

The following refers to two matters; an attempt to interest in the cause of Church Extension an extremely rich old lady, who was one of Dr. Begg's parishioners, and a recommendation of a young minister with a view to Chalmers using his influence in order to his appointment to a vacant charge. With reference to the latter subject, I would call attention to the fact that Dr. Begg asks for nothing on behalf of his friend unless in the event of Dr. Chalmers being asked by the patron to recommend a man. This is a very different thing from the recommendation system against which Dr. Begg so persistently protested:—

"LIBERTON MANSE, *December* 3, 1835.

"MY DEAR SIR,—I have been anxious to see you for some time, but have not been able to call. I fear . . . will, after all, do nothing. I spent two hours upon her, and, I fear, in vain. She speaks of waiting till the Assembly meets, but I fear she will die before that. She mentioned again her Cowgate plan, but when I proposed that she should consult with you she seemed to start. I fear it will end in talk, but I mean to be at her once more.

"I am very anxious that Mr. . . . should get Melrose. He has been long on the Duke of Buccleuch's list, and it would be of vast importance to get a man of his talent and energy placed in such a region. If you are applied to (which is very likely), I think you would greatly advance the best interests of the Church by recommending him. But I fear you will think it very forward in me to give an opinion on such a subject. Anything more of country associations? We must appeal away from individuals to the great mass of the Scottish people, and wealth may flow in from unexpected regions, whilst such people as . . . may be courted and beset for ever in vain. They have not the root of the matter in them.—I am, with the deepest respect, my dear sir, yours most sincerely, JAMES BEGG."

It may be stated in passing that Dr. Begg's friend was not the highly respectable minister who was actually appointed to Melrose. But his friend's subsequent career fully justified Dr. Begg's recommendation of him.

The following letter relates to the same subject of forming associations in aid of Church Extension:—

"LIBERTON MANSE, *May* 7, 1836.

"MY DEAR SIR,—Mr. Cochrane[1] has no doubt informed you of the result of our two meetings in regard to the plan of sending agents to explain and advocate your important scheme. I fear that unless some decided measures are adopted, your object will not to any extent be promoted. A committee[2] has been appointed to recommend a plan of procedure, and to fix upon the persons best qualified to undertake the work. But there appears to be a want of interest in the matter, and an idea amongst some that you should only send to a few cases of peculiar destitution. My idea, and that of others, is that you should embrace all Scotland, and appoint agents to visit every Synod. They should act under your express authority, and with fixed instructions. Their object should be twofold: (1.) to collect money everywhere in behalf of your fund, and especially to form com-

---

[1] The Rev. James Cochrane, afterwards minister of Cupar, was at this time secretary of the Church Extension Committee.—T. S.

[2] I presume that Dr. Chalmers had written to the Assembly's committee recommending them to send deputations over the country; and that what Dr. Begg calls "a committee" was a sub-committee appointed by them. To me it is of special interest that the idea was suggested to Dr. Chalmers by the success of my late beloved and revered friend Dr. Duff in calling forth the energies of the people on behalf of Foreign Missions. The following is Dr. Hanna's account of the matter :—

"Dr. Chalmers had been much struck by the effect of a tour made by Dr. Duff in 1835, through the towns and parishes of Scotland, which had awakened the Church and country to much greater missionary zeal, and had drawn forth an enlarged liberality. From this, as well as from the effects of political meetings held widely over the country, he became convinced that for many purposes the platform was more effective than the press—that the living voice had a power which the dead letter never can exert. This power he resolved to employ on behalf of his favourite scheme; and having in 1836 obtained the General Assembly's sanction, a sub-committee on Church Extension was formed for the express purpose of organising a system of meetings to be held extensively over the country, at which well-instructed deputies were to appear and plead the cause in the most popular and effective manner. The issue was most encouraging" (Hanna's "Life of Chalmers," vol. iv., pp. 31, 32).—T. S.

mittees in aid of it, and receive the names of *annual* subscribers; (2.) to endeavour to set on foot new churches where these are required, or, where the people are not yet prepared for that, to induce them to appoint missionaries, for whom, in due time, places of worship will be erected. They should keep these two objects ever in view, and in every proper way endeavour to promote them."

"*May* 10, 1836.

"This letter I had begun some days ago, but had not time then to finish it. I see that the committee meets on Monday first; and as I must be at my father's sacrament, I am very sorry that I shall not be able to be present. It would be of the greatest importance if you would send them a list of agents. I fear it will never do to let any one take the matter up who pleases; both because few will do it on such terms, and because it is most important that your new attack should be conducted, not at random, but with all the effect of regular well-governed troops. Old Carment, Mr. Macdonald,[1] and every man who, with a sufficient share of prudence, is able to produce an effect on the public mind, should be pressed into the service, and the result would undoubtedly be great.

"My main object in writing is merely to state that many (such as Dr. . . . &c.), though very good men, seem not at all aware of the vast power of the engine you are about to set to work; and that *your word alone* is able to carry the measure into effect, if you could either come over[2]—if it were only to one meeting—or send on Monday written instructions on both the points to which I have referred.

"I do not mean to say that no one is to act but these agents. But the whole responsibility of the movement should be vested in men receiving express instructions from your committee.—I am ever, dear sir, with the utmost respect, yours, &c."

Those who knew Dr. Begg only in his latter years cannot fail to be struck, on the perusal of the above letter, with the earliness of his forming, and the persistency with which he held, his conviction of the potency of an appeal

---

[1] Of Rosskeen and Ferintosh respectively.—T. S.

[2] From Burntisland, whither this letter is addressed.—T. S.

to the people of Scotland, by earnest agents, acting under express instructions, and exercising "a sufficient share of prudence." Any one who was familiar with Dr. Begg a few years ago, especially any one who had occasion to co-operate with him in the conduct of any enterprise, might suppose that the letter should have borne the date of 1876 instead of 1836. From first to last it is manifest that his sheet-anchor in every storm was an appeal to "the people of Scotland," and especially to the Highland people, whom he knew and trusted, as they knew and trusted him.

The following letter intimates the opening of the campaign, and indicates the part in it which was assigned to him:—

"LIBERTON MANSE, *September* 20, 1836.

"MY DEAR SIR,—I have just returned from Falkirk, where we had a splendid meeting last night. Some of the Glasgow clergy were there, with myself and Mr. Hogg.[1] Mr. Candlish should have gone, but did not, owing, I suppose, to other business. Mr. Forbes of Callender took the chair. You will be pleased to learn that a letter was read to the meeting from Lord Dundas,[2] stating that he has resolved to erect and endow a church at Grangemouth at his own expense. Mr. Forbes subscribed £200 for another church in the parish of Falkirk, and before the meeting broke up, £300 were subscribed towards the object. I am sure that the whole sum required may easily be secured.

"Mr. Paul would intimate to you that the arrangements are completed respecting your coming here. I am only anxious to know at what hour you will arrive at Newhaven on Saturday, that I may come down for you. If you can preach *a very short sermon* after my lecture, as well as baptize my child, it will be very gratifying to me and the people. But I leave this entirely to yourself.

"Dr. Aiton of Dolphinton has undertaken to accompany me to the north, at which I am very glad. We appear at Arbroath on the evening of Tuesday next. Therefore we

---

[1] J. M. Hogg, Esq., of Newliston.—T. S.

[2] Who two years later (1838) was created Earl of Zetland.—T. S.

must start by the north mail on the Monday afternoon. But I shall have time to go with you to Dalkeith.

"I intend to try the plan of annual subscriptions in the north, as well as local erections. I am sorry to give you so much trouble; but a single line in reply, stating by what boat you come, will be gratifying.—I am ever, &c."

Dr. Aiton, who was Dr. Begg's associate on this occasion, was a co-presbyter of my father, and I knew him very well from my boyhood. He was a man of considerable ability, and of great eccentricity. He was the author of many books, some of which were not without value. As he was very thoroughly "Moderate," I remember that there were local pleasantries as to the unequal yoking of the pair, and sundry references to Deut. xxii. 10. Probably they were chosen to act together in order to make it manifest that the movement was no party one, but that the whole Church was interested in it. They seem to have pulled well together. The following letters give a chronicle of their proceedings:—

"BRECHIN, *October* 2, 1836.

"MY DEAR SIR,—As I have got a frank from Mr. Chalmers, I beg to give you a short account of our proceedings. We came to Arbroath on Tuesday morning. We found a new church required there, and, by dint of many calls and much persuasion, we stirred up the people to resolve to have one built immediately. A large committee is appointed, and £105 are already raised. We called also on the great men in that neighbourhood, including Lord Northesk, Duncan of Parkhill, &c. &c., and I hope we shall carry from that place at least £30 (including collections, &c.) for the central fund. We thought this pretty well for a start.

"The next day we went to Forfar. We found Mr. Clugston most friendly; but whilst the new church was open, the little old church (formerly a meeting-house) was shut up and useless. We advised the people at once to erect a third church in a better situation; and as a churchyard is also required, we advised them to secure land around the new church for that purpose, which might be a sort of endowment in the meantime to aid the seat-rents. To all this they consented. We had a large public meeting; a large and zealous committee was appointed; one man promised £20, and a collection was also made on the spot for the central fund. I may mention that in all places we supplied the committee with subscription papers.

"Next day we went to call for a zealous man called Mr. Hawkins, at Dunnichen, and he has resolved to begin a church in a village called Letham. He gives ground, stones, wood, value at least £100, perhaps £200, and £50 to begin. We called on an old gentleman called Greenhill, from whom we received £6 to your fund. We saw another large proprietor called Mudie of Pitmuir, and he gave £5 to your fund. A Mr. Jardine of Middleton, who has chiefly built the Friockheim church, we saw also; and he is most knowing upon the whole question, and a zealous churchman. Dr. Aiton addressed the people of Letham in the evening, and I the people of Friockheim, and both subscribed a small sum, formed committees, and manifested deep interest. I gave the people of Friockheim a full explanation of the endowment question.

"Yesterday Dr. Aiton went to Carnoustie and Arbroath, and I came here. At Carnoustie a *fourth* church will be erected. We saw the minister, and he says there are 1200 persons there, two meeting-houses, and *no* church. Many of the people are zealous churchmen; and £16 are there, which the minister is willing to devote in aid of the erection. Dr. Aiton took over subscription papers.

"After I came here I went out to call for . . . . I had a long discussion with him respecting the Church, and beat him off at every point. Not only so, but I told him and made him confess that the Church is becoming stronger every day, and that Voluntaries and Radicals, instead of overturning it, are only striking its roots deeper. He is a poor creature, and I completely defeated him upon the endowment question, made him change colour once and again, and left him much better informed about the Church than I found him. He would not subscribe to the Assembly's fund *at present*, though he was very good-humoured at last, and came to the door with me. I promised to send him Dr. Cooke's discussion, which I shall do with a kind note.

"I next called on Lord Panmure (for we are determined to see all these men, if possible, face to face); but his lordship was unwell with gout, and not to be seen by any one. I sent him up a message, stating who I was, whence I had come, and what my object was. Last night I addressed, for an hour and a half, a meeting here, and collected for your fund £2, 15s. I also preach here twice to-morrow, and collect for the same purpose, and I go to Forfar again in the evening. Dr. Aiton preaches twice at Arbroath and once at Montrose, where I join him to-morrow.[1] We are determined to spend Monday and Tuesday there, to have a meeting on Tuesday evening, and, if possible, to start a *fifth* church there.

"I am more than ever convinced of the vast importance of deputations, and I am sure that our way of conducting them is the best, viz., *public* meetings and sermons for the common people, and *private* meetings and conversations with the men of influence.

"There is another thing which must be done immediately. A cheap journal must be published at headquarters, to range with information through all Scotland. I saw Frazer, the publisher, before I left Edinburgh, and he seems willing at his own risk to undertake it. A penny for the stamp, and three-halfpence or twopence worth of information—news respecting the nature and progress of the Church—more matter than the *Christian Herald* contains. I am sure that 20,000 of such a publication would circulate in Scotland, and cut up by the roots all the strongholds of Radicalism. If you are in Edinburgh, perhaps you would speak to Frazer. A word from you would secure the object. . . .

"I saw an account of your splendid doings at Edinburgh with great delight. I am sure that you will soon see a great harvest as a reward of all your toils.

"We have had very hard work this week; but I am quite strong and well. I shall write you again from Aberdeen. You may meantime mark down those *four* churches to the account of this mission. I am, &c."

---

[1] Probably a mistake for "Monday."—T. S.

"ABERDEEN, *October* 10, 1836.

"MY DEAR SIR,—I think the last thing I mentioned in my former letter was the conversation I had with .... I was astonished to find him next day in the front of the gallery of the new church at Brechin, as he never enters the Presbyterian church. I gave him another lecture on the importance of the objects which the General Assembly's Extension Committee has in view. At Forfar, where I was in the evening, I found the people very zealous, and that they had collected more money. But, as they are generally poor, I left all the collections with them to aid in building their church. Dr. Aiton, on the same Sabbath, preached twice at Arbroath, and at Montrose in the evening. You will see all the collections in the paper which I sent. On Monday I called for Sir James Carnegie of Southesk, and met Dr. Aiton at Montrose. We had very hard work there, and I am sure that, had no deputation been sent to that town, the people would have slept for years yet. A half-filled chapel was the grand argument why thousands should be given over to perdition. We successfully argued down that idea; so much so that the leading man connected with that place of worship gave £20 for a new church. Two are to be built. But as there is not much zeal amongst the people of the place, we collected, before we left the town, as much as to make sure of the erection of both. I also had a meeting in the mill-yard of the people of a spinning-mill, and answered all their difficulties so completely that many of them are to have a public meeting on the subject, and are to give a week's wages each towards carrying the object into effect. The magistrates will perhaps give a site on which the church may be erected. On Thursday we lectured at Stonehaven, and got upwards of £35 for your fund, and on Friday we came here. We think we shall have two new churches started here. We have already got some money for each, and we hope to get more. On Tuesday we go to Banff, and on to Inverness. We have now started *eight* churches. You shall hear from us as we go on. Dr. Aiton is most zealous and useful. We have a public meeting here this evening. Perhaps it would be well to have the reports of our proceedings put into some of the Edinburgh papers. I have addressed large congregations here on the subject.— I am ever, &c."

"FOCHABERS, *October* 13, 1836.

"MY DEAR SIR,—As I have got a frank from Col. Grant, I write you an account of some more of our proceedings. I think I mentioned that we had started two new churches in Aberdeen, for which nearly £600 are raised. Ground for one of them, worth £15 a year, has besides been given by persons interested in the object, for £4 a year. Our meeting at Aberdeen was most splendid. Great crowds could not obtain admittance.

"We went on Tuesday to Banff, where the Synod of Aberdeen received us with great cordiality, and resolved to have a public meeting that evening in the church. The church was full, and the leading men of the Synod took part in the proceedings. They also passed some strong resolutions in regard to Church Extension within their own bounds, a copy of which they promised to transmit to you. There were between forty and fifty ministers present; and they said that any of them would go on a mission anywhere in aid of your cause. The minister of Banff is immediately to have a missionary; and two persons there who are anxious to have an additional church, put down their names for £5 each as soon as one shall be begun. Next day, when we started, the members of the Synod followed us with showers of thanks, and a great enthusiasm prevailed.

"We came yesterday to Cullen, the seat of Col. Grant, M.P. for Morayshire. The parish of Cullen requires to be divided, and a new church erected at a place called Portnocky, containing a population of 800 persons, nearly [1] miles from any church. We explained this to Col. Grant, and he said that he would give ground for the building—an acre—and a donation towards the object, and that he had no doubt that it could easily be accomplished if an endowment could be secured. Properly speaking, this is church the *tenth* that we have started into prospective existence.

"We came to Fochabers an hour ago, and we have written to the Duke of Richmond requesting an interview, and I write this while we wait his grace's orders. We go on to Elgin to-night, where we hold a public meeting to-morrow, as well as at Forres. Mr. Macfarlane of Renfrew, whom we picked up at Aberdeen, goes to Keith this night to hold a

[1] Number illegible.—T. S.

meeting, and we all meet at Inverness on Saturday, where we hold a meeting on Saturday night. Upon the whole we have been most amazingly successful, and I am sure we have spared neither labour nor earnest anxiety. I shall conclude this when I see the Duke of Richmond. . . .

"We have just returned from seeing the Duke of Richmond. He is most favourable to the whole scheme, and very well informed on the subject. He told us that he thought several churches more are required in this neighbourhood, and that he had given orders to his factor to inquire respecting them, and is resolved to have them built. From what he said I believe he will build two at least at his own expense. He promised to write us very soon on the subject; and when I requested him to write to you, he said he would do so with much pleasure. We told him that nothing would give so much pleasure to the Church of Scotland as his doing what he proposed. We came away greatly pleased with our visit, and I am convinced that you will hear something from his grace soon at which you will be delighted. We explained to him the central fund, and he seemed fully to understand its value, but said he would consider of it after the wants of his own neighbourhood were supplied. When I proposed to give him your address, he said that your name was enough without any address. Every nobleman in Scotland should be visited; and I am sure the result would be great.—I am ever, my dear sir, yours with great respect and affection,

"JAMES BEGG."

This very interesting series of letters suggests many reflections. The reader can scarcely fail to be struck with the low scale of the contributions which were given, and which are represented as almost magnificent. No doubt there is much more money in the country now than there was then. But the habit of giving has been acquired by multitudes of our people of all ranks to a degree then unthought of. This is one of the particulars in respect of which the former days were *not* better than these. Still, there has been only a beginning made; and few among us realise the great truth taught in the words of the Lord Jesus, "It is more blessed to give than to receive." As long as the people of Britain pay £150,000,000 a year for drink, and £950,000 for foreign missions, humiliation and amendment befit us better than boasting or self-gratulation. But we should err in the other direction if we despised the day of small things.

The letters indicate the perfectly confidential terms subsisting betwixt their writer and the noble man to whom they were addressed. Few men were better able to enlist in a good cause all the energies of ingenuous men. They felt it an honour and a privilege, over and above the blessedness of well-doing, to serve along with or under him. Few men were more sensible of this privilege than Dr. Begg. Hence the tone of deferential frankness which characterises the letters.

Although this northern tour was the most extensive that Dr. Begg made in the advocacy of Church Extension, it was not the only one of the two letters following the first intimates an intention of visiting West Lothian, and complains of the apathy of Dr. Simpson of Kirknewton, the convener of the Sub-Committee on Deputations. This visitation was probably not carried out, as the second letter, written ten days after the former, gives an account of a visit to Berwickshire, and an intention to visit Peeblesshire:—

"LIBERTON MANSE, *August* 16, 1837.

"MY DEAR SIR,—I have just received your kind letter, and am glad that no objection will be made by Dr. Simpson to our efforts. At the same time, I think he should do more than this. He should plan and arrange deputations for all parts of the country, and send them forth with express instructions. If he merely allows us to do what we please, what is the use of such a committee as his? Besides, the whole thing proceeds on the idea that there is enough of zeal, which only requires to be *permitted* to display itself, instead of which any zeal which did exist is almost cold in this part of the country, and requires to be powerfully stirred.

"At the same time, Dr. Aiton and I have resolved to start and do what we can in Linlithgowshire next week, after your meeting. I mentioned this to Dr. Simpson yesterday, to see whether he would give us the authority of his committee. He said he must first call a meeting for the purpose. Here then is another delay, and it prevents my writing to the places which we intended to visit. I rather think I shall write Dr. Simpson to say he may save himself the trouble of calling a meeting, and start upon our own authority as members of the Synod's Committee, which still is unpleasant.

"I saw Mr. Cuthbertson on Sabbath, and he looks forward with much pleasure to seeing you. Lord Wemyss also sent his regards to you, and expects you to lunch with him on Tuesday. My gig will be waiting for you on Monday evening next, at 7 o'clock. Mrs. Begg sends her best regards, and I am ever, &c.

"*P.S.*—I see nothing doing at Dumfries, Aberdeen, Inverness, or Perth. Dr. Simpson should send some one to stir them.—J. B."

It is the old story of the push of the actors and the *vis inertiæ* of the directors: Sir Arthur Wellesley in the Peninsula had his Sir Harry Burrard and his Sir Hew Dalrymple, Dr. Begg had his Dr. Simpson. But Dr. Begg had this advantage over the great hero, that he could always reckon with absolute confidence on the sympathy and aid of the director-in-chief of the movement. No man was ever more methodical than Dr. Chalmers, so long as method was essential to the furtherance of the end in view; but no man was less fettered by routine, or stood less upon forms, if the end could be better promoted without them. The second letter is as follows:—

"LIBERTON MANSE, *August* 26, 1837.

"MY DEAR SIR,—We had a most admirable meeting at Dunse on Thursday, Sir Hugh Campbell, M.P. for Berwickshire, in the chair. Many persons of importance in that region were present, and the collection amounted to £17, 14s. This, however, only convinced me of what might be done in that region. Sir Hugh was very kind, and urged us to come to his house. If we could have done so, much good might have resulted. The Countess Dowager of Breadalbane lives near that, Sir John Pringle, and many more, all of whom should be waited upon personally. Besides, there should be meetings at Greenlaw, Earlston, and Lauder; and indeed in every parish. You must, therefore, send down two men immediately to follow up what has been so well begun. They are sure of success. Fourteen clergymen were present, and all zealous. Some of them should be sent to other regions. In a word, your plan is the only one that will do the work. Mr. Goldie[1] is willing to spend two weeks in Fife immediately. He should be instructed to proceed forthwith, along with Messrs. Murray and Anderson.

"I stupidly forgot to answer Mrs. Chalmers' truly kind letter; will you give her my best regards, and say that if I can promote her object I shall be truly glad. Mr. Cuthbertson promised to look out for a well-behaved boy, and I shall do the same; but Mrs. Chalmers must not depend upon our success.

"I may mention that Sir H. Campbell is in great spirits about the elections. I am, &c.

"*P.S.*—I go to Peebles and Innerleithen to-day.—J. B."

These letters, never designed for publication, indicate nothing more clearly than the intensity of the love which their writer bore to his Church. He truly took pleasure in her stones, and favoured her very dust. What must it have cost him and Dr. Chalmers, and hundreds of others, to whom those stones and that dust were equally dear, to be conscientiously constrained to abandon that Establishment of which they had been the chief defenders and extenders? It was as the cutting off of a hand or the plucking out of an eye. But I must not anticipate. In giving in to the General Assembly of 1837 the report of the Committee on Church Extension, Dr. Chalmers spoke warmly of the services of the deputies, and made special reference to the interview of Dr. Aiton and Dr. Begg with the Duke of Richmond, and to the meeting of the latter with the millworkers at Montrose.

Not far from the beginning of this volume I stated that

---

[1] Minister of Coldstream.—T. S.

Dr. Begg's politics were what he regarded as Old Whiggism, the Whiggism of 1688. But he often deemed that *that* Whiggism was better represented by the Conservative party than by that party which, calling itself Whig, he regarded as having lapsed into Radicalism; and, demagogue as he was sometimes called, and advocate as he ever was of the people's rights, he had always a heart-horror of Radicalism. But in his political creed at this time the fundamental and almost the sole article was the Church of Scotland, its extension and its endowment. Now the Whigs, represented by Lord Grey and Lord Melbourne, had been in power from 1830 to the end of 1834, and had refused to consider the claims of the Church to a redistribution of her own endowments, or to a grant from the Treasury for the endowment of extension charges. The Duke of Wellington and Sir Robert Peel came into office on the last day of 1834, and in the speech from the throne stated that the attention of Parliament should be called to these claims. This was matter of great joy to Dr. Chalmers and to all his fellow-labourers in the Church Extension cause. But Sir Robert Peel failed to command a majority in the House of Commons, and in April 1835 Lord Melbourne returned to office, as little disposed as ever to do anything for the Church of Scotland. Comparing what the Conservatives had promised to do, and probably would have done had they been able, with what the Whigs had so persistently refused to do, the most prominent advocates of Church Extension regarded Conservatism and their cause as one. At this time a public dinner was given at Dalkeith to Sir George Clerk, M.P. for Midlothian; and I find from the newspapers of the day that Dr. Begg was the only clergyman present. He not only acted as chaplain, but in answer to the toast of "the Church of Scotland," made a powerful attack on the Government, and expressed a confident hope that Sir Robert Peel might soon displace them. But a time soon came when the question was more vital than any relating merely to the extension and endowment of the Church, and neither of the political parties would imperil its own party interests by introducing and carrying through a measure which might have preserved the unity of the Church; and Dr. Begg and others had to learn the lesson so hard to be learned by earnest and generous souls, "Put not your trust in princes." At this time the Edinburgh Annuity-Tax was a burning question, which was once and again discussed in the Presbytery of Edinburgh. It is evident that it was considered seemly that the city clergy, whose interests were at stake, should not take a prominent part in the discussion, and therefore a large share of it fell to the lot of Dr. Begg, who, of the extra-city ministers, was the most capable of taking a leading part in a debate. He not only defended ably the interests of his brethren, but regarded the agitation in opposition to the tax as a phase of that Voluntaryism which he abhorred.

The delivery by Dr. Chalmers in London of a course of lectures on Church Establishments was, in its manifold bearings on the questions of the day, a most important event. The lectures were delivered in April and May 1838. In his visit to the metropolis the lecturer was accompanied by Dr. Begg, and it is from his pen that we have one of the fullest accounts of the impression that was made. I need therefore offer no apology for transferring that account, and a portion of the paragraph with which the biographer of Dr. Chalmers introduces it. "Speaking of the opening lecture, the leading journal of the day said, 'If the interior of the structure correspond in any degree with the simple and massive grandeur of the porch, these lectures will doubtless challenge the admiration of after ages, scarcely more as an imperishable monument of the Doctor's genius than as an invaluable contribution to the permanent literature, and, above all, to the higher interests of the country. From the first word that escaped the lips of the lecturer till the concluding sentence, which died away amid the acclamations of the audience, the vivid interest was sustained with a deep and unflagging intensity.' At the second lecture, the seats reserved for peers and members of Parliament were at an early hour crowded to overflow, and so difficult was it to pack the room aright that for more than a quarter of an hour after the time fixed for opening, the lecturer could not proceed. The third lecture witnessed a still denser crowd, composed of a still higher grade, and manifesting a still higher enthusiasm. At the fourth and fifth lectures an American clergyman was present, who tells us: 'The hour at which the lecture was to commence was two o'clock. I thought it necessary to be beforehand in order to secure a seat. When I arrived I found the hall so perfectly crammed that at first it seemed impossible to gain admission; but by dint of perseverance I pushed my way onward through the dense crowd till I had nearly reached the centre of the hall. Though the crowd was so great it was very obvious that the assembly was made up principally of persons in the higher walks of life. Dukes, marquises, earls, viscounts, barons, baronets, bishops, and members of Parliament, were to be seen in every direction. After some considerable delay and impatient waiting, the great charmer made his entrance, and was welcomed with clappings and shouts of applause, that grew more and more intense till the noise became almost deafening.'[1] The concluding lecture was graced by the presence of nine prelates of the Church of England. The tide that had been rising and swelling each succeeding day now burst all bounds. Carried away by the impassioned utterance of the speaker, long ere the close of some of his finest passages was reached, the voice of the lecturer was drowned in the applause, the audience rising from their seats, waving their hats above their heads, and breaking out into tumultuous approbation. Nor was the interest confined to the lecture-room. 'Nothing,' says

---

[1] "Glimpes of the Old World," by the late Rev. J. A. Clark, D.D. Vol. ii. pp. 96, 97. London, 1847.

Dr. Begg,[1] 'could exceed the enthusiasm which prevailed in London. The great city seemed stirred to its very depths. The Doctor sat, when delivering his lectures, behind a small table, the hall in front being densely crowded with one of the most brilliant audiences that ever assembled in Britain. It was supposed that at least five hundred of those present were peers and members of the House of Commons. Sir James Graham was a very constant attender. The sitting attitude of Dr. Chalmers seemed at first irreconcilable with much energy or effect. But such an anticipation was at once dispelled by the enthusiasm of the speaker, responded to, if possible, by the more intense enthusiasm of the audience; and occasionally the effect was even greatly increased by the eloquent man springing unconsciously to his feet, and delivering with overwhelming power the more magnificent passages—a movement which, on one occasion at least, was imitated by the entire audience, when the words, *the King cannot, the King dares not*, were uttered in accents of prophetic vehemence, that must still ring in the ears of all who heard them, and were responded to by a whirlwind of enthusiasm, which was probably never exceeded in the history of eloquence. Some of us sat on the platform beside the Doctor, and near us were the reporters. One seemed to leave the room every five minutes with what he had written, so that by the time the lecture was finished, it was nearly all in print. On the day of the first lecture, which commenced at two o'clock, and terminated about half-past three, some of us went round by the city, and when we reached our dinner-table at five o'clock we were able to present to Dr. Chalmers a newspaper, I think the *Sun* or *Globe*, containing a full report of his lecture. Nothing was more striking, however, amidst all this excitement, than the

---

[1] "Dr. Begg, along with other members of the Church Extension Committee, accompanied Dr. Chalmers, and, availing themselves of so favourable an opportunity, succeeded in obtaining about £5000 in the metropolis."

childlike humility of the great man himself. All the flattery seemed to produce no effect whatever on him; his mind was entirely absorbed in his great object; and the same kind, playful, and truly Christian spirit that so endeared him to us all, was everywhere apparent in his conduct. I had the honour afterwards to be introduced to the Duke of Cambridge. He immediately introduced the subject of Dr. Chalmers. "What does he teach?" said His Royal Highness rapidly. I intimated that he taught theology. "Monstrous clever man!" said the Duke, "he could teach anything." I had heard Dr. Chalmers on many great occasions, but probably his London lectures afforded the most remarkable illustrations of his extraordinary power, and must be ranked amongst the most signal triumphs of oratory in any age.'"[1]

It may be noticed, in passing, that the historian of the "Ten Years' Conflict" very properly dwells upon the fact that these lectures, thus enthusiastically received by such an audience, contained an explicit statement of the claim of spiritual independence on the part of the Church of Scotland, the rejection of which by the Legislature caused the Disruption of the Church.

[1] Hanna's "Life of Chalmers," vol. iv., pp. 37-40.

CHAPTER XXI.

NON-INTRUSION CONTROVERSY.

IN the years after 1838 the question came to be not as to the extension, but as to the existence of the Church of Scotland. We have already seen the fate of Lord Aberdeen's bill. The Duke of Argyll introduced a bill into the House of Lords, which would have been thoroughly acceptable to the Non-Intrusion party in the Church, being practically a legalisation of the veto law. But it was opposed by leading men of both political parties, such a Herod as Lord Dunfermline entering into amity with such Pilates as the Earls of Haddington and Aberdeen to oppose it. The measure was approved in the General Assembly of 1841 by a large majority, on the motion of Dr. Candlish. But the change of Ministry occurred. Sir Robert Peel came into power, and in the expectation that his Government would deal with the matter, the Duke of Argyll's bill was not proceeded with. Meantime, as deputations had done so much to further the extension of the Church, recourse was had to the same method of enlightening the people as to the vitality of the principles for which she was contending. Dr. Begg was one of the most efficient of these deputies, and rendered good service to a good cause.

In 1839 a movement was made which told most powerfully on the controversy which was being carried on respecting the independence of the Church and the rights of her people. I refer to the institution of the *Witness* newspaper, under the editorship of Mr. Hugh Miller. I have not been able to ascertain precisely the part which Dr. Begg had in the origination of this movement. But I have always understood that that part was a prominent one; and I know that the relation which subsisted betwixt him and Miller to the last day of the life of that notable and noble man was one of cordial friendship and of mutual respect. We may have occasion to notice in the sequel that they did not always agree in opinion. This will neither surprise nor distress us. But each ever regarded the other as an honest and fearless champion of what both regarded as a righteous cause, although there might be shades of difference in their views as to the ways in which that cause could best be advanced. Dr. Begg and the editor of the *Witness* had much in common. Sturdy maintenance of their views, no shrinking from controversy, if not a certain degree of liking to it, a general agreement in political sentiment—Conservative Whiggism as opposed to Radical Whiggism, but all subordinate to Christian principle and an earnest desire for the glory of God—these were the bases of the cordial friendship between the two men. And there were points of difference so great as to bar the access of that rivalry which through human infirmity often militates against the perfection of friendship even among good men. The oratory of the one was as much outside the province of the other as the science of the latter was outside the province of the former. It never occurred to Miller to aspire to oratory, or to Begg to cultivate science, any more than it occurs to any of us to emulate the birds in their flight. I am confident of being pardoned for stepping aside a very little from my direct way to pay a humble tribute to a man who not only did invaluable service to the cause which Dr. Begg had so much at heart, but who also, in a still higher department, in days of the prevalence of a shallow and boastful science, lived as a practical exhibition of the compatibility of sound science with simple faith.

But what I have to do with in connection with the *Witness*

is the fact, or rather the two facts, that Dr. Begg was a frequent contributor to its columns, and that it contains full and appreciative reports of his public appearances. I have before me a collection of articles from the *Witness* which Dr. Begg had transcribed for insertion in his Autobiography. In accordance with the rule which I have prescribed for myself, of giving all the matter which has come into my hand manifestly designed by him to be incorporated in that Autobiography, I shall present these extracts in the order of their dates.

The first is an account of a disgraceful attack made on Dr. Begg at Ellon in Aberdeenshire, and described by himself.

"SHORT NOTES OF A RECENT VISIT TO PART OF STRATHBOGIE AND ABERDEENSHIRE.—BY THE REV. JAMES BEGG, OF LIBERTON.

(*From Witness, April* 15 *and* 25, 1840.)

"The following hasty notes may possess some interest at the present moment.

"On the afternoon of Tuesday, March 31, I started by the Aberdeen mail for the now famed district of Strathbogie.

"One enters this district, so called because it is traversed by the river *Bogie*, between thirty and forty miles beyond Aberdeen, Marnoch and the celebrated Foggyloan being on the right. The aspect of the country is wild, and although agriculture is rapidly advancing under the fostering care of the Highland Society, yet, in most parts of Banffshire and Aberdeenshire, one may see such remains of the olden time as a horse and an ox or cow united in the same yoke, and everywhere miserable huts and vast districts of uncultivated land. The parish churches, too, are in general very paltry, although here and there a few good specimens are beginning to be seen. Strathbogie was till lately a very wild, uncultivated district; indeed, I was told it was little better than a vast morass, whilst we all know it was scarcely thoroughly reformed, and till now a stronghold of Moderatism. But agriculture has of late been making immense strides, and the face of the country is rapidly changing; and a similar improvement is at present vigorously advancing in the moral aspect of the scene, by the divine blessing on the new modes of spiritual husbandry recently introduced. Huntly, the only one of the parishes in which I spent any time, is truly an interesting place. It is well situated on a rising ground—an old seat of the powerful Gordon family, and the remains of their ancient castle, as well as a beautiful modern residence, are in sight of the town. The Duchess of Gordon is held in the highest esteem, and has, by the erection of schools and otherwise, been eminently useful. In Huntly there are several meeting-houses, and especially a Popish chapel, lately finished. It was formerly three parishes, which were united in the days of spoliation by the influence of the landlords—not to benefit the people, but to save expense. This may account in some measure for the growth of dissent. The same system was practised to a great extent in Aberdeenshire, and indeed in most parts of Scotland, during the last century, often with the concurrence of the clergy, who, being mere nominees, durst not resist,—or who were bribed into silence by receiving two or three glebes instead of one. These matters ought to be revised now that the pernicious effects of that system are clearly seen.

"I arrived at Huntly on Thursday, April 2, and soon after was waited upon by Dr. Christie, a most agreeable man, and the Rev. Mr. M'Kenzie, a licentiate of the Church, who is now appointed to labour in the parish of Glass, a gentleman who has acted a most noble and disinterested part in the present struggle, and whose talents and Christian zeal equally entitle him to the active support of all friends of the Church. Soon after, I saw many zealous friends of non-intrusion, and, I trust, of Christian truth,—persons who seemed perfectly alive to the magnitude and importance of the present struggle, and who seemed ready to make any sacrifice for the cause of the Church and Christian people. I never saw a more interesting people. Their desire to hear the Gospel is perfectly wonderful. They listen with the most eager interest; and, week-day or Sabbath, an audience may be collected on the shortest notice. The kind of preaching lately introduced appears to be perfectly new to them, and I do trust that great and eternal good will be the result. Like the rest of my brethren who have been there, I was, of course, duly served with an interdict from the Court of Session. It was given me whilst standing in the open street by an officer, accompanied by two witnesses. The officer himself smiled at the affair, seemed ashamed of it, and, I understood, came to hear the sermon; whilst a decent man, from the parish of Glass, who stood by, said, 'I dinna ken wha gied him authority to order you no to preach, but I'm sure it wasna Him wha gied you your commission.' A large audience assembled at seven to hear the sermon, and remained for nearly two hours and a half. The Rev. Mr. Macintosh of Tain preached a sermon in Gaelic at six o'clock to the Highlanders, who in all parts of the world thirst after the Word of God in their native tongue. I took up my residence in the house of Mr. Lawson, a most excellent man, the kindness of whose family I shall never forget. Next day the Rev. Mr. M'Kenzie and I set out for the Alford district, which was always reckoned the stronghold of the intrusion party. Many threatenings of personal violence had been uttered against any non-intrusionist who would venture there, and we were told to provide steel caps, proving that the fiendish spirit of persecution exists amongst a few of the people, chiefly the lairds, factors, &c., if they had the power of gratifying it,—proving also that such men are convinced that their cause cannot stand the test of argument, but flies before exposure like chaff before the wind. This is the true reason, I rather think, why public meetings are so much disliked, even by some of the clergy, who were themselves quite ready to meet the people upon other questions. The advocates of non-intrusion feel that the more their objects, arguments, and past struggles against violent settlements, and in favour of Christ's supreme and sole Headship in His own Church are known, the more will they commend themselves to the approbation of Christian and intelligent men. Therefore we had no scruple in going. The district of Alford is a beautiful strath on the banks of the Don, nearly twenty miles from Huntly by the best road. On our way we passed through Gartly, the excellent minister of which has stood by the Church and fulfilled his ordination engagements. We passed the church and manse of Rhynie, the wild and upland parish of the leader of the seven suspended ministers. We also saw the place, the court of an inn, where from a thousand to twelve hundred persons at present meet every Sabbath in the open air to hear the ministers sent by the Commission; and we spoke to a most intelligent watchmaker in the place, who is a warm and devoted friend to the Church in her present movements. We learned here not only that the great mass of the Church people now attend the preaching station, but also all the Independents, except about a dozen, and that it is very painful to see Mr. Allardyce sometimes obliged to pass this vast assemblage as he goes to and from the parish church to preach to the handful that remain. We halted at the residence of Mr. Lumsden of Clova, a very large proprietor, about twelve miles from Huntly, and a man of great influence, from whom we received great kindness, and who is a strenuous maintainer of the principle of non-intrusion. We learned from him the great evils which had flowed from the abuse of patronage in that district of Scotland before such a check as the *veto* existed, as also the evils which had proceeded from the inconvenient and unchristian union of parishes. This gentleman seems to be a genuine Presbyterian reformer of the best school. After a beautiful ride along the banks of the Don, we came to the Bridge of Alford, the sort of head-quarters of that district. We soon learned from the people that the statements in the newspapers had been grossly exaggerated, and they seemed indignant at the idea that they should have been so misrepresented. About four hundred people had met there a few nights before in hopes of hearing Mr. Macnaughtan, who had not time to go. The man said, 'The schoolmasters and the lairds hae been riding about on their *shalts* (ponies) to persuade us against non-intrusion, but they hae come little speed.' Another said, 'If Mr. Macnaughtan had come, he would have seen that there are as many non-intrusionists here as could, if they chose, *eat* all the rest.' A third told us that Mr. Paull's letter had been circulated in the district; 'but,' said he, 'I got Mr. Gray's answer, and I was delighted wi' it, for it cuttit um up *sae clean;*' and a fourth expressed his surprise that the newspapers (referring to a Radical print in Aberdeen), which formerly fought the people's battles, had on this occasion 'turned their backs and gaen ower to the side o' the lairds and Moderate clergy.' In a word, I have not often seen a peasantry so thoroughly full of the old Scotch principles and feelings, and I was, of course, agreeably surprised, as I was also when I found the same admirable leaven in strong existence in Eskdale and Wigtonshire. In such districts the Moderate system has existed for years, but some of the people have Boston, Flavel, and the Confession of Faith in their houses, and there are amongst them strong recollections of better days. Gordon of Alford was in former times sent to London to endeavour to secure the repeal of the Act of Queen Anne. Malcolm of Leochel-Cushnie was an excellent man, and his memory is much revered. The people seem most anxious to have a minister in this district who will act upon the principles of the Evangelical party, and most eagerly inquired at us whether such a thing could not immediately be by the authority of the General Assembly. They said his church would be crowded. They spoke in very kind terms of some of their present ministers. It was whispered, no doubt, however, amongst other things, that some of them were 'gran' farmers,' and had great 'skill o' nowt,' and instead of being alarmed and nervous, as some say they all are, at the suspension of ministers at Strathbogie, we heard of some who were expressing great anxiety, in the strong Aberdeen accent, to hear if any such good things were likely to 'come up their wy.'

"The public meeting we had at Leochel-Cushnie that evening was certainly one of the most splendid I have seen. It was just like a west country tent-preaching, such a number of fine-looking people, and so well dressed. They came showering down the hills in every direction, although one could not divine where they came from, and stood in a dense and eager crowd for more than two hours. There must have been at least 1000 people—some say 1200—and they had come from fourteen parishes. It was beautiful to see the vast multitude uncover at once, as by magic, the instant the psalm-book was opened, and delightful to hear the voice of such hearty praise rising in that distant valley. When the daylight failed, two willing assistants stood on the same table with me, and held up the two gig lamps on the right and left, whose light shone on the interesting faces of the people, whilst I stood and spoke in the midst; and at length, when the resolutions were proposed by most respectable men in the meeting, in favour of the great principle of non-intrusion, and of the popular party in the General Assembly, the whole hands went up at once like a forest, and a long shout of enthusiasm was echoed back amidst the darkness from the distant hills. The meeting, after a psalm and prayer, broke up with the utmost harmony. We were loaded with thanks, and entreated to come to many neighbouring parishes, and some of the people told us that they had partly been induced to come to the meeting in consequence of the threatenings uttered by a neighbouring minister, 'wi' a face as red as the fire,' against all who would go to hear those 'dangerous' men.[1]

"Our meeting at Tullynessle, a small parish on the other side of the Don, took place on Saturday, at four o'clock. It was held in the premises of Mr. Smith, at Mountgarry, one of Mr. Paull's elders, a venerable man, and a decided non-intrusionist. Mr. Paull is well liked amongst his people, but our meeting was large; we had again to adjourn to the open air, and there strong non-intrusion resolutions were passed, and a petition adopted, which the elder was the first

---

[1] "As Matthew Henry would say, Nothing provokes human curiosity so much as a strenuous attempt at concealment. It may illustrate the kindness and zeal of the people of this district to mention that our host, Mr. Murray, innkeeper at Muggarthaugh, although we and our horse remained one night with him, would not allow us to pay him a single farthing whilst we were travelling in such a cause. As we stood at the door of the inn next morning, and looked round the vast circle of hills, with scarcely a human being within sight, except such as were busy plying their daily toil, so that a whole army with Claverhouse at their head might have sought in vain for the crowd of the previous evening, we thought of the vast importance of the Church Establishment, by means of which a free Christianity is carried into all such regions, and of the madness of some of our higher classes in trying to force such a people into the ranks of dissent or heathenism, merely to gratify their own tyrannical dispositions, even at the expense of their worldly interests. No men are so deeply interested in securing popular, efficient Gospel ministers as landlords, and no landlords have benefited so much by Christianity as those in Scotland; and that just in the proportion in which they have yielded to the desires of the people for a pure Gospel, warmly and faithfully preached. Give the Scotch people this, and they ask little more; they will be found the most easily governed people in the world. Without this, the land that we saw would be a desert, and the people savages."

to sign, and which the other people were busy subscribing when we left. It was now past six o'clock, and we proceeded past the church of Tullynessle, a very paltry building, but with a good manse, &c., which stands at the foot of a vast black Aberdeenshire-looking hill, over which we passed as the nearest road to Huntly, where we arrived at nine o'clock, after passing the churches of Clatt and Kennethmont.

"On Sabbath, April 5, I preached twice at Huntly to very crowded and most attentive audiences—the place of meeting containing about 1000 people, and a considerable number not being able to find admittance. Between sermons there was a very numerous and interesting Sabbath school, which I had great pleasure in attending. It was established by Mr. Lewis, of Dundee, and the children and young people are making great progress. Many of the grown-up, and even old people, attended, and listened to the lessons with eager interest. The main stream of population and anxiety in the place is now turned towards this place of worship. Not only is the parish church nearly deserted, but many Dissenters and some Roman Catholics regularly attend it, the latter declaring that that church—it was formerly the Popish chapel—was once a 'dark place' to them, whereas they now see the light and rejoice. The same results have appeared more or less in all the parishes. The preachers are attended by large audiences everywhere, and an uncommon interest prevails; indeed, I never saw anything like it. News from the South is eagerly expected, and all eyes are turned towards the ensuing Assembly. The people seem quite prepared for the deposition of their ministers, as a step now forced upon the Church, in consequence of their own tyrannical and refractory proceedings; they say, 'We cannot go back to hear these men;' and if the Moderator were advanced to the chair of the Assembly by the votes of Strathbogie, I should say, from what I heard everywhere, that Dr. Hill would get few votes. The seven brethren are, it is understood, anything but pleased with the recent proceedings of Dr. Cook in the case of his own son, in which he seems to have left them rather in the lurch. The language of his conduct seems to be, 'I have no wish to be deposed, I assure you, gentlemen, nor to have the license taken from my son,—it may do very well for you in Strathbogie, but it won't suit me.' Perhaps the men of the cold 'east neuk' of Fife were afraid of a troop of preachers being sent over.

"On Monday morning, at half-past eight, I had a farewell meeting with the people at Huntly, and even at that early hour there was a good and most interesting congregation. I proceeded immediately afterwards to Aberdeen, and thence to Ellon.

"It occurs to me to mention, in addition to what I have already stated in regard to Huntly, that when there I was very anxious to discover in what way the proceedings of the Commission of the Assembly had operated amongst the people, and by what steps they had been brought to their present interesting state. I found that formerly they knew little about the affairs of the Church, and took almost no interest in her struggles. The great stream of ecclesiastical politics swept past almost unheeded; and even when the case of Marnoch began to excite general interest, the people of Huntly never dreamt that they would be drawn into the vortex. 'The first time I ever heard such an idea suggested,' said a most respectable man to me, 'was after the stormy meeting of Presbytery, at which it was resolved to proceed with Mr. Edwards' trials in defiance of the General Assembly and the people. A decent old man' (I think he said a Seceder) 'came into my house immediately after and said, "Your minister will be suspended for what he has done to-day."' Immediately after the news of the suspension of the seven brethren came upon the district like a thunder-clap. The people scarcely knew either its cause or probable effect; and as Mr. Walker was personally much esteemed, a feeling of general dislike was the immediate result. Indeed, it would have been wonderful had no such feeling existed in such circumstances. But when Mr. Candlish explained the matter fully to the people in the yard of the inn—the only place to which he could then get access—the tide was instantly turned. His sermons and speech appear to have produced a powerful effect, and the interest has since been continually increasing. The people speak with much affection of all the ministers who have been there—of Mr. Guthrie, Mr. Moody Stuart, Mr. Macnaughtan, Mr. Lewis, and others, and every Sabbath new converts are made. One excellent lady, now a zealous non-intrusionist, told me that she had only been hearing for three Sabbaths the 'Commission ministers,' and that she was formerly quite opposed to them; and I heard of a person who had gone for the first time on the Sabbath that I preached. Those left in the old church, however, although few in number, are not deficient in zeal. And it is an instance of good brought out of evil to see them, as I did, taking all their children with them to church, even the smallest,—which they never did before,—for the purpose of increasing the attendance. One has heard of *preaching*, but I had never seen anything like *hearing* 'out of contention' before. In a word, it is impossible to suppose any combination of circumstances out of which more good is likely to spring to the long-neglected district of Strathbogie than the recent painful proceedings forced upon the Commission of the General Assembly. But I must proceed to Ellon.

"Ellon is far from and very unlike Strathbogie. It is on the east coast, sixteen miles from Aberdeen, on the road to Peterhead. It is a small place, amidst a well-cultivated country, in fact only a hamlet, the whole parish containing scarcely more than 2000 souls, and yet within sight of the parish church there are three dissenting places of worship, besides several in the neighbourhood—so much for Moderatism in its worst form, which has long been rampant in this neighbourhood. It is ever to be kept in view that there are various shades and degrees of Moderatism, from Dr. Muir and Dr. Ferrie down to Mr. Pirie of Dyce and Mr. Ellis of Culsamond, although unfortunately, like a spoiled bunch of grapes—to use the figure of another—the good and the bad hang too perseveringly together. A friend of mine, himself one of the party, says there are 'Moderates' and '*dead* Moderates,' and the district of Ellon seems to have had some of the worst samples. The present minister is well known as a man of talent, and I believe diligent in the discharge of his duty. The former was one of the most inefficient of his class for good, and there are still some singular specimens in the neighbourhood. Throughout part of this district there is besides a bad leaven of Scottish Jacobitism, which seems to retain all the hatred of Presbyterianism and of serious religion, against which our ancestors had so many struggles. Such is the low state of vital religion in the district that a most excellent Evangelical minister mentioned to me that he is often pointed and laughed at by the people of the surrounding district; and what would you think of individuals who, in regard to the appointment of an Evangelical minister, could say, 'We don't want any of your praying devils'?

"The meetings at Turriff and Ellon are sufficient to illustrate the moral state of the people, even although it was said in excuse for the latter that it was the 'market day.' It inverted all my ideas of mobs to see a mob of farmers, booted and spurred, doctors, factors, &c., to hear that some elders of the Established Church were amongst the number, whilst the humbler classes of the people—mostly Seceders, I understood —were well behaved, and anxious to be informed. I have been present at many riotous meetings, at Paisley, Dumfries, and elsewhere, and therefore was the less moved; but for deliberate, low, and apparently hired ruffianism, I never saw anything to equal the meeting at Ellon, except an awfully blasphemous exhibition by avowed atheists at Dundee, which Scotland will not soon forget. They were truly '*fierce for moderation.*' There is, however, something intellectual even in the uproar of weavers,—they will debate a point with you, and often with great talent; but there is something intensely gross and sensual in the irruption of a coarse, ignorant, and ungodly squirearchy. Such a scene proves in what a state Moderatism in its worst form leaves a population. It scarcely varnishes over the innate depravity of human nature, far less tends to change it, which nothing but the Gospel and Spirit of God can do; and the 'quietness' of which ministers sometimes boast, in such circumstances, will be found, when it is stirred, to be only like the quietness of a putrid pond. It is of immense importance to bring out the real state of the case; for a scene in a country district of Scotland only equalled by the Popery of Galway and Tipperary, and worse than mere heathenism is generally known to produce, proves that depravity is not confined to towns or the lower classes, and ought to teach senators that if an Established Church is to be of any use, they must take care that it shall really diffuse a knowledge of Christianity among the people. Such a scene proves that the spirit of persecution is as strong as ever, wherever fallen human nature exists unchecked, or perhaps only inflamed into greater hatred; and in the glaring eyes and red, maddened countenances of men who had previously taken the precaution partly to deprive themselves of reason, that they might assail without shame a minister of Christ whom they had never seen before, and whose object was to promote their best interests, one could more vividly imagine some of the striking scenes of the Word of God, and the days of the thumb-screws. We seldom see man in his demon aspect. We may dream that he is changed, and it is useful, though deeply painful, to see him as he really is—'hateful and hating,' 'gnashing his teeth,' and exhibiting his 'desperate wickedness,' as he did in opposing our Saviour and His apostles. It serves to confirm our faith in the divine testimony, and, as a worthy man who was present at the Ellon meeting said—'Sir, we maun just expect it, for before Christ takes to Himself His great power and reigns, Satan will break forth into opposition.' How unlike the fine peasantry of Alford and Wigtonshire, the intelligent shepherds of Eskdale and Selkirk, or indeed anything to be found in Scotland generally beyond the dregs of our large cities. Before I left the place, which I did with deep pity for the people, I distributed a number of tracts, and I have no doubt that ere long a reaction will take place, and an opportunity will occur of letting in the light more effectually. Such a visitation as has been made in Strathbogie would be of great use in other districts of Scotland.

"I spent the night with Sir William Seton, whose high character is well known, and who is a great blessing to such a neighbourhood. Next evening I lectured in a Secession chapel in the neighbouring parish of Belhelvie. I have remarked, particularly in all the distant country parts of Scotland, that the Seceders in general seem to retain their original principles. The ministers often are Voluntaries, but not the people; and it is truly gratifying to reflect upon the vast amount of good which must have been done by evangelical Dissenters in districts where the Established Church has been inefficient, or perhaps worse than useless. What a glorious thing would it have been had the Seceders in this country, as in Ireland, been ready to join their forces with ours, now that the objects of the Testimony are being rapidly secured. Let us hope and pray that we may yet see such a glorious issue of all our struggles. It is melancholy to think that some of the pretended followers of Erskine are now the main obstacle in the way of the accomplishment of his fondest wishes. They should study the history and doom of Edom.

"Aberdeen itself is making vast progress. With such a staff of able and efficient ministers, with so little dissent, with its beautiful new university nearly completed, and with so many parochial schools, it may be justly said, although much remains to be done, to be one of the most hopeful cities in the kingdom. What a change since Rutherford was there of old! The non-intrusion cause is also very powerful, as was evident from the tone of the vast public meeting which I had the honour to attend; and when their new Church paper is started, under the able and spirited management of Mr. Troup of the *Montrose Review*, the best results may be anticipated. The friends of truth in Scotland must seize the press, and wrest it from the degraded hands in which it is often at present found. In travelling I have had occasion to see much of its immense power for good or evil, and the vast advantage of such publications as the *Scottish Guardian*, the *Witness*, and the *Christian Herald*, especially in districts where the ministers are hostile. In all the extreme districts of Scotland these papers are now found, and it is scarcely possible to imagine any cheaper or more effectual way of promoting the diffusion of sound principles than by widely circulating them, as all the country people are anxious to read newspapers. Means must also immediately be adopted, if the Church of Scotland is really to be efficient, for planting and maintaining preachers or ordained ministers in the destitute districts of Scotland. I have seen many a most necessitous district lately, and on former occasions, where the people are literally 'perishing for lack of knowledge,' but where the idea of erecting a church in the first instance is entirely out of the question. The first movement must be made from without, and it was most melancholy to think, whilst looking on these masses of heathenism, that unemployed preachers were walking the streets of Edinburgh whilst such multitudes had none to break to them the bread of life,—multitudes who never will apply to the committee at Edinburgh for relief, although that committee sits till doomsday, and who are every day sinking in torpor, and passing into eternity without hope. Let the Church then arise, and a portion of the Church Extension funds be immediately devoted to this object, and we shall soon set up a light in every dark place, till the whole land is filled with brightness. At present our efforts only reach the able and the willing—the worst cases are entirely overlooked; and besides, if the living agency is first brought to bear, the stone and lime will soon follow. We shall soon then, by the divine blessing, neutralise, and, by Christianising, bring over to the other side the heathenism and torpor which at present are the heaviest dead-weights in the opposite scale. I trust Dr. Clason's Committee 'on the Employment of Probationers' will not lose sight of this object, the immediate importance of which can in no view be exaggerated. If, in addition to all this, the Assembly would only declare against the Act of Queen Anne altogether, while she stands fast in her present noble position, there would arise an instant response from tens of thousands more in all parts of the kingdom. The people all hate patronage as cordially as their fathers did, and wherever I have been the only fault they find with the Church is that she does not go far enough."

Our next extract relates to certain proceedings in the Synod of Dumfries. Probably the latter part of it is from Dr. Begg's pen, though published editorially.

"SYNOD OF DUMFRIES: INDEPENDENCE AND NON-INTRUSION.

(*From Witness, April* 29, 1840.)

"The following overture was proposed by Dr. Duncan, of Ruthwell, seconded by Sir Patrick Maxwell: 'The Synod of Dumfries humbly overture the venerable the General Assembly of the Church of Scotland, that they adhere to their previous resolution relative to the independent jurisdiction of the Church in all spiritual matters, and to support the principle of non-intrusion involved in the Act of 1835 anent calls, and that they continue their exertions to procure some legislative enactment whereby the present unhappy collision of the civil and ecclesiastical courts may be terminated, and the obstructions thereby occasioned to the peace, extension, and prosperity of the Church removed.'

"After a short discussion, this overture was rejected by 37 to 26—majority, 11.

"Mr. Shaw, of Langholm, next proposed an overture calling upon the Assembly to pronounce a sentence of disapprobation, and put an effectual veto upon the illegal procedure of such ministers as have been deserting their own charges, and intruding into the parishes of their clerical brethren. A long discussion took place.

"Finally the overture was carried by 28 to 18—majority, 10.

(*Editorial Remarks.*)

"It is not a little interesting to see the furious recoil of the Moderate clergy against the information which has lately been so successfully diffused in their parishes. No more certain evidence of success could be desired than such pathetic outcries. Owls and bats scream and flutter when light is let in. The Synod of Dumfries, still a region of comparative darkness, at the suggestion of Mr. Shaw, of Langholm, who, of course, is well known, has sent an instructive overture to the Assembly on the subject. The following passage from a violent and outrageous speech by the said rev. brother, in defence of Christian meekness, as a preface to the overture, is admirable. 'Before the intrusion of these rev. agitators, our people were remarkably quiet and orderly, never interfering in any way with Church politics. *But it is truly lamentable,*' of course to the Intrusionists, '*to perceive the change that has taken place,* and the evil spirit which has been engendered amongst them in this respect.' We, of course, all know the meaning of this. We trust the good cause in Eskdale will go on and prosper. The meeting at Langholm was very effective. Hence Mr. Shaw's rage at Messrs. Cunningham and Begg. We trust the Non-Intrusion Committee will take encouragement from such authentic testimonies to the success of their efforts, especially in such interesting districts."

The next extract, from the *Witness* of 15th April, 1840, is part of an account of a

"NON-INTRUSION MEETING AT ABERDEEN.

(*From Witness, April* 15, 1840.)

"The Rev. Mr. Begg of Liberton spoke next. He had listened with pleasure to the very interesting statements which they had just heard, and he was sure he spoke the sentiments of the friends of non-intrusion when he said that they would be delighted if any satisfactory measure were passed in Parliament, by whatsoever party it were introduced. He hoped they would in this question keep clear of politics. It did the gentleman who represented them great honour that he stated in the outset of his address that he did not come there to further any political object whatever. From the beginning he had given this cause his most zealous support, and they were much indebted to all, in both Houses of Parliament, who had done their best to procure a satisfactory settlement of the question. He agreed with the very rev. principal, that no settlement would be satisfactory which did not completely establish the rights of the Christian people, and he felt persuaded *that no measure would give that satisfaction which did not go the length of abolishing the Act of Queen Anne, by which patronage was established.* (Cheers.) That Act was passed avowedly against the best interests of the Church of Scotland; had been used as an engine of tyranny to the people, and at the present moment they were bitterly reaping the fruits of its policy. It was his firm opinion that they would never be able to combine these two elements—the people's power and the patron's rights. *They must cast the patron overboard;* he was the Jonah that had raised the storm; they must go down to 'the side of the ship' and cast him out, and then they would have a calm. (Cheers.) The rev. gentleman then replied at length to the charge brought against the popular party in the Church, that they were grasping at more power, and adduced a great deal of evidence from the history of the Church of Scotland to prove that the Moderate party had all along been the most intolerant. He quoted the forced settlements of Shotts, Nigg, Torphichen, and Muckart, and gave a graphic account of the proceedings attending each case. He then came to the Auchterarder case, and from that to Marnoch, where he dealt rather humorously with Peter Taylor of Foggyloan, the only party who had signed Mr. Edwards' call. Peter, he said, was innkeeper at Foggyloan, at which inn the majority of the Presbytery of Strathbogie had been accustomed to dine. He had been told, however, that even Peter had bitterly repented the step he had taken in putting his name to the call. The call usually runs, 'The male heads of families,' &c.; but in the case of Marnoch it must have read thus, '*I*, Peter Taylor, being destitute of a parish minister, invite you, Mr. Edwards, to minister to me and my family, and I promise you the whole manse and stipend of Marnoch in return for your services.' (Laughter and cheers.) In the days of the old supremacy it was usual to select some decided Intrusionist to ordain an unpopular minister; but on one occasion they chanced to select a man for this service who was in favour of the people's rights. That minister in ordaining the presentee said, 'I appoint you stipend-lifter of this parish.' (Laughter and cheers.) For this he was rebuked by the Presbytery; and on the cause being brought before the Assembly he was sentenced to be rebuked there also, when he leant over the seat, and coolly said, 'Come awa wi' yer rebuke, Moderator, it will brak nae banes.' (Laughter.) And so it would have been in Marnoch. Mr. Edwards could only have been ordained as stipend-lifter of the parish, and if the Moderate party had got their will he would have been so at this present moment; they would have ordained Mr. Edwards to be minister to Peter Taylor had the Commission tied their hands behind their back in a quiet way to prevent them from doing mischief. He then noticed the following encouraging circumstances in connection with the present movement—First, influential men of all parties were now convinced that something must be done. This was the universal impression, with the exception of those who were prejudiced against the people. These he would give up. They were what he would call 'dyed in the wool;' and to expect them to change their views was to expect to see a moral miracle. He would also give up most of the Dissenters, who had an interest in breaking down the Establishment. Secondly, the Rev. Dr. Cook of St. Andrews had given in to the Church. It was generally supposed that Dr. Cook had advised the majority of the Presbytery of Strathbogie in the present case, and had winked at the ecclesiastical authority of the Church. Now, it so happened that his own son had received a presentation as assistant and successor in a parish in Fife. The call to this young man was signed by his father; but though he had preached three years in the parish the people were now up in arms against him, and the Commission of the Assembly prevented the Presbytery from taking him on trials. What did Dr. Cook do in this case? He had abetted the rebellion of the Church, if rebellion it was—he submitted to the Commission. (Cheers.) For this his brethren in Strathbogie were much grieved with him, but he (Mr. Begg) viewed it as a symptom of returning to a sounder state of mind, and as an encouragement to hope that others of the Moderate party would follow his example. Thirdly, the young men in the Church, and those coming into her, were almost all Non-Intrusionists. Meetings had been held in the Divinity Halls, and it had been ascertained that out of 300 students 242 had declared in favour of non-intrusion, and many of these had sent memorials to the Assembly on the subject. Thirty-six students had declared against the non-intrusion principle. Oh, it would be very interesting to get hold of their names, and publish them all over Scotland, that it might be known what kind of men they were. If they could get this done, he believed it would be found that they were men depending on absolute patronage—men who could not get into the Church by the door, and were afraid that the ladder to the window was about to be taken away. (Cheers.) Fourthly, it was admitted on all hands that the Court of Session in granting the interdicts against preaching the Gospel in Strathbogie, went beyond its power. When in Huntly, he too was served with an interdict; but what did he do? Why, Christ told him, 'Go ye into all the world and preach the Gospel to every creature.' The Court of Session says, 'You shall not preach the Gospel to one soul in this parish.' I obeyed my Master. (Cheers.) They the (Non-Intrusionists) would submit to pains and penalties for disregarding these interdicts; but no complaint had been made against them yet; no man had yet been put in jail; and if they now attempt to do so, they would find a rather heavy arrear to bring up, that it would be a rather difficult task to put eighteen or twenty ministers in jail for preaching the Gospel, and determining to prevent a man from being intruded on a reclaiming people. Fifthly, hundreds and thousands of people in every direction were now flocking to hear the Gospel, who formerly cared little about its precepts or practice. In Strathbogie, where he had just been preaching, the people were not satisfied with the discourses delivered to them on Sabbath, but came out in great numbers on the Monday morning at half-past eight o'clock. Such was the desire now to hear the truth in that district, and multitudes, he believed, would bless God through eternity for the visits which had been paid them, and the sermons preached among them on this occasion. (Loud cheers.) In other districts the anxiety to hear the truth was equally remarkable. At Alford, such was the fear of a certain party lest the light should get in amongst the people there, that on hearing of Mr. Macnaughtan's intention to visit them, they collected a parcel of fiddlers together, and laid a scheme to get the people to dance rather than let them hear him speak. Nay, more, they sent men out with blackened faces to frighten him! He (Mr. Begg) was told that if he dared to go to that district he would need to take a steel cap with him; but notwithstanding this remark, and the treatment Mr. Macnaughtan had met with, he determined to go, and thither he went, and had the satisfaction of addressing a meeting of a thousand people in the open air. (Cheers.) There he stood till it was dark, and then two men held lanterns—one on each side of him—while a series of resolutions were passed, praise and prayer offered up to God, and the minds of the people enlightened, notwithstanding they had lairds and lords, ay, and ministers opposed to them; these were against them, but the people were with them. (Applause.) In Tullynessle the people were also with them. One decent man said to him, 'They sent me Mr. Paull and Mr. Pirie's letter, which I read; but I got Mr. Gray's answer, and was delighted with it; it cut up the other letter clean.' (Applause.) He went to Ellon on Tuesday; there he was not so successful. He could not obtain a place to preach in within doors, but he got a wood-yard, and regretted to learn since that the poor man who gave the use of it was likely to suffer loss, the Intrusionists in the town and neighbourhood having resolved not to employ him again. A good number of people came out to hear him. Some of them were drunk; some of them were respectably dressed, and some of them were boys. They began to shout and laugh, and make faces. They induced the boys also to laugh, and they assailed him with eggs. One decent man remarked that this was not more than might be expected under the *yoke* of patronage. (A laugh.) He had been pelted with stones before, but never with eggs. However, there he stood and declared the truth, until two ferocious-looking men came up to the platform and threatened personal violence. He was told afterwards, though he could not vouch for the fact, that these two men were offered a bottle of whisky by one party there to 'go up and throw Mr. Begg down.' In these circumstances he could not proceed further at that time. But did not conduct of this kind show what a desperate cause the Intrusionists had to maintain? Nevertheless, he believed there was a spirit of intelligence abroad which would thwart all their opposition. A reaction would yet take place, even in that district, and when this did happen, he trusted the friends of the truth in Aberdeen would not fail to send out men to explain the question of non-intrusion. (Cheers.) But a reaction had already taken place, for, on the evening of the next day, one of the Seceder ministers, much to his honour, frankly gave them his place of worship. Many other Dissenters, he was glad to say, had given them assistance in their present struggle for the people's rights. There were some opposing them, for this reason: if they could get Evangelical religion and Evangelical ministers out of the pulpits of the Establishment, they would soon get quit of the Moderates—the more rickety the house the easier it would be pulled down.—Mr. Begg then read a statement from a document lately issued by the Central Board of Dissenters in Edinburgh, and deduced therefrom the fears of Dissenters lest the popular party should succeed in their present struggle. He remarked, however, that the Central Board comprised but a small section of the Dissenters of Scotland, and had little influence. He then alluded to the election of delegates to the Assembly in the Edinburgh Town Council, and called attention to the remarkable fact that the extreme ultra-Tories had united with the extreme ultra-Radicals to put in two Moderates!

He then concluded thus—This is just a struggle for the rights of the Christian people of Scotland, and it must—it will succeed. When the Ark of God was brought into the temple of Dagon, down came the image of the idolaters on the floor; and though the infatuated worshippers put him up again, he fell a second time, and his fall was greater than the first, for his hands and his head were chopped off. Now the image of patronage had been set up in the temple of the Lord. When the principle of non-intrusion was introduced, down came the image, and what were the moderate party doing now, but trying to raise him up again, and bind him up that he may frown and scowl on the Christian people. And what are we labouring for but to pull him down again, by all proper means? Nor shall we rest satisfied until we shall have cut off his head and his hands, and thrown him over the wall, that the people of Scotland may no longer be subjected to his tyranny. (Much cheering.)"

Dr. Begg was a member of the General Assembly of 1840, and took an active part in its proceedings. The two following extracts contain reports of his most important speeches.

"GENERAL ASSEMBLY: STRATHBOGIE CASE.

(*From Supplement to Witness, May 28, 1840.*)

"The Procurator moved—'That the General Assembly, having heard counsel for the complainers, find that the Commission had not exceeded its powers, dismiss the complaint, and find and declare the seven ministers of the Presbytery of Strathbogie, complainers in the cause, to have been duly suspended.'

"Mr. Begg (Liberton) rose to support the motion made by the learned Procurator. That motion referred to two matters: first, to the power of the Commission to entertain the question brought before them, and to give the deliverance upon it which they did give; and secondly, to the nature of that deliverance itself—chiefly to the former. In regard to the power of the Commission, he thought that might be established first of all by the general terms upon which the Commission was appointed. He would even take the exception which was quoted and dwelt upon by the rev. doctor who opened the debate (Cook) as in the strongest manner confirmatory of the power of the Commission, and the duty of the Commission, to take up and dispose of that question when it came before them. What were the terms of that exception? The terms were, that they shall advert to the interests of the Church on every occasion, and take care that the Church and the present Establishment thereof shall sustain no injury until the ensuing Assembly, provided always that this general care be not extended to particular affairs and processes before Synods, and to matters that are not of universal concern to the Church. Therefore, although the case of Marnoch had arisen wholly after the rising of last Assembly, and although consequently no remit had been made to the Commission, it concerned *the whole Church*, according to the admission of all parties, and especially of the learned counsel to the seven rev. complainers. The issue of it might be the demolition of our Church Establishment as it is now constituted. (Hear, hear, hear.) They had heard of a special remit of the case of Marnoch to the Commission, by which they were empowered to judge and determine in regard to any appeals or references which might be subsequently made in regard to that case. It appeared that the seven suspended clergymen admitted their knowledge of the authority of the Commission to take up the matter, because in their resolution, after the sentence of suspension had been passed, they declared that the Presbytery find that as ministers of a Church established by law, and owing obedience to the law of the land, they must, from a regard to conscience, and to avoid the penal consequences, refuse obedience. Then followed an expression of deep regret at being obliged to adopt such a course, *as thereby they were acting against the authority of their superior Church courts.* It was very extraordinary to any one acquainted with the history of the Church to see gentlemen on the other side of the House questioning the power of the Commission to take up such questions and decide upon them. In the days of old the Commissions of Assembly were the main agents in carrying through a series of forced settlements—(disapprobation from the Moderate side; 'Hear, hear,' from the other side)—by which the feelings of the people were outraged; no more outraged, however, than were the laws and principles of the Church. Even the celebrated case of Inverkeithing, which gave rise to a large secession, and to the manifestoes of several parties in the Church, was decided originally by a Commission, and that before it came before the Assembly at all. On that occasion Principal Robertson dissented from the sentence of the Commission, not on the ground of its want of power, but because having full power they did not exercise it for the purpose of coercing conscientious ministers to settle unacceptable presentees upon reclaiming congregations. (Hear, hear, hear.) The title of that document was, 'Reasons of dissent from the judgment and resolution of the Commission on March 11, 1772, resolving to inflict no censure on the Presbytery of Dunfermline for disobedience in reference to the settlement of Inverkeithing.' The great fault now found with the Commission was that they had prevented a minister from being thrust upon a parish against whom almost the whole people dissented. (Hear.) The essence of the whole lay there. A new idea—(laughter)—had been discovered by the Moderate party in regard to the power of the Commission, and that grand discovery had probably been made because, unfortunately, the Commission now had shielded the Christian people against violent intrusion. (Hear, hear, hear.) In regard to the emergency itself in which the Commission had to interpose, impartial men could scarcely differ in this, that if they were to have a Church at all, if they were to have any body of men acting together, there must be order, and for its preservation the inferior courts must be subordinate to the superior, except on the ground of conscience, in which case they were entitled to leave the Church. (Laughter from the Moderate side.) The gentlemen who laugh should be told that this was the grand doctrine maintained in days of old—(laughter from the Evangelical side)—and that the essence of Principal Robertson's manifesto consists in its maintenance (to an extent indeed to which I could not subscribe).—Mr. Begg, after quoting part of Principal Robertson's reasons of dissent, made an extract from Dr. Cook's evidence on patronage, to show that he (Dr. Cook) was not the least strenuous in maintaining the power of the superior judicatories. To evade this general reasoning, it was argued that when the civil law interfered all obedience to the Church courts should cease, and the Church should immediately become a passive instrument in the hands of the supreme power in the State. What was this but the old Erastian heresy that was contended against by our ancestors, and for opposition to which multitudes shed their blood? (Hear, hear.) What was the ground of all the struggles in the reign of Charles II.? Chiefly prelacy; but it also regarded the supremacy of the crown in ecclesiastical matters; and their ancestors thought that when they came out from that bloody struggle the yoke of Erastianism had been broken off the neck of the Church of Scotland for ever. During the whole of the last century the civil courts had refused to interfere, on the ground that the Church had been recognised in the Confession of Faith as having exclusive power in spiritual matters. Why did the civil courts interfere *now?* Because the power of the Church, which was formerly exerted *against* the people, is now exerted *for* them. (Hear, hear.) The Church had thrown herself between the people and their oppressors, saying, 'You must trample our spiritual jurisdiction under foot before you can trample on the rights of our congregations.' (Hear, hear.) The civil court was forcing its way through them merely for the purpose of intruding—he did not speak of motives—(laughter from the Moderate side)—ministers upon unwilling parishes; and the object of the Church was to stand between. What had the Presbytery of Strathbogie done? They had voluntarily made a breach in the ranks of the Church; they had said in effect to the civil court, 'You do not require to make your way through us, for we will just lie down, and let you walk over us.' When the Church of Scotland was opposed by many of the high and mighty, when there were many enemies *without,* she must put down mutiny and insubordination within, however painful the task, and he was sure it must have been very painful for the Commission. (Laughter.) He would take leave to say, and he was sure the saying would be re-echoed by thousands and tens of thousands in Scotland, that the Commission was entitled to, and would receive, the best thanks of the people of this country—(loud cries of 'Hear, hear,' and 'No, no')—and since reference had been made to the district of Strathbogie, he would take upon him to say, that, however these sentiments might be disliked in some quarters, nowhere were the proceedings of the Commission more relished than in that quarter.—The rev. gentleman sat down amidst loud cries of 'Hear, hear,' from the members, and vehement marks of applause from the spectators in the galleries, interrupted with loud cries of 'Order' from the Moderator's side of the House, in the midst of which

"Mr. Robertson of Ellon rose to order. He trusted the House would have so much respect to its own dignity as to prevent those marks of approbation from being allowed.

"Mr. Bennie had no objection to support the dignity of the House so that it was done impartially. But he could not agree while the applause from one side was quietly submitted to, though applause from the other side to their friends was immediately complained against. (Hear, hear.)"

"GENERAL ASSEMBLY: CONTINUATION OF THE DEBATE ON NON-INTRUSION.

(From Witness, May 30, 1840.)

"The Rev. Mr. Begg of Liberton then rose, and said that he did not mean to reply to the speech which they had just now heard. He was sure they would agree with him that it would have been a sad pity if the rev. doctor (Bryce) had not been permitted to continue a member of this Assembly, for he (Mr. Begg) thought that the statements which he had just made, and the extreme love which he had expressed for Lord Aberdeen's bill, were in the highest degree fitted to convince the Assembly, and the country, that it was not the bill which they desired. (Hear, hear.) One reason why he (Mr. Begg) would not reply to the previous speech was because Dr. Bryce was one of those convenient speakers who answer their own speeches as they go along. (A laugh.) After alluding to the controversy betwixt Mr. Robertson of Ellon and Mr. Cunningham of Edinburgh, he continued that the question had assumed a very definite shape—whether this House shall approve or disapprove of Lord Aberdeen's bill. He at once admitted that he could not, in any degree, approve of the bill. This was to all of them a matter of serious disappointment, because they expected, upon what they reckoned good grounds, that some measure would be introduced to which they could, in some measure, give their assent. In contemplating, through the medium of the public press, the proceedings of the House of Lords, they supposed that there was some intimation given that there would be some concession by which they could conscientiously have closed, at least for a time—('Hear' from the Moderate side)—with the provisions of the measures introduced. More particularly when statements were made to the effect that the patrons of the land were willing to make concessions, it was expected that the bill would embody some of these concessions, whereas it now appeared to be a mere declaratory enactment; therefore the alteration of its clauses could not affect its essence. It was impossible to improve that bill so as to make it satisfactory, except the *principle* of it was changed, and a totally different one introduced. What was it that the Church has been contending for of late? Her spiritual jurisdiction might be regarded as only an incidental question, though it had now become the most important of the two. The point originally agitated was, whether the pastoral relationship could in any case be properly constituted without the consent of the people implied, or expressly given. The General Assembly, and the Presbyteries of the Church separately, came to the determination, in 1834, that it could not be formed without the consent of the people, at least implied in the absence of dissent. It was vain, therefore, to mystify the question by pretending that there were various interpretations of the word '*non-intrusion.*' There could not by any possibility be two interpretations, for it expressed the simple proposition that no minister be intruded into a parish 'contrary to the will of the Presbytery*.' (Hear, hear, hear.) The question was, since it is admitted by Lord Aberdeen himself, in the most upright and straightforward manner, and since it has been reiterated by the honourable baronet (Sir George Clerk), that the bill did not and never meant to guard that principle, the Church of Scotland had no alternative left her but to reject this measure, if she wished to maintain her ground as a consistent Church of Christ—except she wished to violate all her declared principles, and was prepared to declare herself to the country as a traitor to the cause of God. If they approved of it, they must proceed to do those things which they had already refused to do. For example, they must proceed to induct Mr. Young into the parish of Auchterarder

* Qu. 'people'?—T. S.

and Mr. Edwards into Marnoch,—they must virtually pronounce censure on all the past proceedings of the Church. He knew not what the consequences might be in regard to the country if such a traitorous resolution were adopted, but he knew the consequences if they were for an instant to give in to any plan or measure by which they were compelled to acquiesce in the sentiment that it is possible for the Church, in any circumstances, to intrude a minister. In the days of old, when the Church, in violation of what always was a fundamental principle of her government, thrust ministers into reclaiming parishes, she required to apply to the civil power for protection in exercising that shameful tyranny. The statement stood upon the minutes of the Assembly that application was made to the Lord Advocate for the aid of the civil power, and ministers were carried into parishes in the midst of bayoneted soldiers. Were the Assembly—were those who would acquiesce in the present bill and the decisions of the civil courts—prepared to do these things over again? Mr. Begg then quoted an extract from Dr. Cook's evidence on patronage with reference to the parish of Shotts, in which he stated that he would not have recourse to the assistance of the military in the settlement of ministers *if he could help it!!* (Considerable laughter.) Even Principal Robertson would have gone as far as that admission, for he probably was not an *amateur* of dragoons. (A laugh.) There were yet individuals in the Assembly who were prepared not to use the military, only if the people would consent to take the minister without the military. This bill professed to countenance the principle of ecclesiastical jurisdiction to some extent, and it was mainly on that ground that its defenders had maintained it. All this was founded on a single parenthetical clause, and it had been conclusively proved that that clause gave no protection to the Church. It gave protection in giving effect to certain reasons written down, but not against the encroachments of the civil court. It was said that they wished an independence which was not within the bounds of possibility, which could not co-exist with the independence of the State. They wished no Popish supremacy in the Church. They wished it to stand on the ground on which it was placed in the Confession of Faith, which is part of the law of the land, as a Church of Christ, having a government in the hands of Church officers distinct from the civil magistrate. Unless they had the power of interpreting the limit of their jurisdiction, and of giving effect to it in spiritual things, their independence was but a name. This was the controversy which their ancestors had maintained in all past periods—the only difference being that their ancestors contended against a single despot, but they themselves against the encroachments of what was called the civil authority. The very essence of the whole lay in our claim to interpret and define the limits of our own ecclesiastical jurisdiction; and as the bill takes for granted that the civil court has decided the law for us even in spiritual matters, it is radically and fundamentally defective. The State can only legitimately interfere with the temporalities. The hon. baronet (Sir George Clerk) would give the Church to the full extent the power of determining absolutely in every case in regard to the settlement of ministers. What was the reason that even in England no bishop could be compelled to ordain a man without his own consent, although he could be compelled to induct him into a benefice after he had been ordained? But the proposal at present before them was to degrade the Church of Scotland beneath that level, and to deprive her of her solemn judicial power, and to prevent her from giving effect to her own law in regard to settlements. He (Mr. Begg) had no such faith as some gentlemen seemed to have in the judicious exercise of the judicial power of the Church, even if it were conceded to them. He gave no opinion, however, upon that, except to the extent that if it were granted fully it might clear them for a time of their present difficulty. Yet it would not be in any degree a satisfactory or certain settlement of the great question of non-intrusion, because it did not appear to make intrusion impossible. His principal objection to it was one of principle, for he did not think that the Church court was entitled to intrude. But suppose such a power recognised by a civil sanction, and that they proceeded without an Act to attempt a series of righteous decisions, he had no such faith in Church courts as to make him believe that they would not very speedily relapse into the old system. Dr. Simpson had referred to the students of theology, and it gave him (Mr. Begg) joy to think of so many excellent young men. But would any one acquainted with

Church history deny that in 1735 the Assembly was as much opposed to the intrusion of ministers as it is at present? At that time they sent a deputation to London to have the law of patronage repealed, and the people were admonished to offer prayers for the success of the enterprise. Next year the Assembly passed a solemn declaration against intrusion, but in a few years the spirit of the Church entirely changed, and as the people were protected by no general law, cases of intrusion arose. Ministers were deposed because they would not take part in these proceedings, and in the face of all considerations, they went on in this course until at length 100,000 were driven in thirty years from the Church of their fathers.—The rev. gentleman then referred in illustration to the cases of Jedburgh, in which all the parishioners, except five, were in arms against Mr. Douglas, the presentee, in consequence of whose settlement 2000 left the Church in one day; to the case of Biggar, in which it was objected, and admitted by the Presbytery, that the voice of the presentee could not be heard in the church, notwithstanding which he was settled; and the case of Kirkcudbright, in which the presentee was stone-blind. And in this last case, it was very amusing to see the extent of clerical ingenuity, for it had been specifically stated by the court who sustained the presentation of the blind man, that the objection to his want of sight would have been all very well in Popish times, when there were so many *hocus pocus* ceremonies that it was impossible such a presentee could see how to perform them, but that now the objection was totally inapplicable and irrelevant where the Gospel was administered in all its simplicity. (Loud cries of 'Hear, hear.') He had brought forward these instances for the sake of those on the other side of the House, and in the expectation that they would be brought to look upon and contemplate them in the same way as the wanderers—referred to by the rev. doctor (Macleod)—were now brought to view the bare bones of the Macdonalds. (Loud applause.) He might also ask, in reference to another subject, if those who were on his side were not among the foremost in driving the battle from the gates when the Establishment was threatened to be overthrown by the Voluntaries? (Hear, hear, and great cheering.) It had been alleged that ministers of the Church had addressed the parishioners of men holding different sentiments—that they had propagated sentiments which were fitted to bring the civil law into contempt, and particularly in the west, where the people are notorious for obedience to the law. (A laugh.) He admitted he had been guilty in that respect—('Hear, hear,' from the Moderate side)—guilty of having, to the utmost of his ability, explained to the people of Scotland what he conscientiously believed to be the sound and Scriptural view of the question. Did not the Assembly sanction such agitation as to the important subject of Church Extension? No opposition was given to agitation when they were defending the Church against the Voluntaries; and on his side of the Church, he might state, they were foremost in the ranks in driving the battle from the gate. The Church of Scotland must look to *them*—(laughter from the Moderate side)—and to men of similar principles—('Hear, hear,' from the popular side)—to defend her against the attacks of the Voluntaries. Admissions were made on the opposite side of the House which the sagacious Voluntary might turn most effectively against the Church. It was admitted, for example, that the compact between Church and State prevented them from exercising her spiritual jurisdiction. ('No' from the Moderate side.) If they allowed the Court of Session to interpret the limit of their power, they gave to Voluntaries a weapon with which they would beat down any Establishment upon earth. (Loud cries of 'Hear.') There had been agitation on the other side, too, though on a small scale—(a laugh)—and conducted chiefly by the less knowing of the party, for the most of them are well aware that the great mass of the people of Scotland held opinions entirely and diametrically opposed to theirs. (Cries of 'Hear.') Therefore, although there had been meetings on the other side sufficient to show that they had no objection to the *principle* and *practice* of agitation, they opposed it not because it was agitation, but, like Lord Galloway, because it was not in favour of those principles which *they* have adopted, and of such a bill as that now before them. It was necessary to agitate. Any one who remembered the proceedings of last Assembly must know that the great argument——

" A. E. Monteith, Esq., reminded the speaker that he had digressed from the subject before the House.

" Dr. Cook said Mr. Begg had expressed nothing more than

that it was his opinion that such an inference might be drawn from what had been stated in the Assembly.

"Mr. Begg said that the subject was introduced into the debate by a rev. doctor from the west. They had heard much addressed to their fears; they had been told that unless they had accepted of this bill there was no relief, and they might only expect the destruction of the Church. If she did accept of it she was infallibly gone as a Church of Christ in this land, if those against whom they were contending were determined to persevere in their present measures. (Hear, hear.) He saw nothing for the Church but either a glorious dissolution from the State, retaining all her principles entire, or the abandonment of her principles—the prostration of herself at the feet of the State, and her utter extinction piecemeal from the desertion of the best of her people. It appeared to him that although the Church of Scotland was a poor Church (and her poverty was principally owing to the faithful contending for her present principles), yet, being free, she was a noble Church. When they looked to all the Churches of the Reformation fettered and prostrated before the civil power, and thought of their own Church, free and independent, though supported by the civil power, he felt that she was a noble specimen of the Church of Christ. The question was now tried with regard to her whether it was possible to have a Church Establishment and at the same time maintain her ecclesiastical freedom as a Church of Christ, and the rights and privileges of a Christian people. If by their vote they gave the slightest countenance to any individual in determining that question so as to peril the existence of our spiritual independence—so as to peril or endanger the rights of the people, he saw nothing for it but dissolution to the Church. But if they stood true and united within, he had no fear of their enemies from without. Truth was great—it had prevailed in times past over far mightier difficulties, and he trusted that by the aid of the great Head of the Church, whose prerogatives they were endeavouring to defend, the Church would again be rescued from danger and perplexity; they would not fear: God Himself would defend and protect her, and that right early."

There is generally a comparative lull in the ecclesiastical

cyclone after the meeting of the General Assembly, and so an opportunity is given for the consideration by the inferior courts of matters relating to the regulation of minor ecclesiastical affairs, many of which, though minor, are of great importance. But at such a time as 1840, there was and could be no lull. The subject of non-intrusion was all in all. In July, the subject of Lord Aberdeen's bill was discussed in the Presbytery of Edinburgh. The *Witness* of 4th July contains a report of the speeches, and a most interesting leader on the discussion, manifestly from Hugh Miller's own pen.

"PRESBYTERY OF EDINBURGH: LORD ABERDEEN'S BILL.

"Mr. Begg, after a short pause in the court, said that as none of the older brethren seemed inclined to speak, he would respectfully submit a few remarks. There was no need to reply to the speeches of Dr. Muir and Mr. Penney, as they had so often before heard what these gentlemen had advanced, and more especially as they had never once looked at, or attempted to answer, the conclusive argument of Mr. Cunningham. There was, however, one remark of Dr. Muir that had the semblance of novelty, though in reality it was neither new nor applicable. He alluded to what Dr. Muir had said about the translation of ministers. They did not in that case advocate intrusion any more than in the case of a first ordination. Much had been said about the corruption of human nature, and the consequent danger in admitting the people to a voice in the choice of their spiritual guides. That corruption they admitted to at least as great an extent as their opponents. But it was surely absurd to take refuge from the corruption of the people in the purity of the patron. An argument which had been made use of by Dr. Muir would, if carried out, lead to the destruction of patronage. Dr. Muir had supposed the case of a parish in a state of apathy and heresy, and had stated it to be the duty of the Church to find a man able to rouse from the one and to combat the other. Now, as it was arranged at present, it was impossible for the Church to exercise her own judgment in the choice of a fitting individual. She could not move till the patron made his choice. Dr. Muir, to carry out his own principle, ought to be an anti-patronage man, as under patronage there was no opportunity for such a choice as that for which he (Dr. Muir) argued. He (Mr. Begg) must, however, say that he wondered to hear any man speaking of heresy and apathy in connection with the support of a measure for the purpose of bolstering up that very system under which such evils had been fostered. He was loth to believe, both when this bill was before the Synod, and when it was discussed in the Assembly, that Lord Aberdeen was anything but a friend. Now he was better informed. He now knew that his lordship was neither more nor less than the exponent of the defeated minority in the Church, and that the Dean of Faculty was his accredited friend. Lord Aberdeen had denounced their proceedings, and had gone so far as to say that there were some of them he would not object to see imprisoned. That just meant that he would do as Charles II. did, if he were as independent of public opinion as he was. But there was one admission of his lordship which was important. In recommending his Declaratory Act, he had told the House of Lords that the Church, though it had disobeyed a deliverance of that House, would not disobey an Act of Parliament, which was very different from a mere judgment of their lordships' House. Such a judgment was not law. Here Lord Aberdeen admitted that the Church of Scotland was not rebellious in having refused obedience to that judgment. It was a most important admission coming from his lordship, that they stood on strong legal ground, and were not exposed to the charge of rebellion. The fact was, that their enemies had found that the thing was at a dead-lock. Since the Church would not obey, there was no power to compel her. This was a defect which Lord Aberdeen wanted to supply by his bill. He wanted to give authority to the Court of Session and the House of Lords to enforce their decision. That clearly was the character of the bill, and they might plainly see the position in which it would put them. Looking to the reason of the thing, they had just as much right to look over the shoulder of the judges in the Court of Session, and review their proceedings, as they have to come and review the proceedings of the Church. But the object of the bill was to erect a court of review over the Church. They had heard a great deal from the learned gentleman who seconded the motion of 'I think,' and 'I believe,' and 'my professional opinion is'—(laughter)—and the learned gentleman had assured them on the strength of these asseverations that the whole question of qualification was left entirely open in the bill. But it so happened that they could refer to Lord Aberdeen's own interpretation—and what did his lordship say? Speaking of the question of qualification, he had said that the bill did not, and was not intended to leave the Church courts at liberty to give effect to their convictions of the inexpediency of admitting a presentee. The plain and manifest object of the bill was to give power to compel the Church to admit presentees, whether the expediency of their admission was approved by her or no. They had heard in the course of the discussion that there was no Act on record in the history of the Church similar to this, except the Act of 1612, which compelled ordination under pain of horning. That was an important circumstance, as it enabled them to identify the principles of the supporters of the bill with those of some of the worst men that Scotland had ever produced. When Carstairs went to London on matters connected with the Act of Queen Anne, he found that it was meditated to pass two other bills; one of them was for the abolition of the Assembly, and the other to compel the Church to do exactly what the Earl of Aberdeen wants—namely, to force the Church to grant admission in every case of a presentation. Carstairs warded off this by telling that he would rather use the whole of his influence with the people of Scotland to cause them to submit to the Act for restoring patronage than have these new enactments. The time soon came when the Church courts did not need the coercion which it had been contemplated to impose, for they became themselves the willing instruments of intrusion. And now, when the Church is alive to the sinfulness of such procedure, and refuses any longer to be the instruments of such tyranny, men are rising up to do the very thing—to impose the very compulsion, which Carstairs was the means of averting. And further, Lord Aberdeen had denounced the Commission as unrecognised by law. The Assembly had supported the obnoxious deed of the Commission, and his lordship's good will to it was more than suspected. Thus is his lordship coming in to do the work which the men of Queen Anne's day left undone, because they did not venture to do it. And yet they had men imploring them to accept that bill, and so secure their peace, in a style so ludicrous that he thought he saw the smile of the learned gentleman (Mr. Penney) through his own pathetic —— (Laughter.) The question had long ago come to this, that patronage, the root of the mischief, must be destroyed. For that purpose a vigorous, a determined, and a sustained agitation would speedily be undertaken. The Earl of Haddington had talked of compelling the Church to do its duty in the settlement of presentees. Was he to drag the Presbytery to the church of Marnoch? Was he, by force, to hold down their hands upon the head of Mr. Edwards and ordain him to empty walls? Perhaps he thinks that the mere passing of an Act of Parliament will cause the submission of the Church? Dr. Muir had failed to administer a fitting rebuke to his lordship, but it became them to let it be known that they would not sell their birthright for a mess of pottage—they would not consent to hold the means of temporal subsistence on the condition of such degradation, being well assured that to do so would be to accept the wages of iniquity. (Applause.)"

"The present struggle threatens to be a protracted one. But there is no lack of symptoms on the part of both the friends and the opponents of the popular principle which indicate the final result. Our readers will find a full report in our columns of the proceedings of the Edinburgh Presbytery at its meeting of Wednesday last. The chief business of the meeting arose out of the present position of the Church in connection with the attempt of the Earl of Aberdeen to convert into law the mischievous absurdities of the Dean of Faculty; and the decision arrived at by the Presbytery, by an overpowering majority, and after a discussion of six hours, was to petition Parliament against his lordship's bill as directly subversive of the spiritual independence of the Church, and wholly at variance with the genius of Presbytery. No report, however literal, can convey an adequate idea of a debate so animated and interesting as that which took place on this occasion,—there is a vast difference between a series of speeches spread over a few closely-printed columns and a spirit-stirring *viva voce* discussion; but our report must be very defective indeed, if it does not convey the impression of strength contending with weakness, and show that there was much feebleness and much timidity on the one side, and much courage and great power on the other. The cause backed by the decision of our law courts, and by a considerable portion of the wealth and a large proportion of the aristocracy of the country, must ultimately go down, for there is no heart and no strength in it.

"We fain wish we could give our readers at a distance some such idea of the late meeting of Presbytery as we ourselves have had an opportunity of forming. The Presbytery of Edinburgh is the most ancient in the kingdom. It may be regarded as the nucleus of the Scottish Church. According to Knox, 'before that there was any public face of the true religion in this realm, it had pleased God to illuminate the hearts of many private persons, who, straightway quitting the idolatry of Papistry, began to assemble themselves together.' They elected out of their number good and judicious men, such as 'God by His grace' had best qualified for their elders and teachers; and from this small beginning, principally within the town of Edinburgh, arose the Presbyterian Church of Scotland. There is nothing to mark the antiquity of the Presbytery in the hall in which they assemble. It is a modern erection, lighted from above, with a few portraits suspended on the walls, and a bust or two placed on brackets. There is a gallery for strangers, of limits all too scanty on occasions such as that of Wednesday last, and the members occupied the area below. From a front seat, which we were fortunate enough to secure, we could overlook the whole. The parties, instead of being ranged on opposite sides, were mixed up together, and apparently for a very excellent reason—the Non-Intrusionists were all too numerous, and their opponents too few. The original Presbyterians bid fair to fill all their own house as at first; and if Moderatism insists on retaining its own side, it must proceed forthwith, as in the days of Gillespie, to eject and expel.

"Some of the better-known names in the Presbytery are borne by men of very striking appearance. Dr. Muir is an eminently handsome man, thin, gentlemanly, dignified, tastefully dressed, with a well-formed head of moderate size, such as a phrenologist would expect to find on the shoulders of a person rather of fine taste than of comprehensive genius. We would have deemed him quite in his proper place in the Upper House of Parliament either as a lord spiritual or lay. Dr. Gordon is also a strikingly handsome man, but with a much more remarkable development of head. It is a head of the Melancthon type—high, erect, with an overpowering superstructure of sentiment on a narrow base of propensity, and a forehead rising, as in the case of Shakespeare and Sir Walter Scott, to the top of the coronal region. Combe in one of his phrenological works gives a print of a similar head, and states that among the heads of many thousand criminals which he had examined, he had in no instance found a resembling development. If, however, the Earl of Aberdeen carry his measure, prisons will be quite the place to find them in, and the phrenologist will require to modify his statement by a note. Among the figures of the younger members of the court, that of Mr. Guthrie is one of the most striking. He is an erect, lathy, muscular man, of rather more than six feet two inches, who would evidently not have been idle at Drumclog, and who, if employed at all, could not be employed other than formidably. Though apparently under forty, the hair is slightly touched with grey, and the features, though beyond comparison more handsome than those of his ancestor the martyr, bear decidedly a similar cast and expression. The appearance and figure of Mr. Cunningham is scarcely less striking than that of his friend Mr. Guthrie; he is tall, but not so tall, though rather above than below six feet, and powerfully built. His head is apparently of the largest size—of the *nemo me impune lacessit* calibre, and the temperament is of that firm bilious cast which gives to size its fullest effect.

"Mr. Cunningham commenced the debate in a speech of tremendous power. The elements were various. A clear logic, at once severely nice and popular, an unhesitating readiness of language, select and forcible, and well fitted to express every minuter shade of meaning, but plain and devoid of figure; above all, an extent of erudition, and an acquaintance with Church history, that in every instance in which the argument turned on a matter of fact, seemed to render opposition hopeless. But what gave peculiar emphasis to the whole was, what we shall venture to term the propelling power of the mind—that animal energy which seems to act the part of the moving power in the mechanism of intellect, which gives force to action and depth to the tones of the voice, and impresses the hearer with an idea of immense momentum. There were parts of Mr. Cunningham's speech in which he reminded us of Andrew Melville when he put down Bishops Barlow and Bancroft, and shook the lawn sleeves of the latter; and we could not help wishing that, by any possibility, circumstances should be so ordered as to afford an opportunity of trying conclusions face to face with the Earl of Aberdeen.

"His powers of sarcasm are great, and of a peculiar character. He first places some important fact or argument in so clear a light that there remains no possibility of arriving at more than one conclusion regarding it. He then sets in close juxtaposition to it the absurd inference or crooked misstatement of an antagonist, and bestows upon his ignorance or his absurdity the plain and simple name. White is always white with Mr. Cunningham, and black black, and he finds no shade of grey in either. His confidence in matter of fact, based on an extent of erudition recognised by all, tells, with a crippling effect, on his opponents. He referred during his speech to the often-repeated sophism regarding the non-intrusion of the Reformers—Knox, Calvin, and Beza. What, he asked, do the Earls of Aberdeen and Dalhousie know of the opinions of these men? This much and no more. Lord Medwyn inserted in his speech on the Auchterarder case a few partial and garbled extracts from the writings of Calvin and Beza, which, in their broken and unconnected state, seemed to bear a meaning at variance with the principles which the men in reality held. Mr. Robertson of Ellon quoted the passages at second-hand, not omitting even the errors of his lordship's printer. The Earls of Dalhousie and Aberdeen quoted them at third-hand from Mr. Robertson; and such is the entire extent of their lordships' information on the subject, and such the amount of their authority. He then proceeded to show what the non-intrusion of the Reformers really was,—that they all held with the ancient fathers the doctrine for which the Church is now contending;— 'there is no member of this Presbytery,' he added, 'who will question the fact.' And he was quite in the right,—no member did question it. He offered to prove further, that Dr. Muir on the agitated question holds exactly the principles of Cardinal Bellarmine, and the doctor took particular care not to demand the proof.

"Mr. Cunningham was followed by the Lord Provost of Edinburgh, a gentleman who has been a reformer all his life long, and who evidently feels that, in the present struggle, he is occupying exactly his old ground. He was listened to with much respect. His remarks were characterised by a vein of sound good sense, and much gentlemanly feeling. Dr. Muir then rose to express his approbation of the Earl of Aberdeen's bill.

"How, we asked, when listening to the powerful logic of Mr. Cunningham, will Dr. Muir contrive to find answers to arguments such as these? We might have spared ourselves the query. Dr. Muir did not attempt finding answers to them. He spoke as if no one had spoken before him. He reiterated all his old assertions, and assured the meeting that he was thoroughly conscientious and quite in earnest. Pascal could mortify his senses by shutting his casement on a delightful prospect. Dr. Muir restrains the reasoning faculty in the same way out of a sense of duty, and eschews argument as a gross temptation. When convicted of an absurdity, he talks of persecution, and clings to an exposed misstatement with the devotedness of a faithful nature true to a friend in distress. He carries, on every occasion, all his facts and all his opinions home with him—nothing adds to their number, nothing diminishes them—and when the day of battle comes, he bring them out with him again. His troops fight none the worse of being killed; they rise all gory, like Falstaff's opponents, and fight by the hour; his antagonists complain, with Macbeth, that his dead men come to 'push them from their stools.'

"He was followed by Mr. Penney, a smart gentleman, who is tedious with very marked effect, on the same side, and succeeds when he is particularly pathetic in making his audience gay. He was liberal in tendering to the Presbytery the benefit of his law, and generously advised them to submit to the Court of Session, without cherishing the remotest expectation of being paid for his advice. He excels, too, in divinity. His speech gradually rose into a sermon, and when he came to the most serious part of it the gallery laughed. He was succeeded in reply by the Rev. Mr. Begg of Liberton.

"Of all the gentlemen whom the caricaturists have failed in rendering ridiculous, Mr. Begg has escaped best. Some of the others are striking likenesses. There is no likeness in the case of Mr. Begg. There is no exaggeration of feature or figure for the artist to catch, and so he has caught none. He is a young good-looking man, rather above the middle size, with a well-developed forehead—frank, vigorous, and energetic. His brief speech contained one or two pointed hits, which told with excellent effect, and a historical statement of much importance in its bearing on the Earl of Aberdeen's bill, and which will probably be new to the great bulk of our readers.

"He was suceeded by the Rev. Mr. M'Farlane. We are admirers of the good sense and poetical feeling of Hervey, whereas Mr. M'Farlane seems to admire only his style. He rounds his sentences after the same model, and leaves out only the poetry and the good sense. His flowers are all gum-flowers. Pliny speaks of an orator who used to set his periods to music; we are convinced that if Mr. M'Farlane were well watched he would be found modulating *his* periods by the full symphonies of the Jews' harp. All feel, however, that when delivered in public they want their necessary and original accompaniment; and we think the reverend gentleman should benefit by the hint. A respectable and sensible man, a Seceder, sat beside us: 'Ah,' he exclaimed with a groan, 'a weak brother.'

"The Rev. Mr. Bennie followed in a sparkling, witty speech that at once awakened the gallery, and cost the Moderator a considerable amount of trouble. All was extempore — there was not an idea which did not bear reference to some previous remark from the opposite side, and yet every sentence had the point of an epigram. The laboured dulnesses of an inane and feeble mind have rarely been more pointedly contrasted with the spontaneous felicities of a mind singularly ingenuous and fertile than on this occasion. Drs. Clason and Gordon followed in addresses brief, but of great moral weight, and conceived in an admirable spirit, and the whole was wound up by Mr. Cunningham.

"Nothing more tended to the spread of the Reformation than the public disputations between the Reformers and their opponents. There was breadth of principle and force of argument on the one side, united to generous feeling and conscious integrity—and merely sophistry, meanness, misstatement, and the disreputable shifts of a petty ingenuity on the other. On every occasion on which they met, the better cause invariably prevailed; and the people saw and felt that it did. Good argument is always popular argument. If Dr. Muir and his friends really wish well to the people of Scotland, they could still hold by their peculiar opinions and yet be of great service to them. All that is necessary is to grant their opponents such opportunities of meeting with them in the various parishes of the country as they afforded them at the meeting of the Edinburgh Presbytery on Wednesday last."

The two extracts following relate to a particular phase of a matter of vast moment—the subject of pauperism, in which Dr. Begg all through his life took a specially lively interest. Alas that his warnings, and those of Dr. Chalmers, were treated by cotemporaries as Cassandrine prophecies.

PRESBYTERY OF EDINBURGH: CHURCH-DOOR COLLECTIONS.

(*From Witness, October* 3, 1840.)

"Mr. Moody Stuart brought up a reference from the kirk-session of St. Luke's, arising from an application which was made to them by the treasurer of the charity workhouse, requesting them, in terms of a resolution come to by that body, to send in to the funds of the workhouse the collections made at the doors of the church on each Sabbath.

"Mr. Paul moved—'That the Presbytery having learned, with the deepest regret, the intended attempt of the managers of the Edinburgh Charity Workhouse to obtain possession of the collections at the unendowed churches within the city, an attempt which must necessarily be productive of great inconvenience and injury to the congregations of these churches, and will certainly prove of no avail to the charity workhouse, in so far as regards the collections in question, inasmuch as its effects would be not to provide any addition to the workhouse funds, but to compel the congregations to resort to a more convenient means of making those contributions which are essential to the maintenance of their places of worship. The Presbytery regret this attempt the more, because, if persevered in, it will lead to very disastrous consequences; but as the Presbytery are most unwilling to contemplate the necessity of such results, before adopting any resolution on the subject they appoint a committee to take this matter into consideration, to confer with the managers of the workhouse, in the hope that the necessity of doing so may yet be prevented.'

"Dr. Simpson, Mr. Wood, and Mr. Candlish spoke in support of the motion.

"Mr. Begg most cordially agreed with all that had been so well said, but thought the Presbytery ought to regard this not as an isolated case, but as part of a general system. He believed it first began in Brechin, and had since been attempted in Haddington, and at various other new churches. It had now come to the capital, and it fell to the Presbytery of Edinburgh, in the face of all Scotland, to give a decision on the question. Even though the managers should decline to avail themselves of these church-door collections, any ratepayer might force them to appropriate them; for since the law had decided that all church-door collections were liable to be taken for the support of the poor, it was in the power of any ratepayer to say that he would not pay one farthing of his assessment till the managers had taken the collections. It was therefore important that they should contemplate in their settlement of this matter not only the immediate result that would flow from it, but some suitable remedy that would reach to the root of the evil. If it were not put an end to, he had no doubt that the collections in the city churches generally would entirely cease, and that this example would spread throughout the kingdom. Even already, in all assessed parishes, the feeling was spreading that in giving collections the people are only saving the pockets of the heritors, and these rapacious proceedings would only increase that feeling. He wished to press upon the heritors of Scotland this consideration, that, in the first place, £40,000 a year was collected at the church doors in support of the poor, and this depended entirely upon the sanction of the Church. The General Assembly had only to do what some were disposed to do—and what, if they followed this example of going to the full stretch of their rights, they might do—issue an edict to all ministers and elders in the Church prohibiting this system, and the thing would be put an end to at once; and not only so, but there were 7000 men, ministers and elders, who gave their gratuitous services in superintending the distribution of this money among the poor. If these men were paid at the low rate of £50 each, the result would be that £350,000 would be required for the expense of machinery alone, while at present the whole assessment of Scotland only amounted to £100,000. This was a most important question, and might settle in a very summary way a controversy of vast importance at present agitating the kingdom. Dr. Alison has proposed that the present mode of supporting the poor should be entirely changed, and that an assessment should be raised, amounting to £80,000, for their support. (Hear, hear.) Sheriff Alison thinks that £1,200,000 a year will be necessary, or more than four times the whole cost of the Church Establishment! A committee of the Presbytery is at present engaged in deliberation on this important question, but if the present attempt is persevered in, that committee may be dissolved, for if the collections are swept away, nothing will remain but to have recourse at once to the English system of poor-rates. (Hear, hear.) As to the case of Edinburgh, the managers of the charity workhouse were by far too well off already. They received from the city churches £2000 a year, whilst no meeting-house in the city gave them a penny. (Hear.) This was never the original design of these collections, and was a most improper innovation. When the system was first begun, the intention was to distribute the collections among the poor of each congregation by the kirk-session. It was never meant to be handed over to a parcel of nondescript persons called managers, who might be respectable men indeed, and many, he believed, were so, but they were never intended to come in place of the elders. The effect of the measure would be to put a premium on dissent,—to raise up a barrier in the way of Seceders returning to the Church, for every seceding congregation now returning to the Church must do it under the certainty that their collections might be seized upon. The very men who formerly put a barrier in the way of Church extension, now put a barrier in the way of Church union. The Church must put a stop to this. It would be easy to place a box in every lobby, and send round the elders to collect the sums there deposited. He would regret if this were found necessary; for he was a friend to the parochial collections, and wished to continue and extend them. But if the question came to be whether the parochial collection of the Church Establishment was to be put down—for if the Church was not extended, she must be extinguished—he had no doubt the Church would know how to answer it. (Hear, hear.) He thought the Presbytery should not only adopt the resolution, but overture the Assembly to appoint a committee to confer with the landed proprietors of Scotland in order to have a legislative enactment for some change in the present system.

"Mr. Guthrie spoke.

"The motion was then unanimously agreed to.

"Synod of Lothian and Tweeddale: Collections at New Churches.

(*From Witness, Nov.* 14, 1840.)

"Dr. Aiton moved the appointment of a committee to consider this subject. As an overture had been sent up by his Presbytery on this subject, he felt inclined to state to the Synod the views he, in common with all his brethren in the country, entertained on this important subject. He felt strongly, but he would endeavour to express himself temperately, as became one moderate in all matters of the Church. But guided as he was by this desire, which he hoped was natural to him, nevertheless he must say, that in the history of human folly he had not observed anything more cruel or infatuated than the course of conduct now complained of. He did not know, neither did he care, whether the legislative aristocracy or the executive departments were most to blame, because the result was the same to the Church; for on every hand in these matters she had got nothing but hard and heavy blows from the birth of Presbytery in Scotland. The Establishment had not only been kept half naked and half starved, but she had been otherwise stunted in her growth, hampered in her proportions, and distorted in all her members. When the population of Scotland scarcely amounted to one million, church accommodation hardly adequate to that number was provided. In course of time the population increased rapidly, but instead of divided parishes, *many* of them were united. Manufacturing villages rose like mushrooms, and became towns, and even cities; and ironworks were erected, employing thousands of persons, and expending millions of money every year. But instead of providing new churches, the strong arm of power was raised to prevent even the little old parish church from being enlarged so long as the heritors could manage to keep one stone of it standing upon another. Parishes a hundred square miles in extent, in earlier times, had a small pastoral population clustered into a fertile corner, with a few herds' houses, distant half a score of miles from the then 'clachan,' or from each other. The church was placed amid the general mass of the people, beside the smithy, the wright's shop, and the cobbler's stall. In time agricultural improvements advanced rapidly. Bogs and moors were converted into fertile fields, and a swarming population was spread over the whole parish. The people complained that they were far from Gospel ordinances, and that the church should be removed from a distant corner to the centre of the parish. But when the aged and infirm thus asked the bread of life, a stone was thrown in their face—an Act of Parliament was passed (1707) prohibiting any church to be moved without the consent of three-fourths of the heritors. Dissenters broke off from the Church, and Episcopalians began to raise their head. In reference to the churches erected in this way, the Establishment demanded that equal justice should be dispensed to all; and as their collections went to the heritors' pockets for behoof of the poor, so, it was argued, should the collections of dissenting chapels be applied to the same purpose. But the Court of Session found (1739) that this money might be appropriated as the managers might please to direct. Thus there was a pressure kept on the Establishment, and a premium offered to Dissent. But this finding of the Court of Session was ruinous even to the landed interest, inasmuch as it gave rise to parochial assessments. Under every discouragement from the Church herself, chapels of ease began to be raised, and as these congregations were similar to the Dissenters in everything but their attachment to the Establishment, they expected that they would enjoy the benefit of their own collections. But no; every penny collected at their plate was put into a box and carried away to the pockets of the heritors. Hence chapels of ease could not compete with dissenting churches. In this way the Establishment drifted fast towards the minority. She dropped astern of her people, and would in time have been left, as an old hulk, to rot at her leisure. But fortunately a man rose amongst us with the head and the heart of a Knox. And he has done more for the Presbyterian Establishment of our Church than any since the period of the two Reformations. Unaided by one sixpence from the public purse, and unsupported by many men in public stations, he has raised two hundred churches in about four years. Endowments were asked by the people from the Legislature; but no, said they, we will build jails, and bridewells, and penitentiaries enough, but no churches; we will give batons to our police, but no Bibles to our poor; we will pay constables, endow a rural police, and fix salaries on judges, jailers, and hangmen, but we will not endow your clergymen. In other words, we will punish rather than prevent crime, although the one method costs ten times more than the other. Nay, worst and last of all, they have not only refused to feed the skep, but when the industrious bees have begun to lay up stores for themselves, the lazy drones are come, numerous as the locusts of Egypt, to rob them of their own honey. In plain speech, the heritors are with sacrilegious hands laying their greedy grasp on the pence which our poor are willing to pay for a preached Gospel which they must otherwise want. The demand made on Israel of old for bricks, while the material was withheld, is nothing to this. In our case the straw is withheld by the Legislature, and when the bricks are made, notwithstanding, they are wrenched out of our hands by the Court of Session, and still we must, without money and without price, give them to the perishing souls of our overcrowded population. The State are, or ought to be, nursing fathers to the Church; but what parent would put the foot of his own child into an iron boot, and, however much the child might grow in stature, would refuse to enlarge it? But the State parent adds screws to the ankles, pincers to the toes, and drives down wedges at the top. This is not only cruel but infatuated, as it is killing the goose with the golden egg, and breaking the egg to the bargain. But Tartars will be caught if matters are to go on in this way. The Church will be roused, not to retaliate, but to redress her wrongs. Men of all parties will unite in protecting their interests, and promoting the spiritual good of the poor. They will not, they ought not, quietly to submit. Let a committee be formed, and an overture transmitted to the Assembly. Let appeals be made to our congregations, and let all culprits be told of their guilt and their danger.

"Mr. Begg remarked that the subject was of immense importance in itself, and in its bearings on the moral condition of the people, and therefore on the state of pauperism. Everything which made the house of God inconvenient was a direct cause of pauperism. If people were not at church, they both sunk into heathenism, the great parent of poverty, and they could not of course give their penny at the church door. The obstacles, therefore, to such improvements as have been suggested ought, if possible, on every ground to be removed. He rejoiced in the appointment of this committee, and hoped they would direct their attention to the general subject of collections as a mode of supporting the poor, and as a peculiar part of the Scottish parochial system. A short history of that system would exhibit the outrageous injustice and impolicy of the present attempt to seize the collections of the unendowed churches. At the Reformation it was proposed to divide the immense sums of the Popish Church into portions, one of which was to go to the maintenance of the poor. The whole, however, was seized, and when a small pittance was extorted back for the support of the clergy, the Church herself most disinterestedly contrived by her collections and judicious management to make this fraction contribute towards the comfort of the poor also. But now there is a refinement proposed even on this. The pittance is now to be withheld in the case of our new churches—the teinds are not to be given up—the Government is to give nothing—the ancient property is all to be kept—every obstacle is to be thrown in the way of Church Extension, and every premium given to dissent; and yet, when in spite of every obstacle new churches are erected, their collections are to be seized, and still the Church, thus trampled on, is expected to stand as a barrier against the demand for the entire overthrow of the present system of supporting the poor. The real state of the matter is not understood even by men who profess to speak and write on the subject, and a calm firm statement of facts may serve to convince the landholders and aristocracy, as well as the poor of this land, of their own true interests, and the glaring cruelty and absurdity of recent attempts at aggression. He hoped the committee would carefully consider the matter in all its bearings, and report fully and clearly to next meeting of Synod."

At the same meeting of the Synod of Lothian and Tweeddale, an overture was moved by Dr. Candlish for the abolition of patronage. Dr. Begg made a short speech in support of the overture, which is thus reported :—

"SYNOD OF LOTHIAN AND TWEEDDALE: OVERTURE ON PATRONAGE.

(From Witness, Nov. 14, 1840.)

"Mr. Begg said that he rose chiefly to correct an assertion of Dr. Simpson's, reasserted also by Mr. Bridges, which was not correct. He had said that the patrons endowed the Church. Now, whatever may be the case in other countries, it would have been much nearer the truth had he said that in Scotland the Church had endowed the patrons. After the Reformation they got a large portion of the Church lands, and afterwards, as a result, obtained the patronages connected with these lands. At the Revolution, when patronage was abolished, a compensation was given to the patrons, but when it was restored they retained the compensation—they kept, in the words of our fathers, 'both the purchase and the price.' So that no one could say, with the shadow of a ground, that the Church was endowed by the very patrons by whom she had been deprived of her property. There might be single cases, such as that of Mr. Gladstone at Leith, where the church and endowment were presented on condition of the patronage remaining in the hands of the donor.

But he thought it was to the lasting honour of the Presbytery of Edinburgh that they refused to receive a church coupled with such a condition. In that case, however, patronage had been created by an express Act of the General Assembly, and the fact had been founded on here, which only showed them the extreme jealousy with which they ought to look upon all such measures. As to the probable success which would attend their endeavours, it was a serious and a natural question. It was too true that Scotch matters are treated with contempt in the British Parliament; but would England refuse to repeal the Act of Queen Anne if Scotland, on the ground of Scripture and the Treaty of Union, declared against it? If the people came forward, and firmly and calmly demanded from England, on the ground of the national faith, which has been outraged, that patronage should be destroyed, would England contemptuously refuse to do it —would she say, when all the circumstances were fully explained, that she would persist in her unrighteous conduct, though she saw the contention it created, the many evils it had inflicted on Scotland? Would she persist in preserving the union merely by superior physical force, and at the same time trample on the constitution of our Church and of the country? He could not bring himself to believe that she would do so. The people of Scotland would be with them; there was nothing about which they were so unanimous; and, considering the history of patronage in the Church— how it was opposed to Scripture, and was only part of the errors of Popery—how it had been twice shaken off, and only restored in violation of the Treaty of Union—how it had caused secession, heathenism, pauperism, and many evils—he had no doubt whatever that truth and justice would ultimately prevail, and that it would be for ever abolished. He wished the people of Scotland every success in their present righteous and noble struggle."

I have thought it well to introduce in continuity the autobiographical materials which Dr. Begg had collected from the columns of the *Witness* for the year 1840. I have now only to add a few fragments collected from the same quarter. In the earlier part of the year we find him in various parts of the country addressing enthusiastic meetings on Non-Intrusion, sometimes in connection with Dr. Guthrie or other Edinburgh ministers, and sometimes alone. No place can be got for holding a meeting in Thornhill, but a large one (proportionately) is held at Canonbie, and another at Stranraer. His name is also frequently introduced by the speakers at Intrusion meetings, coupled with those of Dr. Cunningham and Dr. Candlish, as the arch-disturbers of the peace of the Church. From some of the extracts already given it has been seen that he was a member of the General Assembly of 1840. In addition to the two speeches already given, he spoke from time to time on various points. In that Assembly an anti-patronage overture, by 71 members of the House, was presented. From the fact that he presented it to the Assembly it may be presumed that he was its originator. From the length of time occupied in the discussion of the Strathbogie case, it was not found possible to enter on the consideration of the overture. In this Dr. Begg reluctantly acquiesced, but gave distinct warning that the question must be faced ere long :—

"Mr. Begg observed, that as the debate had been prolonged to so late an hour there had been no time to take up the subject of patronage yesterday, and he did not mean to propose that it should be taken up now, in consequence of the overwhelming mass of business. All that he wished was to advert to the fact, as he felt perfectly certain that great anxiety prevailed amongst thousands throughout the country to learn in what way the Assembly disposed of the question. It was evident that a large number of persons had formed decided opinions on the subject, from the great number of overtures sent up. One of these laid on the table of the House, calling for the abolition of patronage, was signed by no less than 71 ministers and elders, members of the Assembly. He, however, thought it right to give fair notice to the Assembly that it was intended to commence immediately to bring the matter under the serious consideration of the country, in order to obtain a remedy for this grievance. He was persuaded that not only a large number of persons were convinced that this was the only effectual way of terminating the present conflict, but it was every day becoming clearer that many more, whose minds were in a transition state, would be convinced by next Assembly that, in the words of our sagacious ancestors, 'the order whilk God's Word craves cannot stand with patronage and presentations to benefices.'"[1]

In the course of the summer I find him in Ireland, attending, along with Mr. M'Cheyne of Dundee and Mr. Maitland Makgill, a large meeting held in Belfast to express sympathy with the Church of Scotland. His speech is not reported; but from the opening sentence of Dr. Cooke's speech it appears that it was in whole or in part on the subject of patronage. Dr. Cooke said—"Mr. Chairman and Christian friends, I have been specially gratified with the declaration of my friend Mr. Begg, that as patronage and freedom can never be reconciled, no quarter should be given to the system. The question is now between patronage and the Church of Scotland, and patronage or the Church must fall. So long as patronage submitted to be modified by the Veto Act, the minds of the Christian people and the Church courts had a posture of independence and freedom; but when the voice of the Christian people is silenced, and the ecclesiastical authority is, in things ecclesiastical, superseded by the civil power, independence and freedom are no more, and nothing remains but the tame submission of slaves, the struggle of freemen, or the endurance of martyrs. Yes, sir, when unrestricted patronage would enchain the Church, nothing remains but to enchain patronage."

As patronage, or rather anti-patronage, was at this time the subject that was in the ascendent in Dr. Begg's mind, it is probably to this period that we are to ascribe the following imperfectly dated note addressed to Dr. Chalmers. It pos-

---

[1] *Witness,* June 3, 1840.

sesses great historical interest, and it is to be regretted that its date can only be conjectured:—

"LIBERTON MANSE, *Thursday*.

"MY DEAR SIR,—I have requested Mr. Johnston to present you with a copy of the 'Anti-Patronage Library,' a work whose publication was superintended by Cunningham and myself. I was much delighted to hear that if the Church question is not properly settled before the Assembly, it is your intention to take up anti-patronage ground. This I think is, humanly speaking, the only prospect of safety. And I fondly hope that you will find in the 'Anti-Patronage Library' unanswerable arguments in favour of such a course from Scripture, reason, and history. Indeed the work, although small, contains all that can be said on the subject. If others could be persuaded to read it, our ministers would be prepared (all our people are prepared already, for they are ahead of the Church courts in this matter) to join a bold and decisive movement in May next, which would bring the English nation to its senses.—I am, &c."

On the 11th of August, the evening before the meeting of the Assembly's Commission, a great meeting was held in Edinburgh for the formation of an association for the repeal of patronage. The venerable minister of New Monkland was among the speakers; but his son, on account of the lateness of the hour, contented himself with merely reading the motion which he had to propose. A month later a meeting with the same object was held at the instance of the Tradesmen's Association. Dr. Begg made a most eloquent speech, which was cheered to the echo. He was seconded by a journeyman joiner in an equally effective speech. This was after Dr. Begg's own heart. He was no vulgar radical, and in the speech before me he pays a glowing tribute of admiration to the Marquis of Breadalbane, and to Mr. Fox Maule, and Mr. Maitland Makgill Crichton; but he loved the people, and believed in them, and they loved and believed in him.

In an article in the *Witness* of the 19th of August 1842 on the inconsistency of the *Scotsman* on the subject of patronage, I find the following statement: "The country is deeply indebted to Mr. Begg for proving, in his admirable lecture on patronage, all the statements which were thus made many years before by the *Scotsman*; he has filled up their outline by many striking details, and has made it plain to the meanest capacity that the privilege which the Scottish congregations enjoyed of electing their clergymen . . . was taken away, and patronage re-established, in 1712, by Oxford and Bolingbroke, to further their schemes for betraying the country into the hands of the exiled family. And the passing of this Act is shown to have been an act of the basest treachery for the accomplishment of the vilest purposes." This would seem to refer to a published lecture on the subject; but I have not been able to find any other reference to such a publication. Nor is it in the collection which Dr. Begg had begun, several years before his death, to form of his published writings. But he was aware that this collection was very incomplete. The loss of this one is regretable on literary grounds, but not in any great measure on ecclesiastical or controversial, as he doubtless repeated the substance of the lecture on many occasions and in many forms. But I do regret not to have before me what appears to have been the first of that series of pamphlets in which Dr. Begg was ever ready to express his sentiments on important questions as they successively became prominent.

CHAPTER XXII.

THE BEGINNING OF THE END.

THE abolition of patronage was advocated, not only as right in itself, and as consistent with the order "whilk God's Word craves," but also as affording a solution of the extreme difficulty in which the Church, the civil courts, and the Legislature found themselves. It would not indeed have improved the position of the Strathbogie ministers in their relation to their ecclesiastical superiors, nor settled the other cases which were pendent. But it would have made the recurrence of such cases impossible; and a *modus vivendi* might perhaps have been found if it had been secured that these cases could never be used as a precedent. But then the evil was that those who were unanimous in reprobating the encroachments of the civil courts, their denial of spiritual independence as belonging to the Church and its courts, were not unanimous in regarding patronage as an unmixed evil, or as a usurpation which might properly be redressed without compensation to those who held what had come without question to be regarded as a civil right. It is admitted by all that the grand and stately mind of Dr. Chalmers moved more slowly than the minds of younger men. And the enemies of the Church, and the "Moderate" party within the Church, were ready to misrepresent or to exaggerate the extent to which the younger men propelled the noble fathers. I find, for example, a reference to this in the *Witness* of 10th March 1841. It occurs in an article, manifestly by Hugh

Miller, in which he is endeavouring, by internal evidence, to identify the author of a certain article in *Fraser's Magazine* with the late Dr. Cumming of London. It is so exquisite that I cannot resist the temptation to make the extract a little longer than my proper purpose demands:—

"That portion of the internal evidence in the article before us, which depends on style and manner, seems very conclusive indeed. Take some of the avowed sublimities of the Rev. Mr. Cumming. No man stands more beautifully on tiptoe when he sets himself to catch a fine thought. In describing an attached congregation, 'The hearers' prayers rose to heaven,' he says, 'and returned in the shape of broad impenetrable bucklers around the venerable man. A thousand broadswords leapt in a thousand scabbards, as if the electric eloquence of the minister found in them conductors and depositories.' Poetry such as this is still somewhat rare; but mark the kindred beauties of the writer in *Fraser*. Around such men as Mr. Tait, Dr. M'Leod, and Dr. Muir, 'must crystallise the piety and the hopes of the Established Church.' What a superb figure! Only think of the Rev. Dr. Muir as of a thread in a piece of sugar-candy, and the party of the Dean of Faculty and Mr. Penney, joined to that of some four or five hundred respectable ladies of both sexes besides, all sticking out around him in cubes, hexagons, and prisms, like cleft almonds in a bishop cake.' Hardly inferior in the figurative is the passage which follows: 'The Doctor' (Dr. Chalmers) 'rides on at a rickety trot, Messrs. Cunningham, Begg, and Candlish by turns whipping up the worn-out Rosinante, and making the rider believe that windmills are Church principles, and the echoes of their thunder solid argument. A ditch will come; and when the first effects of the fall are over, the dumfoundered Professor will awake to the deception, and smite the minnows of vetoism hip and thigh.' The writer of this passage is unquestionably an ingenious man, but he could surely have made a little more of the last figure. A dissertation on the *hips and thighs of minnows* might be made to reflect new honour on even the genius of the Rev. Mr. Cumming."

I should not have quoted this passage, had I had any idea

that it was intended or fitted to cast any ridicule on Dr. Muir, a man who was deservedly held in the highest estimation by all who knew him. But the object of ridicule was not Dr. Muir, but the absurd language of the writer of the article; and the absurdity of it consists in the grotesqueness of the representation of *such* a man in such a position.

In the earlier half of 1841 Dr. Begg was, in his turn, moderator of the Presbytery of Edinburgh, and on this account alone we should have been without any statement of his views on the important matters which were discussed in the meetings of the Presbytery during these eventful months, as of course he had no right either to speak or to vote. But there was another reason for his silence. In the reports of several meetings of Presbytery we find the statement that the Presbytery sat with one or other of the members as moderator *pro tempore*. The explanation of this is that he was incapacitated for duty by an attack of that painful and depressing malady to which, I believe, the special designation has been given of *morbus clericorum,* or clergyman's sore-throat. That this should have befallen him will surprise no one who has traced his career and noticed the immense amount of his speaking in very large churches and in the open air. Now for the first time, and probably for the last, I regret that Dr. Begg kept no diary or journal. The spiritual exercises of such a man at such a time might have been of interest and value, and it would have been well if we had possessed a record of them. In the absence of such a record we can only infer from what we know of the character of the man that he would employ his enforced leisure in very solemn dealings with his God and Saviour, and in very earnest searchings of his own heart, and very humble acknowledgments of his defects and shortcomings. I cannot doubt that tribulation wrought in him patience, and patience experience, and experience hope. Nor can I doubt that this enforced cessation from public duty was one of the means which God employed for preparing his servant cheerfully to make the sacrifice which, at the call of duty and conscience, was so soon to be required at his hands.

After spending the latter half of 1841 in Devonshire, he returned in an improved but still a feeble state of health. His announcement of his return is accompanied with a statement of an extremely painful matter. I must give it in his own words:—

"LIBERTON MANSE, *December* 28, 1841.

"MY DEAR SIR,—I much regret that certain negotiations, which I have found it necessary to carry on for twelve months past with the heritors of this parish, for the purpose of securing certain improvements in the construction of Liberton church, which recent events have proved to be absolutely essential, have come unexpectedly at length to an unsatisfactory termination. I have, therefore, respectfully to crave the paternal advice and interference of the Presbytery of Edinburgh. I shall be glad to have an opportunity of laying the whole facts and documents of the case before the Presbytery, or any committee that they may appoint, and I venture fondly to hope that the Presbytery will not find my proposals unreasonable, and that they will be able, in an amicable way, to obviate the difficulties which have arisen, or otherwise to advise me what to do.

"I may take this occasion respectfully to inform the Presbytery, with much thankfulness to the Giver of all good, that my health is now, after a tedious illness, nearly quite restored, and that I have the delightful prospect of an early restoration to the discharge of all my duties, although, for some time yet, by the advice of my medical friends, I am prevented from any exertion in the way of public speaking.— I am, my dear sir, your affectionate brother in the best of bonds, JAMES BEGG.

"To the Rev. the Moderator of the Presbytery of Edinburgh."

A committee was appointed accordingly; but I do not find any notice of their ever having reported. I believe that the dispute had reference to the acoustic qualities of the church, to whose defects, and the strain of his voice which these defects entailed, Dr. Begg imputed his illness. I have no doubt that the defects existed, as indeed they did in most of our large churches. But that they were the cause of Dr. Begg's illness, or that they would have been removed by the alterations which he suggested, is more questionable. It is no disparagement to him to suppose that the irritation of his malady and the depression occasioned by his enforced cessation from his loved work, made him less tolerant of contradiction than he usually was. As after this he had a good deal to do with the construction of many churches, and as he exercised a most vigilant care over the acoustic arrangements, it is not improbable that many Free Church ministers and congregations lie unconsciously under a debt of obligation to the heritors of Liberton.

The proceedings in which Dr. Begg was thus precluded from taking part, constituted an epoch in the history of the Church of Scotland which I have called "the beginning of the end." The action of the Government—and both parties had been in power during the period—and of Parliament had made it patent that the Church, as it then was, could not long remain an Established Church. And the action of the minority of ministers within the Church in defying the spiritual acts of its supreme court, and ostentatiously fraternising with the ministers whom that court had solemnly deposed, made it equally patent that it could not, as it then was, long remain one Church.

The Assembly of 1842, of which Dr. Begg was not a member, adopted the CLAIM OF RIGHTS, a document which will not soon cease to be regarded as one of the most important in the records of ecclesiastical history. It was composed by Mr. Murray Dunlop. Its adoption was moved by Dr. Chalmers and seconded by Dr. Gordon. With all the calmness of a legal document, it is distinguished by a stern and uncompromising statement of high principle, and of a determination to stand by that principle at whatsoever cost. In seconding its adoption, Dr. Gordon, one of the meekest and most venerable of men, began as follows :—

"I second the motion for the adoption of this overture, with a hope which I am not willing to relinquish, that when our claim of right is brought before an enlightened legislature—before high-minded and honourable men—they will not refuse at least a patient perusal of that claim; and I have the conviction, which I am as little willing to relinquish, that if they do give it a patient perusal, they will see the justice, and therefore the policy of acceding to it. But, sir, if unhappily it should be otherwise,—if they have resolved on refusing what we think reasonable on our part to ask, I feel for one that we are bound, as honest men and as Christian ministers, with all calmness and with all respect, but with all firmness and determination, to tell them that we cannot carry on the affairs of Christ's house under the coercion of the civil courts; and however deeply we may deplore the loss of those advantages which we derive from our connection with the state, if ultimately the legislature determine that they will not listen to our claim, then those advantages we must relinquish, because we could not hold them with a good conscience."

The Claim of Rights was addressed to the Queen. The Marquis of Bute, the Royal Commissioner, with a disclaimer of approval of its contents, agreed to transmit it, and in due course Sir James Graham, the Home Secretary, with a similar disclaimer, intimated that he would lay it before Her Majesty. The answer of the Government was not given till the January following, and it was uncompromisingly unfavourable.

Meantime events had been proceeding. Various attempts were made to devise a *modus vivendi*, and had failed. The Duke of Argyll's bill, which was substantially reproduced in the House of Commons by Mr. Campbell of Monzie, was thrown out on a technical objection, and the decision of the House of Lords in a second Auchterarder case proceeded on grounds altogether incompatible with the Church's possession of any measure of spiritual independence.

In these circumstances it was agreed that a CONVOCATION should be held of ministers favourable to non-intrusion and spiritual independence. It was called by a circular, signed by thirty-one of the most venerable ministers of the Church. It met on the 17th of November 1842, and was attended by 423 ministers. Its proceedings were private, and beyond the two series of "Resolutions" which it adopted, until quite recently no account was given to the public of its proceedings, although their general character was of course no secret. I have been so long in the habit of regarding my friend Dr. William Wilson as one of the most judicious of men, that I have considerable hesitation in expressing my doubt as to his maintenance of that character, when he inserted in his "Memorials of Dr. Candlish" a paper of notes of the proceedings, taken by a most respected member of the Convocation. That the notes were taken in absolutely good faith is as certain as almost anything can be, for they were taken by the late Dr. Henderson of Glasgow. But they are only brief jottings, never intended for publication; and I think it would have been better that they had not been published.

There is no doubt that these notes produce in the mind of the reader an impression that Dr. Begg was less zealous than his brethren, or more cautious as to committing himself. I have the testimony of several members of the Convocation that it was not so. In fact, the only question of any consequence betwixt him and them was as to what should be regarded as constituting a refusal on the part of the Government and the Legislature to amend what the supreme judicial court had declared to be the existing law. The members of the Convocation were unanimous in holding that a *refusal* to amend that law would necessitate a disruption. But hitherto the Government had not given an unfavourable answer to the Claim of Rights.

They had only delayed unduly in giving an answer at all. Dr. Begg and some others held that this delay might *justify* a disruption, but did not *necessitate* it. But after some argument he heartily acquiesced in both series of Resolutions. After a little while the small ground of contention was removed. The letter of Sir James Graham, of 4th January 1843, was an absolute and decided refusal to grant the Claim of Rights; and so the condition which Dr. Begg and some others considered necessary to compel a disruption was fulfilled.

The actual Disruption of the Church of Scotland was an event not only to be remembered by those who took part in it, and by those who witnessed it, but to be held in constant remembrance by succeeding generations. The steadfastness with which so many men went forward in what they regarded the path of duty called forth alike the sympathies of friends and the admiration of generous foes; and not all their foes were ungenerous. It may be quite freely admitted that in some cases unduly strong expressions may have been employed in speaking of the conduct of those who "stayed in," and especially of those who got new light on the subject at the last hour. But the deed itself was a noble one, and could have been done only by courageous men.

Between the meeting of the Convocation and that of the General Assembly, some still entertained hopes that a disruption might be prevented, but it was a hoping against hope. The Government expected that faint-heartedness would invade the host at the decisive moment, and Sir James Graham afterwards admitted that he had been misled by information from Scotland as to the numbers that would "come out."

It is no part of my duty to add another to the numerous descriptions of the Disruption. I confine myself to a brief statement of Dr. Begg's relinquishment of one of the most desirable positions that a minister of the Church of Scotland could occupy. On the Sabbath after the Disruption Dr. Begg entered the parish church of Liberton for the last time. His infant child was baptized by his friend, Mr. Charles Marshall of Dunfermline. At the close of the sermon Dr. Begg, with great emotion, bade farewell to such of his people as were not to accompany him in quitting the Established Church, but expressed a hope that between him and a large proportion of them there would be no separation. He explained that the minister, office-bearers, and people of the Edinburgh United Presbyterian Church, of which Dr. George Johnstone was minister, had most generously agreed to give the Free Congregation of Liberton temporary accommodation in their place of worship, altering their own hours of meeting in order to accommodate them.

On the following Sabbath the great body of the people of Liberton crowded to overflowing the Nicolson Street church. As they converged by the several roads, and asked one another whether the minister had yet come, they naturally agreed to await his arrival. In due time he left the manse, and in descending the steep incline at whose top it stands, met the minister who had been sent to preach the church vacant. He civilly saluted him, and told him that he had made all necessary arrangements for his visit, however unwelcome might be the occasion of it. Then he passed the first of the groups of waiting people, who unconsciously formed a procession behind him. This was enlarged at one and another cross-road, and thus the Parish Minister of Liberton entered on the new stage of his career as the Free Church Minister of Newington.

END OF VOL. I.

SHORT LIST OF PUBLICATIONS
OF
JAMES GEMMELL,
10-15 GEORGE IV. BRIDGE,
EDINBURGH.

LONDON..........	HAMILTON, ADAMS, & CO.; SIMPKIN, MARSHALL & CO.
EDINBURGH..........	OLIVER & BOYD; J. MENZIES & CO.
GLASGOW..........	J. MENZIES & CO.; PORTEOUS BROTHERS.

THE CREATION.

Just Published, in 1 thick 8vo vol., (663 pp.) cl., price 12s. 6d.

DISSERTATIONS ON THE PHILOSOPHY OF THE Creation, and the First Ten Chapters of Genesis, Allegorised in Mythology; containing Expositions of the Ancient Cosmogonies and Theogonies, the Invention of Hieroglyphics, and of the Ancient Hebrew Language and Alphabet, etc. By WM. GALLOWAY, M.D., L.R.C.P.E., etc.

"An able and exhaustive treatise, . . . bears throughout the stamp of study pursued *con amore.*"—*Dundee Advertiser.*

REUSS ON THE CANON.

In 1 thick 8vo volume, price 9/.

HISTORY OF THE CANON OF THE HOLY SCRIPTURES IN THE CHRISTIAN CHURCH. By EDWARD REUSS, *Professor in the University of Strasburg.* Translated from the Second French Edition, by Rev. DAVID HUNTER, B.D., *late Scholar and Fellow in the University of Glasgow.*

"It is a book I highly value."—PROF. A. B. BRUCE, D.D., *Free Church College, Glasgow.*

"The book is a most valuable and useful one."—PROFESSOR WM. MILLIGAN, D.D., *University, Aberdeen.*

"I have long known the book, and have found it very stimulating. —PROF. A. H. CHARTERIS, D.D., *University, Edinburgh.*

"A most scholarly and comprehensive work. The most complete on the subject we know of."—*Christian Age.*

"Wide knowledge of Church history, impartial judgment of the evidence of facts, keen historical insight, are certainly not lacking in the History of the Canon. . . . . Its accuracy is guaranteed by the fact that all the proofs have been revised by the author himself."— *Literary World.*

Demy 8vo, cl., with Illustrations, price 7/6.

LECTURES AND SERMONS BY MARTYRS.

CONTAINING SERMONS AND LECTURES BY

RICHARD CAMERON. ALEXANDER SHIELDS.
ALEXANDER PEDEN. JOHN LIVINGSTONE.
DONALD CARGILL. JOHN WELLWOOD.
WILLIAM GUTHRIE. JOHN WELCH.
MICHAEL BRUCE. JOHN GUTHRIE.

With Preface by JOHN HOWIE, of Lochgoin; and Brief Biographical Notices of the Authors of the Sermons, by the Rev. JAMES KERR, Glasgow.

ILLUSTRATIONS.—Grassmarket of Edinburgh—Canongate Tolbooth—Martyrs' Monument, Greyfriars—The House where Cameron was Born—Netherbow Port, Edinburgh—Greyfriars' Churchyard—Monument at Airsmoss—Bothwell Bridge.

"These sermons were first published by the celebrated John Howie, of Lochgoin, in 1779. This edition having long since become very scarce, if obtainable at all, it was a good thought to have it reprinted. This has been done under the careful editorship of the Rev. James Kerr, of Glasgow. . . . No one that values the contendings of Scotland's martyrs should be without a copy."—*Covenanter.*

Crown 8vo, cloth, price 2s. 6d.

THE SCOTTISH CHURCH AND ITS SURROUNDINGS,

IN EARLY TIMES.

BY
ROBERT PATON,
MINISTER OF KIRKINNER.

"The story of the introduction of Christianity into Britain is one full of picturesque incident, no less than of historical and antiquarian interest; and in a series of short sketches, to which he gives the title of 'The Scottish Church and its Surroundings in Early Times,' the Rev. Robert Paton has shown that he knows how to take advantage of this circumstance. . . . His sketches are vigorous and animated. . . . He writes very well."—*Scotsman.*

"We have here a delightful little volume. . . . . It presents, in a very attractive form, the chief facts belonging the first seven centuries of our era and pertaining to Scotland."—*Presbyterian Churchman.*

WORKS BY REV. HUGH MARTIN, D.D.

Second Edition, demy 8vo, cloth, price 7s. 6d.

THE ATONEMENT;

IN ITS RELATION TO
THE COVENANT, THE PRIESTHOOD, AND THE INTERCESSION OF OUR LORD.

"A volume written with remarkable vigour and earnestness."—*British Quarterly Review.*

"Something like theology. We wish our young divines would feed on such meat as this. Dr. Martin teaches a real substitution and an efficient atonement, and has no sympathy with Robertson and his school."—*Spurgeon.*

"In these days of lax and shallow theology, it is refreshing to come upon a volume like Dr. Martin's. The subject is one of surpassing importance, and upon the treatment of it the author brings to bear extraordinary powers of reasoning, warmed and animated by a soul that has felt the blessedness of an interest in the Atonement. . . . . The whole volume is one of no ordinary kind."—*Rock.*

Second Edition, demy 8vo, price 7s. 6d.

THE SHADOW OF CALVARY;

GETHSEMANE—THE ARREST—THE TRIAL.

"It will be seen that Dr. Martin holds very definite theological views, and that he is not ashamed nor afraid to proclaim them. . . . . These lectures, abounding in powerful appeals and stern warnings, are not deficient in tenderness and reverence."—*Scotsman.*

Second Edition, demy 8vo, price 7s. 6d.

THE PROPHET JONAH:

HIS CHARACTER AND MISSION TO NINEVEH.

"To ordinary readers we can thoroughly recommend it as a good, sound, full, practical exposition of the Prophet Jonah."—*Daily Review.*

"A good specimen of the author's power of exposition, and is certain to be useful to those who intend to devote special study to the book whose contents are discussed."—*Glasgow News.*

"We are gratified to find that this excellent work on the book of Jonah, published some years ago, has reached a second edition. The book is no less rich and varied in matter and earnest in spirit, than it is vigorous in style."—*R. P. Witness.*

"Dr. Martin is well known as an able author. His 'Jonah' is a work of considerable merit, ... and is written in an attractive and interesting style."—*Courant.*

Crown 8vo, Second Thousand, 357 pp., price 5s.

THE STORY OF DANIEL:
HIS LIFE AND TIMES.

BY

P. H. HUNTER.

MINISTER OF ELIE, FIFESHIRE.

"The difficult task has been skilfully done. It has resulted in a graphic and vivid historical biography as engrossing as a volume of Macaulay; and proving that, whatever else there may be, there is, at all events, a warm interest in the ancient documents. If books like the 'Story of Daniel' were more common, modern faith in the flesh and blood reality of the Old Testament saints would not be so exclusively an intellectual effort as it now often is."—*Scotsman.*

"Mr. Hunter has done his work very thoroughly, laying under contribution a throng of writers, ancient and modern, and gathering into a focus the scattered rays of light which they shed upon one of the dimmest periods of history."—*Glasgow Herald.*

"It is an honest piece of work, and will be found, by most people who see it, very readable and very useful."—*Outlook.*

HAUSSER'S (LUDWIG) THE PERIOD OF THE REFORMATION (1517 to 1640). Edited by WILHELM ONCKEN, *Professor of History in Giessen University.* Translated by Mrs. G. STURGE. 1 thick volume, cr. 8vo, 800 pages, price 7s. 6d.

"It would be difficult to find a book better suited to give a just and comprehensive view of the subject. Not its least valued characteristic is the connection which it enables the reader to perceive in periods which are commonly studied by themselves."—*Spectator.*

"We recommend it to all who wish to understand the history of Europe since the sixteenth century. Once opened it will be read."—*The Watchman.*

Cr. 8vo, cl., 220 pages, price 2/.

THE TRUE PSALMODY; or, The Bible Psalms the Church's only Manual of Praise. With Prefaces by the Rev. Drs. COOKE, EDGAR, and HOUSTON; and Recommendations from Eminent Divines.

"'The True Psalmody' is a book that is calculated, we firmly believe, to convince any mind that is open to conviction, that the Psalms alone are to be employed in the service of God and that the use of hymns is wholly unwarrantable. It is seldom in these days of 'liberal views'—that is, of wholesale corruption of doctrine and worship—that we meet with a new publication which we can heartily and unreservedly commend."—*Reformed Presbyterian Witness.*

THE ONLY HISTORY OF THE WESTMINSTER ASSEMBLY.

Fourth edition, in 1 vol., cr. 8vo, cl., 6s.

HISTORY OF THE WESTMINSTER ASSEMBLY OF DIVINES.

BY THE LATE
PROF. WM. M. HETHERINGTON, D.D., LL.D.,
FREE CHURCH COLLEGE, GLASGOW.

EDITED BY ROBERT WILLIAMSON, D.D., ASCOG.

With Notes and Fac-similes of Title-Pages of the Original Editions of the Confession of Faith, the Catechisms, Larger and Shorter; and the Directory of Church Government and Ordination of Ministers.

"The value of the present edition has been greatly enhanced by the care and judgment with which Dr. Williamson of Ascog has readjusted its contents, and added what brings its information into accord with the light of the latest discoveries."—*Free Church Record.*

"Comparing this edition with the book when first published in 1843, its enhanced value is great."—*Scottish Congregational Magazine.*

"An admirable edition of a valuable work at a *reasonable price.*"—*R. P. Witness.*

"In paper and in topography the edition is superior to its predecessors, and we expect that, for many years to come, this will be the standard edition of a standard work."—*Covenanter.*

Important Work in Defence of Church Establishments.

Crown 8vo, cl., 5/.

STATEMENT OF THE DIFFERENCE BETWEEN the Profession of the REFORMED CHURCH OF SCOTLAND as adopted by Seceders, and the Profession contained in the New Testimony and other Acts, lately adopted by the General Associate Synod: particularly on the POWER OF CIVIL MAGISTRATES RESPECTING RELIGION, NATIONAL REFORMATION, etc. By the late THOMAS M'CRIE, D.D., *Author of* "*Life of John Knox,*" etc. With Preface by Prof. SMEATON, D.D., Edinburgh.

"Apart from the editor's commendation, anything from the pen of so masculine a reasoner, and so well practised a writer as Dr M'Crie, must be worth reading; and whoever wishes to study the important subject here treated of, will do well to have the little book beside him."—*Scotsman.*

In 2 vols., price 3s. 6d. each (sold separately) Demy 8vo, cloth.

THE MODERN SCOTTISH PULPIT:

SERMONS

BY EMINENT PRESBYTERIAN MINISTERS.

"*Scotch Sermons* are not all bad, though the name has gained an unenviable notoriety; for here are discourses as 'sound as a bell.' Sydney Smith called Scotland 'the knuckle-end of England;' but as to gospel preaching we have always regarded it as the choicest part of the three kingdoms; and so it is, and so shall be, by the grace of God."—*Rev. C. H. Spurgeon.*

Crown 8vo, 232 pp., price 3s. 6d.

OUTLINE OF THE HISTORY OF

PROTESTANT MISSIONS.

From the Reformation to the Present Time.

A CONTRIBUTION TO RECENT CHURCH HISTORY.

By Dr. GUSTAV WARNECK.

Pastor at Rothenschirmbach.

Translated from the Second Edition

BY

Dr. THOMAS SMITH.

Professor of Evangelistic Theology, New College, Edinburgh.

"Dr Smith's translation of Dr Warneck's able and valuable treatise will prove of great value, and cannot fail to stimulate and encourage the efforts which have already effected a hopeful commencement—for it is little more than a commencement—in the mission work entrusted to the Church of Christ."—*Aberdeen Journal.*

"It presents a careful summary of Protestant Misson work, from the Reformation to the close of the eighteenth century, and deals more fully, though in a sort of statistical and commercial fashion, with the operations that have been carried on in the mission field during the present century."—*Scotsman.*

EDINBURGH UNIVERSITY: a Sketch of its Life for Three Hundred Years. Demy 8vo, sewed, price 1s.

"In these pages an admirable as well as an accurate account is presented of the story of the College of Edinburgh since its foundation."—*Liverpool Mercury.*

"We recommend this historical sketch to our readers as useful and entertaining."—*Dundee Courier and Argus.*

IMPORTANT WORK ON BAPTISM.

Crown 8vo, cloth, price 2s. 6d.

CANDID REASONS FOR RENOUNCING
THE PRINCIPLES OF
ANTIPÆDOBAPTISM.

By PETER EDWARDS.

The following treatise, written by a man who was for ten years a Baptist minister, we very earnestly recommend to the careful study of those who desire to make themselves acquainted with the argument in favour of infant baptism. The book contains this argument summarily stated, and most logically defended. There is probably no treatise in the English language on a Theological subject in which the reasoning is closer. We consider that its careful perusal is fitted, by the blessing of God, to lead Christian parents to understand clearly the ground on which the ordinary doctrine of the Church is maintained, and to value, more than many do, the privilege of obtaining the recognition of the church-membership of their children; and we are not without hope than many of our Baptist brethren may be led by it to re-examine the grounds on which they have hitherto regarded the baptism of infants as being without Scriptural authority.

> ROBERT RAINY, D.D., Principal, Free Church College, Edinburgh.
> GEORGE C. M. DOUGLAS, D.D., Principal, Free Church College, Glasgow.
> W. H. GOOLD, D.D., Edinburgh.
> GEORGE SMEATON, D.D., Professor, Free Church College, Edin.
> W. LINDSAY ALEXANDER, D.D., Edinburgh.
> JAMES BEGG, D.D., Edinburgh.
> JAMES MACGREGOR, D.D., St. Cuthbert's, Edinburgh.
> ROBERT JAMIESON, D.D., St. Paul's, Glasgow.
> JAMES MACGREGOR, D.D., Professor, Free Church College, Edin.
> HORATIUS BONAR, D.D., Edinburgh.
> THOMAS SMITH, D.D., Edinburgh.
> JOHN KENNEDY, D.D., Dingwall.
> WILLIAM WILSON, D.D., Dundee.

THE VOICES FROM THE CROSS. By Rev. MALCOLM WHITE, M.A., *Blairgowrie, Author of "The Symbolical Numbers of Scripture,"* etc. Foolscap 8vo, sewed, 1/.

"Will, we trust, be read with pleasure and profit by a large circle of readers."—*Presbyterian Churchman.*

"Good, and is suggestive of thought."—*Family Treasury.*

"We have perused this excellent little book with great pleasure, and, we trust, with spiritual profit. Quite at home on the subject he has chosen, and treats it in a very instructive manner."—*Dundee Courier and Argus.*

Crown 8vo, cloth, 178 pages, with portrait, price 2s.

LIFE OF
ROBERT SMITH CANDLISH, D.D.,

MINISTER OF FREE ST. GEORGE'S CHURCH, AND PRINCIPAL OF THE NEW COLLEGE EDINBURGH.

By JEAN L. WATSON.

"A most admirable sketch of the character and work of the late Dr. Candlish. . . . . This is a most seasonable publication, and should be read by all who want to get a concise and comprehensive account of the important principles and controversies with which Dr. Candlish was much identified."—*Daily Review.*

"In selection, arrangement, and graphic description, the little volume is all that could be desired."—*Edinburgh Courant.*

Crown 8vo, cloth, price 2/.

LIFE AND TIMES
OF
THOMAS BOSTON:
PASTOR OF ETTRICK.

By JEAN L. WATSON.

"That the autobiography is so little known is much to be regretted: it is a picture of one of the most momentous periods in the religious history of Scotland; it is, moreover, the mirror of a life spent in high communion with God, and gifted with a vision penetrating far into the kingdom. Miss Watson's 'Life' is based upon this larger work, and abundant extracts are given from it. She has selected her materials wisely, and the result is a book which cannot fail to interest."—*British Messenger.*

New ed., cr. 8vo, cl., 233 pp., 1/6.

SELECT SERMONS
BY
THOMAS CHALMERS, D.D., LL.D.

With a *Tribute to his Memory*, by the late DR LORIMER.

"Judiciously selected, and will serve, as far as printed words can serve, to convey to a new generation an idea of the power and eloquence which entranced their fathers. It is fitting, too, that Dr. Lorimer's funeral sermon should escape any hostile criticism. From an evangelical and Free Church point of view, it is a noble *éloge*."—*Scotsman.*

Cr. 8vo, cl., 203 pp., with Two Portraits and Engraving of Gairney Bridge. Price 1s. 6d.

THE ERSKINES:
EBENEZER AND RALPH.

BY
JOHN KER, D.D., AND JEAN L. WATSON.

"This is the joint production of a distinguished U.P. divine and a well-known Free Church authoress. They have succeeded between them in making a very readable book. . . . . It is written in an agreeable and attractive style, which is certain to ensure its popularity."—*Edinburgh Courant.*

Crown 8vo, cl., price 1/6.

LIFE
OF
ANDREW THOMSON, D.D.
BY
JEAN L. WATSON.

"The compiler of a brief life of the well-known Dr Andrew Thomson has done her work with conscientious care evidently, ... will be found of interest to many as a record of the life of a very able, manly, and large-hearted Christian minister."—*Aberdeen Free Press.*

"Her biography will be prized by many admirers of its subject."—*Scotsman.*

THE KITTLEGAIRY VACANCY; or, A New Way of Getting Rid of Old Ministers. By JOHN PLENDERLEITH. 143 pp., cr. 8vo, *sewed*, 1s. 6d.

"This is an excellent satire on the democratic spirit which manifests itself too often in the heartless treatment of ancient ministers, who deserve well of their Church and people."—*Presbyterian Churchman.*

"A very clever story of the difficulties which beset certain ministers—especially of the old school—in the smaller towns of Scotland, and perhaps in England also. . . . Many of the characters are well drawn, and the remarks of the ministers' clerical colleagues on their conduct and the harm they were doing to the 'cause' are cleverly put."—*The Bookseller.*

"'The tale of Dr. Howliston's persecution is remarkably well told.'—*Dundee Courier.*

"A story of ecclesiastical troubles, trenchantly exposing the scandals often associated with the selection and treatment of ministers. . . It will be read with interest."—*Literary World.*

163 pp., crown 8vo, cloth, 3s.

BIBLICAL GEOGRAPHY
IN A NUTSHELL.

Containing many of the most Recent Identifications, with Map.

BY

MARGARETTA SHEKLETON.

With Introductory Note by AMBROSE W. LEET, D.D., Incumbent of Bethesda Chapel, Dublin.

"This work will, by the blessing of God, go far to supply a want hitherto only too practically felt by thousands of Sunday-school and other students of the Scriptures. Its 166 pages of well-arranged matter offer, at a reasonable charge, such an amount of useful information as to show that the much esteemed Christian authoress has expended upon them a marvellous amount of labour, knowledge, and skill. Every diligent Sunday-school teacher in the kingdom should possess this instructive and eminently helpful handbook of the Bible." —Rev. J. ORMISTON, *British Protestant.*

"The book will be found of real service in the systematic study of the Scriptures."—*Scotsman.*

Fcap. 8vo, price 1/6.

OUR MOTHER:
A LIFE PICTURE.

BEING

A LIFE OF MRS. KRUMMACHER,
Wife of the Author of "The Suffering Saviour," etc.

Translated from the German by a well-known Author.

"Deep appreciation of the purity and peace of home-life enables German writers to depict it as no others can. . . . . possesses all the pathos, sweet simplicity, and lofty teaching which characterise the best German story-writers. The translation is beautifully done. A Capital gift book."—*Irish Baptist Magazine.*

THE CROOK IN THE LOT; OR, THE SOVEREIGNTY AND WISDOM OF GOD IN THE AFFLICTIONS OF MEN DISPLAYED; together with a Christian Deportment under them: being the Substance of several Sermons on Eccles. vii. 13; Prov. xvi. 18, and 1 Peter, v. 6. By the Rev. THOMAS BOSTON. 16mo, *cloth,* price 8d.

Demy 16mo, in Ornamental Cloth Covers.

BIOGRAPHIES

OF

SCOTTISH REFORMERS, PREACHERS, MARTYRS, etc.

BY JEAN L. WATSON.

LIFE OF RICHARD CAMERON. 70 pp., with View of Monument at Airsmoss, and of Falkland Palace, price 6d.

LIFE OF HUGH MILLER. 132 pp., with View of Bass Rock on Cover, price 9d.

LIFE OF RALPH ERSKINE. 99 pp., with Portrait, price 9d.

LIFE OF EBENEZER ERSKINE. 104 pp., with Portrait, price 9d.

LIFE OF THOMAS GUTHRIE, D.D. 106 pp., with Portrait and Illustration on Cover, price 9d.

LIFE OF DONALD CARGILL. 60 pp., with Views of Glasgow Cathedral, and Martyrs' Monument, Edin., price 6d.

LIFE OF ROBERT MURRAY M'CHEYNE. With View of his Church in Dundee, price 9d.

LIFE OF THOMAS CHALMERS, D.D., LL.D. With View of Kilmany Church, 134 pp., price 9d.

LIFE OF NORMAN MACLEOD, D.D. With Portrait and View of Barony Church on cover, price 9d.

"This well-known authoress has spent a long life-time in getting up these admirable stories of the heroes of Scottish Church history. She knew many of the heroes personally. She has a quick eye, is shrewd, thoughtful, receptive. She has a most fascinating and instructive style. There is no resisting her glowing pages. She has done a noble work for Scotland in telling these stories. Such reading as this is wholesome, invigorating, refining."

BY ROBERT MACGREGOR.

LIFE OF JOHN MACDONALD, D.D., "The Apostle of the North." 96 pp., price 9d.

THE JESUITS: a Sketch of the Origin and Progress of the Society of Jesus. 110 pp., price 9d.

MEMORIALS OF THE BASS ROCK. 136 pp., price 9d.

BY JOHN KER, D.D.

THE ERSKINES: EBENEZER AND RALPH. With Engraving of Gairney Bridge, price 6d.

"These biographies are well written. The leading events in each life pass rapidly before us, and the story is so well told that the reader will find it difficult to lay down any of the 'Lives' until he has finished it."—*Reformed Presbyterian Witness.*

Just Published, Demy 16mo, cl., 123 pp., with Portrait, price 9d.

THE LIFE AND TIMES OF
GIROLAMO SAVONAROLA.
BY
ANNIE C. MACLEOD.

"The author is a daughter of the late Dr. Norman Macleod. She has done her work extremely well."—*Scotsman.*

"To those who have little time to read, desire to read profitably, and for the young who must necessarily begin their studies of great subjects with short books, this life of Savonarola can be most confidently recommended as a slight sketch of Florence in the fifteenth and sixteenth centuries, and also of that time."—*Edinburgh Courant.*

PULPIT TABLE TALK. Containing Remarks and Anecdotes on Preachers and Preaching. By EDWARD B. RAMSAY, M.A., LL.D., F.R.S.E., *Dean of Edinburgh*. Third Edition, fcap. 8vo, sewed, 1s.

THE STORY OF MY HEART DISEASE; or, the Experiences of a Dyspeptic. Dedicated, without Permission, to all Invalids. By MOSES GREEN. Cr. 8vo, sewed, 1s.

THE SAINT'S EVERLASTING REST; or, a Treatise on the Blessed State of the Saints, in their Enjoyment of God in Heaven. By the Rev. RICHARD BAXTER. Abridged by BENJAMIN FAWCETT, M.A. New edition, 12mo, cloth, 1s. 6d.

A METHOD OF PRAYER, with SCRIPTURE EXPRESSIONS Proper to be Used under each Head. By the late Rev. MATTHEW HENRY. 16mo, cl., 1/.

OUR CHILDREN FOR CHRIST; a Plea for Infant Church Membership, with a full Discussion on the Mode of Baptism. By Rev. SAMUEL MACNAUGHTON, M.A., *Preston*. Cloth, 9d.

"These arguments will no doubt be regarded as convincing by the numerous sections of the Christian Church who accept the doctrine."—*Scotsman.*

"Free from all controversial bitterness."—*Daily Review.*

Demy 16mo, cl., with frontispiece, price 6d.

THE WATER-CRESS BOY.

BY

JEAN L. WATSON.

"This is a fresh, pretty little story of a struggling and penniless artist, who, at the crisis of his career, was saved from destruction by a little water-cress seller, who dreamily murmured one of his Sunday School texts as he passed the desperate man. . . . . The story is pleasantly and sympathetically told, as might be expected from its coming from Miss Watson's pen."—*Edinburgh Courant.*

Demy 16mo, limp cl., frontispiece, price 6d.

WILLIE'S BRINGING-UP.

BY

JEAN L. WATSON.

AUTHOR OF "BYGONE DAYS IN OUR VILLAGE," ETC.

"Forms a wonderfully true picture of Scottish peasant life. Must have been drawn from nature."—*Fifeshire Advertiser.*

"The story is well told."—*Christian Treasury.*

"This is a nice story very becomingly told in simple language. . . . It is true to the life, as few readers will fail to see."—*Hawick Express.*

Crown 8vo, 689 pp., price 7s. 6d.

THE LAND OF THE MORNING:

AN ACCOUNT OF

JAPAN AND ITS PEOPLE,

BASED ON A FOUR YEARS' RESIDENCE IN THAT COUNTRY, INCLUDING TRAVELS INTO THE REMOTEST PARTS OF THE INTERIOR.

BY

WILLIAM GRAY DIXON, M.A.,

Formerly Professor in the Imperial College of Engineering, Tôkiyô.

With 21 Original Illustrations by J. BAYNE, and a Map.

"A book of interest, ... gives us the impression of trustworthyness and solid value. Full of facts, shrewdly estimated and compared. . . . all the appearance of reasonableness and impartiality. . . . full of pleasant pictures, and for this, as well as for graver reasons, well worth reading."—*Spectator.*

"Taken altogether this volume, with its excellent map and its occasional and appropriate illustrations, is almost a model of its special class of books—clearly the outcome of thorough acquaintance with the subject in hand, and written in so full and interesting a style as to be the pleasantest possible vehicle of information."—LITERARY WORLD.

"Any one who wishes to learn all about the Japanese—their history, manners, and laws—could not find them better described than in this volume. . . . The style of the author is very pleasing, and from the fact that it is a narrative of personal reminiscences the interest is kept up throughout."—ROCK.

JOURNAL OF A VOYAGE TO AUSTRALIA, by Cape of Good Hope, Six Months in Melbourne, and Return by Cape Horn, including Scenes and Sayings on Land and Sea. By SINCLAIR THOS. DUNCAN. *New and enlarged edition, with frontispiece and map.* Cr. 8vo, cloth, 3s.

THE IVY SERIES.

In foolscap 8vo, neatly bound in cl., price 1/ per vol.

THE HISTORY OF SUSAN GRAY.
THE BASKET OF FLOWERS.
THE BABES IN THE BASKET.
THE HISTORY OF LUCY CLARE.
DISRUPTION MEMORIES; being the Personal Narrative of a Lay Voluntary. With Remarks on the Present Condition of the Church.
THE CASTLE OF PICTORDU.

"These are all neat interesting little stories that will delight young people."—*Scotsman.*

"The 'Ivy Series' is a marvellous instance of what art and taste can accomplish with materials by no means expensive. The books of this series are quite cheap, and yet they are clearly printed and beautifully bound."—*Fifeshire Advertiser.*

"No better gifts at the price could be placed in the hands of children who have just learned to read."—*Dumfriesshire Herald.*

"Elegant as is the style in which these books are got up, that is far from being their only excellence. . . . are admirably adapted for Sabbath School Prizes. The stories are such as young people delight to read."—*Banffshire Reporter.*

"For Sunday School libraries or prizes no works could be better suited."—*Dundee Advertiser.*

"They will be a valuable addition to any library for the young."—*Invergordon Times.*

THE SCOTS WORTHIES. By JOHN HOWIE, of Lochgoin. *New edition, with notes.* 464 pp., 32mo, sewed, price 6d.

James Gemmell, Edinburgh. 15

In foolscap 8vo, neatly bound in cloth.

THE ANCHOR SERIES
OF
BOOKS FOR THE YOUNG.

The following are now ready, price 1/6 each.

UNCLE TOM'S CABIN. By Mrs H. B. Stowe.
LUCY CLARE, and THE BABES IN THE BASKET. In one vol.
THE BASKET OF FLOWERS, edited by Dr G. T. Bedell, Philadelphia; and THE HISTORY OF SUSAN GRAY, by Mrs. Sherwood. In one volume.
THE PRINCE OF THE HOUSE OF DAVID. By Rev. J. H. Ingraham.
GLENCOE PARSONAGE. By Mrs A. E. Porter.
THE KING'S DAUGHTER. By Pansy, Author of "Ester Ried."
THE JUDGE'S SONS: a Story of Wheat and Tares. By Mrs E. D. Kendall.
STRAWBERRY HILL. By Clara Vance, Author of "Andy Luttrell."
BARBARA. By the same Author.
THE TALBURY GIRLS. By the same Author.
EVA: a Book for Girls, translated from the Dutch of Andriessen. By G. S. Grahame.

"They are handy, legibly printed, and attractively bound, most suitable volumes for a Sabbath School library. . . . As now presented, they are a marvel of printing, binding, and cheapness."—*Edinburgh Courant.*

"May be commended to the notice of teachers and others, as prize works for juvenile readers. They are tastefully got up at a very cheap rate, and the choice made in the selection of favourite stories is all that could be desired."—*Dundee Advertiser.*

Just published, 8 vols. crown 8vo, price 2/ per vol., New Edition of

WILSON'S TALES OF THE BORDERS
AND OF SCOTLAND.

Each Volume Complete in itself—Volumes sold separately.

CONTENTS OF THE VOLUMES.

VOL. I.—The Vacant Chair—Tibby Fowler—My Black Coat; or, the Breaking of the Bride's China—We'll have another—The Soldier's Return—Grizel Cochrane; a Tale of Tweedmouth Moor—Sayings and Doings of Peter Paterson—The Prodigal Son—Sir Patrick Hume: a Tale of the House of Marchmont—Charles Lawson—The Orphan—The Seeker—Squire Ben—The Fair—Archy Armstrong—The Widow's Ae Son—The Death of the Chevalier de la Beaute—The Procrastinator—Ups and Downs; or, David Stuart's Pilgrimage—The Cripple; or, Ebenezer the Disowned.

Vol. II.—The Leveller—The Bride—The Smuggler—The Dominie's Class—The Henpecked Man—I Canna be Fashed; or, Bailie Grant's Confessions—The Poacher's Progress—The Royal Bridal; or, The King may come in the Cadger's way—The Faa's Revenge: a Tale of the Border Gipsies—The Outlaw; or, the Maiden of Ledwick—The Broken Heart: a Tale of the Rebellion.

Vol. III.—The Guidwife of Coldingham; or, the Surprise of Fast Castle—The Adventures of Launcelot Errington and his Nephew Mark: a Tale of Lindisferne—Judith the Egyptian; or, the Fate of the Heir of Riccon—The Deserted Wife—The Unbidden Guest; or, Jedburgh's Regal Festival—The Covenanting Family—The Festival—The Simple Man is the Beggar's Brother—The Unknown—The Solitary of the Cave—The Order of the Garter: a Story of Wark Castle—The Red Hall; or, Berwick in the year 1296.

Vol. IV.—Perseverance—The Irish Reaper—Edmund and Helen; a Ballad—Roger Goldie's Narrative—Trials and Triumphs—Laidley Worm of Spindleston Haugh—Johnny Brotherton's Five Sunny Days—The Hermit of the Hills; a Ballad—The Minister's Daughter—The Faithful Wife.

Vol. V.—The Poor Scholar—Reuben Purves; or, the Speculator—The One-Armed Tar—Midside Maggie; or, the Bannock of Tollishill—The First and Second Marriage—The Twin Brothers—Leaves from the Diary of an Aged Spinster—Madeline of Roeclough—The Adopted Son—The Doom of Soulis—The Baron's Vow.

Vol. VI.—Leaves from the Life of Alexander Hamilton—The Wife or the Wuddy—Willie Wastle's Account of his Wife—Polwarth on the Green—Bill Stanley; or, a Sailor's Story—The Recollections of a Village Patriarch—The Whitsome Tragedy—The First Foot—The Persecuted Elector; or, Passages from the Life of Simon Gourlay—An Old Tar's Yarn.

Vol. VII.—Coldingham Abbey; or, the Double Revenge—The Heroine—The Story of Dugald Glen, the shepherd of Dilston—The Mysterious Exchange—The Chase: a Passage from the History of the Rebellion—The Thriftless Heir—The Foundling; or, the Heiress of Castle Gower—The Fugitive—Lottery Hall—Fatal Secret—The Sabbath Wreckers: a Legend of Dunbar—The Blacksmith of Plumptree—Mary Armstrong—The Monks of Dryburgh.

Vol. VIII.—The Lost Heir of the House of Elphinstone—The Countess of Cassilis—The Mysterious Disappearance—Patrick O'Flannigan—The Siege—The Avenger—The Stepmother—The Freebooters of Coldstream—Mary Merton—Seven Lights—The Lord of Hermitage—Red Eric and Lord Delavel—The Two Sisters.

"Mr. James Gemmell adds to the literature of this time of year in a very pleasant way. He produces a new edition of 'Wilson's Tales of the Borders.' It is not, as we understand it, to be a complete work, but is to contain a selection of some of the best stories. .... If the first two volumes, which we have received, are to be taken as specimens of what the others will be, then a distinct good is to be done to the reading public by their issue."—SCOTSMAN.

"Mr. Gemmell's reissue is one of the neatest and cheapest we have seen, each volume being of crown 8vo size, handsomely bound, with gilt top, and published at two shillings certainly a very moderate price for a book of 224 pages. ..... All who wish, in the words of Sir Walter Scot, to read of, 'Lovers' sleights, of ladies' charms, of witches' spells, of warriors' arms,' cannot do better than procure these volumes, which contain quite a store-house of material bearing upon the hills, glens, and folk-lore of Scotland."—LIVERPOOL MERCURY.

www.ingramcontent.com/pod-product-compliance
Lightning Source LLC
Chambersburg PA
CBHW080329170426
43194CB00014B/2500